HOW THE QUEEN REIGNS

DOROTHY LAIRD

HOW THE QUEEN REIGNS

An authentic study
of the Queen's Personality and Life Work

THE WORLD PUBLISHING COMPANY

CLEVELAND AND NEW YORK

Published by The World Publishing Company
2231 West 110th Street, Cleveland 2, Ohio

Library of Congress Catalog Card Number: 59–7750

FIRST EDITION

CONTENTS

LIST OF ILLUSTRATIONS

*The following photographs will be found in sequence
after page 128*

LIST OF ILLUSTRATIONS

AUTHOR'S FOREWORD

I AM a journalist, not, unfortunately, a historian. This book
came to be written because, about nine years ago, the Editor
of the *Scottish Field*, of which I am London Correspondent,
asked me for an article about Buckingham Palace. A Member of
the Household kindly lent me Mr. Clifford Smith's fine book on
the Palace, and I gradually became enthralled by the long history,
the devoted service and unique position to-day of the British
Royal Family. As time went on, I missed increasingly *one* book
in which would be gathered an account of all sides of the
Sovereign's work. As this changes with the individuality of each
Sovereign, it would require also some form of profile or character
study of Her Majesty. (Mr. Dermot Morrah's scholarly study
The Work of the Queen had not then been begun.) Eventually I
had the temerity to think of writing it.

Throughout the period of almost three years involved in the
writing I have received constant and quite invaluable help from
many Members of Her Majesty's Household. It would be pleasant
to record my gratitude to each by name, but they prefer to be
thanked collectively. Similarly, I am deeply indebted to members
of Government Departments, who must remain anonymous.

Throughout, I have had time, trouble and kindness from a
very large number of people, many of them distinguished, many
the highest expert in his or her particular field, all of them
extremely busy. They have patiently answered obvious, or difficult, or sometimes silly questions. They have directed me to the
best books on their particular subject and to other experts. They
have carefully read and corrected—and sometimes re-corrected—
my efforts to understand and put upon paper the involved
matters which were crystal clear to them. Others have had
nothing to do with my assessment of their subject, but have been
good enough to read, correct and comment upon the draft
afterwards. Others again have contributed an anecdote or fact.
Still others have given time and trouble to no effect, because I
have not been able to make use here of their information.

It is impossible that this book has been compiled without error, but it *must* have some merit because so many wise persons have put so much into it. I am only sorry I was not able to make better use of my magnificent opportunities.

The names of some—but not by any means all—to whom I am deeply indebted and exceedingly grateful follow here:

Members of Her Majesty's Household.

The Admiralty; The Air Ministry; His Grace the Duke of Argyll; Mr. E. O. Asafu-Adjaye, H.E. The High Commissioner for Ghana; Joseph Asscher, Jnr., Asscher's Diamant Maatschappij N.V. Amsterdam; J. F. Austin, Messrs. Ede & Ravenscroft, Queen's Robemakers; H.E. The High Commissioner for Australia.

Sir Henry Arthur Benyon, J.P., The Lord Lieutenant of Berkshire; Leonard and Margaret Boden; Henry Bowman, British Honduras; The British Leprosy Relief Association; British Transport Commission; British White Cattle Society.

The late Douglas Chandor and Mrs. Chandor; The Church Information Board; The Colonial Office; Rt. Rev. Frederick William Thomas Craske, Bishop of Gibraltar; Antony Craxton, B.B.C.; The Crown Office, Palace of Westminster; Terence Cuneo; Customs and Excise Board.

The Royal Danish Embassy, London; E. R. Davis, Clerk of the Lieutenancy of Berkshire; Rear-Admiral Peter Dawnay, M.V.O., D.S.C., Flag Officer, Royal Yachts; Miss Lydia de Burgh; Brigadier-General Harry Disston (Retd.), N.Y.N.G., New York City; Hon. George Drew, Q.C., H.E. The High Commissioner for Canada; Rev. Andrew Drummond Harcus, then Gen. Sec. Free Church Federal Council of England and Wales; H.E. Sir Ambrose Dundas, K.C.I.E., C.S.I., Lieutenant Governor of the Isle of Man; Stephen Dykes Bower, M.A., F.R.I.B.A., F.S.A., Surveyor of the Fabric, Westminster Abbey.

The late Rt. Hon. W. E. Elliot, C.H., M.C., D.Sc., F.R.S., M.P., and Baroness Elliot of Harwood.

Lady Foot.

His Eminence Cardinal Norman Thomas Gilroy, D.D., Roman Catholic Archbishop of Sydney; J. Haydon W. Glen, LL.B., Town Clerk of Kingston-upon-Hull; The Rev. John Gwinnett, Chaplain, H.M. Tower of London.

Edward Halliday; W. E. D. Halliday, Registrar of the Cabinet of Canada; Rt. Rev. Percy Mark Herbert, K.C.V.O., D.D., Bishop of Norwich, Clerk of the Closet; The Home Office; The Editor, *Homes and Gardens*; The Rt. Hon. Dame Florence Horsbrugh, G.B.E., M.P.

Mr. Mohammed Ikramullah, H.E. The High Commissioner for Pakistan; Sir Thomas Innes of Learney, K.C.V.O., LL.D., F.S.A. Scot., The Lord Lyon King of Arms.

Sir Robert Knox, K.C.B., K.C.V.O., D.S.O., Sec. Political Honours Scrutiny Committee.

C. D. Laborde, Master in charge, Harrow football; The Rev. John Lamb, C.V.O., D.D., Minister of Crathie; E. J. Langdon, High Sheriff of the City of Gloucester; Professor John Le Patourel, M.A., Ph.D., Professor of Medieval History of the University of Leeds; J. G. Links of Calman Links (Trading) Ltd.; His Excellency the Earl of Listowel, P.C., Governor-General of Ghana; The Rev. J. B. Longmuir, T.D., M.A., Principal Clerk of the General Assembly of the Church of Scotland.

Cecil Mann, M.V.O., The Queen's Jeweller, Messrs. Garrard; The late H.H. Princess Marie Louise, G.C.V.O., G.B.E., C.I., R.R.C.; His Grace the Duke of Marlborough; Donald and Valerie Marr; Mr. Matthew Mbu, then Commissioner for the Federation of Nigeria in London; Sir Iain Moncreiffe of Moncreiffe, Bt., Ph.D., Unicorn Pursuivant; Rt. Hon. Rt. Rev. Henry Colville Montgomery Campbell, M.C., D.D., Bishop of London; Mrs. William Shepherd Morrison, Wife of the Speaker of the House of Commons; Noel and Gwen Murless.

H.E. The High Commissioner for New Zealand.

H.E. Madame V. L. Pandit, The High Commissioner for India; F. E. G. Pearson, The Methodist Missionary Society; Sir Arthur Penn, G.C.V.O., M.C., Treasurer to H.M. Elizabeth the Queen Mother; The Rev. Jocelyn Henry Temple Perkins, C.V.O., F.S.A., D.C.L., Sacrist and Minor Canon of Westminster Abbey; The Privy Council Office.

The Rabbi of the Spanish and Portuguese Synagogue; The Rev. J. H. Ransom, Rector of Gt. Bromley, Essex; Miss Flora Robson, C.B.E.; Rolls Royce Ltd.

Colonel Norman R. Salew, O.B.E., D.L., Sec. to the Lieutenancy of Essex; Mrs. Marjory Savery, Oji River Settlement, E. Nigeria; Peter Scott, C.B.E., D.S.C.; Rt. Rev. Dr. Robert F. V.

Scott, D.D., Ex-Moderator of the Church of Scotland; Sir Ambrose Sherwill, C.B.E., M.C., Bailiff of Guernsey; Major Sir Henry Gray Studholme, Bt., C.V.O., M.P., then Vice-Chamberlain of the Household; Shahid Suhrawardy, C.V.O., then Prime Minister of Pakistan; The Royal Swedish Embassy.

Godfrey Talbot, O.B.E., B.B.C.; Sir Colin Thornley, K.C.M.G., C.V.O., Governor of British Honduras; The Treasury, 10 Downing Street.

W. G. N. Walker, Chairman, Jute Industries Ltd.; The War Office; The Hon. Sir T. Clifton Webb, K.C.M.G., Q.C., formerly High Commissioner for New Zealand; Norman Wilkinson, C.B.E., P.R.I.; Miss Carolynn Wood; Alderman Frederick Woods, ex-Mayor of Chelmsford.

I am also grateful for generous permission to quote from copyright material which has been received from:

The Rt. Hon. Earl Attlee, K.G., P.C., O.M., C.H., to quote from his Speech to the Oxford Law Society, 1957.

Mr. Humphry Berkeley, for a passage from "The Finances of the Monarchy", *The National and English Review*.

Messrs. Cassell and Co. Ltd., for passages from *A King's Story* by H.R.H. The Duke of Windsor, *Dawn of Liberation* by Sir Winston Churchill and *The English Empress* by Count Corti.

The Rt. Hon. Sir Winston Churchill, K.G., P.C., O.M., C.H., M.P., to quote from his speeches.

Messrs. Collins, Sons and Co. Ltd., for a passage from *Fulness of Days* by the Earl of Halifax, K.G.

Messrs. Hodder and Stoughton, for passages from *The Life of Cosmo Gordon Lang* by J. G. Lockhart.

Messrs. John Murray (Publishers) Ltd., for a passage from *King George V, a Personal Memoir* by John Gore.

Sir Harold Nicolson, K.C.V.O., C.M.G., for passages from *King George V, His Life and Reign* (published by Constable).

Messrs. The Oxford University Press, for a passage from *Government and Parliament* by The Rt. Hon. Herbert Morrison, M.P.

Messrs. Penguin Books Ltd., for passages from *The Queen's Government* by Sir Ivor Jennings.

The Editor of *Theology*, for a passage from "Crown Appointments in Theory and Practice, with Special Reference to the English Episcopate" by R. H. Malden, Dean of Wells.

CHAPTER ONE

The Task

"Royalty is a Government in which the attention of the nation is concentrated on one person doing interesting actions. A Republic is a Government in which that attention is divided between many, who are all doing uninteresting things."

The English Constitution, Bagehot

"She is a true daughter of her father—and with that we are well content."

Leader in the *Daily Mail* on Friday, February 8, 1952

". . . it is my resolve that under God I shall not only rule but serve. This is not only the tradition of my family; it describes, I believe, the modern character of the British Crown."

The Queen, opening the Australian Parliament, Canberra, February 15, 1954

AT an unknown moment in the early hours of February 6, 1952, Queen Elizabeth II succeeded her father, King George VI, as Head of the Commonwealth. She became the forty-second sovereign of England since William the Conqueror, her sixth Sovereign Queen, and one of the seven reigning monarchs of Europe.

She had succeeded to the greatest and most permanent office of our civilisation.

She was now titular head of Office, Law and Honour throughout a vast Commonwealth. Her subjects and citizens numbered five hundred and thirty-nine millions. She was official Head of the Church of England, yet was Queen to millions of believers of other faiths.

She was twenty-five years old.

What would be demanded of the new Queen? How far was her inheritance one of ceremony and figurehead duties only? Would she wield real power, even in a strictly constitutional monarchy?

How will her character, her concept of her duties, so change the age in which she reigned as to make it as instantly distinctive in the future as are the Victorian or the Edwardian eras?

*   *   *   *

King George VI, her father, died peacefully in his sleep at home in Sandringham House, which had been built for his grandfather, surrounded by the wintry woodlands and frosty pastures of Norfolk, a countryside he loved.

In tropical Africa, over three thousand miles to the south, and three hours earlier in time, Queen Elizabeth II succeeded King George VI in the strangest and least likely circumstances which have yet attended accession to our historic throne. The Queen is the first sovereign in our modern history whose instant of accession cannot be known, the only sovereign since King Edward I—who was absent on a crusade when his father, King Henry III, died in 1272—and King George I, who was in Hanover—to succeed to the throne of England when overseas.

Yet an earlier accession might have taken place in Africa. The Prince of Wales was on safari in Tanganyika in 1928, when the near-fatal illness of King George V caused him to be sent for in great haste.

The moment of succession to the throne must always be historic and moving. The new monarch steps across the wide gulf from comparatively carefree princedom to a position of unequalled honour, incalculable responsibility and great loneliness, of which only death will relieve him. Almost always there is warning of, and mental preparation for, the approaching change of status. There was no such preparation for Queen Elizabeth II.

Sixth of our Sovereign Queens, she was the first to mourn the death of a parent upon succession. Of her predecessors, both Marys fought against opposition to gain their thrones, and indeed Queen Mary II was a Queen Regnant in name only. Queen Elizabeth I, although secretly forewarned, with her unfailing sense of situation, appeared amazed and overpowered when members of her sister's Privy Council arrived at Hatfield to do her homage. She sank to her knees, exclaiming, "*Domino factum est istud, et est mirabile in oculis nostris!*" (This is the Lord's doing, and it is marvellous in our eyes.)

Gentle, portly Queen Anne sat in St. James's Palace, awaiting half-hourly, scribbled bulletins on the extinguishing life of her brother-in-law, King William III. She received the news of his death from the Bishop of Salisbury, who drove hard to the Palace with the news, just as the Archbishop of Canterbury and the Lord Chamberlain were to drive through the night from Windsor Castle to Kensington Palace to the young Queen Victoria with the news of the death of her uncle, King William IV.

How did the news come to Queen Elizabeth II?

Princess Elizabeth and the Duke of Edinburgh were at the beginning of a tour to Australia and New Zealand by way of Kenya, which they were undertaking as deputies for King George VI, whose ill-health had enforced his withdrawal. They flew out from London Airport on January 31, 1952, their departure watched by a worn, tired and courageous man who had won the deep affection of his peoples for his lifelong quiet devotion to his family during the fifteen years of his reign, and for his upright sense of duty to his Commonwealth.

Princess Elizabeth went first to Kenya. There, after a few days of busy public duty, she and her husband retired to Sagana Lodge, the hunting lodge presented to them as a wedding present by the people of Kenya, which lies on the banks of the Sagana river in the Aberdare Forest. The highlight of their few days' happy holiday was to be a night of game-watching from a little hut, called Treetops, perched on a platform in the branches of a giant fig-tree overlooking a water-hole and salt-lick in the Aberdare Mountains game reserve.

It was a memorable night.

The bush was alive with game. Even before Princess Elizabeth gained the house in the trees, a large herd of forty-six elephants loomed out of the bush, almost directly between her and the tree. There was a tense moment, although the Princess showed no sign of it, as she quietly crossed a stretch of open ground, close to the leading elephant, and gained the ladder to safety.

A record number of animals was seen at the pool that night. Treetops had a wide view of the water-hole, and artificial "moonlight" created by searchlights had encouraged the game to come out. It had been expected that the Princess would watch the spectacle for some hours and then retire to rest, but she was so enthralled by it that she sat for nearly the whole night watching the scene through her field glasses. She was wearing russet-coloured tailored slacks and a yellow shirt. When the night became chilly she slipped a cardigan over her shoulders. Several times she exclaimed how much her father would enjoy it.

She thoroughly enjoyed the amusing antics of a troop of baboons, which she fed on sweet potatoes. She watched elephant and rhinoceros. She saw a battle between water-buck, and followed through her glasses the slow withdrawal of the defeated buck, which was badly wounded and fell, to lie motionless close to the far edge of the water. In the morning, when it was safe, she sent one of the party over to see to the wounded buck, but it was dead.

In the morning The Queen, who everyone thought was Princess, went back to Sagana Lodge. It was a wonderful morning, and she was delighted with her night of adventure. She fished that morning in the stream close to the Lodge, had a good catch—better than her husband's—and was in tremendous spirits. As one who was with her that day recalls, she was "looking very, very, pretty".

It was the last day of the holiday break in the official programme. The Queen and the Duke of Edinburgh took things easily. Only a few members of the Household had come with them to Nairobi and Sagana; the main party was awaiting them at the port of Mombasa, on board the liner *Gothic* in which they would voyage to Australia. Next day's plans were that the Princess and the Duke of Edinburgh would inspect three battalions of the King's African Rifles at nearby Nanyuki and then fly down to Mombasa, where, after a round of official duties, they would embark in the *Gothic* and sail for Australia.

The fig-tree observation post was so small that there was not room on one night for the whole of even the attenuated royal party, which was divided into two. Among those who were going to spend the second night up the tree was Major the Hon. Martin Charteris, Private Secretary to Princess Elizabeth (now Lieutenant-Colonel the Hon. Martin Charteris, C.B., M.V.O., O.B.E., Assistant Private Secretary to The Queen). He went from Sagana Lodge across the valley to the Outspan Hotel which was closer to Treetops, and which was also the headquarters for the Press who were covering the visit. Here he lunched before going to Treetops. About 1.30 p.m. local time, Major Charteris was just walking to his car when someone touched him on the shoulder and told him he was wanted in the telephone booth. Here he found, not a telephone call but the reporter from the *East African Standard*, as white as blotting paper. He was blindly turning over and over a packet of cigarettes with one hand. Without preliminaries the reporter said abruptly,

"The King is dead."

It was a profound shock. But it was almost instantly believed because, although the death of the King was utterly unexpected, it was not unlikely.

The news had been received by the *East African Standard* in Nairobi through a Reuter message, and they had immediately contacted their representative at Outspan. No official news had come through, nor had any arrived at Sagana Lodge, where Major Charteris immediately contacted Lieutenant-Commander Michael Parker, the Duke of Edinburgh's Private Secretary. (The reason, it was discovered later, was that the Governor of Kenya and almost all his staff were on the train from Nairobi to Mombasa, and the cipher telegrams were piling up in an almost empty Government House.) Commander Parker tried to get confirmation from the radio, and although he did not intercept any announcement, he did get an indication from the tone of the programmes. By this time other reporters at Outspan were getting messages from their papers. It was obvious that the news was all too true.

* * * *

Sagana Lodge has one sitting-room, which runs right through the house. This has a wide bay window, overlooking the bright tropical garden. Commander Parker went round on to the lawn outside the window and managed to attract the attention of the Duke without The Queen seeing him. Commander Parker beckoned him urgently. The Duke came out and was told the news. He went back and broke to his young wife that her beloved father was dead and that she was now Queen. The time was 2.45 p.m. local time, and 11.45 a.m. Greenwich Mean Time, on Wednesday, February 6, 1952.

She took the news bravely, "like a Queen".

No one can tell before the event how a person will measure up to the great moments of destiny, when those with hidden reserves of character and training can withstand a shock which would overwhelm a weaker personality. Princess Elizabeth was only twenty-five: there had been no previous testing-point in her life.

It was with a feeling of complete ignorance of what awaited them that her Household and staff rallied to the young Princess who had just become their Queen. At Sagana Lodge, the joyous holiday air was instantly extinguished. An atmosphere of uncomfortable hush settled upon the Askari soldiers, the drivers, the policemen and staff. The sun still shone on the bright flowers and the strange African plants and trees in the primitive garden. In the forest across the valley elephant, lion and rhinoceros roamed or slept undisturbed. The wild, natural setting of the African scene gave a dream-like quality to the accession of the Sovereign, a sudden impact with history which had recurred always dramatically throughout the centuries, but never before in such a setting.

The quality of The Queen was from the first instant apparent. Even those who knew and loved her best were amazed at the maturity, the control with which she took the crushing news of the death of the father who was so dear to her. From the first The Queen was entirely in command of the situation.

In the white-painted, panelled sitting-room where The Queen learnt that she was Sovereign, there is a little hall where were kept the fishing rods now laid aside, then a few steps lead down into the room itself. The great bay window through which Commander Parker had attracted the attention of the Duke frames a magnificent view of Mount Kenya. There are easy chairs covered in red and grey chintz, and a big stone fireplace. Between fireplace and window there is a desk.

At that desk The Queen sat down to the first tasks of her reign. Perhaps fortunately there was no time to ponder: there was much to be done. With her own hand she wrote out the telegrams to her hosts in the Dominions who were awaiting her, not cancelling but indefinitely postponing her visit to them.

The Queen was asked what she wished to be called.

(There is no compulsion to be titled by the name by which the heir has been christened or is known. Queen Victoria was christened Alexandrina Victoria, King Edward VII was christened Albert Edward, and King George VI was christened Albert Frederick Arthur George.) The Queen was christened Elizabeth Alexandra Mary, and she could have chosen to be known by any of these names, or by any other. But she has always signed herself Elizabeth, and she replied at once,

"Oh my own name—what else?"

Thus simply was The Queen's title chosen.

Meanwhile a cipher telegram had arrived from London, which requested permission to call the first part of the Accession Council —that part which authorises the proclamation of the Sovereign and which in normal accessions is immediately followed by the second part, which is attended by the Sovereign, and at which he declares his intention to rule according to the law.

The answer to this request, and the cables to the Dominions had to be signed. There was a moment's discussion whether The Queen would be right in signing "Elizabeth R." (Regina) before the Accession Council had been called. The point, hitherto academic, had never been considered, but it was decided that The Queen should do so, and this snap ruling was afterwards found constitutionally correct.

The Duke of Edinburgh busied himself primarily with plans for the immediate return to England. These may seem to have been inevitable now, but there were many problems at that instant of decision. It was decided to fly to Entebbe in Uganda (where there was an airfield at which long-distance aircraft could land), in the Dakota of East African Airways, which was waiting at nearby Nanyuki airfield for the planned flight to Mombasa on the following day. Fortunately the Argonaut *Atalanta*, in which The Queen had flown from London Airport to Nairobi, had just made a second flight with the Members of the Household to Mombasa, and was still there. The rendezvous at Entebbe was arranged, and packing was hurriedly set in motion.

The Queen remembered everything. She gave a signed photograph and present to each member of the staff. It was a very moving moment. The Africans mourned with their Queen, and her chauffeur threw himself down to kiss her shoes.

Soon the car, with the standard of Princess Elizabeth flying, was driving over the red dirt roads on to which the mauve-blue blossoms of the jacaranda were falling, towards Nanyuki airfield. The town was incongruously beflagged for its great day which never came. Crowds of sad-faced Africans lined the streets in sympathetic silence.

It was nearly dark when the car drew up at Nanyuki airfield, which lies exactly on the Equator. Flares had been set out round the edge of the field, but were not lit because the grass was tinder-dry and there was danger of starting a bush-fire.

There had been no opportunity to organise mourning. The Queen wore a flowered beige dress with a white hat and gloves. The Duke of Edinburgh had borrowed a black tie to wear with his grey suit. The Press waited on the edge of the airport. They were themselves much moved, and a member of The Queen's Household paid tribute to their decorum and bearing. The Press photographers, in response to a request, held their cameras on their arms but took no pictures of the young woman who had just become their Queen. So there are no photographs of The Queen on the day of her accession in Africa. Presentations were briefly made. The iron training of British royalty enabled The Queen to turn for an instant to wave and smile before entering the aircraft in which she left Kenya.

The five-hundred-mile flight to Entebbe through the dark African night was dramatic. The stars were clear and brilliant. Bush-fires were burning below. It was during this flight that a typical message of sorrow and allegiance was received *en plein* from Mr. Winston Churchill, the Prime Minister, on behalf of the Cabinet, which ended: "The Cabinet in all things awaits Your Majesty's command."

The Dakota in which Her Majesty was travelling was the first of the two aircraft to land at Entebbe airfield. There The Queen was met by Sir Andrew Cohen, Governor of Uganda, and his wife, who were in deep mourning not initially for the King, but for a family bereavement. Shortly afterwards, just as the Argonaut *Atalanta* landed from Mombasa, a violent tropical thunderstorm broke out, which delayed departure for three hours.

The Queen and her little party waited in an airport building. Then, at 11.47 p.m. local time and 8.47 p.m. Greenwich Mean Time, The Queen walked out across the wet tarmac, under brilliant stars, to board the *Atalanta*, the same aircraft in which she

24

had said good-bye to her father, The King, only a week before.

Throughout the long, trouble-free flight of 4,127 miles, by way of El Adem in Libya to London, The Queen maintained the same remarkable composure. Yet it must have been a time of great strain for her.

At last, within ten minutes of the originally appointed time—in spite of the long delay at Entebbe—the Argonaut touched down at London Airport on the darkening afternoon of February 7. There on the apron The Queen could see a dark group of the great men of her Realm, headed by three men who will be numbered among Britain's Prime Ministers, standing in line waiting to acknowledge their Queen. Wearing mourning which had been hurriedly sent from the *Gothic*, with the flame-lily diamond brooch which had been given to her by the children of Southern Rhodesia in her lapel, Queen Elizabeth II walked slowly and firmly down the steps into her new life of unremitting responsibility.

*   *   *   *

The Queen had entered into one of the most complex of all jobs. She is the bond and symbol of the Commonwealth. The Commonwealth has no common race, no common language, nor religion, nor landscape, nor flag: we share only The Queen. She alone unites us.

This, paradoxically, is most marked in countries of the Commonwealth which are Republics, because they share with us this one symbol only, The Queen, whom they acknowledge as Head of the Commonwealth.

There has always been, in any form of Government, some visible symbol upon which the people can centre their patriotism. Each nation has its own way of centring patriotism; there are many common bonds. For instance, the citizens of the United States place great symbolic value on their flag. The Norwegians, while truly loyal to their recently re-founded and much-loved dynasty, all share a great and deep love for the scenery of Norway, so that reference to its fjells, its snows, its fjords meet instant response from all Norwegian hearts.

The Members of the Commonwealth receive their similar stimulus and response from our Royal Family. The Sovereign lends what might, for want of a worthier word, be called *glamour* to all manner of worthy but otherwise rather dull projects. The Queen, by meeting and talking with the people on whom we all depend because of their stoical devotion to monotonous duty, gives them an experience which cannot be bought. In these days money can buy its way into a great many places, so that it is beyond price to have a sphere which is entered not so much from attainments of birth or bank balance, but from service.

The Monarchy links us to our past, and in so doing gives our troubles perspective and our efforts a future. The Queen stands as a link with our history over the past thousand years. During these past centuries how many calamities and crises have been surmounted! That feeling of an abiding link with the past gives us great inner strength in time of trouble. We feel linked to our history through our Queen.

The Monarchy enables only the best of our past to live into the future. As Sir Winston Churchill said at the Coronation Luncheon in Westminster on May 27, 1953:

"A great battle is lost: Parliament turns out the Government. A great battle is won—crowds cheer The Queen."

The Sovereign must stand for everyone. She must be above and outside of all partisan activity; she must be as impartial to the views of different sections of her community as it is possible for a human being to be.

Above all, she must give to an elected Parliament—of whatever political persuasion—her full backing and help, for that Government then represents her Country. This was a part of her duties which was somewhat imperfectly interpreted by Queen Victoria, although she was so great a Queen in much else. But it was understood to a masterly extent by King George V and King George VI.

The Sovereign has no need to be swayed by the ordinary political expediencies, and the people, knowing that, may sometimes feel that the Sovereign's outlook can be closer to theirs than that of a political party. This can come about only because the Sovereign has no direct power.

A Sovereign masks change. The outer ceremonies continue and forge us to history, whatever far-reaching innovations may be finding their way to the Statute Book. It is in many ways easier for a progressive party to put through unprecedented legislation without alarming the country when the familiar ways of government are expressed by a Sovereign, and continue unchanged, than it is in a republic.

The Queen also appears as something outside the common run of humanity. We all want to know in what way a young woman charged with such abnormal responsibilities remains an ordinary person. Everything about her seems interesting—and not only to us, but to vast numbers of republicans. The Queen's life is more interesting, more full of memorable moments than ours, and is yet more constricted, more pressed upon by duties and more disciplined. We are intrigued because The Queen is a person and not a formula devised to fit a need—although some of her critics would appear to think that she can be as easily moulded—because she is a human being and not aloof from the sudden tragedies or the repetitive pin-pricks of life. We are constantly interested in watching, discussing and thinking about her way of life.

The Queen is strongly linked to the family symbol. Indeed, so much has a happy family life become identified with the British Royal Family that it is doubtful whether a Sovereign could sustain his sovereignty were this shattered. The value of the family is tremendous, it is universal and it is fundamental.

We think, "There is Queen Elizabeth II: she has everything in the world, but look, she chooses to spend her leisure much as we would, with her husband, her children, her dogs, in her own home in the country." We are reinforced in our belief that the greatest and basic happiness lies in such a simple and sound way of life.

The trouble is that we want our Queen to be a human being—but a perfect human being. We want personality without peccadillo, beauty without vanity, modesty without shyness, a sense of duty without dullness, a sense of humour without ever laughing at us, a life devoted to our service 86,400 seconds a day every day of her life. In short, we want what no human being could ever produce (and how we should hate them if they did)—perfection.

To be positive without offending her subjects' susceptibilities is perhaps the hardest yet basically the most important part of

The Queen's lot. She must submerge her personal point of view for the good of the job, yet she must never permit herself to be a mere cipher.

So much for the public and representational part of The Queen's life as Sovereign. What of her constitutional part?

Does she wield real power or has Parliament, which has hewn away her political prerogative, entirely turned her position into a sinecure utterly without power?

The Queen's direct power is almost nil, as practically her every official action is "By the advice of her Ministers".

"The Queen can do no wrong" is a phrase one often hears. One theory is that originally the simple phrase "The King can do no wrong" was evolved because as absolute Monarch he was the sole judge of his actions. So, if he maintained that he was not wrong, whatever he did could not be proved wrong. But the common sense of the British people could not believe that any human being, even a King, could be infallible. It was on this issue that the Civil War was fought, and although King Charles I's sons in turn inherited the Throne from which he had been deposed, no longer was it possible for a Sovereign to claim that all his actions were dictated by Divine Right. Therefore the device was evolved that the King's command must always bear a Minister's signature. If things went wrong, the Minister could always be used as the whipping boy. Moreover, it also ensures that ministerial advice is always available to the Sovereign in all decisions.

But, strangely, it is a paradox to say that the Sovereign is without power. The Sovereign strongly influences his or her age. The reigns of Queen Victoria, King Edward VII, King George V and King George VI, even the brief reign of King Edward VIII, are strongly marked by the personality of the Sovereign. The personality of the Sovereign sets a seal upon his age far more than does the statesman who wields infinitely greater power, the Prime Minister. Who would speak of the not-so-distant past in terms of, "it was the time of the Campbell-Bannerman Ministry"? The average person would hardly know what you meant, but if you mention "in the middle of King Edward VII's reign", an instant mental picture is called up.

In general terms, the Sovereign has only three main powers

left: the right to be consulted, the right to encourage and the right to warn. These are by no means to be despised.

In crisis, whenever it is humanly possible, the Prime Minister or responsible Minister must inform the Sovereign of the situation and how it is proposed to deal with it. At all times, to the Sovereign comes an immense bulk of papers, and the study and knowledge of what they contain are the tools for her job.

The Sovereign stands for all the people whether in or out of power, whether within the jurisdiction of the Parliament of the United Kingdom or the many Parliaments of the Commonwealth, or whether ruled directly from the Colonial Office. The Sovereign is always there, whatever party is in power. The Sovereign cannot change by a jot the decisions of any of her Governments, but she can point out to them where she thinks they may be making a mistake. She can advise and warn. This very considerable power has never been put better than in the frequently-quoted words of the great Victorian constitutional writer, Bagehot, supposing the thoughts of a wise King:

"I do not oppose, it is my duty not to oppose, but observe that I *warn*." Supposing the king to be right . . . he could not help moving his minister. He might not always turn his course, but he would always trouble his mind.

In the course of a long reign a sagacious king would acquire an experience with which few ministers could contend. The king could say, "Have you referred to the transactions which happened during such and such an administration, I think about fourteen years ago? They afford an instructive example of the bad results which are sure to attend the policy which you propose. You did not at that time take so prominent a part in public life as you now do, and it is possible you do not fully remember all the events. I should recommend you to recur to them, and to discuss them with your older colleagues who took part in them. . . ." The King would indeed have the advantage which a permanent under-secretary has over his superior, the parliamentary—that of having shared in the proceedings of the previous parliamentary secretaries. These proceedings were part of his own life; occupied the best of his thoughts, gave him perhaps anxiety, perhaps pleasure, were commenced in spite of his dissuasion, or were sanctioned by his approval. The parliamentary secretary vaguely remembers that something was done in the time of some of his predecessors, when he very likely did not know the least or care the least about that sort of public busi-

29

ness. He has to begin by learning painfully and imperfectly what the permanent secretary knows by clear and instant memory. No doubt a parliamentary secretary always can, and sometimes does, silence his subordinate by the tacit might of his superior dignity. He says: "I do not think there is much in all that. . . . Many errors were committed at the time you refer to which we need not now discuss." A pompous man easily sweeps away the suggestions of those beneath him. But though a minister may so deal with his subordinate, he cannot so deal with his king. The social force of admitted superiority by which he overturned his under-secretary is now not with him but against him. He has no longer to regard the deferential hints of an acknowledged inferior, but to answer the arguments of a superior to whom he has himself to be respectful.

What is the Sovereign's advice worth? Given a well-disposed and dedicated Sovereign (such as the British people have almost come to regard as their right), it is worth a great deal. Today the Head of the Commonwealth meets more people than practically anyone in the world, reads almost as much paper as any statesman, is evenly informed because she does not spend periods out of office. The Sovereign is able by her freedom from the political pressures to take a longer and clearer view.

The Sovereign is the oil in the wheels of the Commonwealth, constantly working to ease us into a harmonious whole instead of splintering us into antagonistic particles. It is the Sovereign's job constantly to smooth out the differences of opinions and upsets on all levels in all countries of the Commonwealth, both on public occasions and at home in the privacy of an Audience.

This job will continue for the rest of her life; she will enjoy many magnificent experiences, live in comfort, and even in luxury, be always regarded with immense interest and affection. But there will be no occasions when all the worries of the world can be light-heartedly thrown aside, no weekends without work, no carefree holidays, no remission from responsibility.

Who would apply for such a job?

Certainly not, one feels, a young girl of twenty-five, happily married, delighting in quiet country things. The late Mr. Horace Smith, who taught The Queen riding, recounted in his memoirs, *A Horseman Through Six Reigns*, that Princess Elizabeth once said to him that if she had not been who she was, she would like best to be a lady living in the country, with lots of horses and dogs. That is a dream far removed from the course of destiny. But the Royal Family has been brought up and conditioned from childhood to a concept of vigorous and self-effacing service.

When I had the privilege of being presented to the late Princess Marie Louise, granddaughter of Queen Victoria, and of talking to her for some time in her home, I was immensely struck by the ingrained attitude of service which was apparent in everything she said. "We are brought up in a tradition of service," she said. "Never to lend our name to any enterprise or charity to which we do not give our time, our thoughts, our interest."

Who could better have taught The Queen the royal tradition of service than her father? King George VI's quotation from *The Pilgrim's Progress* in his Christmas broadcast in 1950 was most fitting to himself:

"Like the pilgrim, we have gone forward, only to fall back. Like him, we have fallen back, only to press onward once more. We have passed through the valley of the shadow of death, but, always with the determination natural to our race and training, we have kept our eyes fixed on the far-off delectable mountains of peace and good will. And like the pilgrim, every one of us had his own individual burden to shoulder. Too often we have laid it down for a brief respite, only to be obliged to pick it up again and find it even heavier."

Now the weary man's burden had been relieved while he lay asleep, and had been laid upon the young, strong, willing but untried shoulders of his daughter.

Of course there was much ahead which would delight, excite and thrill Queen Elizabeth II, much which would touch and move her, many deep and wonderfully satisfying experiences, and the warm content which comes from doing one's best for the cause in which one believes.

But the young Queen had seen her father, the King, exhausted and white after the strain of public duties, tired and worried over the political tidings disclosed in the perpetual official Boxes. She had seen eagerly-planned family events put aside time and again for the press of duty. She can have been under little illusion as to the task demanded of her.

When Princess Elizabeth of York was born, she stood third

31

from the Throne; but her uncle, the Prince of Wales, was only thirty-one years old. She was her parents' first child, and a son born to them would have taken her place in the Succession. It was not very likely that she would ever succeed to the Throne. Yet on February 6, 1952, at the age of twenty-five years, ten and a half months, she was Queen.

What manner of person was she? How has she developed under the stress of office? Six and a half years, thousands of pictures and millions of words later, Her Most Excellent Majesty Elizabeth by the Grace of God, of the United Kingdom of Great Britain and Northern Ireland and of Her other Realms and Territories Queen, Head of the Commonwealth, Defender of the Faith, is still an enigma, imperfectly understood by millions.

CHAPTER TWO

The Woman who is Queen

"The most wonderful thing I ever saw in my life was the moment when she lifted the sword and laid it on the altar—she was putting her whole heart and soul to the service of her People."

A Bishop, speaking of The Queen's Coronation.

"She is so calming." An Artist.

"A lot of laughing goes on in this house."

A Member of the Household at Buckingham Palace.

EVERYONE knows what Queen Elizabeth II looks like. Even children hardly able to talk instantly recognise The Queen's features—the mid-brown hair, the arched, strong eyebrows, the direct grey eyes, the wide mouth with its straight upper lip, the head beautifully poised on the long neck. Almost everyone knows The Queen's voice, with its clear, youthful tones; her swinging walk; her gentle movements.

Yet, in a strange way, everyone does not understand her personality. Many people who recognise The Queen's qualities and her preferences are not able to envisage her as a living person. The Duke of Edinburgh or the Queen Mother seem to them—on the surface at least—much more easily understood as people.

Incidentally why is it that comparisons are so often made between members of the Royal Family? The duties required of them are not the same. We do not need a series of carbon copies of "the perfect Royal Personage", but different, hard-working and sincere Royalties, all in their own way doing their best for the Commonwealth. Where we are so very fortunate is that The Queen, who must have a constant sense of her responsibilities, *is* Queen; that the Duke of Edinburgh, whose keen intelligence and quick wit enormously stimulate and enliven royal occasions,

33

is in a position where he can give scope to these qualities; and that the Queen Mother, after a lifetime of support and help to her husband The King, can now in turn support her daughter The Queen, with what amounts to her genius for public relationships.

Those close to The Queen find it difficult to understand the general public's haziness about her personality, because no one near The Queen, in whatever capacity, is in any doubt about the kind of person he or she serves. I was almost taken aback when a notably unsentimental member of the Royal Household, when trying to describe The Queen to me, spontaneously exclaimed, "You see she is GOOD—she is fundamentally GOOD." Because, in this disillusioned age, there is something a little disconcerting in coming up against someone—especially a young and very good-looking woman—who is GOOD. It conveys a sense of goody-goodyness, and this is where so many people go wrong about The Queen. They understand that The Queen is good, and some modern reflex action makes them feel that she must therefore also be somewhat dull. Or perhaps they feel that everyone in public life to-day is in some way "phoney", and therefore they search for some shadow upon her character which would make her in their eyes more "human". It is worthy of notice that the world's scandal press, in spite of diligent attempts, has found so little to whisper about The Queen.

This is not an account of The Queen written by one who is in direct contact with her. The Queen, quite rightly, is inaccessible to the Press. But it is the result of talking to scores, probably hundreds, of people who either work closely in contact with The Queen, or are close to her in one aspect of her life. This is not a mass of random adjectives heaped together to build up a sparkle-and-sugar figure of a fairy Queen, but an attempt to write a sober and objective account of a remarkable young woman in a uniquely important position.

It is the *same* woman who has been described to me by all the people with whom I have talked, by a High Commissioner to the Court of St. James, and a Moderator of the Church of Scotland, by a Member of The Queen's Household, by a woman who has entertained The Queen in her home, by another who has been The Queen's house guest, by a diplomat and by The Queen's Jeweller. Indeed, many of these dissimilar people who have spoken about The Queen have used exactly the same phrases in which to describe her. The Queen's character has grown and developed, but it has not changed since she was as a child steadfast, serious, truthful, imaginative and sympathetic. The Queen's light burns steadily. She has a great and constant loyalty to her family and friends, a fine gift for friendship and intimate human relationships. The Queen arouses and holds deep affection in those round her.

What is the character of The Queen?

The most important attributes of The Queen are perhaps her sincerity, her consideration for others, and her staying power. It is hard to think of qualities more needed for the long years of queenship. The Queen is a lovely woman, but much more is needed than beauty, which must fade; she has a zest for life and travel, but the enjoyment of strange, new experiences may eventually pall—great and helpful though these qualities are.

The Queen feels deeply within herself the power and force of what is good, and her life is deliberately dedicated to furthering everything in which she believes. Princess Marie Louise, writing with sympathetic understanding of The Queen's task, chose her word with care when she described it as a "vocation". It is as a vocation that The Queen has entered upon her sovereignty.

One of the Bishops who was near her at the time of her Coronation described to me, several years later, the moment at which The Queen offered her Sword upon the High Altar of Westminster Abbey:

"It was a most moving experience, being close at hand, watching her Coronation. She never thought of the crowds of people. She was completely taken up in her Act of Dedication. The most wonderful thing I ever saw in my life was the moment when she lifted the sword and laid it on the altar—she was putting her whole heart and soul to the service of her People."

The Queen can see the underlying meaning in what would otherwise be dull and repetitive duties. Her whole-heartedness, I am told by those best qualified to know, makes them realise what a privilege it is to work with her.

"The Queen has an inflexible standard of right and wrong," a cleric who is close to The Queen said to me.

Queen Elizabeth II does demand an impossible standard from herself. Yet she does not ask impossible standards from others. This is strange. It is extremely rare to find the highest and most inflexible personal standards combined with a warm compassion and tolerance, especially in someone young. Always, she is trying to do her very best.

Another eminent man of the Church, who had been close to The Queen at a time of crisis, said, "I was just amazed at her—the strength and ability of her mind, her sure grasp of affairs, her sense of real concern with and compassion for her people. She has a great sense of vocation. She is a woman not only graceful in her humanity, but full of the grace of God."

The Queen is conscientious, perhaps even over-conscientious. She is a planner, a hard worker, sometimes a worrier. She has a very high concept of the duties of queenship. An excellent reporter of the old school once said to me that he always considered the men under him as "percentage men". From A he would expect a 60 per cent job, from B an 85 per cent job and so on. The Queen expects from herself a 100 per cent job, and measures her results in minus points from complete achievement, whereas most of us sun ourselves in our plus marks. Yet occasionally—very occasionally—housewives who have probably failed to turn out the spare room this week, journalists who have scamped confirming a plausible statement, or lie-abouts who are doing practically nothing useful at all can be heard making petty critical remarks about some tiny aspect of The Queen's job which could not rate more than $\frac{1}{2}$ per cent at the most, as though they themselves were perfect. They are, however, only a very small minority. The vast majority of people fully acknowledge that The Queen attains a fantastically high achievement in a gruellingly hard lifework.

Because The Queen is never entirely satisfied with herself, she pays a great deal of heed to criticism. She ponders and considers how she can do better. She seeks advice from those she trusts, but she is not easily turned from a course of duty which she feels inwardly is right.

The Queen has an immense inner core of courage—the courage that faces fear.

She also has a deep respect for courage. Her childhood heroes of the war included many of the men decorated by her father with the Victoria Cross or the George Cross, and whose stories she pressed him to tell her. There were sad hearts in the schoolroom of Windsor Castle on the day it was known that Wing Commander Guy Gibson, V.C., D.S.O. and bar, D.F.C. and bar, had been killed.

Courage in the face of the enemy is not the only courage which The Queen admires. Recently she spoke with deep interest of watching a television programme in which a number of blind showed how they had adapted themselves to their new limitations. "What wonderful courage they have," she said. "And they were so gay. How they laughed at the mistakes they made." She had obviously been greatly touched.

She has an imaginative understanding and respect for others. A friend of hers said to me, "She has a very warm sympathy with people. She is just like her mother, always thinking 'How can I help So-and-so?' "

Lady Foot, writing from the tragic crisis of Cyprus, where her husband was Governor-General, gave me generous permission to quote from her account for the Red Cross of The Queen's visit to Jamaica where, in happier circumstances, Sir Hugh Foot was Governor-General at the time of The Queen's visit. This so vividly and naturally sets down The Queen's constant qualities that I am quoting it almost in full:

VISIT TO JAMAICA

By Her Majesty The Queen, Patron And President Of The British Red Cross Society

Lady Foot

Her Majesty the Queen is Patron and President of the British Red Cross Society. During the time when we in Jamaica had the privilege and unforgettable joy of having her among us each one of us looked for something in her—each one of us found what we were looking for. We had not known the meaning of the Queen's Majesty. We had so often read and heard of it—but when we saw her moving among us we knew what the Queen's Majesty was. A cool, quiet dignity, a thoughtful receptiveness, a serenity of mind, a sweet absorption and radiance coming from infinite gentleness and mercy. Those of us who belong to the Red Cross saw particularly this last and lovely characteristic—this rare virtue: Mercy—the Queen's Mercy—and felt enormously elated at the thought that we had for our Patron and President not only the Queen of England but a Lady whose mind and manner exemplified the true principle of the Red Cross.

I will always treasure the wonderful experience of being close to the Queen for three days and have stored in my mind many pictures and many incidents both small and big. I would like to write a few of the incidents which illustrate the beauty of the Queen's Mercy and thoughtfulness.

I remember first the incident of the little old country lady. It happened on the drive across the Island from Montego Bay to Kingston. I was in the second car following the car in which the Queen and the Duke of Edinburgh and my husband were travelling. My companion was the Lady Alice Egerton, Lady in Waiting to the Queen. It had rained during the night and the sun had come out in a cloudless sky and all the banks looked greener and all the bougainvillæa and hibiscus looked more brilliant and fresh and every tree looked more beautiful than ever before. I have crossed the Island along that road countless times but never have I seen Jamaica look more lovely and fresh and festive than it did on that day. And the people lined the sides of the roads—Jamaican country people, men and women and children in their gay holiday clothes, people who had waited for hours by the roadside in order to catch a glimpse of the Queen, patiently and cheerfully, quite prepared to spend the day. And we in the second car were moved to tears to see the expressions on the faces of those who had seen her—to hear them exclaim, to see the women embracing each other in wild excitement, the children leaping and jumping about and the men, open-mouthed, hat in hand, rooted to the spot, silent and spellbound. All the time Lady Alice and I kept a watchful eye upon the car in front of us. Many times the car slowed right down at the Queen's request because she had seen in that endless mob one person proffering a bunch of flowers. And the Queen stretched out her arm with a smile and a word of thanks and took the flowers.

But there was one time the Queen did not see the little old lady by the side of the road until the car had gone past. And she turned right round in her seat and waved and gestured to us, pointing to the old lady who was standing there holding in her hand a bunch of country flowers which must have been a fragrant posy of sweetness when she had gathered it in the morning but after hours of being held in a hot hand under a hot sun looked very wilted and tired. We knew of course what the Queen meant us to do and we stopped and spoke to the old lady and took her little bunch from her and took down her name and address so that she should have a little note of thanks from the Queen the next day. Lady Alice knew that the Queen would want to write and at the first stop as soon as she got out of the car the Queen said, "Alice, did you thank the old lady? Did you ask for her address? I am so sorry I did not see her in time, but we will write and thank her." She smiled and turned to speak of other things but I could only stand in silence and wonder at the gentleness of her mind and the sensitive understanding of one who with her vast preoccupations and endless duties is always mindful of not causing disappointment to those who have paid their own personal tribute to her no matter how humble.

Then later when we approached Linstead and drove into a sudden rainstorm the Queen again showed the greatest concern for the cubs and brownies who were lining the road. She spoke of her anxiety as a mother would speak, "They are so wet, poor little children, they will catch colds." And so throughout the days, her anxiety for instance that all letters of thanks going out to the many who had sent flowers or fruit should contain a specific reference. "I do not like to thank for flowers; I like to say what kind of flowers I have received and thank for them specifically." Her insistence that she should see every one of these tributes and have them by her. We had gifts from very humble country people—gifts of coconuts and sugar-cane, and one lady from Manchester sent a bunch of "celery grown in my own garden by my own hand for the Queen". All these gave her pleasure, the orchids and the sugar-cane, the roses and the celery, the carnations and the coconuts. We had rows of wooden steps built up against the window-sills in the wide porch off her bedroom—we had them built because we knew flowers would come but we had never thought of the produce and I must say that when the steps were banked high with bananas, coconuts, sugar-cane, celery and the great baskets of orchids and flowers, the sight was unforgettable and very symbolic of the variety of sweetness which is strewn in the path of a Queen.

Her Majesty was greatly concerned about the illness of the then Leader of the Opposition, Mr. Manley. In those days when we all caught the infection of her happiness and youth and gaiety those of us who were with her all the time were very moved by her consciousness of the one unhappiness which cast its shadow upon those sunny days. Many, many times during the day she would enquire after him and every day she sent messages to Drumblair.

And on the last night of her stay when she went up to dress—to put on her lovely gown (which she herself told me in great glee was "new for this splendid occasion") and to be adorned in all her splendour of Crown jewellery for the Banquet and Reception at King's House she asked whether our children would like to go up to her room to see her when she was ready. So the children went and filled their eyes with her beauty and she, in the happiest and most youthful manner, pirouetted in front of them and spoke to them in her bell-like and touchingly childish voice and seemed to enjoy showing herself to these entranced small creatures just as much as they enjoyed seeing this unforgettable sight.

These then are a few of the incidents which come to my mind, illustrating the thoughtfulness of our Queen and Patron. There were, of course, many, many others but all the time the most wonderful thing about this attitude of hers is that it is her own way of life. These are not things that can be taught, nor did we at any time feel that she had these spontaneous demonstrations of extraordinary concern for others out of a sense of duty. The Queen always seems to be tuned in on a special wave-length of her own, one that tells her that this one is sick and that one is wanting for comfort and the other is left out in the cold. And when the voice on that wave-length reaches her, her reaction is immediate, to bring comfort and happiness wherever it may be.

The Queen is slow to condemn. Even when she is brought face to face with a ghastly crime, as when she signs the reprieve of a murderer, she tries to puzzle out why a human being came to do such a dreadful thing. To her a criminal must be a most unhappy person, or he would never have taken such desperate measures.

When involved personally—and how much harder it is to be forgiving when we are personally affected—The Queen is completely lacking in vindictiveness. On one occasion, when a newspaper reporter whom she had formerly trusted had published a malicious and inaccurate article about her, one of her ladies-in-waiting said with emphasis that she intended to cut the reporter at the next available opportunity.

"Oh, don't do that," exclaimed The Queen spontaneously. "He is a nice man."

The Queen hates people to be hurt, either physically or mentally. Even as a child she was unusually understanding. The perplexities and deep wounds to the heart which her family suffered when her much-loved "Uncle David" decided to abdicate, the reluctance of her father to accept the Crown and the sense of duty which made him do so, made a deep impression on her.

So did the war. She spent most of the war years at Windsor.

For part of the time, for fear of an attempt upon the Heiress Presumptive, she was restricted in her movements even within the Great Park. Her father and mother were able to join their family only irregularly; their deep concern and anxiety were obvious to her. The war struck a family blow when, only a few days after Princess Elizabeth had thoroughly enjoyed the christening of little Prince Michael of Kent, she learnt the unbelievable news that his father, her Uncle George, had been killed. Many of the young Guards officers who had been stationed at Windsor were killed or wounded.

After her succession, when she gave a subscription to the Blue Cross, in aid of animal welfare, she asked that the money should be used "to save a horse from slaughter". A beautiful Suffolk Punch mare, aged only six, from a farm that was being mechanised, was in consequence purchased, suitably renamed Regina and put to the useful job of carting on Wimbledon Common.

The Queen has a good understanding of the ways in which she can help people. For instance, I know of several instances when she went privately to the theatre, and when the last thing she wanted was to become the centre of attention. However, she gave the management permission to announce her visit to the Press at the time of the fall of the curtain, so that the play could have the benefit of the publicity.

"She is patient and cheerful," said a Member of the Household. "When you think of all the demands made upon her, it makes you appreciate all the more how she conducts herself so cheerfully. Of course, being human, she does sigh occasionally about some particularly irritating detail, but fundamentally she does not complain about the things she has to do; she does them as part of a Queen's duty."

She is a good loser—note her immediate and sincere congratulations to Sir Gordon Richards, when he achieved his lifelong ambition to win the Derby, at the expense of The Queen's Aureole which was second.

The Queen is not an intellectual, but she has an immense store of common sense. Fortunately—and in a way rather pathetically—The Queen has had to learn much about life from paper. The deadly formal phrases of the long reports from the official Boxes, in which documents are brought to her, need strong-willed application before they spring to life. They are concentrated meat, and they unfold, to the careful reader, the story of our times. But without unflinching concentration they are just a mass of words. Much background knowledge and mental discipline is needed fully to grasp their meaning. The Queen reads her despatches methodically and with great interest. (I have seen a long document read by Her Majesty; a statement which was wrong had been changed, not only the first time it was made, but on every subsequent reference. A typing error was queried. There were other quiet and sensible little comments. The document had been most carefully read.)

The result is that what The Queen reads, she understands, she remembers, and she acts upon. She is immensely well informed. Her knowledge is thorough and well-grounded: it is very much more than that of an intelligent and fact-seeking member of the public—or of any one Government Department—because her sources of information are so much wider and more up to date. When she wishes special amplification and background information it is readily available, but already, in the ordinary course of her day's work, she sees nearly all the papers that go on a Prime Minister's table.

Reading and understanding this mass of paper which comes to The Queen is an exhausting task.

Never forget, The Queen is by instinct and desire a countrywoman. As a countrywoman The Queen is slow-growing and sturdy in her qualities; to be compared rather with a fine tree than a showy annual. She likes things and she likes people that *last*, and she is willing to work for a long time ultimately to reap the right result. The Queen is indeed a countrywoman by temperament, by outlook and by taste.

"The Queen does not seem to need to get up and fidget," said an artist to me, to whom The Queen sat, "she is so calming."

I once stood within a few yards of the Royal Family at a horse show where the people round her, although doing their best not to be inquisitive, could not help looking a great deal at The Queen and the Royal children, who were then quite young. Although The Queen knew that her children—restless like all children—were the focus for all eyes, let alone the relentless lenses of a score of Press cameras, she was calm and relaxed. The Queen did not fuss the children, but left them free to enjoy themselves until they required restraining, and then she did it in a quiet, easy way. Watch The Queen among horses, how her quiet and steady movements—never hurried, never startling—instil confidence.

A Member of the Household said, "Look at those corgi dogs—you know how corgis are always barking and other people are always shouting themselves hoarse at the dogs. But not The Queen. She never raises her voice to them, and yet, somehow, they always obey her and keep close to her."

The Queen rules her household in this same quiet manner. When she has given her confidence to those around her, she then stands back and allows them freedom to do their job according to their high standards—in which she believes implicitly—without fussing or confusing them with contradictory orders. The Queen does not change her attitude, even if her people are subject to criticism and attack. She backs them up. Every man or woman who has served in the Forces knows what that quality means in their Commanding Officer.

Constancy is not easy to describe. The Queen is not a fireworks kind of person. She does not lend herself to bright little anecdotes, because she is not unexpected. We know what to expect of her, and that we can always rely on her.

The Queen creates an atmosphere of trust and sincerity round her: she is steady in affection. She has outstanding qualities of steadfastness. She never takes up an interest or a person on impulse, to drop them again just as lightly. She is a serene person in a firmly-rooted setting.

It is just as well that The Queen is a balanced person, when you realise that her apparently serene life is lived out against a background of perpetual crises. There is a popular concept that The Queen is "away from it all", exempt from all the anxieties, worries and frustrations of the average life. True enough, The Queen is relieved of the ordinary woman's burden of waking up in a cold house and going down to make the breakfast day after day, month after month. But instead she wakes up every day to the knowledge of tensions, quarrels, potential and actual dangers in the Commonwealth and all over the world. There are few political headaches (only those which are purely party affairs) which she does not share. All the crises come to her *before* they are resolved, whereas the general public generally only hears about them when they have been cobbled together.

Everyone knows that the burden of cares pressing upon the politician in office is a constant strain, sometimes resulting in illness and even death. The increase of pace and pressure with every year is recognised. The Queen is always in office. The Queen, of course, cannot make policy. But she is there to implement it, to make power acceptable by her presence, to be informed and to comment, to soothe quarrels and to work always for the general unity.

The Queen is very strong indeed, and stands up to work which would knock many people flat. She finds it easier to work in heat, which affects her remarkably little, than in extreme cold, which she feels intensely. Nevertheless in the spring and summer of 1958 she suffered a series of heavy colds, and one attack of sinusitis, and was slower to shake them off than might have been expected in one of her age and natural strength.

She plans sensibly when she has a hard day in store. Never a particularly late-night person—nor is the Duke—she goes early to bed on the days before a heavy programme.

One usual feminine form of relaxation is not much used by The Queen. She does not relax in spending binges as do so many women. Perhaps this is because she has little time to visit shops—except for shopping for Christmas presents in one or two famous stores, goods are generally brought to her in the Palace. More probably it is a matter of temperament. The Queen is a careful shopper. She likes to get value for her money, and is careful about the lasting quality of the goods she buys. Particularly she does not like to pay fancy prices for children's clothing. The children's clothes have big hems for letting down—you can see the tell-tale line on some of Princess Anne's winter coats. All the Royal Family's country clothes are worn until they are decently shabby.

Perhaps this is because Princess Elizabeth grew up during the war, when economy was continually urged upon her.

For The Queen, buying clothes is part of the job, and to begin with she suffered from the unkind criticisms sometimes made about her dress. Although line and fashion can never be a really major issue in her life, she has recently shown considerable fashion-consciousness, and with great success. The Queen buys her clothes methodically and according to plan. Otherwise this considerable item in her budget might reach truly staggering figures.

Whenever practicable, The Queen wears her father's robes, and as the Sovereign's robes have considerable trains the difference in height creates no difficulty.

She has a great love for the things she has always known, and for possessions she has acquired from those she loves. For example, when she was made Lady of the Garter, her father presented her with her jewelled Garter Star. This was of the square shape introduced in Georgian times. Later, King George VI reverted to the more elongated and elegant Carolean Star, worn in the days of the Stuarts. Although The Queen appreciates the beauty of the Carolean Star, now that she is in turn Sovereign of the Order she continues to wear the Georgian Star on her Garter mantle, just because it was a gift from her father.

The Queen has so little liking for the ostentatious that it was six years after she came to the throne before she ever wore her most valuable brooch, which is the third and fourth part of the Cullinan diamond, a story told in full in a later chapter.

The Queen likes her jewels as she likes her friends, for their associations and for the memories they bring her, as well as for their qualities.

Although King George VI used to marvel that his daughters were so much less shy than he had been as a boy, The Queen has always been accustomed to being a little apart. She is thoughtful and sensitive. It takes her a little time to be on really close terms with someone, and by the circumstances of her upbringing she knew intimately few of her contemporaries except Princess Margaret. It is not as easy for her to relax absolutely with other people as it is, for instance, for Princess Alexandra of Kent, who was at boarding school.

How much more difficult it would have been for The Queen, with her compelling sense of duty, if it had not been for marriage with the more relaxed Duke of Edinburgh. Would even her iron health and unflinching resolution have been able to stand up to the unremitting strain?

The Duke of Edinburgh's easy confidence in his public duty, his ability to produce spontaneously a pleasant *bon mot*—often of such a high standard of wit that it remains, in cold blood, extremely quotable—his way with people were and are of incalculable value. His searching mind, his ability (so rare these days) to see the wood in spite of the trees, lend a special value to his rôle as Consort. The Duke of Edinburgh has the wise and wide interests which were invaluable in the Prince Consort to Queen Victoria, plus the invaluable lighter touch.

Particularly in the early days of Princess Elizabeth's public appearances, there was a marked difference in her ability to be at ease according to whether her husband was, or was not, with her. On the other hand, the Duke of Edinburgh gained just as much from The Queen; pleasant and apparently engrossed participation in long and sometimes deadly dull official functions was not something that came all that easily to the Duke.

Meeting large crowds was something of an ordeal for The Queen at first, especially when she became the principal figure. From the Press reports of The Queen's tour of Canada in 1951 as Princess Elizabeth, one gains the impression that, to begin with, she was overwhelmed by the enthusiastic reception of the crowds, to such an extent that she smiled much less than had been expected. The reports go on to say that the warmth and friendliness of the crowds in Manitoba, Alberta and British Columbia as she travelled westward broke down her reserve so much that when she returned eastward to the Atlantic and spent thirty-six hours in Montreal, she was entirely relaxed and at home with crowds just as enthusiastic and overwhelming as those she had met previously in Ottawa and Toronto with reserve and restraint.

This is not an entirely false picture, but like many day-to-day reports it is an over-simplification. The impact of the North American Continent is a very powerful one, all the more so to those who must continually fill the centre of the stage. Probably The Queen did find this surprising and perhaps, at first, daunting. But those of the Household who were lucky enough to be in attendance were continually amazed at The Queen's resilience, and found she was more relaxed after the first week and became more used to it. "My memory is of someone going not from weakness to strength, but from strength to greater strength," said one man who followed the whole Canadian Tour.

The Queen armed herself for her public duties by being perfectly prepared for two main reasons; she would not dream of the discourtesy of taking part in a ceremony or attending a function without understanding what it was all about, and because it was less of a strain when she knew exactly what she had to do.

She was not a ready improviser, and did not always find it easy to change course suddenly in the middle of a carefully planned engagement in order to take in some newly-arisen situation. This presented difficulties for her in the early days of her public engagements, especially when her husband, who is superb at improvisation, was not with her. With practice, and still more with confidence, The Queen has become more flexible. She is freed from an almost too strict regard for the clock, without losing her marvellous punctuality.

"Now they enjoy things when they go wrong," I was told, only the other day, by a Member of her Household throughout her reign.

All the same, The Queen's shyness is possibly not entirely mastered, and possibly it never will be completely subdued.

At the opening of the extension to the Baltic Exchange, the shipping and grain market in London, a couple of years ago, The Queen entered the building very close to where I was standing. She was looking absolutely lovely. She was wearing a deep apricot-coloured lace gown, embroidered in gold thread, and over it the blue riband of the Garter. On her head sparkled the marguerite tiara given to Queen Mary by the Marys of Great Britain and Ireland at her wedding, and which Queen Mary gave to The Queen at her wedding. Round her throat was a triple diamond necklace. In her ears swung chandelier finely-cut diamonds, an heirloom gift from her father. She looked like a being from another world, utterly without cares. She knew well most of the notabilities at the door, and she laughed and joked with them in a completely relaxed way. Then she came forward to enter the Room, which was filled with many hundreds of people. Her pathway was lined with people, every head was turned towards the door, nearly a thousand people staring at her. There was a little pause before she entered the Room: and The

Queen took a deep breath and stiffened for one instant—then, a composed and relaxed figure, she moved forward among those hundreds of eyes.

Even as recently as 1957, before The Queen spoke on television to her subjects in Canada, she was so tensed up, so worried, that she could not bear to think about it. "It is so absolutely irrevocable", she said (quite accurately) to one of her Household.

Even after it was over, she was pent up with nervousness about opening the Canadian Parliament next day. Certainly it was by no means the first Parliament she had opened, but she still felt it to be an ordeal.

"I always have butterflies when I open Parliament," she remarked.

The Queen must always appear unruffled and composed.

It is not only in times of political crisis that The Queen must appear calm and composed in public, she must show the same calm whatever the turmoil of her heart during personal anxieties. On the day before her father underwent his lung operation—an operation she knew to be critical—Princess Elizabeth did not remain in the comforting unity of her family, but went out, pale but smiling, to take part in a film première in aid of nursing funds, which she had previously promised to attend. Only a fortnight after her father had undergone that severe operation, while he was still a very sick man, the Princess had to fly across the Atlantic to take up the considerable ordeal of her first independent Commonwealth Tour. She had to mourn her father in public, and her courage and dignity, and that of the widowed Queen Mother, is something that we who witnessed it will never forget.

Perhaps even more difficult are occasions when The Queen has had to live out personal crises in the public eye. It is known that she suffered agonies as a young woman at an unresolved period of her courtship when there were well-meaning but embarrassing calls of "Where's Philip?" when she appeared in public. At the time when Princess Margaret was having to make a fundamental emotional decision in her life, it cannot have been pleasant for any of the Royal Family to appear before the inquisitive gaze of the public. When a bubble of rumour was blown up regarding a completely mythical "rift" between The Queen and her husband at a time when he was overseas attending the Opening of the Olympic Games in Melbourne, she had a barrage of prying eyes around her at the time of their happy reunion. No, it cannot be easy. No sense of duty, no training in the world, no fortitude, can make the constant pressure of millions of eyes and ears anything but a continual strain.

At the same time The Queen has much happiness from her many encounters with the public. She knows sincerity when she sees it, and gains great happiness from the sincere affection of her many friends in every possible position throughout the Commonwealth. The sight of a smiling, friendly face glimpsed through the car window, or a simple, heart-felt letter from one of her subjects can bring her rewarding joy.

One reason why her public engagements are much easier for her now than then is that even The Queen is now beginning to re-meet people instead of everlastingly meeting new ones. She will always enjoy meeting a person for the second, third and subsequent times more than the first. She is surrounded by old friends of many years' standing. Checking up from available accounts of accessions over some centuries shows that no Sovereign, on accession, made fewer changes in the people round the Throne. The Queen took over her father's Household *en masse* and retained them in her service, at the same time finding place for those already employed around her. Nearly all the changes between her father's Household and hers to-day have been caused by time. The Queen's steadfastness is a quality of immense value to those who work for her and know her trust is not lightly withdrawn.

But however much support The Queen can and does get from her millions of loyal subjects, it would be almost impossible for her to sustain the burden of her position without the happiness of her personal surroundings.

The family comes first with most people, not least with The Queen. She was a happy daughter, growing up in a happy family. It was a curiously isolated and quiet life at the centre of a whirling and confused world, a still axis round which revolved the passions and furies of the warring world outside.

The Queen has inherited her sense of duty from her father: her interest in and sympathy with the lives of other people from her mother. The Queen has a considerable likeness to Queen Mary too.

The Queen has always been happy and relaxed within a family circle, but the Duke, with his wide circle of friends and experiences, his different approach to what was going on around him, gave The Queen a new concept of modern life. Her interests and her pleasures were multiplied.

It is a thousand pities for The Queen's happiness that she had only four short comparatively carefree years as the wife of a naval officer before her father's death brought upon her at the age of twenty-five the full burden of sovereignty.

But it is not so often realised that The Queen gave to the Duke of Edinburgh what he had never known, and that is the happiness of a secure and constant home. All sailors are wanderers, and so particularly appreciate the security and stability of a happy home. Furthermore, the Duke had twice been exiled, with all that means in insecurity and rootlessness. He had been brought up partly in Greece, partly in France, partly in Germany, and partly in England and Scotland. He had served throughout the war at sea. Although he had always regarded the home of his uncle, Earl Mountbatten of Burma, as his, Prince Philip had never really had a home of his own until The Queen made it for him in the unlikely setting of a palace.

The Queen and the Duke of Edinburgh do things together. They plan together the children's upbringing, the year's programmes, the research into the background of the events they attend, all the details of their two extremely busy lives.

They like the same kind of life. They both enjoy fun, but are fundamentally serious. They are extremely idealistic. They are hard-working. They are conscientious. They enjoy finding things out, and will take immense pains to do so. They like people who do things. They like all sorts of different kinds of people, and neither is in the slightest degree a "snob".

The Duke of Edinburgh is more outspoken and more easily irritated by rudeness or impertinence. He has possibly less patience with interminable formal affairs; he is extremely quick-witted and indeed has one of the most spontaneous and delightful wits in the country. He is more accustomed to "roughing it"— but do not think The Queen was "brought up in a hot-house";

she thinks nothing of going out and staying out in the vilest weather. But fundamentally they like the same people and the same things, and they share the same ideals.

The Queen has shown perspicuity and sympathy in the highest degree in her relationship with her husband. When they married, the average man sympathised deeply with the Duke's equivocal situation as a man inferior in rank to his wife. That feeling has quite vanished. Everyone appreciates that the Duke is doing a magnificent job.

When they married, The Queen fought to preserve for her husband the naval career for which he was trained and which he loved. When the Duke's keen mind grasped the immense but self-made potentialities of his job, The Queen saw to it that he had the amplest scope.

Although the Duke of Edinburgh, I am told by one who knows him well, does not care "a docken leaf for position", The Queen secured his place—because The Queen's husband has no place by right—by giving him in February 1957, by Letters Patent under the Great Seal, the style and titular dignity of a Prince of the United Kingdom of Great Britain and Northern Ireland, and early in her reign (October 1952) by a Warrant signed by her assigning to him "Place, Pre-eminence and Precedence next to Her Majesty".

By the Regency Act of November 19, 1953, Prince Philip will become Regent in the event of the death of The Queen during Prince Charles's minority, instead of Princess Margaret, as would have been the case under the existing Regency Act of 1937. The Home Secretary, Sir David Maxwell Fyfe (now Lord Kilmuir), announced to the Commons that: "I am authorised to say that Princess Margaret shares the desire of The Queen that if a Regency should become necessary, Prince Philip should become Regent."

The Queen has not forced upon Prince Philip any large part in ceremonial affairs. At the Coronation he took part only as a royal duke, being the first to kiss the hand of The Queen, his wife, in fealty. But The Queen appointed him President of the Coronation Committee, which decided matters behind the scenes, and President of the Mint Committee, which advised on the designs of seals, coins and medals.

At the Opening of Parliament he does not even wear a duke's

robes over his naval uniform when he escorts The Queen to her place on the Throne.

He was not present at the earliest of The Queen's Birthday Parades, and takes part now as Colonel of the Welsh Guards and not as Consort of the Sovereign.

The Queen and the Duke of Edinburgh are very nearly perfect complements of each other's strengths and weaknesses. They make a wonderful combination.

What kind of mother is The Queen? is a question often asked.

"The Queen is really an ordinary mother," said a Member of the Household. "She did not much like sending her son away to school—what mother would? But she was very philosophical about it, and has been extremely careful not to ask for special privileges for Charles. When he went away to school, she was very anxious to hear every little detail about how he was getting on from those who saw him. But she did not fuss him."

The Queen is on easy terms with her children. I have watched her with Prince Charles, talking away to each other as though they were contemporaries, while she has enormous fun with the effervescent Princess Anne. The Queen has always entered into the children's games; she has been an engine driver, a porter or a policeman, an extra hand at snap, a companion on a morning ride as the occasion demanded. She takes the children very much for granted when they are with her, talks to them easily and naturally as people, never considering that they require a special kind of face or manner, as do some people who are basically ill at ease with the young.

The Queen and the Duke—because of course both parents together bring up the children, as in any ordinary family—have an extremely hard job.

I had the privilege, a few years ago, of writing some small books about the royal children, and on one occasion a message was passed to me by one of the Household from The Queen:

"Prince Charles must be brought up to be a good man, because if he is not a good man, how can he possibly be a good king?"

The Queen is seeking to bring up her children as ordinary children, enjoying a wide circle of friends and a normal range of interests. It is a simple enough ambition, yet it is extraordinarily difficult to achieve. The interest of the ordinary public, whetted by the Press, radio and television, has increased vastly in recent years. When the royal children are recognised, they are all too often exposed to a barrage of curiosity. When Prince Charles went to the Hill House Pre-Preparatory School in Hans Place, on one morning, when a spot check was made, nearly two hundred housewives and about thirty photographers had assembled to watch this one small boy go into school.

Parents whose children were in school with Prince Charles found themselves rung up by their friends and asked for details about Prince Charles. A few parents did ask their sons many questions about him, but on the whole his schoolmates behaved remarkably well.

When Prince Charles went away to Cheam School, this, as a boarding school in its own secluded grounds, would appear an easier place to protect him from public curiosity. Yet on no fewer than sixty-eight of the eighty-eight days of his first term, in the autumn of 1957, stories about Prince Charles, or about the school and its staff, were featured in the London Press alone. Matters grew to such a head that what had been a happy and contented school was being turned into a place of mistrust and suspicion where no one knew who—if anyone—had been responsible for the latest story in the Press.

As a result, in the Christmas holidays the editors of the London papers were invited to Buckingham Palace, where they met The Queen's Press Secretary and the Headmaster of Cheam School, who explained to them what the constant surveillance and attempts at bribery had meant in terms of the school's happiness, and how impossible the situation had become. The editors were plainly told that if such close attention was paid to even the smallest detail of Prince Charles's schooldays, The Queen and the Duke of Edinburgh would be forced to remove him from Cheam and to educate him privately. Fortunately the result was a complete curtain in the London Press on minor gossip about Prince Charles at school.

The world outside hardly realises how alike The Queen and Princess Margaret are in many things. They over-simplify the characters of the two sisters, forgetting that The Queen too loves to play duets on the piano, to sing the choruses of old songs and to play family games such as Scrabble or charades, as an antidote to the anxieties of the day. Both sisters are country lovers, they enjoy long walks or rides in beautiful country, whatever the weather. Yet they are neither of them athletic or games players. Although they took their bronze life-saving medals for swimming, they do not seem to swim much now. They are extremely good friends, although their different lives prevent them from seeing as much of each other as they did.

Who are The Queen's personal friends? is often asked.

I have been told by one who knows The Queen well that her closest woman friend, other than her sister, is undoubtedly Miss Margaret MacDonald, her Dresser, who has been her companion and confidante since those days when Princess Elizabeth was in her charge when King George VI and his family moved into Buckingham Palace. What the Queen owes to Miss MacDonald's care and helpfulness could never be set down in words.

So close is the rapport between The Queen and Miss MacDonald that it has been called "almost telepathic". She is of medium height, trim and slim, beginning to go grey, a capable, decided, much-travelled woman of the greatest efficiency, loyalty and integrity, on whom The Queen relies implicitly.

The Queen comes into contact with more people, probably, than any but a dozen other people in the world. Friendship has grown with those whom work and interests have brought into recurrent contact with her, and with whom that indefinable reciprocal sympathy has flourished. The Queen has exceptionally wide interests and sympathies, therefore her friends are drawn from an exceptionally wide range. They are of all ages (she has never had any trouble in getting on with those either older or younger than herself), of many races and creeds.

But to The Queen old friends are best, because she is happier with a person the longer she knows him or her. She has many true friends among people considerably older then herself. Her father's counsellors and Household have always been devoted to her. Owing to the war, she has few really intimate friends from her schoolroom days, although she made some good friends in the Sea Rangers and the A.T.S. Her closest contemporary women friends are probably to be found among her ladies-in-waiting.

The Queen's circle of personal friends is not to be found among the ultra-fashionable nor "café society", but among pleasant hard-working people, often with a country background.

Such are the Duke and Duchess of Beaufort. He is her Master of the Horse, a delightful man with a great knowledge of horses, who is also The Queen's remote relative, being descended from John of Gaunt, son of King Edward III, and whose wife, a descendant of King George III, is a closer kinswoman.

Many of The Queen's friends are to be found among her Household and employees. The Queen "lives above the shop": her place of work and her home are combined. The people who work for her are very much more a part of her family life than is the case with the average employer and employee. It is essential that they should get on well together.

Contrary to report, not many of the Household have enjoyed close contact with the Royal Family before being appointed. When they arrive, they are immediately made welcome and put on friendly footing. The Queen and the Duke of Edinburgh normally address the Household either by Christian or nicknames, while a Member of the Household says "Ma'am" or "Sir" when addressing The Queen or the Duke of Edinburgh.

The Palace has a young Head. The Queen is not stuffy or old-fashioned in her way of thinking, and she does not like stuffy or old-fashioned people round her. She is courteous by nature and upbringing. There is a lot of laughing and joking in the Royal Family circle. The Queen and the Household share many jokes, but The Queen is studiously careful that she should never appear to laugh at anyone.

"The Queen is very quick on the uptake," I was told by someone in close contact with her.

Everything is decided and carried on at a brisk, decisive pace. The Household works normal office hours at Buckingham Palace. In addition, there are many occasions when The Queen is working late, either on her Boxes or on public engagements, when Members of the Household are required to be on duty.

It used to be the custom for the lady-in-waiting to live wherever The Queen or Queen Consort might be during her period of waiting, and similarly for the male Members of the Household to be constantly on call. Queen Victoria, indeed, disregarded wives to almost the same extent as the old-time Royal Navy or Colonial

Service, and had little compunction in taking her married Household with her for months to Scotland or the Isle of Wight without considering their domestic arrangements. Times change in Palaces as elsewhere, and the job of serving The Queen as a Member of her Household has changed with it.

The Queen's lady-in-waiting no longer lives in at Buckingham Palace, and goes home after her day's work like anyone else, unless perhaps she has accompanied The Queen on a very late evening engagement or has an early start next morning, when she may occupy the bedroom of the suite which is always set aside for her. No lady-in-waiting, private secretary or equerry normally goes with The Queen and the Duke of Edinburgh when they go to Windsor for the "weekend" (which is frequently only one night).

But when the Court is in residence in Windsor, or when The Queen is at Sandringham, Holyrood or Balmoral or on a regional or overseas tour, then Members of the Household accompany her. On such occasions The Queen and the Duke of Edinburgh share their relaxations with the Household, and they take part together in many games and amusements.

The Queen always bears in mind such things as school holidays when she is arranging the rotas of duties for her ladies-in-waiting with her Mistress of the Robes, Mary, Duchess of Devonshire.

The Queen is always remembering the interests of those around her. At her Coronation, in spite of all she had on her mind, she seemed to forget no one. A woman who worked as a V.A.D. inside the Palace that day told me that just as The Queen was leaving her room to go to the Abbey, she sent a message to them to come to the entrance hall, so that they could see her there.

A dressmaker told me, "She is the easiest person to serve. She puts you at ease at once, and is always trying to think how she can make your job lighter."

The Queen relaxes most quickly in the open air: it is her way of shaking off tiredness. On the morning after her Coronation, she was out early in the grounds of Buckingham Palace, riding side-saddle on Winston, in training for her Birthday Parade. On the morning after her return from the strenuous French State Visit, she went out riding with her family in Windsor Great Park very early next morning.

Whatever the pressure upon her, The Queen always gets into the open air, at least in the garden, every day. When she is staying at Buckingham Palace she goes off briskly into the grounds in all kinds of weather, accompanied often by Princess Anne and always by the dogs. At Windsor she often rides in the early morning, leaving the rest of the day free for work. At Balmoral and Sandringham she is out of doors all the time she can spare from her paper work.

With horses, The Queen can relax completely and forget everything except the present moment.

When The Queen is completely engrossed, her face reflects her emotions almost as transparently as does Princess Anne's. I remember watching The Queen during the Olympic Games in Stockholm, when her own horse, Countryman, was fulfilling the heavily-marked and highly technical dressage test of the combined horse trials. Dressage is for experts, but as Colonel Frank Weldon, Captain of the British gold-medal team and individual bronze medallist, remarked to me then, "The Queen really understands dressage." Again and again, in the early mornings at Windsor, where the team in training were her guests, The Queen had watched the long hours of practice for just this moment. She knew every movement and point of the complex routine by heart. She urged her horse through every stage by motion of hand and nodding head, visibly counting the horse's steps as he reined back. And as Countryman left the arena she gave a delighted smile and a "thumbs up" signal to Princess Margaret.

At horse shows I have watched her face when she is seeing the great masters of horsemanship taking their horses round a really difficult jumping course. Her love of the art of horsemanship goes far beyond the natural desire that the British horses should win. She goes with each horse every inch of the way, and you can see her "riding" a reluctant horse into the fences. She delights in watching the great masters of pace and judgement, whether they are the D'Inzeo brothers from Italy, or our own Colonel Harry Llewellyn, Miss Pat Smythe or Mr. Peter Robeson.

But her heart is truly on the side of those battling against bad luck. At Richmond horse show some years ago a small boy, who has since become an international rider, had to make an extra round after what seemed, on the face of it, a hard decision by the judges, although of course it was an exact interpretation of the rules. The Queen was with that lad every inch of the way, and when he ultimately won, she turned to her lady-in-waiting and laughed with spontaneous delight.

I have heard The Queen laughing like that—young, carefree, happy—in the distance in Buckingham Palace.

The Queen is great good fun when at ease. This has been emphasised to me time and time again by those who have been in close contact with her.

"We had no idea The Queen could be so gay," said the wife of an artist who accompanied her husband to Buckingham Palace when he painted Her Majesty. "She was radiant," and the Scottish artist made use of a homely Scottish phrase which the Queen Mother would understand, "She absolutely cawed the feet from us."

"The Queen enjoys an amusing story, and likes a neat or comical turn of phrase," said another person who is in close contact with the Queen.

"A lot of laughing goes on in this house," said an official at the Palace.

As everyone knows, The Queen has one hobby which over-rides her other relaxations, with the exception of the time she spends with her family. That is her love of horses. From the time she was a very little girl, and rode with Owen, the stud groom at Windsor (who died only recently in retirement at a great age), she has had a tremendous interest in horses.

Many small girls go through a phase of adoring their ponies and their riding, but afterwards drop it. With The Queen it has always been rather different. She is extremely fond of riding. She is a good, competent rider, although not in the top flight.

Where The Queen excels is in the far less common sphere of horse management. Even when she was very young she was insatiable in her search for knowledge of stable care. She realises that it is the long weeks of training and care behind the scenes that really count in making a good horse, as much as the few hectic minutes of competition. She is never so busy nor so far from home that she is not constantly in contact with her Stud Manager.

The Queen is a real expert about the breeding of horses, their training and care. It is significant that, although there are many owners of racehorses in England, and many of them are extremely astute and wealthy men, The Queen is almost alone in making racing pay. This is not because she has bought vastly expensive bloodstock bred by other people, but as the just reward for her instinct for horses. "She has great knowledge and love of horses," commented a racing expert close to The Queen.

The Queen's racehorses are in two categories, and both have done well for her.

There are the horses which she owns (and almost always breeds) herself, of which she bears all the expenses and collects all the winnings. They are trained by Captain Cecil Boyd Rochfort at Freemason Lodge, Newmarket. Of these, the greatest so far was her bright chestnut Aureole, which she bred herself and which won £36,225. He is now at stud at Sandringham.

Then there are the horses bred by the National Stud, and leased to The Queen for their racing life. Up to the death of the late Lord Lonsdale, these young horses were leased and raced by him, thereafter they were leased and raced first by King George VI and now by The Queen. The Queen pays the racing expenses of these horses, and their winnings are equally divided between The Queen and the National Stud. When they retire from racing, they are returned to the National Stud. These horses are trained by Mr. Noel Murless at his beautiful stables at Warren Place, Newmarket.

It was with a National Stud horse that The Queen won her first Classics race in 1957, the filly Carozza which won The Oaks. The Queen had two horses in the race, and her other runner Mulberry Harbour was the better fancied. Carozza was in front three furlongs from home, but was tiring and being overhauled rapidly by the Irish challenger Silken Glider in the last furlong. The two mares passed the post so close together that a photo-finish was called upon, and bets were freely given and taken in the few minutes until the plate was developed. Both jockeys thought they had won. The photograph showed that The Queen's Carozza had stayed to win by a nose, or as *The Times* described it next morning "the width of a nostril". A tremendous and sustained cheer went up when the result was known.

The Queen thoroughly enjoys racing. She goes to see the

horses, not to see the frocks, or even primarily to meet her friends. She is tending to spend more of her rare leisure time in visiting studs and stables, and less in going to the actual race-meetings, as it is breeding and stable management which interest her most.

The Queen is not interested in betting. There is absolutely nothing of the gambler in her make-up.

Some people who love the thoroughbred horse have no use for his less aristocratic brethren. But The Queen is interested in all horses, and in the way in which their conformation is suited to meet the special demands of their work.

She was one of the first people in Britain to appreciate dressage, which is the advanced training of a horse in flexibility and obedience, for a long time looked upon as some kind of foreign nonsense by many of our horsemen, who thought it spoilt the natural courage of the animal. It is now generally considered that a highly disciplined good horse will inevitably beat an equally good undisciplined horse, just as trained soldiers will beat undisciplined individuals.

The Queen, together with the Queen Mother, the Duke of Beaufort and Colonel V. D. S. Williams (the father of Mr. Dorian Williams, the television commentator), put up the money to retain Mr. Bertie Hill's good combined trials horse Countryman for the British Olympic team. The Queen gave permission for the horse to be entered in her name; and so he became the first royal horse to win an Olympic Gold Medal.

I saw The Queen's face as Countryman passed her on the gruelling cross-country section on the second day. It mirrored conflicting pride in how well her horse was going with concern as to how he should fare in the remainder of this arduous course. Fortunately The Queen did not see Countryman straddled across the top bar of a *trakena* (a stout timber fence set in a ditch, by then filled with heavy mud), with his legs slipping in the mud on either side. It was a terrible moment, saved by Mr. Hill's calm control of an exceedingly dangerous situation, and the horse's own unconquerable courage.

When, that evening, a fire broke out near the Swedish Cavalry stables where the British horses were quartered, and the tired horses had to be led to safety, The Queen did not content herself with enquiring whether the horses were all right, she went to the stables herself next morning.

The Queen is interested in army chargers, her carriage horses, in farm-horses and pit ponies. I can hardly imagine a situation in which a horse would not momentarily deflect her interest from the matter in hand. Horsemen all over the world regard The Queen as a real authority on their subject.

How thankful we should be that The Queen has a hobby in which she can relax entirely, moreover a healthy relaxation which gives her exercise and takes her into the open air.

Naturally enough, each Sovereign's hobby differs. King George V, her grandfather, rather unexpectedly relaxed completely with his stamp collection. He also was completely engrossed when yacht-racing—unfortunately Queen Mary actively disliked being afloat—and shooting, at which he was a great expert.

King George VI, The Queen's father, enjoyed every form of country activity. He preferred walking up game to shooting from a butt. He loved gardening, especially landscape gardening. Perhaps he was at his happiest when clearing a prickly tangled undergrowth and tending an enormous bonfire.

The Queen's hobby is neither gardening nor collecting stamps, although she does a little of both, but everything to do with horses. She rides frequently when at Windsor or in the country, although she does not ride in the Row in London as King George V did. Her horses are not specially valuable thoroughbreds, but good, well-mannered hacks, of whom she is very fond. Although she often sends a token exhibit to Royal Windsor Horse Show (where she has been a prize-winner in the driving classes) and often lends one of her horses for the Parade of famous horses at "The Horse of the Year Show", she has never gone in for riding show-hunters or show-hacks.

Where The Queen has competed is in flat-racing, and with such success that she was twice leading owner on the flat in the first six years of her reign. Since her accession she has not so far owned a horse trained under National Hunt rules. She was much distressed when Monaveen, the fine steeplechaser which she owned in partnership with the Queen Mother, was fatally injured on the racecourse. However, she often goes with the Queen Mother to watch her horses run.

Her other hobbies and interests are walking in the country; having a gun-dog; farming; deerstalking; picnics with her family; reading—in spite of the vast amount of official reading she has to do, she still enjoys reading autobiographies and biographies and amusing novels; watching television; seeing films; going to the theatre, especially to well-acted modern plays; listening to music as well as playing music; Scottish country dancing; driving a car; walking and playing with the dogs, and a mass of other activities for which she has more inclination than time.

Now that we have been thinking about The Queen's character and her personality, let us look again at a picture of The Queen, and consider what reveals the character in her face.

When Signor Annigoni first met her, he was immediately struck by the lovely poise of The Queen's head. Others have reacted to her clear and steady gaze, her sweetness of expression and her most beautiful colouring. In expression The Queen varies considerably, grave, thoughtful, occasionally withdrawn, compassionate and amused by turn. She never looks lovelier than when her eyes and mouth are lit by her warm and slightly shy smile, and there is something infectious (and in a way touching) about her occasional spontaneous and very youthful laugh.

The particular qualities of The Queen's appearance are well shown on those occasions when she, at a Royal Film performance, meets the most beautiful women in the film world, all in their best "bibs and tuckers", and without any effort holds every eye.

The value of The Queen's beauty should never be underestimated. It has been a great draw in attracting the interest and appreciation of millions of people upon the woman who is the leader of the Commonwealth.

But of what use would good looks be, without the inner warmth of heart and sincerity of purpose which impel The Queen? This is not a pretty actress assuming the part of a Queen. This is a woman of long lineage and firm purpose, to whom her sovereignty is her vocation and who has promised herself to her vocation as Queen as solemnly as a priest to the church or a doctor to healing.

This is our Queen.

CHAPTER THREE

The Queen's Back-room

"The Queen has on her table nearly all the documents that go to the Prime Minister."   Jennings.

"This interminable amount of desk work . . ."
The Duke of Windsor about the Sovereign's routine work.

"She has an amazing way of sucking facts out of the dullest document."   A Member of the Household.

"She is extremely well informed."
     A Commonwealth Prime Minister.

THE Queen's programme contains differing types of commitments which recur at differing distances, and which form the pattern of her life.

There is the *annual* pattern, as a result of which The Queen usually spends Christmas at Sandringham, Easter at Windsor, part of August and September at Balmoral, and much of the time between at Buckingham Palace.

In each year there are also a number of *recurring public events* which The Queen attends. These include the Opening of Parliament, the Royal Maundy Service, the Royal Garden Parties and attendance at the Cenotaph Memorial Service on Remembrance Day.

Equally a part of her normal life are the *visits overseas*—either State Visits to foreign countries or, on an ever-increasing scale, stays in other parts of the Commonwealth. These do not take place at regularly spaced intervals, but, when viewed from a distance of time, will be seen to be roughly spaced in biennial groups.

Within the framework of these main themes are placed all the irregularly recurring engagements such as regional tours (which themselves follow a careful pattern), the celebration of centenaries, the opening of important new buildings, reviews of troops and

63

associations, and the whole wide range of events which The Queen, by her attendance, marks as important to the Nation's progress.

But the background to the whole design is the *daily* pattern of The Queen's life. This is the least known part of The Queen's duties, and yet without it everything would fall apart. This chapter will deal chiefly with that daily pattern and with the way in which The Queen attends to her State papers, her correspondence and plans, how she orders her Household and how she gives Audiences, and sits to artists—her "back-room" work.

The obvious place to start is with the planning of The Queen's programme. A programme of such special complexity requires very careful planning. It would be the easiest thing in the world by just a few too many good-hearted but over-enthusiastic acceptances to plunge The Queen's programme into complete chaos.

Even as it is, many thinking people are deeply concerned at the incessant demands made upon The Queen.

Fortunately The Queen has a strong constitution, but, all the same, it is understood by those closely concerned—her family and Household, Government and other officials, as well as her doctors—that she cannot possibly keep up the pressure of such exacting years as her Coronation year, the period of the World Tour of 1953–4 and the heavy programme of 1957, involving four State Visits and a stay in Canada.

1958 was a rather easier year, with little overseas travelling.

1959 is again a very heavy year, involving as it does the extensive tour of Canada and visit to the United States in connection with the opening of the St. Lawrence Seaway in the summer, and the intensely interesting visit to Ghana, her first Sovereign African territory, and to Sierra Leone and The Gambia late in the year.

The way The Queen's programme is planned is this:

In the early winter The Queen's programme for the next year is thought out. She discusses with the other persons concerned what will be her principal engagements in the following year. The Queen and the Duke of Edinburgh talk everything over together, as they always do. Ministers, both in the United Kingdom and in the Commonwealth overseas, are consulted about possible plans.

The permanent officials of the Household give the benefit of their experience. The Queen's physician, Lord Evans, who keeps a watchful eye on her health, gives his views. There are always far more things that The Queen is asked to do, and that she would like to do, than there is time in which to do them. What will be, under the circumstances, the best possible solution is most fully discussed between all the people concerned. It is not a quick nor a secret decision, but a very carefully considered plan to make the best possible use of The Queen's time.

All this takes place in November and December. By Christmas The Queen's general plans for the next year are fairly firm, although of course any suddenly changing condition or emergency would result in extra engagements being slipped into the diary.

When The Queen sees how crowded her programme is in the following year, she begins to plan out her daily life. For instance, she knows from experience that before a State Visit overseas or a Commonwealth tour, many hours must be firmly reserved for the necessary working-up of her knowledge of the place, its personalities, its problems and its policies. She must also allow a quite considerable amount of time for selecting and fitting the clothes she will take with her.

The number of Audiences that The Queen has time to give, as well as the people to whom she gives them, are therefore linked with her future plans.

But whatever the special duties which The Queen may be undertaking at any time, a heavy and constant hail of problems falls daily upon The Queen, whether she is in London or the country, in Britain or overseas. Modern life is seldom without its crisis, and every crisis is laid before The Queen.

Whatever else changes in the life of The Queen, one thing is constant—the stream of Red Boxes or, more properly, Boxes—the despatch cases in which most of the official papers come to Buckingham Palace. These papers are sorted by her Private Secretaries and either laid before her by them personally, or collected in a single box and sent up to her. Red Boxes can be of almost any rectangular size or shape, and some are even green or black! A usual type of Red Box is covered with scarlet or dull red morocco leather, has a brass handle at one side for carrying, and a lock at the other, and is lettered "The Queen" in gold. Each Government Department has a number of Red Boxes used for carrying despatches to The Queen. (Similar Red Boxes, but untitled, are used within and between Government Departments for any documents of special secrecy and are also used within Embassies and Legations overseas.) Some of the Sovereign's Red Boxes are extremely old and must have carried many historic—and even more long and dull—despatches in their time.

The Queen has passing before her all the information needed for making her, increasingly as her reign lengthens, the most fully informed person in the world.

The amount of information at hand within any Government Department is infinitely greater than that available to even the most fortunate of outsiders. The Queen has sent to her the fruits of not one but *every* Government Department, not only from the United Kingdom Government but *throughout* the Commonwealth. All background information such as Blue Books, White Papers, reference books and so forth are of course available to her, although such sources suffer from the inevitable lapse of time required for printing and are always "yesterday's stuff" compared with to-day's report. The Queen's news is as recent, her information as accurate and her means of checking up as good as that of any statesman.

For atmosphere and public opinion, The Queen sees papers of every political persuasion. Anything unusual in the way of reporting or comment about royal affairs is always drawn to her notice by the Household. Occasionally, even now, there are reports in the Press which suggest that The Queen is "blinkered" in her newspaper reading, and only sees the staider journals. This is quite untrue. The reason perhaps is that a special "Royal" issue of *The Times* is printed, costing sixpence instead of fourpence. It is only the paper which is different; the contents are the same.

She also gets a large number of periodicals ranging from the highbrow to the popular. She reads *Hansard*, the official verbatim account of proceedings in Parliament. As a relaxation The Queen enjoys looking through the illustrated magazines, and when she has time reads the country and sporting magazines, with special interest in those devoted to riding.

Because The Queen is Queen, a certain number of her contacts are formalised and stylised by her position. This occurs to some extent with everyone holding a full and responsible job in the centre of the world's stage: there simply is not time to-day to browse around, picking up leisurely impressions and meeting people in a casual way.

But statesmen, "even television personalities", as the Duke of Edinburgh himself reminded us in a pithy approach to the problem as it affects his own children, do have a period of obscurity in which to develop as normal people. For The Queen, owing to the pressure of public interest, and the extra need for security in wartime, when she was growing up, this was hard to achieve.

The Queen therefore supplements our normal channels of getting information by developing an extra sense.

"She has an amazing way of sucking facts out of the dullest document," one of the Household told me.

She draws facts and impressions too out of those around her. Here the most important person in her life—in this respect as in every other—is the Duke of Edinburgh. He has a particular gift of winkling out useful information, often in formal circumstances. He believes that an important part of his job is going out to places where interesting things are going on, finding out about them, and coming back to tell The Queen. He has the time, energy, initiative and ability to supplement The Queen's constant contacts with statesmen and high officials by getting to know the scientist, the research worker, the educationalist, the social welfare worker and in general the man on the job.

The Queen's Household also plays an important part in widening and deepening her knowledge of the world. Members of the Household—in spite of what uninformed critics sometimes write of them—are able men and women, with an unusually large first-hand experience of many parts of the world.

In addition The Queen meets "the top brass" of the whole world—really meets them—but an account of this must wait until the chapter on "The Queen as the Commonwealth Hostess". Far from being "shut off", The Queen knows more world leaders, in more spheres, than almost any other person.

But what of that mythical person, "the man in the street"? The Queen has an insatiable curiosity about her fellow men. She is just as interested in the ordinary fellow as she is in the great statesman, and she eagerly drinks in impressions of the ordinary way of life.

An artist told me that he painted The Queen in the Yellow Drawing Room of Buckingham Palace, which overlooks The Mall. The Queen sat very quietly, but occasionally she became so interested in the people she was watching through the curtains that she craned her neck and unconsciously changed her position to get the last glimpse of some little incident which had caught her interest.

Yet that view must be very familiar to her. Even as a little girl she liked to stand for long periods behind the net curtains of the Palace, looking out across the bare, gravelled forecourt to the ornamental railings and gates (of which, incidentally, the Royal Family have the "undressed" view where policemen's raincoats hang behind the pillars, hidden from public but not from royal eyes) to the groups of people clustered on the pavement, the nurses and children and dogs going for their walks, and to the traffic which mills incessantly round the Victoria Memorial.

Miss Crawford, her governess, tells us in her book *The Little Princesses* that Princess Elizabeth used also to watch from the windows of 145 Piccadilly for the homeward passing every evening of the familiar van horses; and how the Royal children used to watch and wave to one particular elderly woman who was always at the gates of Buckingham Palace to see them off to Windsor every weekend, and of how worried they were one week when she failed to be there.

When The Queen attends public functions, everything is spruced up to an abnormally high level of fresh paint, colourful bunting and new clothes. The Queen once complained jokingly, after visiting a College of Art, that the art students had all been so brushed and tidy, and not in the least the hairy, unconventional crowd she had been led to expect.

But even the most copious application of whitewash cannot really disguise what things are like.

While reporting a royal occasion in some setting which I know at ordinary times, I have sometimes tried to see the scene through The Queen's eyes, and to guess how far it would be

68

possible for her to see through the festive trappings to the ordinary, humdrum life of that place. The answer is: surprisingly much.

All the same, The Queen always enjoys things which are not specially put on for her, and that is one reason why she so much enjoys television. She likes the outside and direct transmissions and also the documentaries, from which she learns a good deal about ordinary people's lives.

A tremendous advantage enjoyed by The Queen is that the information she gets is accurate, or at least can be quickly checked. (This is one of the greatest privileges of authority.) As a result, as a Commonwealth Prime Minister, after several audiences with The Queen, remarked to me: "She is extremely well informed." In almost the same words, I have heard that comment about The Queen dozens of times from people in different fields.

Having talked about the way in which The Queen's programme is planned, and the general way in which The Queen keeps herself informed, it is certainly time to come to the backbone of all her information—her paper work.

Sovereigns can be divided sharply into those to whom their paper work was a source of strength, and those to whom it was an awful bore. Like Queen Victoria, King George V and King George VI, the present Queen is fortunate in that—tedious though it may often be for her to return to her Boxes at the end of a long, hard day—she recognises that the spirit of history is contained in them, and that they are the basic tools for a Sovereign's job.

King Edward VII and King Edward VIII frankly hated the Boxes. They would have liked to spend all their time in making use of their talents for getting on with people.

In his book, *A King's Story*, the Duke of Windsor remarks:

The ceremonial façade that provides the public with a romantic illusion of the higher satisfaction of kingship actually disguises an occupation of considerable drudgery.

This fact was hardly a discovery for me. From long observation of my father's activities, I knew only too well what I was in for. The picture of him "doing his boxes," to use his own phrase, had long represented for me the relentless grind of the King's daily routine.

The Queen's work is divided between periods of intense and unremitting duty with many public duties and Audiences, and "easies" when The Queen lives in the country and spends all possible time out of doors.

But the paper work goes with her everywhere, always.

Even when The Queen is overseas, the most important papers follow her. When she goes abroad for a short visit only, The Queen does not necessarily appoint Counsellors of State, and therefore absolutely everything must be done by her as usual, either in an hour snatched from her heavy programme during the State Visit abroad, before she goes, or immediately she gets back.

When The Queen goes overseas for a longer time, she appoints Counsellors of State to take care of routine affairs in Britain. Such Counsellors of State, of whom any two members form a quorum, can and do deal with routine signature of documents of not very great importance, but they cannot appoint peers, appoint a Prime Minister or dissolve Parliament.

In addition to the special exceptions in regard to the dissolution of Parliament and the granting of ranks, titles and dignities of the peerage the Letters Patent command the Counsellors not to receive homage and not to approve and sign "any warrant, fiat, submission or other document set out in the Schedule hereunto annexed".

This Schedule specifies:

Awards of honours decorations and medals,

Precedence to rank among nobility

The use by British subjects of foreign Orders in the United Kingdom

Issue of writs in Peerage claims for the determination of abeyances

Disbandment of Regiments and other Army Units and changes in Army and Air Force dress

Matters arising in connection with the General Assembly of the Church of Scotland

Amendment of Statutes of Orders.

(This is, of course, theoretically to prevent power being seized from the Sovereign when he or she is out of the country.)

Few people realise that Counsellors of State are only appointed with regard to affairs of the United Kingdom. Commonwealth matters always go direct to The Queen, wherever she is.

Only if The Queen is ill is a Regent appointed.

The *signing* of documents is only one part of The Queen's work: she must *know* their content. She must always be informed of the latest developments. Her meetings with the Heads of other States in their own countries are certainly not the time for her to be behindhand with her information!

How, then, does The Queen fit it all in—the planning, the background work, the mastering and signing of the contents of the Boxes, the planning of her Household and her private life? An imaginary "ordinary day" in the life of The Queen at Buckingham Palace goes something like this:

The Queen wakes up early in her room on the north and sunless side of Buckingham Palace. Outside her open windows is a stretch of green lawn, broken by fine trees. Against the wall is the border, where in season are planted thousands of colourful tulips received as a gift from Queen Juliana of the Netherlands. Beyond the wall, which is topped by revolving spikes, traffic hums along Constitution Hill (which is dead flat), and beyond the trees of the Green Park red London buses shimmer on Piccadilly.

The Queen breakfasts early in private with her husband. This is invariably the custom wherever they are staying. They have the opportunity to discuss together the day ahead of them. Their personal letters come direct to them. Princess Anne, and Prince Charles if he is at home, come along from the children's apartments where they have had breakfast, to talk to their parents and to look at pictures in the papers of what "Mummy" and "Papa" were doing yesterday. The royal children do not bow or curtsey when greeting their parents, although they are supposed to do so before running into the arms of their much-loved "Granny", the Queen Mother.

Soon it is time for The Queen and Prince Philip to go to their desks to begin the day's work. The Queen likes to work with reminders of the people she loves around her. Her desk is laden with photographs, and into the corners of the formal studio portraits are often stuck Press photos or private snapshots which have captured the personality of those she loves. She always has flowers on her desk, and these are often long-stemmed, deep-pink carnations of a kind specially grown for her in one of the glass-houses at Sandringham. On The Queen's desk is a wide expanse of fresh blotting paper and a silver tray containing pens and pencils.

On the other hand the Duke of Edinburgh likes the most utilitarian simplicity for his desk. He has a leaning towards new, streamlined devices to speed the flow of his day's work. If the gadget does not live up to what is expected of it, it is thrown out ruthlessly. He considers that business tools should have progressed to a stage when they can look good as well as be efficient. He will not tolerate bad design or tatty finish. The Duke of Edinburgh does not have official papers circulated to him, but he is making important investigations into the leading scientific, industrial and agricultural projects of the Commonwealth, and an immense number of technical and semi-technical books, periodicals and specially-written papers go to him.

But the amount of paper in various forms that comes before The Queen is truly staggering.

When The Queen is seated at her desk, her Private Secretary, Lieutenant-Colonel the Rt. Hon. Sir Michael Adeane, K.C.B., K.C.V.O., and often one or other of her Assistant Private Secretaries, Sir Edward Ford, K.C.V.O., C.B., and Lieutenant-Colonel the Hon. Martin Charteris, C.B., M.V.O., O.B.E., come in with the first instalment of the varied business of the day.

These three men have a most important task.

They deal with all the correspondence between The Queen and her Ministers, whether of the United Kingdom or other Commonwealth Government, unless these are matters normally specifically dealt with by some other Member of The Queen's Household. Government appointments for which The Queen's approval is required go to The Queen through her Private Secretary. He is responsible for The Queen's engagements, whether in the United Kingdom or overseas. He deals with The Queen's speeches and her messages, with The Queen's correspondence and her private papers. The enormous number of congratulatory messages received annually come through the Private Secretary, as do requests from people wishing to present gifts or books to The Queen, or to dedicate books or music to her. The Royal Archives at Windsor fall within his province. For some not immediately apparent reason, the Private Secretary has control of The Queen's Flight, which was originated by King Edward VIII.

The Press Secretary's office, under Commander Richard Colville, C.V.O., D.S.C., R.N., Press Secretary to The Queen, is a part of the Private Secretary's office. Besides dealing with Press and public enquiries, this office arranges and co-ordinates the Press facilities for all functions which The Queen, The Duke of Edinburgh, Queen Elizabeth The Queen Mother and The Princess Margaret attend. This has entailed such major events as State Visits, Tours, the wedding of The Princess Elizabeth to the Duke of Edinburgh, the funerals of Queen Mary and King George VI.

The position of Private Secretary to the Sovereign is of immense responsibility. By the nature of things, every Sovereign must rely on his or her Private Secretary for unstinting help and for impartial advice. The original Private Secretaries to the Sovereign became in turn the Heads of great Government Departments, their royal connection maintained in the title of their office, Lord Chancellor, Secretary of State for Home Affairs and so on. To-day the Private Secretary is the personal servant of The Queen, and not an employee of a Government department; this is an important factor in maintaining the personality and preventing the institutionalising of the Sovereign.

Sir Michael Adeane, The Queen's Private Secretary, is the grandson of Sir Arthur Bigge, later Lord Stamfordham, who was Private Secretary to Queen Victoria, and to King George V. Short, rather bald, military looking, Sir Michael is an excellent organiser and administrator, a man with a fine war record in command of a battalion of the Coldstream Guards, and a man above all things devoted to the Sovereign. He served on the staff of two Governors-General of Canada before the war. He succeeded Sir Alan Lascelles as Private Secretary at the beginning of 1954. Before that, he was Assistant Private Secretary to King George VI, and afterwards to The Queen when she succeeded to the Throne. "You will generally find him somewhere in the background, talking quietly to someone very important," is how he was described to me by someone who knows Sir Michael very well.

The Queen has two Assistant Private Secretaries. They work in direct contact with her, and mostly take direct control from her of rather less important matters than those in the care of Sir Michael Adeane.

Sir Edward Ford has served three Sovereigns, as he was for a time tutor to King Farouk of Egypt, and afterwards Assistant Secretary to King George VI. His father was Lionel Ford, the well-known headmaster of Repton and Harrow. He has a degree in Greats from Oxford. After coming down from the University he spent some time in Canada, was called to the Bar, and served with the Grenadier Guards throughout the war.

Lieutenant-Colonel Martin Charteris was formerly Private Secretary to The Queen when she was Princess Elizabeth. He served in the King's Royal Rifle Corps during the war, and was one of the few survivors when the troopship *Yorkshire* was torpedoed and sank in the Atlantic in 1940. He has a gift for getting on with people which has stood him in good stead when planning many of the Overseas Tours, on many of which he has accompanied The Queen.

The Private Secretaries are none of them Civil Servants. If they belonged to the Civil Service of the United Kingdom it would not be easy for them to handle matters on The Queen's behalf which might be no concern of the United Kingdom Servant.

Like the rest of the Household they are The Queen's personal servants. As such they stand in the same relation to each of the countries of the Commonwealth of which Her Majesty is the Head.

The papers the Private Secretaries bring to The Queen are of the most varied kinds. The Government Departments have contributed letters, reports and submissions to The Queen. The principals of institutions write to The Queen asking her to honour with her presence the celebration of their centenary or any other milestone in their history, perhaps the laying of the foundation stone for a new science block. The Lords-Lieutenant of counties, and Lord Mayors and Mayors of cities and towns urge The Queen to visit them.

Many individuals write to The Queen. Perhaps something has gone wrong in their lives, and they turn to The Queen for help—

the mother of a man condemned to death for murder, a widow about to be evicted from a tied cottage, the parents of a grievously sick child. Whenever any of these letters raises a problem which is within the scope of a Government Department, The Queen will have it sent to the head of that Department of her Government, often asking her Secretary to arrange for her to hear the outcome of the matter.

Some of The Queen's letters are spontaneous messages of loyalty from individual subjects who are unknown to her, and from these The Queen often gains much pleasure. Sometimes naïve and delightful letters are received from small children. All are answered.

Even now *all* letters addressed to The Queen go to her first of all. Then, after The Queen has abstracted some of them, the rest go to her Private Secretaries for further winnowing. Every one of the many letters she sees is considered by The Queen, who either writes her decision on the document or letter or tells her Private Secretary what to do about it.

The Queen receives many requests for telegrams of congratulation on the occasion of diamond weddings and centenaries, and she takes a personal interest in these. When an account of the work she did every day was written before she went to the United States in 1957, The Queen made a note that these congratulatory messages had not been mentioned, and that fifteen hundred such telegrams are sent every year. She also changed a statement that "all the Red Boxes go to Her Majesty", to "not quite all the Red Boxes go to The Queen, as these are sorted by her Private Secretaries before she sees them". The Queen is scrupulous in claiming nothing to which she feels she is in any way not fully entitled.

Almost every letter that comes to the Palace is answered, and it is answered courteously and promptly. A comparatively small Palace staff keeps up a very high standard of clerical efficiency. At times of rejoicing or sorrow—when naturally our thoughts turn to the Sovereign—this is only achieved by working, when necessary, very long hours.

When the day's correspondence has been dealt with, there comes the turn of the official documents, which form the most important part of The Queen's work. The Queen must as Head of State, and always acting on the advice of her Ministers of the United Kingdom, approve a tremendous and widely varied number of decisions, actions and appointments, both at home and in relation to what were once known as the Colonies and are now called the non-self-governing territories.

From the other countries of the Commonwealth of which she is Queen come many documents requiring her approval. Although many matters in these countries are done in her name by the Governor-General, acting on the advice of the Ministers of that country, The Queen's approval is required for many things such as Letters of Credence, Alliances, Formation or Disbandment of Regiments, Appointments of Ambassadors, Honorary Surgeons, A.D.C.s and so on.

Then drafts of programmes for forthcoming visits have to be gone through. The Queen's trained eye reads a draft programme as a seaman reads a chart, quick to spot hidden dangers. The programme is always submitted by The Queen's hosts and she will of course adapt herself to what they wish, but as a result of her experience she can point out places where trouble is likely to occur. Perhaps the timing is too tight to allow for slowing down so that crowds gathered on the road may see The Queen, or for The Queen to change. These plans go to and fro between host and Queen many times before they are drawn up in final detail.

When The Queen is asked if she will approve a certain appointment, she will probably initial the document "Approved—E.R."

The Queen signs a great number of official documents, and she puts her pen to all the papers placed before her which require her approval. They become State Documents after The Queen has signed them. When The Queen has finished her business with the Private Secretaries, there are often the heads of other departments of her Household who wish to see her.

The Lord Chamberlain (the Earl of Scarbrough, K.G., P.C., G.C.S.I., G.C.I.E., G.C.V.O.) does not see The Queen as frequently as do the Private Secretaries, although he is the Head of The Queen's Household, the Chairman of the Household Committee and the Chairman of the Committee of Royal Warrants of Appointments.

All Court ceremonial falls within the Lord Chamberlain's

province. He has to do with precedence; uniforms; styles and titles; the flying of flags; all the arrangements for royal weddings and funerals, for garden parties and indeed for all ceremonial occasions with which The Queen is connected; and with communication with Commonwealth countries about ceremonial matters when The Queen is on tour. The Lord Chamberlain organises the ceremonial connected with State Visits to the United Kingdom. He it was who announced the regulations governing the presentation of débutantes at Court, and who announced The Queen's decision to dispense with these Presentation Parties in favour of extra Garden Parties.

Moreover, the Lord Chamberlain, as Head of The Queen's Household, is responsible to The Queen for all Appointments with a capital "A".

He is responsible for the Lords and Grooms-in-waiting, the Ecclesiastical and Medical Households, for the Gentlemen at Arms, the Yeomen of the Guard and the Royal Company of Archers, for the Gentlemen Ushers and the Sergeants at Arms, for the Marshal of the Diplomatic Corps and the Central Chancery of the Orders of Knighthood . . . for the Royal Library, the Chapels Royal, the Windsor State Apartments, and the official grace and favour apartments, for the regalia and a host of other matters—not excluding The Queen's swans!

The Lord Chamberlain is also responsible for stage censorship and for the licensing of certain theatres, as a result of a protest in the 1570s by the Puritans of the City of London when they attacked stage players. The Lord Chamberlain was then in charge of the entertainment of the Court, and he took the players under his protection.

The number of appointments to The Queen are considerable, although many of them are of a chiefly honorary nature. (Vital departments, such as the Private Secretary's hard-working office, consist of so few people that many a "big business" executive would blink if he saw how few Secretaries, secretaries' secretaries, clerks and typists are required to run The Queen's business.)

The Household, as listed in the invaluable *Whitaker's*, consist of 311 persons in England and Wales, and 67 persons in Scotland. But of these only between 60 and 70, including clerks and typists, are working full time for The Queen, the remainder being chiefly honorary appointments. For instance there are 50 members of the Ecclesiastical Household, and 23 members of the Medical Household, both strictly part-time categories. In some cases, one person holds two or more posts, for instance the Duke of Hamilton and Brandon is the Lord Steward (an appointment connected with everything "below stairs", but whose duties are in part discharged by the Master of the Household) and hereditary Keeper of Holyroodhouse and a Brigadier of The Queen's Bodyguard for Scotland—all more or less honorary appointments to-day. Sir Michael Adeane is listed both as the Queen's Private Secretary and as an extra-Equerry. The Assistant Private Secretaries are also extra-Equerries, as are some retired Members of the Household such as Sir Alan Lascelles and Group Captain Peter Townsend. The Rev. M. F. Foxell is sub-almoner in the Royal Almonry as well as Deputy Clerk of the Closet and sub-Dean of the Chapels Royal.

The Lord Chamberlain is also responsible for presenting to the Sovereign Addresses from the House of Lords.

The Queen therefore has plenty of matters about which she consults her Lord Chamberlain. She generally sees him about 11 in the morning or at 2.30 in the afternoon, but he does not have an Audience every day, as do the Private Secretaries.

Perhaps he presents to The Queen an Address from the House of Lords. Perhaps there is the date of a garden party or an investiture to fix. Or there may be a State Visit pending, in which case there is necessarily much planning between The Queen and the Lord Chamberlain.

All matters affecting the appointment of Members of the Household require careful consideration, because The Queen's Household holds a most responsible position. The Members of the Household are in close contact with The Queen and therefore must not only be able and trustworthy, but also congenial.

As a token of his high office, the Lord Chamberlain received upon his appointment a long white rod from the hands of The Queen. Should The Queen pre-decease him, it would be his last act of service to her to break it ceremonially over her grave, as the Earl of Clarendon, his predecessor, broke his white rod over the grave of King George VI.

The man holding this responsible post is the Earl of Scarbrough who has been described to me as "a very silent and a very shrewd gentleman. If you ask him for advice, he will give extreme consideration to the point, and will then give you exceedingly good advice." He was born in 1896, served in both World Wars, in the First in France with the 11th Hussars, in the Second as an acting Major-General; he has been a Conservative M.P., an exceedingly able Governor of Bombay and Parliamentary Under-Secretary for India and Burma. He has written a history of his old Regiment, and is extremely interested in Asiatic affairs. He is Grand Master of the United Grand Lodge of Masons of England, and was installed by the late King just a year before his death. He is a good horseman and shot, and a non-smoker. The Queen has stayed at his home of Sandbeck Park in Yorkshire for the St. Leger.

The Countess of Scarbrough is also a close friend of the Royal Family, and is an extra Lady of the Bedchamber to the Queen Mother.

For household matters with a small "h"—the day-to-day running of the Palace and estates, and the many matters concerning staff—The Queen talks with her Master of the Household, Major Mark Milbank, C.V.O., M.C. He has to do with everything on the domestic side of all five homes of The Queen—Buckingham Palace, Windsor Castle and the Palace of Holyroodhouse, which are State property, and her two private homes of Sandringham and Balmoral Castle. And Buckingham Palace alone is the largest home in Britain, with approximately 600 rooms. No two persons have come to the same total, because of the difficulty of deciding whether this or that windowed space is a small room or a large cupboard. Windsor Castle, Pepys considered, even 300 years ago, as "the most romantick castle in Europe".

Staff matters on such a scale are a considerable headache, especially as the benefits of the welfare state have lessened the unusualness, if not the value, of the extremely good medical care always available to the staff. One much appreciated "perk" is the many delightful little houses which are set aside for members of the staff, especially perhaps those at Windsor and at Sandringham.

Among the chief detail duties of the Master of the Household are arrangements for the Royal Dining Room and staff catering, including the selection of wine from the royal cellars. He issues invitations to State Banquets (in the name of the Lord Steward) and to those lunching or dining privately with The Queen. In collaboration with the Lord Chamberlain's department he organises official entertainments.

The Master of the Household also has several of those intriguing and slightly inconsequential spheres of authority within the Household which have grown up through the centuries; he issues the Court Circular, and is in charge of both the Court Post Office and the Palace Police.

Major Milbank is very tall—about six foot three inches—and is a distinguished-looking man. He was born in 1907 and is heir to a baronetcy. He was educated at Eton, served in the Coldstream Guards throughout the Second World War, and has first-hand overseas experience, before the war as A.D.C. to the Governor of Bombay (yes, for part of the time to his present chief, the Earl of Scarbrough) and after the war as Comptroller to the Governor-General of Canada. He enjoys country things. He is a first-rate shot. In his job he is a good judge of people, tactful and a good administrator. "He is always cool, calm and collected."

Under the Master of the Household are The Queen's personal servants and the staffs of the various Royal Residences. Neither their work nor that of the officials in the various Household Departments receives much publicity. But it is continuous and it is vital. On their devotion and efficiency depends to a large extent the personal well-being of Her Majesty—wherever she is—and the smooth running of her several houses.

The Queen also has occasion to see the Keeper of the Privy Purse at frequent intervals, although not every day, generally after lunch at 2.30 in the afternoon. The appointment is now held by Lord Tryon, and his department is responsible for all the money matters connected with The Queen's expenses, with the running of the Palaces and the extensive estates, with The Queen's charities, donations and subscriptions (in themselves a considerable duty), with the Balmoral bursaries (the Scottish word for scholarship), the Royal almonry and Royal Patronage.

Rising costs affect The Queen at least as much as the rest of us, and his is the thankless task of trying to cut as good a coat as formerly when the price of cloth is continually rising.

In addition he is responsible for the Commemorative medals (such as The Queen's Coronation medal), for the Presentation Prizes, medals and cups and for the allocation of seats in royal boxes.

In general the Keeper of the Privy Purse has to do with all the estate and money matters, with The Queen's Solicitors, with all the correspondence with the Crown Lands department and in certain cases with the Ministry of Works.

He also deals with The Queen's thoroughbred studs and Ascot Racecourse, with the Duchy of Lancaster (private lands held by The Queen as Duke of Lancaster, and with the Duchy of Cornwall (the estates which are the inheritance of the Heir to the Throne).

He has to do with two categories of Appointments: the pages of honour and the Military Knights of Windsor.

He has also the supervision of The Queen's stamp collection— which, incidentally, is far from the least valuable of The Queen's possessions!

The Keeper of The Queen's Privy Purse writes the cheques and settles the bills. As is well known, The Queen does not often handle money, accounts being submitted in due course to the Privy Purse. He is also Secretary of the Royal Victorian Order, which is important and takes a lot of time and thought. One change that the Queen made in 1957 is believed to be because of the request of the Keeper of the Privy Purse. The Queen has discontinued The Queen's Bounty for Triplets of £1 for each child given to the parents of triplets or quadruplets, a charity instituted by Queen Victoria and for which there is no real need in the changed social conditions happily prevailing to-day. The parents often preferred to retain the royal cheque as an interesting family treasure, and the accumulation of an ever-increasing number of issued but not cashed cheques was a bother in keeping The Queen's accounts. The parents continue to receive from The Queen a message of congratulation, which they can keep as a memento.

Lord Tryon, the man with this unenviable task, was born in 1906, went to Eton, commanded the Fifth Guards Brigade at the end of the Second World War and has useful Commonwealth experience as A.D.C. to the Governor-General of Canada.

He is essentially a soldier and a countryman, a man of the land, a very good shot and a fisherman. He is a pipe-smoker. He is extremely good at running estates, and has a country property near Salisbury. "His job is very much more a matter of running estates than just palaces," I was reminded.

The Queen's consultations with her Lord Chamberlain, her Master of the Household, her Keeper of the Privy Purse, are no mere matters of form. I asked a Member of the Household how much The Queen has to do with the domestic side of Buckingham Palace.

"Why, she runs the place," he exclaimed.

These are Members of her Household whom The Queen sees most frequently. But many others are summoned from time to time, when something special has to be discussed.

The Queen sends for the Housekeeper of Buckingham Palace to discuss some large purchase, such as a large renewal of linen, or to consider whether the upholstery in a certain room really must be renewed this year, or if it can "do" another year. Buckingham Palace is far from being in a glossy state of brand-newness everywhere. Some of the curtains in daily use at Buckingham Palace date back to the reign of Queen Victoria, and not unnaturally they are beginning to show signs of wear. Up to the time of King George VI, it was the custom to take down the hangings in the guest-rooms whenever the visitors departed. This saved some wear, although it caused work. But King George VI found depressing the resultant appearance of the rooms, both from inside and from outside the Palace. The guest-rooms are now kept ready, as The Queen, in this as in so much else, has continued her father's custom.

When The Queen has guests coming to stay, she discusses arrangements for their comfort with the Housekeeper, and goes to see that their rooms are perfectly ready for them. The Housekeeper at Buckingham Palace is Mrs. J. E. Findlater, a Scot like many others who serve The Queen, a quiet lady of rather smart and well-turned-out appearance who holds herself particularly well. She has an extremely pleasant manner and a quiet, observant way of carrying out her work.

The chef sends up the menus every day to The Queen, and is occasionally summoned when she is planning a specially important event. He is Mr. Ronald Aubrey, a middle-aged Londoner, who is dark, tall and robust. Generally The Queen approves the chef's suggestions, occasionally she alters a dish. Sometimes she introduces dishes she has first tasted and liked during her tours. Both The Queen and the Duke prefer simple meals, quickly served, when they are alone. They do not like to linger over their meals.

The Queen is a light eater; she likes good food, plainly and well cooked, is particularly fond of roasts, whether beef, mutton, chicken, pheasant or other game, with the exception of the stronger-tasting grouse, and is particularly fond of very young, succulent, fresh vegetables such as french beans and peas, and also of fresh fruit in fine condition. She does not like very highly flavoured dishes, and she particularly dislikes oysters. She likes a very little of a light and sweet wine such as moselle or sauterne.

There are other Members of the Household who are summoned less frequently. The Queen may see the Deputy Treasurer and Assistant Keeper of the Privy Purse, Commander Philip Row, R.N. about a Household pension or gratuity, one of the subjects under his control, as well as the general control of matters dealt with by the Privy Purse Office.

She may send for the Crown Equerry, Brigadier W. M. Sale, C.V.O., O.B.E., who is in charge of the Royal Mews and all its services, both horses and carriages, and cars, and who combines with the Private Secretary and the Equerry-in-Waiting to look after general travel arrangements.

The Equerry-in-Waiting is in personal attendance upon The Queen during his time in waiting, and works in conjunction with the Private Secretary. He deals with The Queen's private engagements and arranges her private travelling. When there are official visitors or private guests at any of the Royal residences the Equerry meets them and ensures that they are properly looked after. He passes orders to the Officer of the Guard. The Queen has three Equerries, one permanent, Major the Lord Plunket, M.V.O., who also holds the appointment of Deputy Master of the Household, and two temporary service Equerries. These latter Equerries are officers specially selected by the Royal Navy, the Army and the Royal Air Force in turn for duty with the Royal Household for three years. They also keep The Queen in day-to-day touch with their respective services.

No special mention has yet been made of The Queen's Ladies-in-Waiting. Strangely, they have a less busy time during the reign of a Sovereign Queen than they would have in attendance upon a Queen Consort. That is because while they would cope with all sides of the clerical work of a Queen Consort, most letters sent to a Queen Regnant—in view of her Constitutional position in which as Sovereign she is bound by Ministerial advice —are dealt with by her through her Private Secretary and Assistant Private Secretaries.

But there are still a considerable number which are dealt with according to The Queen's instructions by her Ladies-in-Waiting —thanks for letters of congratulation, answers to requests for autographs or photographs, or letters asking where they can see The Queen on a public occasion, letters about the children, instructions to shops, enquiries when people are ill. The Queen herself writes several letters to personal friends and relations, and it is perhaps worth noting, in an age when so many people use printed Christmas cards, because they are so busy, that The Queen finds time to sign every one of her Christmas cards.

The Queen has nine Ladies. This may sound rather a lot, but their duties are different, and there is no occasion on which all are in attendance on her.

Principal among them is, of course, the Mistress of the Robes, who is almost always a Duchess. At present she is Mary, Duchess of Devonshire, a tall, stately woman, whose quiet dignity did much to enhance the Coronation, during which she was always closely in attendance upon The Queen. In this reign she also undertakes the duties which would fall in a king's reign to the Groom of the Robes. She is responsible for organising the rota of Ladies-in-Waiting in accordance with The Queen's wishes— and The Queen always remembers such things as school holidays when arranging which of her Ladies-in-Waiting shall attend her. She also attends The Queen on all State occasions. Sometimes she goes with The Queen on her more important tours abroad, and she sometimes attends The Queen to Windsor at Easter or to Holyroodhouse in July, but she is never regularly "in waiting" in the ordinary sense.

The Queen has two Ladies of the Bedchamber, the Countess of

Leicester and the Countess of Euston, both tall, fair, slim and pleasant, both with wide interests and a knowledge of art. They attend The Queen upon her more important public occasions, but do not go into waiting regularly. Sometimes a Lady of the Bedchamber attends The Queen on an overseas tour.

Then there are the Women of the Bedchamber, generally four in number. They take turns of going into waiting upon The Queen for periods of about a fortnight. During that time the Woman of the Bedchamber, or Lady-in-Waiting as she is generally termed, is The Queen's constant companion, answering letters, making all kinds of arrangements of the more personal kind for The Queen—seeing to enquiries about people who are ill, doing shopping and generally making herself useful. During her period of duty the Lady-in-Waiting attends The Queen upon every public engagement. The Lady-in-Waiting will go to Windsor for the Easter and Ascot visits, when the Court is in residence, and also goes with The Queen to Sandringham and Balmoral.

At the present time The Queen has appointed four Women of the Bedchamber: Lady Margaret Hay, C.V.O., who is the wife of Mr. Philip Hay, Comptroller to the Duchess of Kent, and who has three sons; Lady Alice Egerton, C.V.O., who was with The Queen on her round-the-world tour; Lady Rose Baring and Mrs. John Dugdale (temporary).

Two of The Queen's former Ladies of the Bedchamber, who resigned from regular duties upon marriage, have been appointed Extra Ladies of the Bedchamber and occasionally do a period in waiting. They are the Hon. Mrs. Andrew Elphinstone, C.V.O., and Mrs. Alexander Abel Smith. Both were widows when they entered The Queen's service. Both remarried while in her service, Mrs. Andrew Elphinstone marrying The Queen's cousin.

So much for the correspondence, and for the Members of The Queen's Household whom The Queen may wish to see. There remain the Audiences, one of the most important parts of The Queen's day.

Audiences generally, but not invariably, take place during the second part of the morning. The number of people who have Audience of The Queen over the years of her reign is very great, and ranges over a wide diversity of occupation, background, language and creed.

It is not usually realised that The Queen is entirely alone when she gives an Audience to a member of the Commonwealth. That means indeed that she must be "up in" each of her visitors' subjects, to be able to talk to them—as she does—knowledgeably, interestedly and without ever compromising any of her Governments, about their own background and problems.

Members of Foreign States are received by The Queen, who has with her her Secretary of State for Foreign Affairs, or some other representative of the Foreign Office.

A good idea of the range of The Queen's Audiences is given by this day recorded in the Court Circular. It is not a day selected exactly at random, as the type of Audiences is rather more varied than usual, but it is not particularly heavy. There are many days on which The Queen gives five, six or even seven Audiences, and she may easily have several public engagements as well, in addition of course to the inescapable paper work. The day selected is in 1957.

Buckingham Palace. Dec. 5.

His Excellency Monsieur Mohammed Kabir Ludin was received in audience by the Queen this morning and presented the Letters of Recall of his predecessor and his own Letters of Credence as Ambassador Extraordinary and Plenipotentiary from the Kingdom of Afghanistan to the Court of St. James's.

His Excellency was accompanied by Monsieur Mohammed Ebrahim Nouri (First Secretary), Monsieur Said Waheed Abdullah (Second Secretary) and Monsieur Mohammed Khalid Roashan (Information Attaché) who had the honour of being presented to Her Majesty.

Sir Frederick Hoyer Miller (Permanent Under-Secretary of State for Foreign Affairs), who had the honour of being received by the Queen, was present and the Gentlemen of the Household in Waiting were in attendance.

This is one of the Audiences which The Queen gives at frequent intervals; and is described in greater detail in the chapter "The Queen and Foreign Powers".

Mr. H. T. Andrews had the honour of being received by Her Majesty upon his retirement from the South African Foreign Service.

As the Commonwealth grows and as the Commonwealth countries establish their own diplomatic representation with each other and the rest of the world, so this part of The Queen's Audiences grows with it. The Queen always likes to see members of the Commonwealth Foreign Service when they are in London.

Sir Kenneth Blackburne was received in audience by The Queen and kissed hands upon his appointment as Captain-General and Governor-in-Chief of Jamaica.
Lady Blackburne had the honour of being received by Her Majesty.

Those persons who *represent* The Queen kiss hands upon appointment, that is Ministers with Seals (The Lord Chancellor, the Lord Privy Seal, all the Secretaries of State, the Chancellor of the Exchequer and the Chancellor of the Duchy of Lancaster); Governors-General to self-governing Dominions and Governors to non-self-governing territories, and Ambassadors and Ministers Plenipotentiary, upon appointment. The custom goes back long in our history, and its exact origin is unknown, so far as I have been able to discover.
The Queen receives the wives of these personages, and also the wives of Ambassadors and Ministers accredited to the Court of St. James, a duty which would normally fall to the Queen Consort in the reign of a King.

The Hon. Peter Legh (Vice Chamberlain of the Household) was received in audience by the Queen and presented Addresses from the House of Commons, to which Her Majesty was graciously pleased to make reply.

Communication between the House of Commons and The Queen takes place by means of the Vice-Chamberlain of the Household. (His is a political appointment, combined with the duty of Junior Whip, and will be fully described in the next chapter.)
The Queen's Household is now almost entirely free of party politics, although this was not so formerly. Just over one hundred years ago Queen Victoria caused the fall of Peel's Government by refusing to change her Whig ladies for Tory ladies when Lord Melbourne's Government fell. Now only about a dozen appointments are political, and these are The Lord Chamberlain, The Lord Steward, The Master of the Horse, The Lords-in-Waiting (at present five in number) and the Parlia-

mentary appointments, viz.: the Treasurer of the Household, the Comptroller of the Household and the Vice-Chamberlain of the Household. The Captain of the Honorable Corps of Gentlemen at Arms and the Captain of The Queen's Bodyguard of Yeomen of the Guard are political appointments.

With regard to the political appointments, since the first Labour Government in 1924, the Prime Minister has always left the choice of the Lord Chamberlain to the Sovereign, on condition that he does not vote against the Government of the day. But the appointment could always revert to the Prime Minister if he wished, and he does in fact make a formal submission each time a Lord Chamberlain is appointed—whatever his political persuasion.

This also applies to the Lord Steward, the Master of the Horse and three non-political Lords-in-Waiting, of whom Lord Eldon is one.

To return to the Audiences, The Queen also receives her own Ambassadors and Ministers, both on appointment and when they are on leave from posts, particularly if they are important or in the forefront of some crisis. She also receives Ambassadors and Ministers upon their retirement from the service.

The Queen receives Commonwealth representatives, not necessarily appointed to this country, when they are in London, an expanding part of her work which she particularly enjoys.

A multitude of other people are, at one time or another, received by The Queen, often Cabinet and other Ministers whose work particularly impinges upon The Queen at the time. She has received in Audience such a wide variety of different people that it is difficult to indicate their range adequately, but here are a few examples: the Master Gunner, Royal Regiment of Artillery, and the Director of Royal Artillery, from whom she accepted a Regimental brooch; Bishop Wand, retiring Bishop of London, whom she invested with the Badge of Prelate Emeritus of the Most Excellent Order of the British Empire; the members of the West Indies cricket team; and her new First and Principal Naval Aide-de-Camp. She has received the Minister of Transport and Civil Aviation, who presented representatives of Associations and Unions representing Seafarers and Fishermen, and accepted a copy of the Roll of Honour of the Merchant Navy. She has received the Governor of Virginia and his wife and other distinguished Virginians, presented by the American Ambassador; General Lauris Norstad, Supreme Allied Commander Europe, and his wife; the retiring Permanent Secretary of the Treasury; Commanding Officers and others of Royal Auxiliary Air Force and the Air Division of the R.N.V.R. when they were being disbanded; several Justices of the High Court whom she usually knights during Audience; relatives who delivered up the regalia belonging to deceased Knights of the Order of the Garter and the Order of the Thistle; all the Heads of Foreign States visiting this country; the guests of the Princess Elizabeth Birthday Fund from Southern Rhodesia; her Stud Groom (Mr. Walter Hodges) when she presented him with the Royal Victorian Medal (Gold) to mark his service of fifty-six years; the Permanent Under-Secretary for War on his retirement; the General Officer Commanding London District; and so on and so on.

Whenever a meeting of Commonwealth Prime Ministers is held in London, The Queen sees each Prime Minister or representative of a Commonwealth separately at least once in private Audience, in addition to the considerable number of times she meets him on other occasions.

On some mornings The Queen gives a sitting to an artist. She has innumerable requests from public bodies to sit for portraits. The name of the artist proposed is always submitted to The Queen for her approval. It is impossible for her to say "Yes" every time, but she knows that many of her subjects can never see her face to face, and that therefore all sorts of long-range methods by which The Queen becomes known to her peoples are important, and are part of her job—sitting for her portrait, studio portraits and Press photographs, reports, articles, broadcasts and television appearances, both by the camera's "eavesdropping" on great public occasions, and by direct televiewing. The Queen may not like it particularly, but she takes it in her stride, as part of the job.

When an artist has obtained permission to paint The Queen, he sees one of The Queen's Private Secretaries or her Press Secretary and discusses the pose, the dress and the jewels he would like, and sometimes submits a sketch of the pose he would suggest.

This is, of course, a rough sketch only, and may easily be altered when the artist sees The Queen.

The artist is generally taken up to The Queen's private wardrobe rooms on the second floor of the North wing, and there evening dresses are laid out (for his selection) by Miss Margaret MacDonald, The Queen's Dresser. If he is wise he will come forearmed with some preference among the bewildering choice of The Queen's jewellery. If The Queen approves the artist's choice —and she generally does—then, on the day put aside for the first sitting, she will dress in that evening gown with those particular jewels, and at the time appointed (generally 11 in the morning) the door of the room set aside as a studio (often the Yellow Drawing Room or the Balcony Room) will open, and The Queen will come in, quite alone, and will place herself at the artist's disposal for an hour and a half or two hours. She often talks gaily on a wide range of subjects during these sittings. Sometimes she may seem preoccupied and silent, but always she collaborates quietly and without affectation with the artist. She seldom asks to see the canvas before it is finished. Always she wears the correct dress and the exact jewellery required.

The number of artists to whom The Queen has recently been sitting has not been quite so many. I am told this presages no change of policy, just that The Queen has sat to almost a score of artists and one sculptor (the Nigerian Mr. Ben Enwonwu, one of whose sculptured heads The Queen bought). One artist, well known for his splendid group scenes of great ceremonies and occasions, has had sittings from The Queen for no fewer than five pictures. She feels that there are not so many pressing claims for her portrait as there were, and that a short "breather" will do no harm.

From the artist's point of view, even with The Queen's kindness and helpfulness, it is something of an ordeal. The Queen can just manage to squeeze the time for a maximum of eight or nine sittings. Many artists are accustomed to forty or more sittings, therefore they require to press on full-pelt through every minute of their precious sitting time. To make things easier, The Queen has had made a lay figure of herself, to her exact measurements, on which the clothes and robes can be draped for painting.

The Queen has also to fit in choosing and being fitted for her clothes, a considerable task in itself, "shopping"—which in her case is done chiefly by proxy by a Lady-in-Waiting, or in selecting from goods submitted to her by one or two of the best London shops about once a week—and such necessary chores as having her hair done and visiting her dentist.

All of such duties do not, of course, take place in the same morning, but some of them are always included in any day at Buckingham Palace.

Often—although, according to the Court Circular, not quite as often as at the beginning of the reign—the last persons to whom The Queen gives an Audience are asked to stay to lunch. Whereas invitation to a ceremonial occasion would be arranged through the Lord Chamberlain, an informal invitation of this kind comes through the Master of the Household, who also daily informs the chef of how many people must be catered for at all meals.

Many of the duties listed here will spill over into the afternoon if it is a day on which The Queen has no public duties. But The Queen will always try to break in the afternoon for at least a walk in the garden, and she has tea with the Duke of Edinburgh, if he is at home—as he has less compulsory paper work he can get out and about more frequently than The Queen—and with the children, at 5 o'clock. Then she likes to be with the children for a little.

Sometimes she goes out quite informally to have tea with her friends. I happened to be walking along a quiet suburban street when I recognised The Queen's chauffeur at the wheel of her numberless maroon Rolls-Royce. It drew inconspicuously to the kerb, a little way ahead, outside the home of one of her Ladies-in-Waiting. No sooner had the car stopped than The Queen, quite alone, came quickly down the path and entered the car, which immediately drove off. The painter who was giving an under-coat to the next-door gatepost never even looked up. I learned later (not as the result of special enquiries) that The Queen was a frequent visitor to this house, often bringing the Royal children with her to tea, and that the neighbours whose windows over-looked the garden scrupulously refrained from watching them.

Just before dinner, when Parliament is sitting, The Queen receives a report of the day's proceedings written by her Vice-

Chamberlain of the Household, and describing the tone and feeling of the House as well as the actual business conducted. Once a week, generally on Tuesday evening, and at a time changed from 5.30 to 6.30 to allow her more time with her children, the Prime Minister calls to discuss in person the affairs of State.

If The Queen has no public engagement and no guests have been invited, she and the Duke of Edinburgh have a short and simple meal, and afterwards read or watch television (which is "piped" to her set to avoid disturbance from the busy traffic) or play cards or see a film in the excellent private cinema at the Palace.

On most evenings The Queen must return to her desk for an hour or more to deal with the more urgent papers in her Boxes.

The Queen has neither time nor inclination at the end of a succession of such strenuous days for much in the way of late parties. It is not usually very late at night, and the sound of traffic is not yet stilled, when the lights go out in The Queen's bedroom in the North wing of Buckingham Palace.

CHAPTER FOUR

The Queen and Parliament

"Be it enacted by The Queen's most Excellent Majesty, by and with the advice and consent of the Lords Spiritual and Temporal, and Commons in this present Parliament assembled, and by the authority of the same as follows:—"
Recital to an *Act of Parliament*

"The Queen must make certain that she has a Government in the United Kingdom."
Jennings

"A conscientious constitutional monarch is a strong element of stability and continuity in our Constitution."
Lord Attlee, addressing the University Law Society in Oxford, June 1957

WHEN The Queen opens Parliament—which is usually once a year—it is the one occasion other than her Coronation on which she wears a Crown and Regal Robes. The Queen is driven through the gateway of Buckingham Palace by way of The Mall and the Arch in Royal Horseguards' building to Whitehall, past the Cenotaph, and through Parliament Square to the Royal Entrance beneath the Victoria Tower of the Palace of Westminster. She goes in the Irish State Coach, usually drawn by four grey horses, the Coachman is on the box and four footmen on the step behind. (In 1958, for the first time and to give additional control, a third pair of greys with postillion were put to the coach.) This coach was bought by Queen Victoria from an Irish coach builder when she visited Dublin in 1852, and was afterwards used by her on the very rare occasions in her widowhood when she was persuaded to open Parliament. Up till the war the Sovereign always rode in the magnificent eight-horse State Coach to Westminster to open Parliament, but this has so far appeared only once in Queen Elizabeth II's reign, for her Coronation.

93

In front and behind the coach ride the Life Guards and the Royal Horse Guards, who in their scarlet and their dark-blue tunics respectively on their black horses form the Sovereign's escort. The streets are lined by that good-humoured loyal crowd which is characteristic of London, and is composed partly of its own citizens, interspersed by proud Commonwealth visitors from overseas, and partly of a good number of perplexed but impressed foreigners.

These crowds never see The Queen wearing her crown; on each of the first six occasions when she has opened the Parliament of the United Kingdom at Westminster she has chosen to wear the beautiful diamond diadem (that is, a complete circlet) which is made up of Maltese Crosses interspersed with national emblems, and which was made on the order of King George IV to wear over a Cap of Maintenance. It was not completed before his death in 1830, but has been worn by every Queen Regnant and Queen Consort since the days of Queen Victoria.

On this very formal occasion, The Queen wears some of her finest jewels, and has varied her necklaces and earrings from year to year. She wears evening dress, always a light-coloured, dignified, formal dress, although little is seen of her dress on this occasion. Over her shoulders she wears either the ermine stole, an Accession present from the Hudson's Bay Company, or an ermine jacket. The Duke of Edinburgh, wearing naval uniform, sits at her left side.

When The Queen alights, she is met by some of the highest officials in the land, the Great Officers of State. The Lord Great Chamberlain is present as Keeper of the Palace of Westminster which was declared "the King's Palace of Westminster—for ever" by an Act of King Henry VIII in 1536. The custom of holding Parliament at Westminster is extremely old, and grew out of the King's Councils, of which the first recorded was that of William the Conqueror in 1076, although the earliest royal building on the site was the palace of King Canute the Dane, which was burnt in 1036 and replaced by a probably unpretentious palace by Edward the Confessor, so that he could watch over the great abbey which was being built nearby.

The present Lord Great Chamberlain is the Marquess of Cholmondeley. This is a hereditary office, vested in the de Vere

Earls of Oxford, just as that of Earl Marshal is vested in the Norfolk family. But the direct male line of the de Veres died out in 1626, and the office continued in the female line and was in constant dispute until in 1902 the House of Lords decided that it was jointly vested in the families of the Marquisate of Cholmondeley, the Earldom of Ancaster and the Marquisate of Lincolnshire, each family having the power to nominate their deputy. The office is held by the Cholmondeley family under alternate monarchs, King Edward VII having agreed that the post should be held only for the duration of a reign. As the Earl of Ancaster held it in the reign of King George VI, the nominee of the Lincolnshire family will hold it in the next reign. The Lord Great Chamberlain on such special ceremonial occasions wears the gold key of his office.

The Lord Chancellor, Head of the Judiciary, is also there. His is, of course, a high political appointment carrying Cabinet rank. He wears his gold and black robe used on State occasions, and carries the handsomely embroidered Purse which might contain the heavy Great Seal, but the Great Seal rests in safety in his office in the Westward Tower of the Palace. The Purse, in fact, contains The Speech which Her Majesty will later read from the Throne.

A few steps farther back the Earl Marshal, the Duke of Norfolk, awaits The Queen.

These officials precede The Queen up a short flight of steps to The Queen's Robing Room. (A lift was installed for King Edward VII during the last years of his reign, but The Queen does not use it.)

The Queen and the Duke of Edinburgh pass into their robing rooms. The Queen takes off the diadem and the ermine stole. While she stands, the Robe of State of crimson velvet is placed over her shoulders. Sometimes this is called the Parliamentary Robe, but this is not absolutely correct, as it is also worn by the Sovereign when arriving at the Abbey for the Coronation, and formerly could be worn on other occasions too. The Robe of State is one magnificent garment consisting of an ermine cape evenly decorated with little black ermine tails, and a long train. From The Queen's shoulder to the tip of the train it measures eighteen feet four-and-a-half inches, and the width of the train at the foot is just under four feet. The whole train is completely lined with ermine. It is also turned up with ermine to a depth of several inches, and is banded with two rows of gold lace with filigree gold-work between, and bordered with many ermine tails. It is a fantastically heavy garment. This Robe is made of fine crimson velvet specially woven in England for The Queen's Coronation, the first occasion on which The Queen wore it. The Queen opened her first Parliament in the crimson velvet Robe of State which had belonged to Queen Victoria, and which was also used by the Queen Mother.

On The Queen's head is placed the fabulous Imperial State Crown. This is not as old nor so historic as St. Edward's Crown, which was used at The Queen's Coronation, and is of gold, adorned not too plentifully with precious stones. The Imperial State Crown was made in 1837 for Queen Victoria, but its platinum base is completely covered with jewels. At every movement —and The Queen must be conscious of them all, as the crown weighs nearly three pounds—it flashes and shimmers with the many-coloured fire of the jewels. The Crown contains four rubies, eleven emeralds, sixteen sapphires, two hundred and seventy-three pearls and approximately two thousand, seven hundred and eighty-three diamonds. The base consists of a band of alternate sapphires and emeralds set in diamonds and has in front the enormous second part of the Star of Africa, cut from the Cullinan Diamond, a famous diamond which can be worn as a pendant or brooch. Above is a band of pearls, and then alternate fleurs-de-lys and cross-patees heavily set with emeralds and rubies, including the Black Prince's spinel (a precious stone closely resembling a ruby), which was worn by Henry V at Agincourt. The arches of the crown are formed by branches of diamond oak leaves set with pearl acorns. The four great pearls, reputedly the ear-rings of Queen Elizabeth I, who loved pearls, hang from the crossing. The whole is topped with a jewelled globe and cross.

Below the Crown The Queen wears a cap of purple velvet turned up with ermine.

Although a Robing Room is provided for Prince Philip the Duke of Edinburgh, he has so far preferred to wear naval uniform without the Duke's Parliamentary Robes in the ceremony. When all is ready, The Queen's two Pages-of-Honour step forward, and take up as much weight as they can of the heavy train. This is the heaviest garment that The Queen ever wears, because, although the Coronation Robe of purple velvet, beautifully embroidered with gold and silver thread, was of the same length, it was lined with white silk in place of fur. The Crown weighs heavy and Kings have commented, one after another, on the headaches that they have endured on the day of the Opening of Parliament.

The Pages-of-Honour are dressed in scarlet coatees, the colour which has been the Royal Livery of the Kings and Queens of England since it was brought to this country by King Canute the Dane, with white breeches and stockings and gold-buckled shoes with red heels. They carry their gilt swords, which are generally very popular with the youthful Pages.

The Queen is preceded in procession by her Pursuivants, Heralds and Kings of Arms, Equerries and other Members of her Household, culminating with the peers who bear the Sword of State and the Cap of Maintenance. She is followed by her Mistress of the Robes and Ladies-in-Waiting and other Members of the Household.

The Chamber of the House of Lords has been gradually filling since shortly after 9 o'clock. The Peers are wearing their Parliamentary Robes of scarlet cloth and white ermine. The Judges in their robes are seated on the Woolsack. The Peeresses and the diplomats' wives are in full evening dress with fine jewels. The diplomats, seated on benches to the right of The Throne, wear diplomatic uniform variously frogged in gold with ribands of different orders.

A few minutes before The Queen enters the Chamber, the lights are lowered, and then, as The Queen enters through the doorways flanked by tall Gentlemen-at-Arms, the lights gradually blaze up again. The Queen, the tips of the fingers of her left hand held at shoulder height in her husband's right hand, walks slowly up the three steps to the dais, turns and takes her seat upon the peaked gilded throne chair designed by Pugin, and says in her clear voice, "My Lords, pray be seated." The Duke of Edinburgh sits upon a chair to the left of, and one step lower than, the Throne. (When Princess Elizabeth first officially attended Parliament in 1947 she sat as Heiress Presumptive on a similar chair placed in a corresponding position to the right of the Throne.) The Household ranges itself on either side of her; the Lord Great Chamberlain stands on the steps of the Throne.

In 1958, the historic year in which, for the first time, the Opening of Parliament was televised, The Queen reverted to an earlier form of the ceremony of despatching Black Rod to fetch the faithful Commons to the Bar of the House. It is one of the few occasions on which The Queen has set aside one of her father's innovations, and it was done in order that the historical ceremony seen by millions of her subjects should be as complete as possible.

The Queen waited until she was seated on her Throne before despatching Black Rod (Lieutenant-General Sir Brian Horrocks, K.C.B., K.B.E., D.S.O., M.C.) to summon the Commons to the Bar of the House. This has meant the return of a pause of some three to four minutes at this part of the ceremony, a pause which King George VI found trying, and eliminated by despatching Black Rod to summon the Commons while the King was in the Robing Room, so that they arrived at the Bar of the House shortly after he had seated himself upon the Throne. The Queen followed her father's pattern in this up to 1958.

The Lord Chancellor bows, approaches, kneels on the top step, takes from his Purse the printed copy of The Speech and hands it to The Queen. Her Majesty reads The Speech, which is the Government's declaration of policy for the coming session.

The Speech contains the future programme of the Government in office and has been worked over and approved by the Cabinet. Traditionally it is not changed in any way by The Queen. I am told, however, that if any phrase were found by The Queen to be not to her liking, different words meaning the same thing would be substituted. Possibly the last occasion on which a Sovereign may have changed the *meaning* as apart from the mere *form* of the words of The Speech was at the time of the Schleswig-Holstein crisis between Denmark and Germany, when, according to Queen Alexandra's biographer Troubridge, Queen Victoria insisted that certain aggressive Government statements were smoothed down, as she believed they would lead to a break with Germany.

Queen Elizabeth II, having to hold her head high because she is wearing the Crown, then reads The Speech, which generally takes nine or ten minutes and which is sometimes of most highly controversial material in contrast to her speeches on most other occasions. The Speech always ends with the words "I pray that the blessing of Almighty God will rest upon your counsels." The Lord Chancellor then advances and receives back the copy of The Speech from The Queen.

Then The Queen leaves the Chamber, returning to the Robing Room where she exchanges the Crown for the Diadem, before driving back in State to Buckingham Palace.

This time-honoured scene now generally takes place in early November, as it did over three hundred and fifty years ago when, on November 4, 1605, Guy Fawkes was discovered hiding in the cellars below the Palace of Westminster. Ever since that time the Yeomen of the Guard search the cellars, still being issued for the purpose with lamps, although the capacious cellars have long since been fitted with electric light.

The Queen's Bodyguard of the Yeomen of the Guard is not only the oldest royal bodyguard, but also the oldest military corps in the world. It was formed in 1485 at the Coronation of Henry VII, after the Battle of Bosworth Field. The knee-length scarlet tunics, white ruffs and black Tudor hats worn by the Yeoman of the Guard form one of the most familiar of all British uniforms. The Yeomen of the Guard, who are The Queen's Bodyguard, can be distinguished from the Yeomen Warders of the Tower of London, as the Royal Guard has cross-belts. These belts were originally for supporting arquebuses when mounted, which must have been just about the most cumbrous and uncomfortable form of weapon inflicted upon a guard.

The search is not entirely ritual: the search party is accompanied by officers of the Special Branch of the Metropolitan Police Force, whose duty it is to guard members of the Royal Family and leading statesmen.

Although all seems changeless, the passage of time must bring changes. For instance in 1955 The Queen and the Duke of Edinburgh drove to open Parliament in a closed car. But it was in 1956 that the press of history surged around the Opening of Parliament, which took place on November 6, at the full height of the Suez crisis. Who would think, to look at the pictures of The Queen, erect, serene and smiling in the Irish State Coach, that such a black burden was upon her young shoulders?

CABINET MEETS AS THE QUEEN SPEAKS

ran the headlines in the evening papers. The *Evening Standard* wrote:

Sir Anthony Eden called a Cabinet meeting at his room in the House of Commons today to consider Russia's threat—contained in a message from Marshal Bulganin—of intervention in the Middle East.

The Cabinet remained in session during the Royal Opening of Parliament, although the Prime Minister and one or two other Ministers left the meeting for a short time and took part in the ceremony. The meeting, which continued after The Queen had left Westminster, ended after being in session for more than three hours.

In the House of Lords The Queen took her part in the ceremony with unaltered grace, her clear voice reading:

"My Government will continue their efforts to achieve, by all possible means, a prompt and just settlement of the many problems arising from the grave situation in the Middle East."

As the correspondent of *The Times* wrote next day:

For a few minutes yesterday, at the State Opening of the new session, the clear, calm voice of the Queen reminded the Lords and Commons alike that, in spite of the passionate recriminations of the past week, they all serve one mistress, and are responsible for working in harmony to preserve her justice and the national honour. . . . Once again, in the midst of the dark and thunderous atmosphere of the world, ancient pageantry had shown its power to quiet and uplift the heart.

This Opening of Parliament was unusual in another way. It was the only occasion through the seven hundred years of Parliamentary history that a sister accompanied the Sovereign. The Duke of Edinburgh was unavoidably absent, having already left on his long-promised visit to Australia for the Opening of the Olympic Games. So Princess Margaret sat opposite The Queen in the Irish State Coach to Westminster, and followed her in procession into the House of Lords.

Usually members of the Royal Family who attend the Opening of Parliament enter the Chamber without ceremony a few minutes before the Sovereign. It is not usual for the widow of a Sovereign to come to the Opening of Parliament after her husband's death, and so far the Queen Mother has not attended any Opening of Parliament since the death of King George VI. Incidentally, in the photograph of The Queen and Princess Margaret on this occasion, it will be noticed that the Princess is wearing a tiara. As an unmarried lady, the Princess only wears a tiara on an occasion of State.

When The Queen opens Parliament it is one of the few occasions on which all the parts of the forces that govern us—that is, "The Queen in Parliament"—are physically met together. (Another occasion is when the Royal Assent is given to an Act of Parliament, but the Sovereign seldom attends in person.) Originally Parliament was called at a time when the Sovereign, the absolute ruler, talked things over with the wise men of his realm and received their petitions. After taking counsel, the King then did what he thought best. The presentation of a Bill to The Queen takes the form of words of a petition which the faithful Commons and Lords deliver to their Sovereign. Our law demands that all legislation shall be passed by the two Houses of Parliament, and assented to by the Sovereign. In fact, of course, when a Bill has been read three times by both Houses, and passed, The Queen is almost bound to give her Assent to it.

How much does The Queen have to do with these measures which are first announced in her Speech from the Throne? The Queen does not concern herself with the progress of Bills at all, unless they directly affect the Crown. But she will hear about them and possibly discuss them with her Prime Minister when he comes to see her, and she will read in *Hansard* and in the daily reports from her Vice-Chamberlain of the Household about their reception in the House.

The Lords have now only strictly limited power; they can only delay the passage of a bill by one year, or, if it is a financial bill— the control of the moneybags has always been the jealously guarded province of the Lower House—by one month. Should the Lords refuse to pass a Bill, it could, ultimately, under the provision of the Parliament Act 1911, as amended by subsequent

Acts, receive the Royal Assent, without the concurrence of the House of Lords.

Before a Bill can become an Act, it must receive the Royal Assent. Theoretically, The Queen could refuse her Assent, but this is now scarcely conceivable. The last time on which a Sovereign has said "No" to Parliament was when Queen Anne refused the Royal Assent two hundred and fifty years ago.

How does The Queen give her Assent to a Bill? At what moment does a Bill become Law? Does she sign a Bill? Many well-informed people are just a little hazy about it all. When a Bill, or more probably a number of Bills, have passed all their stages through both Houses, and require the Royal Assent, the Clerk of the Crown, in the Crown Office at the Palace of Westminster, prepares a Commission to appoint the Commissioners who will give the Royal Assent in The Queen's name. This Commission contains the name of the Bill or Bills concerned. It goes from the Lord Chancellor to The Queen in a Red Box, which looks just like the other red leather boxes mentioned earlier, except that it is lettered "Royal Commission".

The Queen signs the Commission, which commands that certain peers who are also Privy Counsellors are to make known to both the House of Lords and the House of Commons on her behalf the Royal Assent to the Acts named in the Commission.

The Commission is returned to the Lord Chancellor, and it is sealed with the Great Seal. This was formerly in itself a ceremonial operation of considerable complexity, but is now done simply by an official in the Crown Office, who takes particular pride in getting a good impression.

The document is then sent to the Clerk of the Parliaments in the House of Lords. At the time appointed, the Peers are assembled on both sides of the House, facing inwards, and the Lord Chancellor and the other Royal Assent Commissioners, who are generally two in number, enter the Lords' Chamber, and sit on a bench in front of the Throne, facing the assembly, and form the third side of a square. Black Rod is called upon to summon the Commons from their Chamber to the Bar of the House of Lords. There, headed by the Speaker and his suite, come the senior members of the Government and Opposition, followed by members of the different parties walking together.

They spread themselves out at the Bar of the House and form the fourth side of the square.

However bitterly the Bill has been contested, it is seldom that basic national unity is not displayed in this manner at the moment when a Bill becomes the law of the land. On one recent occasion only has the Government alone come to the Lords to hear the Bill made law.

The Clerk of the Crown reads out the name of each Bill in turn, and the Clerk of the Parliaments gives the Royal Assent in Norman French, the formula differing somewhat according to the type of Act. For most Acts he says, "La Reine Le Veult" (The Queen wishes it). It is at that moment that the Bill becomes Law.

The most recent instance of the Royal Assent being given in person was not in the Mother Parliament in Westminster, but when King George VI visited Canada in 1939. He then gave the Royal Assent in person to a number of Bills, which thereupon became Law. The Sovereign has not given the Royal Assent in person in Westminster in this century.

So much for The Queen's physical association with Parliament.

The Queen exercises her power only after consultation with wise men of the Realm.

It is the Sovereign's Prerogative to choose the Prime Minister. In some circumstances the choice is clear and straightforward, as, for example, when one Party wins a decisive victory at a General Election. On other occasions the choice is less easy, as when the Prime Minister resigns owing to ill health, or dies in office. On such occasions there may be more than one possible candidate and it is then that The Queen's Prerogative becomes supremely important. It is, of course, open to her on such occasions to seek advice in whatever quarter she sees fit.

As everyone knows, an occasion of this kind arose in January 1957 when Sir Anthony Eden resigned because of ill health.

On Tuesday, January 8, 1957, Sir Anthony Eden, the Prime Minister, travelled to Sandringham following a Cabinet Meeting. The newspapers informed the public that the visit "has no special significance, and its purpose is solely to keep The Queen informed on Government policy."

At Sandringham, Sir Anthony disclosed to The Queen the state of his health, and that a successor would be required immediately as Prime Minister.

On Wednesday, January 9, The Queen returned by road from Sandringham to Buckingham Palace. The more astute newspapers pointed out that she had been expected to remain in Norfolk until early February: it was suggested that she would be having fittings of clothes for the State Visit to France in April.

At 7 p.m. that evening the news was revealed to the public in a statement issued from Buckingham Palace that:

> The Right Honourable Sir Anthony Eden, M.P. (Prime Minister and First Lord of the Treasury), had an audience of the Queen this evening and tendered his resignation as Prime Minister and First Lord of the Treasury, which Her Majesty was pleased to accept.

Bulletins were issued (dated January 8) signed by Sir Horace Evans (The Queen's physician also) and two other doctors, stating that:

> . . . In our opinion his health will no longer enable him to sustain the heavy burdens inseparable from the office of Prime Minister.

Sir Anthony Eden himself made a statement:

> When I returned to this country a month ago [from a visit of three weeks to Jamaica to recuperate after illness] I hoped that my health had been sufficiently restored to enable me to carry out my duties effectively for some considerable time. That hope has not been realised.
>
> I do not feel that it is right for me to continue in office as The Queen's First Minister, knowing that I shall be unable to do my full duty by my Sovereign and the country. I have therefore decided, with the utmost regret, that I must tender my resignation to The Queen, which Her Majesty has been graciously pleased to accept.

For once the centre of activity in crisis switched from Downing Street to Buckingham Palace. Whom would The Queen choose as Sir Anthony's successor? The position was not entirely clear. Two men seemed to have almost equal claims, Mr. R. A. Butler, Lord Privy Seal and Leader of the House of Commons, and Mr. Harold Macmillan, Chancellor of the Exchequer. Other names were popularly mentioned, but the choice among them all lay with The Queen.

Because the arguments put forward in Cabinet meetings are never heard outside the Cabinet Room, except possibly by The

Queen, we shall never know the truth, but the general public believed that Mr. Macmillan and Mr. Butler stood for different viewpoints on the Suez crisis. It is not always understood by the public that a Cabinet decision is a collective responsibility, and that a Cabinet Minister *cannot* "opt out" of a Cabinet decision, except by resigning. Therefore Mr. Macmillan and Mr. Butler were equally committed to the Suez policy.

Only rarely in this century has such a set of circumstances occurred. One such occasion was because of the fatal illness of Mr. Bonar Law, which in 1923 led King George V to choose Mr. Baldwin, who sat in the Lower House, in preference to the Marquess of Curzon; and again when Mr. Neville Chamberlain resigned in 1940, and King George VI sent for Mr. Churchill to form a new Government.

Indeed, "It is for The Queen alone", wrote *The Times* on the morning of Thursday, January 10, "to decide who shall be invited by her to form a Government."

Queen Elizabeth II was thirty years old. She had been almost five years on the Throne. Her husband was unavoidably overseas, and she did not have his support in the sudden crisis with which she was faced.

The Queen took the advice of senior statesmen—Sir Winston Churchill, the Marquess of Salisbury and others. She could properly have consulted any one of the two hundred and eighty or so Privy Counsellors or anyone else. It was obvious that for national and international confidence The Queen's choice must be made swiftly, although the Ministers—who would automatically hand their resignations to the new Prime Minister so that he could re-shuffle his Cabinet as he liked—would carry on until The Queen made her choice known. All morning the discussions proceeded. The Queen made up her mind. Then Mr. Macmillan was called to Buckingham Palace. At 1.41 p.m. he drove out from Downing Street, on his way to Buckingham Palace. The small crowd who saw him arrive guessed his mission and guessed rightly. Just before 2.30 p.m. the official statement was issued from Buckingham Palace:

The Queen received the Rt. Hon. Harold Macmillan in audience this afternoon, and offered him the post of Prime Minister and First Lord of the Treasury.

The Prime Minister kissed hands upon his appointment, and returned to Downing Street after a short interview lasting only twenty minutes. The twenty-hour gap between Prime Ministers had been filled.

Less than an hour later The Queen drove out from Buckingham Palace, smiling, hatless and wearing a mink coat, on her way back to Sandringham. The formation of the Government now lay in her Prime Minister's hands. The crisis was over, although she returned to London two days later on Sunday (and was criticised by the Lord's Day Observance Society for so doing) in order to receive the Oaths of loyalty of such Ministers as were newly appointed and to present to them their Seals of Office.

The exercise of The Queen's prerogative in this matter was acknowledged as the Sovereign's right by all parties. But the Socialist Party regarded the position as inherently dangerous in that it tended to bring The Queen into party politics.

Mr. James Griffiths, Deputy Leader of the Opposition, and temporary leader of the Party while Earl Attlee was in Canada, commented on television, after a meeting of the Shadow Cabinet, that the Conservatives had "placed the Crown in a very difficult and embarrassing position". The Opposition did not question that The Queen had acted with due constitutional propriety, but it was felt by the Socialists that if this were a position which were to recur often, there would be a case for examining the procedure.

During the television interview, Mr. Griffiths was quoted as saying:

"We believe that it is important that parties themselves should decide on their leaders, and that the Crown should not be put in the embarrassing position of having to make a choice between rival claimants for the premiership of the same party. This is bringing the Crown into internecine party warfare, which is very bad for the constitution."

Should the Conservative Party wish to make their own choice of a successor to the Prime Minister in similar circumstances, it has been suggested that the Prime Minister who had been taken ill could first resign from the Party leadership, and the Party successor be chosen before he went to the Palace to tender his resignation as Prime Minister. The disadvantage of this method would obviously be that it would be hard to achieve any measure of secrecy, and that the period of unsettlement which is inevitable during a change of premiership would be longer.

It would be quite impossible for the Sovereign to impose a totally unsuitable choice upon Parliament. Such an unsuitable person would just not be able to form a Government. If he did manage to form a Government from among his friends, he would be voted out of power by Parliament. In this way democracy is safeguarded.

The continuity and unity to the nation which The Queen can give in these and similar times of crisis is one of the great strengths of the monarchy.

The Queen has also the power to prorogue or dissolve Parliament. This is generally exercised in accordance with the request of the Government in order to bring a Session to a close. The Prime Minister asks for the dissolution of Parliament, either at the end of a Government's customary five years of office, or because his Government has been defeated in a major issue in the House of Commons, or because he considers that a strategic time has occurred for appealing to the country. But The Queen also—unlike the President of the Fourth French Republic—has the prerogative to dissolve Parliament at other times, if, for instance, it were thought that Parliament and the will of the people were diametrically opposed. It is almost inconceivable that such a position should occur, but theoretically it would be possible for The Queen to say in effect that "the policy the House of Commons is now introducing is so absolutely different from that which its members supported when they were elected that I think you should have the vote of confidence from the country before bringing in these extraordinary measures". This is only a hypothetical case, but the power does remain.

There is no written power that could make the Sovereign summon Parliament if he or she did not want to, but, to prevent the country being carried on without a Parliament, a considerable number of financial measures are deliberately introduced in Parliament to cover one year only, such as The Finance Bill and the Navy, Army and Air Force estimates. Therefore no person or party could run the country without Parliament, because they would soon run out of money.

Parliament is only dissolved before a General Election. Sessions of Parliament are prorogued—that is to say, discontinued for a time without being dissolved. The custom recently has been to prorogue Parliament for only a few days before the summoning of the new Session, so that there is no long interim period between one Session and the next. In this way the machinery of Government is always available during the long summer recess, and is ready to go into immediate action in crisis.

Parliament is prorogued at a ceremony at which the Sovereign can take part, but has not recently done so in person. When Parliament is prorogued The Queen is represented by her Lords Commissioners at a brief ceremony in the House of Lords. The Queen's Speech, citing various events of the past session, is read by one of the Lords Commissioners, who is generally the Lord Chancellor, and ends by telling Parliament the date, which is always stated, to which they are prorogued. Parliament then disperses until that date.

Parliament is dissolved by a Proclamation made by The Queen. The Proclamation dissolves Parliament and calls for a new one. Thereupon on the Sovereign's Warrant Writs for a new Parliament are issued by the Lord Chancellor, to the Peers individually and for the Commons to the Returning Officers of the various constituencies. The Proclamation is read in the City of London by the Common Crier from the steps of the Royal Exchange, at St. James's Palace, and elsewhere throughout the United Kingdom. The Royal Family habitually cancels any public engagement which may have been made for the day of the election. The Queen has no vote. The Royal Dukes, as Peers, have no vote, as they are entitled to take part in the House of Lords proceedings, although they do not now do so. The Queen Mother, Princess Margaret, and other ladies of the Royal Family are entitled to vote, although they never use their vote, because the Royal Family takes no part in politics.

After a General Election, if a new Prime Minister has been returned to power, the Prime Minister of the defeated party tenders his resignation to The Queen, who thanks him for his services, and asks him to carry on until she has been able to arrange a new Government. She then sends for the Leader of the Opposition Party. Queen Elizabeth II inherited her father's fourth Parliament. Her first Parliament, the fifteenth this century, took place after the General Election of May 1955 when the Conservative Government was returned for a second term of office.

The majority at the General Election may be a small one, but, in the present mainly two-party system, the choice of party from which a Government should be formed presents no difficulties. Even should the number of Liberals or of a new party rise considerably, the problem is not likely to be difficult. The new Prime Minister kisses hands upon appointment, and goes away to form his Government. His new Cabinet is summoned to attend· The Queen to kiss hands and to receive their Seals of Office, which have been delivered up by their predecessors. If they are not already members of the Privy Council, they are sworn.

Members of the new Parliament assembling at Westminster are sworn in. Both Lords and Commons are told that, as soon as they are sworn in, "the causes of Her Majesty calling this new Parliament will be declared to you", a form which emphasises the original form of Parliament, when the Sovereign called his peers and wise men together for consultation. Black Rod is commanded to summon the Commons to the House of Lords to hear "the Lords who are authorised by virtue of Her Majesty's Commission to declare the opening of Parliament".

The House of Commons meets to elect a Speaker, whose office is historic and was sometimes dangerous, as he was the mouthpiece of the Commons to the King. The appointment must be approved by The Queen.

At the Opening of the new Parliament the Speaker, attended by members of the Commons, goes to the House of Lords to seek the Royal approval of his appointment. This is invariably granted. He then goes on to claim the rights and privileges of the House of Commons from the Sovereign in these words:

"My Lords, I submit myself with all humility and gratitude to Her Majesty's gracious commands. It is now my duty, in the name and on behalf of the Commons of the United Kingdom, to lay claim by humble Petition to Her Majesty to all their ancient and undoubted rights and privileges; especially to freedom of speech in debate; to freedom from arrest; and to free access to Her Majesty whenever occasion shall require; and that the most favourable construction shall be put upon all their proceedings. In regard to myself, I pray that if in the discharge of my duties I shall inadvertently fall into any error, it may be imputed to myself alone, and not to Her Majesty's most faithful Commons."

And these privileges are of course always granted.

The Speaker's deputy is the Chairman of Ways and Means, and is proposed by the Government Party. His appointment does not require to be approved by The Queen.

A Cabinet Minister in particularly close contact with the Sovereign is the Secretary of State for Home Affairs. Historically the Home Secretary is The Queen's Secretary, and he is in a special position *vis à vis* Her Majesty, because he advises her on most matters which concern her within the United Kingdom—Tours, Speeches, Title Royal, ecclesiastical affairs and so on.

Apart from the Prime Minister, the members of the Cabinet with whom The Queen has a special relationship are the Lord Chancellor, the Foreign Secretary, the Home Secretary (as has been explained) and also, naturally, the Service Ministers representing the various armed forces.

The Queen takes no active part in the proceedings in Parliament.

The individual members both of the House of Commons and of the House of Lords have a theoretical right of direct approach to the Sovereign; the Lord Chamberlain, as the senior Officer of the Royal Household, acts as The Queen's emissary to the House of Lords, receiving their Lordships' Addresses to The Queen, and returning them Her Majesty's reply. The Vice-Chamberlain of the Household undertakes a similar rôle with the House of Commons. The office of Vice-Chamberlain is one of the political appointments to the Household which change with the Government, and carries with it the post of Junior Whip. (The political appointments which change with the Government are the Lords-in-Waiting to The Queen, who act as Whips in the House of Lords; and the Treasurer, Comptroller and the Vice-Chamberlain of The Queen's Household, who act as assistant Whips in the House of Commons.)

The description of The Queen's reception of addresses from Parliament has been given briefly in the chapter "The Queen's Back-room". When the Queen replies to such addresses she gives her reply to the Officer of the appropriate House. The Vice-Chamberlain goes back to the Commons with The Queen's reply. Carrying his long white staff of office, he stands at the Bar of the House and calls: "A message from The Queen, Sir, in reply to a loyal and dutiful address from this House", and then proceeds up the floor of the House to read the message in front of the Table before delivering it to the Clerk. More important messages from the Crown are delivered by the Prime Minister, the Lord Privy Seal or the Home Secretary, who stands at the Bar of the House and says: "A message from The Queen, Sir, signed by her own hand" before proceeding up the floor and handing the message to the Speaker, who reads it to the House. Mr. Churchill took over this office for the reply to the first petition of The Queen's reign, and with his sense of the drama of history turned this simple ceremony into something memorable.

Certain rules govern the mention of The Queen in Parliament.

The Queen and her actions can be criticised or commented upon by Parliament. But if her actions are going to be discussed, they must be definitely introduced in a Motion, not just brought up during discussion of another Motion.

This applies also to the Heir to the Throne, Governors-General, the Lord Chancellor, the Speaker, the Chairman of Ways and Means, to members of both Houses of Parliament and to Judges of the Superior Court of the United Kingdom as well. It does not, however, apply to Ambassadors.

Nor is it in order in Parliament to "utter treasonable or seditious words, or use The Queen's name irreverently, or to influence the debate".

The Queen's name is used in a purely theoretical sense from time to time. For instance, motions granting money are worded as though the money were granted to The Queen herself. The Queen's recommendation is needed for financial resolutions. Every financial resolution has to be set upon the Order Paper. When it is raised, the Speaker asks whether it has The Queen's recommendation, whereupon a Minister rises and indicates that this is so. The House then resolves itself into Committee to consider the resolution. The Speaker withdraws when money is being discussed. It has been suggested that this is because formerly the Speaker was in very close contact with the Sovereign, and might tell what went on, and what So-and-so said when discussing the giving—or more probably not giving—the money.

There are occasions also when the Sovereign can refuse or argue against the request by the Prime Minister for dissolution. The most controversial of these was the occasion in 1931 when Mr. Ramsay MacDonald, Prime Minister of a minority Socialist Government, at a time of great financial crisis, went to King George V to submit the resignation of the Government and to request the dissolution of Parliament. King George V took the advice of many counsellors, and persuaded Mr. MacDonald, instead of resigning, to try to form a coalition Government instead, which he succeeded in doing. Thus was averted the danger of a period of uncertainty at a time of urgent financial crisis, and when two General Elections had already taken place within a short time. The balance of subsequent opinion would seem to be that, in a period of great danger and difficulty, the King acted wisely. But there is no doubt that many Socialists would not agree. No one questioned, however, that the King had acted with full sincerity and completely within the rights of his prerogatives.

There was another occasion on which the Governor-General, acting as the King's representative, refused a dissolution of Parliament when requested by the Prime Minister. This was in South Africa in 1939, when the issue was the grave one of the declaration of war. The Prime Minister differed from his colleagues in the Cabinet; he did not want South Africa to declare war, and he wanted the matter to be taken to the country. The Governor-General did not believe that the Prime Minister was justified in asking for a dissolution when he was not voicing the opinion of his Cabinet. He refused to accept the Prime Minister's advice. The Prime Minister resigned and the Governor-General requested another member of the Cabinet to form a Government, which he was able to do without difficulty. War was declared.

The advantage of the present use of the prerogative is that it means the Nation can never be forced into a position of doldrums. There must always be the Sovereign, who can bridge any gap, forseeable or unforseeable.

"The Queen must make certain that she has a Government in the United Kingdom," says Sir Ivor Jennings.

This is the great strength of the British system, as against the systems carefully laid down and safeguarded in such lawyer-made Constitutions as those of the United States or France. It is impossible for man, however ingenious, to find a formula to cover all the unimaginable quirks of fate; and in his efforts to pilot his successors through waters which must be unknown to him he is far more likely to be running them on to the rocks.

The Queen herself physically has no contact with the Commons, except at the Opening of Parliament, when they are summoned to hear the Speech from the Throne. She is actually barred by established custom from entering the Chamber of the House of Commons when the House is in Session—which is rather strange when one considers that the Commons' House is situated in part of her own Palace of Westminster. Since the time of King Charles I the only occasion on which the Chamber of the House has been entered by a ruling Sovereign was when King George VI inspected the rebuilt Chamber before it was reopened. This was possible because technically the new Chamber had not yet been taken into use. (When Parliament is not in Session, the building reverts to its status as a Royal Palace.) The Queen, who was then Princess Elizabeth, accompanied her father on that unique occasion.

The Queen's connections with the Palace of Westminster are not many, although signs of the royal link are visible to those with a sense of history. Before the Royal Gallery can be used for any function The Queen's consent is required. Then the Lord Great Chamberlain, Keeper of the Palace of Westminster, writes to The Queen's Private Secretary, who lays the request before The Queen.

Westminster Hall, the magnificent hall built by William Rufus, son of William the Conqueror, almost alone links the Palace with pre-Tudor history. Saved with difficulty in the fire which destroyed almost all the Palace in 1834, it was again saved in the blitz of 1941 when, to get at the beams of the roof already alight, the Rt. Hon. Walter Elliot, C.H., M.C., wielded an axe on the stout timbers of the door whose key was not available, so that the fire in the roof could be tackled from within. Thus a great historic building was saved. Even in recent years Westminster Hall has added to our history. Three Queens mourned here at the lying-in-state of King George VI and as I, in company with thousands of others, passed the coffin guarded by Gentlemen-at-Arms with reversed partisans, the King's mother, Queen Mary, erect in spite of her eighty-four years, accompanied by her bowed, sad-faced son and ex-King, Edward VIII, came out from Westminster Hall.

Only a short time later, Queen Mary lay in state in this same hall.

A few weeks afterwards, I was The Queen's guest in Westminster Hall at one of the many luncheons she held for those who had been fortunate enough to attend her Coronation in Westminster Abbey. The Hall, which had been hushed and mournful when I had last seen it at the lying-in-state, was filled with excited voices and the clatter of glass and cutlery. People known usually as pictures in the newspaper were easing aching feet out of elegant shoes, resting on the stone steps and meeting and re-meeting friends in an atmosphere totally different yet equally in keeping with this historic old Hall, which has witnessed every form of human emotion from the trial of Charles I to the old Coronation banquets, at one of which it is said that the ladies starving in a gallery let down a rope of napkins to which a friend on the floor below kindly attached a cold roast chicken!

*　　*　　*　　*

The Queen has more to do with the Government, and particularly with the inner coterie which forms the Cabinet, than with the House of Commons in general. The Sovereign ruled originally with a Council, remnants of which are to be seen in the Privy Council, which is discussed in the next chapter. Charles II did not like discussing his affairs with "a set of fellows" and formed an inner council of his principal officials, which met in his antechamber or Cabinet at St. James's Palace and was formerly called the Cabinet Council. King George I, who spoke no English, found it extremely tedious to attend the meetings of the Cabinet when he could not understand one word of what was going on, and gradually discontinued coming. The prerogative of the Sovereign to attend a Cabinet meeting has therefore lapsed: it has not been waived. (Incidentally, the King of Denmark regularly attends the meetings of his Cabinet.)

As the King no longer took the chair at a Cabinet meeting, the principal minister (*premier ministre* or Prime Minister, originally a term of abuse) took his place and gradually rose to a position of power. He had, however, no place in the national precedence, until the reign of King Edward VII. The Office of Prime Minister is combined with the much older post of the First Lord of the Treasury, because the First Lord of the Treasury had by far the greatest number of positions in his patronage, and so was the most powerful minister.

In the United States the change of Administration affects a great many more appointments than the change of Government does here. It is said that there are no fewer than 750 persons to be replaced on a change of régime in the United States. In this country there are only about one hundred ministerial appointments which change with the Government.

There are a large number of Crown appointments which are made by The Queen on the recommendation of the Prime Minister, such as the appointments of Bishops and of Lords-Lieutenant of the Counties. These appointments, once made, continue whatever Government is in power.

The requirements of these non-political offices do not vary from one Government to another and the same personal qualifications of ability and experience, character and integrity are needed, whatever party is in power.

The offices of Prime Minister and First Lord of the Treasury are now always held by the one man.

The Prime Minister is in a special position with regard to the Sovereign. The Queen may not attend Cabinet meetings, but she has the right to know all their decisions, although not necessarily their differences. The Prime Minister either writes to her to tell her of Cabinet decisions or sees her to discuss them in person. Usually the Prime Minister sees The Queen once a week, often on a Tuesday evening, but if urgent matters arose he would seek an immediate Audience, or, if this were impracticable, communicate in writing.

The Prime Minister used to write to The Queen every day telling her both about Cabinet affairs and affairs in the House. This letter was of immense importance, because right up to 1916 the Cabinet had no secretariat. Ministers were allowed to make no notes and the only record of Cabinet proceedings was the agenda, which the Prime Minister wrote out, and the rough notes he made during the meeting, which were later incorporated in his letter to The Queen, often written on the Treasury Bench. These letters from the Prime Minister to the Sovereign were an exacting duty, and varied much in content and character according to the Premier and the Sovereign. Queen Victoria thoroughly enjoyed the flattering and amusing letters she received from Disraeli; on the other hand King George V disapproved of any attempt at facetiousness in his Prime Minister's letters. King Edward VIII discontinued the Prime Minister's letters, one of the few lasting changes he made during his short reign.

All Members of the Cabinet must be sworn into the Privy Council. This is to bind them with the severe oath of secrecy which all Privy Counsellors must take and which will be discussed in the next chapter, and to ensure that absolute secrecy is maintained about all matters discussed in Cabinet. Normally there is only one occasion on which this oath of secrecy is sometimes lifted. That is when a Member of the Cabinet resigns following a difference of opinion on a matter discussed by the Cabinet. He has then the right to approach The Queen through the Prime Minister and to ask that he may reveal the circumstances which led to his resignation. This permission is usually granted, but the Cabinet Minister concerned must only explain those circumstances which led to his resignation and must not disclose other occasions on which he differed from the rest of the Cabinet.

A most unusual instance of disclosure of Cabinet information took place in the autumn of 1957 when an enquiry was being made into an alleged leak of information connected with a rise in the Bank Rate. The Chancellor of the Exchequer, Mr. Thorneycroft, was asked by the Attorney-General:

"Have you sought permission of Her Majesty The Queen to disclose information about proceedings of the Cabinet on September 17th and 19th?"

Mr. Thorneycroft: "Yes."

"Has Her Majesty been graciously pleased to give her consent to disclosure of that information?"

"She has, Sir."

Not all members of the Government, of course, are Members of the Cabinet. The numbers have varied with the times and circumstances. Disraeli had a Cabinet of 12, Mr. Macmillan in 1957 formed a Cabinet of 18. There are many Ministers outside the Cabinet. Mr. Herbert Morrison, who has made special research into this subject, is of the opinion that all Ministers who are Privy Counsellors, whether within or without the Cabinet, are "Ministers of the Crown".

There are two kinds of Ministers. There are the Ministers mostly but not entirely of ancient office, who are descended from The Queen's personal servants, and to whom she stands in an historic association. And there are the Ministers appointed by Acts of Parliament with whom her connection is not nearly so close.

Strangely, there is nothing definite in law to compel The Queen to delegate her functions to those Ministers who are the successors of her Royal Servants, although of course in practice their relationship to The Queen gives them just the same powers as those held by Ministers appointed under Acts of Parliament.

The Ministers who are descended from the old Royal Servants are:

(1) The Lord Chancellor, formerly the Chancellor, and the Sovereign's first Private Secretary. He is the Keeper of the Great Seal.

(2) The First Lord of the Treasury, who is also the Prime Minister, who replaced the Treasurer.

(3) The Lord President of the Council, who as head of The Queen's Privy Council has an extremely high position in precedence, coming immediately after the Prime Minister who is himself of lower precedence than the Lord Chancellor. The work of the Privy Council is described in the next chapter, but it does not take up all the time of the senior Statesman appointed to this post, and the Lord President is often available for other duties.

(4) The Lord Privy Seal, who keeps The Queen's Privy or private Seal. This is really his only office, and the post is that of a Minister without Portfolio. He often has the task of leading the House in which he sits.

(5) The First Lord of the Admiralty.

(6 and 7) Secretaries of State for War and Air. It is interesting that the personal loyalty of the Armed Forces to the Crown is such a real asset that the entirely modern Ministry of Air was formed with a Secretary of State at its head in order to maintain a more direct link with the Sovereign and parity with the two senior services.

(8) The Chancellor of the Exchequer, who was formerly a mere clerk, but who to-day is one of the Crown's principal Ministers.

(9) The Chancellor of the Duchy of Lancaster. The Duchy of Lancaster, which looks after the estates held by the Sovereign through inheritance from the Dukes of Lancaster, is not entirely fused with the Crown. The actual estates are widely spread all through Britain, and are administered by a separate office from that of The Queen's Privy Purse or the Crown Lands. They will be more fully described in the last chapter. The Chancellor of the Duchy of Lancaster is estimated to have only an hour or two's work on the Duchy's business each week and is therefore in great measure free to undertake any "spare duties" available.

(10) The President of the Board of Trade is so called because the Board of Trade was originally a Committee of the Privy Council, and as Head of such a Committee he too was in a special relationship to the Sovereign.

Ministers with Seals kiss hands upon their appointment. Should the Sovereign die and a new Great Seal be required, the old Great Seal is damasked (damaged) by a knock by the Sovereign—as light as possible to be effective. The old Great Seal is then customarily given to the Lord Chancellor of the time being as his perquisite. It has been known that an ex-Lord Chancellor and the Lord Chancellor in office have shared the Great Seal, each having one half.

The Queen's relationship to the Upper House differs from her relationship with the House of Commons.

The Queen can of course enter the House of Lords, and indeed she does so at the Opening of every Parliament. It is not usual for the Sovereign to listen to debates in the House of Lords, although Queen Anne came incognito to the House of Lords to listen to a debate about the conduct of the War in Spain. But that was in January 1711.

The House of Lords consists of five types of Peers. The largest group is that of the Hereditary Peers, of whom there are about eight hundred. These consist of Dukes, Marquesses, Earls, Viscounts and Barons. Then there are the Lords Spiritual, consisting of the Archbishops of Canterbury and York, the Bishops of London, Durham and Winchester, and the next 21 Bishops in order of seniority as Bishops. Spiritual Peers hold their seat in the Upper House only while they hold a See.

At the time of the Union with Scotland, when the Scottish Parliament was dissolved, it was agreed that Scottish Hereditary Peers would elect sixteen of their number to sit as their representatives in the House of Lords. These are elected every Parliament. A similar arrangement—except that Peers were elected for life—was in force with regard to Ireland, but no Irish Representative Peer has been elected since 1922, and at the time of writing it is believed that only two Irish Representative Peers remain.

At the opening of The Queen's reign, there were only a handful of "Life Peers" in the House of Lords. The Lords of Appeal in Ordinary, known as the Law Lords, who sit for life, are appointed under the Appellate Jurisdiction Act of 1876 in order to strengthen the legal element in the House of Lords, which is the Supreme Court of Appeal. In 1876 their number was only two: there are now nine.

Queen Victoria was convinced of the necessity for stronger legal representation in the Upper House, and in 1856 she agreed readily to the Government proposal to offer a Life Peerage to Lord Wensleydale. His Letters Patent under the Great Seal granted him a seat in the Lords. But the Peers took a stand, declaring that, although it was quite true that the Sovereign had the prerogative to create a Life Peer, they denied that a Life Peerage could carry with it the right to sit in the House of Lords. It took twenty years for a special Act to be passed to enable Law Lords to be created for life and to sit in the House. The wife of such a Law Lord is called Lady Blank, and his children bear the courtesy prefix of "Honourable". But the title is not inheritable.

Queen Elizabeth II, who was the next Queen Regnant after Queen Victoria, introduced—or rather her Conservative Government introduced—a measure for the creation of Life Peerages.

The Bill provided that women as well as men were eligible. And what a commotion that in itself caused! The reform of the House of Lords is always a very delicate problem, and the introduction of Life Peers was no exception. The first intimation of this revolutionary measure came from the lips of The Queen herself when, in her Speech from the Throne at the Opening of Parliament on November 5, 1957, she announced:

> You will also be invited to approve a measure to permit the creation of Life Peerages for men and women, carrying the right to sit and vote in the House of Lords.

In 1919 an Act called the Sex Disqualification (Removal) Act was passed which removed the disqualification which sex alone formerly carried, for specifically mentioned and widely various offices, professions and occupations, among them membership of the House of Commons. The House of Lords was not made subject to the provisions of the Act and the sex disqualification of Hereditary Peeresses from sitting in the House of Lords has never been removed, though certain of them have made unsuccessful attempts to obtain the right to seats there. The terms of the Life Peerages Act of 1958 do not specifically cover Hereditary Peeresses, so that their position remains the same as it always has been, whereas a new Life Peeress has the right to sit in the House conferred upon her by her Letters Patent in words similar to those of the Letters Patent of a male peer, which state that he shall have, hold and possess a seat, place and voice in the Parliaments. No such words appear in the Letters Patent relating to Hereditary Peeresses.

There is nothing new about Life Peeresses, although their previous history is somewhat murky. The later Stuarts and the First Georges, when they were generously disposed towards their mistresses, sometimes elevated them to the Peerage. It was the Peerage of Ireland that was generally "honoured" in this way, but occasionally Life Peeresses were created in the English Peerage. Take for example the German Ehrengard Melusince von der Schulerburg, who was the mistress of King George I: she was created in the Irish Peerage Baroness of Dundalk, Countess and Marchioness of Duncannon and Duchess of Munster in 1716. Two years later she was created in the English

Peerage Baroness of Glastonbury, Countess of Faversham and Duchess of Kendall. None of their Patents, however, contained the requisite words entitling them to sit in the House.

Before a woman had sat on the benches of the House of Lords as a Member of the Upper House, one woman has sat on the steps of the Throne while the House of Lords was sitting. This was Miss Florence Horsbrugh, who exercised her right as a Privy Counsellor to do so in 1953 when she was Minister of Education, during the passing of the Bill which became The Education (Miscellaneous Provisions) Act, 1953.

The names of the first four women who will sit in the House of Lords as Life Peers were announced (with ten men) in a Supplement to the *London Gazette*, published on July 24, 1958. They were Dame Katharine Elliot, the widow of Mr. Walter Elliot (Baroness Elliot of Harwood); Baroness Ravensdale, baroness in her own right and the elder daughter of the late Lord Curzon (Baroness Ravensdale of Kedleston); Stella, Marchioness of Reading, the widow of the first Lord Reading (Baroness Swanborough of Swanborough); and Mrs. Barbara Frances Wootton (Mrs. Wright) (Baroness Wootton of Abinger), lately Professor of Social Studies, University of London, and a former Governor of the B.B.C. They are all women distinguished in public service.

The Queen decided that the Life Peeresses should wear, at their Introduction, ordinary day clothes under their Parliamentary robes of scarlet cloth. The Queen approved the design of the hat which they wear at their Introduction only. It is a modified form of a male Peer's tricorne, but made in velour and in smaller dimensions than in the past, thus having a softer line to it. For the Life Peeresses a gold cockade has been added to the left side as ornamentation.

At the Opening of Parliament Life Peeresses wear the same robes as a Baron, over evening dress. The Queen decreed that a Life Peeress will bow (instead of the proposed curtsey) with her fellow Peers. But at the Introduction, the part of the ceremony which requires a Peer to raise his hat three times has been waived in favour of the Life Peeresses because of their hair styles.

A Royal Warrant which accompanied the Supplement to the

London Gazette stated that the Wives and Widows of Law Lords and Life Peers, and the Sons and Daughters of Law Lords and Life Peers and Life Peeresses "shall be treated for their style, rank, dignity and precedence in the same way as the Wives, Widows and Children of hereditary Barons".

CHAPTER FIVE

The Queen's Most Excellent Majesty in Council

BUCKINGHAM PALACE, June 25 (1958)
"The Queen held a council at 12.30 o'clock this afternoon.
"There were present:—The Viscount Hailsham (Lord President), the Right Hon. Alan Tindal Lennox-Boyd, M.P. (Secretary of State for the Colonies), the Right Hon. Christopher Soames, M.P. (Secretary of State for War), the Right Hon. Sir Reginald Manningham-Buller, Bt. (Attorney-General), and the Right Hon. Aubrey Jones, M.P. (Minister of Supply).
"Mr. William Grant, M.P. (Solicitor-General for Scotland), and Sir Godfrey John Vignoles Thomas, Bt., were sworn in Members of Her Majesty's Most Honourable Privy Council.
"Mr. W. G. Agnew was in attendance as clerk of the council.
"The Viscount Hailsham had an audience of the Queen before the Council." *Court Circular.*

OCCASIONALLY a short paragraph appears in the daily newspapers stating that The Queen has held a Privy Council at Balmoral or Sandringham or Goodwood—because it is slightly unusual. Only in the *Court Circular* or in the *London Gazette* (in which some of the measures introduced at the Council are also given) do you usually find mention of a Council in the now normal venue of Buckingham Palace (although the Privy Council held at Buckingham Palace by King Edward VII on April 24, 1902, "was the first to be held there in living memory").

So the general public has little idea whether the Privy Council is merely an ancient ceremonial relic or is a tool of significance in the modern working of the Constitution; whether The Queen has or has not any powers in Privy Council, or indeed what takes place at a meeting of the Privy Council. Some have only a fairly vague idea of what and who is a Privy Counsellor, how many of them there are and what, if any, are their privileges. Many may possibly be surprised to know that it took only five years and ten and a half months of The Queen's reign before she had herself presided at one hundred meetings of the Privy Council. Actually more than one hundred Council meetings of the reign had been held, before the Queen's hundredth Council, on December 20, 1957. Two Councils in 1953, six in 1954 and one in 1956 had been held by the Counsellors of State appointed to act when The Queen was overseas.

Although the volume of business conducted by the Privy Council is continually increasing, every effort is made to keep the number of Privy Councils at about the same level, to prevent increase of the very heavy burden of The Queen's duties.

The Privy Council is the oldest part of The Queen's Government. It traces its origin back certainly to Norman times, and most probably beyond, to the ninth century Council or "Witan" of Alfred the Great. Then the King, who required the help of the powerful men of the country to rule, used to summon the great, the influential and the wise men of his realm around him and take counsel. In Norman times this was known as the *commune concilium* and was an assembly of the King's Household, the Great Officers of State and the King's chief tenants. It became known as the King's Private or Privy Council.

It is from this Central Council that the whole administration of the country stems. As affairs became more stable, they became more complex, until they were too unwieldy to be decided by a single central organisation. First of all the financial side separated off under the Treasurer. Then the administration of the Law branched off (although the assemblies at which justice is meted out according to the law are still known as *Courts*).

The growth and transfer of power to Parliament gradually reduced the scope and powers of the Privy Council. But the Council never withered away. At times when the King was most powerful, the Council's power increased. When Parliament was gaining pre-eminence, the Council's power was clipped.

The Privy Council was a much quicker instrument of power than Parliament. (This is still true to-day.) Therefore in times of unrest and rebellion, it was a particularly good way of dealing swiftly with the rebels. That was why King Henry VII used the Privy Council for dealing out summary justice. It could award any punishment short of death. Although it enabled a poor man sometimes to obtain justice against a more powerful neighbour, gradually the Privy Council was used so ruthlessly, and with such disregard for Common Law, that it became much feared. The Council was held at that time in a certain panelled room in a building parallel to the river and on the site of the present Chamber of the House of Commons. From the decoration on the ceiling this room was known as the Star Chamber—a name which became feared. The panelling from this room was taken down when the building was demolished in the nineteenth century and was re-erected in a room in Windsor Castle, which was named the Star Chamber, and where it remains to-day.

The Star Chamber was used by the early Stuarts: it was not until 1641 and the Civil War between Charles I and Cromwell that many important powers, especially with regard to jurisprudence, were removed from the Privy Council by Act of Parliament.

But the Privy Council was not abolished. Its residual powers have continued through the centuries and—strangely—it has recently become of increasing importance to Parliament.

Later I shall try to describe the type of business that is dealt with by the Privy Council, but first of all the meetings of the Privy Council itself.

When The Queen is to hold a Privy Council meeting, those Privy Counsellors who will attend are summoned in the following ancient form:

Let the Messenger acquaint the Lords and Others of Her Majesty's Most Honourable Privy Council that a Council is appointed to meet at the Court of Buckingham Palace on Tuesday, the Twenty-Fourth Day of March, at 10.30 of the Clock A.M.

The Duke of Edinburgh is always informed when a Privy Council meeting will be held.

A note of the business which is to be dealt with at the Council is sent to The Queen previously, so that she can go through it and question anything about which she wants further information.

On the day appointed, the Lord President of the Council, those Privy Counsellors who have been summoned and the Clerk of the Privy Council assemble. Most Council meetings are now held at Buckingham Palace. A Council, however, can be held anywhere, and The Queen has held more Councils outside London than her father or grandfather. In this reign Councils have been held at Windsor Castle, at Sandringham and at Balmoral, where it has usually proved necessary to hold at least one Council during her late-summer stay there. The Queen has occasionally held Councils at country houses where she has been staying, such as Goodwood House, Arundel Castle and Sandbeck Park, the residences of the Duke of Richmond and Gordon, the Duke of Norfolk and the Earl of Scarbrough respectively.

She has even held a Council on board ship, which is a rare proceeding. This was on board the royal yacht *Britannia* at Leith immediately after The Queen returned from her Tour of the Outer Hebrides on August 19, 1956. It was to give her consent to the marriage of Captain Alexander Ramsay, son of Lady Patricia Ramsay and great-great-grandson of Queen Victoria, to Miss Flora Fraser, daughter of Lord Saltoun.

When a Privy Council is held at Buckingham Palace, the room used is generally the 1844 Room, so called from its occupation in that year by Emperor Nicholas of Russia, whose portrait hangs on the silk-hung walls. This room also contains the famous Negro Head Clock, whose eyes are dials recording the hours and minutes. It is a white and gold room on the ground floor below the State Apartments, overlooking the garden.

The Queen always receives the Lord President of the Council before the Council.

When Queen Elizabeth II came to the Throne, this office was filled by Lord Woolton. Then it was held by the Marquess of Salisbury, whose family has strong connections with the office. Probably his ancestor William Cecil, Lord Burghley, who was Lord Treasurer to Queen Elizabeth I, was a Privy Counsellor. His younger son Robert Cecil, the first Earl of Salisbury, was certainly a Privy Counsellor, and was sworn in 1591. Both the second Marquess of Salisbury (1858–9) and the fourth Marquess of Salisbury (1922–4) were Lords President of the Council. The fifth Marquess of Salisbury held the office from 1952 to 1957. Lord Salisbury resigned on March 29, 1957. The Earl of Home was declared and sworn on April 1, 1957, and was succeeded by Lord Hailsham on September 23, 1957. The Earl of Home was also Secretary of State for Commonwealth Relations. Lord Hailsham also has a family connection with the office, as his father was Lord President in 1937.

The office of Lord President of the Council is one of great honour. In the table of precedence, it is ninth after the Sovereign. The only non-royal persons of higher rank are in this order: The Archbishop of Canterbury, the Lord High Chancellor, the Archbishop of York and the Prime Minister. Following the Lord President of the Council in the Order of Precedence are the Speaker, the Lord Privy Seal, High Commissioners and Ambassadors, all taking precedence of Dukes.

Although the Lord President is a Great Officer of State and also a Member of the Cabinet, his duties with regard to the Privy Council do not occupy him full time. He therefore always combines this position with important other work, often as Leader for the Government in the House of Lords. The fifth Lord Salisbury, when holding this office in this reign, once described his duties by saying:

"I am a Minister without Portfolio. In plain English, that means an odd-job man—rather a superior odd-job man."

At the time appointed, the other Privy Counsellors enter the room in order of precedence, followed by the Clerk of the Council. They go up to The Queen, bow, shake hands and go to their appointed places.

The Queen, wearing ordinary day dress and no hat, stands at the head of a small round table. On her right is the Lord President and beyond him the other Privy Counsellors. The Clerk of the Council stands on The Queen's left side facing the line of Privy Counsellors. Everyone remains standing. Then the Lord President reads out the various items from the list of business. The Queen then gives her approval or other instruction.

The Orders in Council are signed by the Clerk of the Council as evidence that they have been approved by The Queen. But The Queen herself signs a Proclamation made in Council. (It is not always realised that The Queen does not sign an Order in Council: once a newly founded University requested the pen "with which His Majesty signed the Order" which founded it.)

In common with so many other British institutions, there is

not a book of rules for the conduct of the Privy Council, only the records of centuries of service. There are many occasions on which a long memory or a fresh viewpoint are valuable attributes to the Clerk of the Privy Council, who is in a position to gain unusual insight into the continuous process of Government. The present Clerk of the Council is Mr. William Godfrey Agnew, C.V.O., who was Deputy Clerk in 1951, and made Clerk in February 1953.

An Order in Council is sealed with the Privy Council Seal. This is a single-sided seal, minted in a press and used to make an impression upon paper, not to affix a seal of wax. It is not a "Seal of Office" and is therefore not handed over by The Queen to the Lord President. A new Seal is made for each office in every reign. The Queen approved a proposal to take the opportunity to change the size of the new Council Seal. Formerly it was one and a half inches in diameter: Queen Elizabeth II's Seal is about two inches in diameter. The increase in size is to present a better balanced appearance on documents. The design is a combination of rose, thistle and shamrock, crowned and supported by lion and unicorn, together with the royal style and titles in Latin. It was designed by Mr. W. M. Gardner, who also prepared the single-sided Seals of the Secretaries of State and made the designs for the reverse of the English and Scottish shillings.

Although there are actually close on three hundred Privy Counsellors, a quorum is three. Usually only four Privy Counsellors are present, although a few additional Counsellors may be present to be sworn.

The Privy Counsellor's oath is probably the most solemn and binding that any British subject can take. The text is kept secret but is to the effect that "you shall keep secret all matters the committee has revealed to you, or that shall be treated secretly in Council". It is because this Oath is so binding that Cabinet Ministers are still required to be sworn as Privy Counsellors before taking office. It is sometimes invoked by Members of the Government when disclosing certain business to the Leaders of the Opposition, in order that the matter which they feel should be known to the Leaders of all Parties should not go further; in effect, "I am telling you this as a Privy Counsellor, and you may not repeat it."

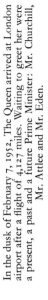

In the dusk of February 7, 1952, The Queen arrived at London airport after a flight of 4,127 miles. Waiting to greet her were a present, a past and a future Prime Minister: Mr. Churchill, Mr. Attlee and Mr. Eden.

In "Treetops," a primitive hotel built in the branches of a giant fig-tree beside a waterhole in the Aberdare Forest, Kenya, Queen Elizabeth II unknowingly succeeded her father, King George VI, sometime in the early hours of Wednesday, February 6, 1952.

At the Camperdown Works, Jute Industries Ltd., in Dundee on June 28, 1955, The Queen (who is accompanied by Mr. W. G. N. Walker, the Chairman) has spotted a flaw in the processing; she laughs mischievously towards the Duke of Edinburgh, who is generally so quick to notice anything unusual. The happiness of The Queen and the Duke of Edinburgh lightens their lives of duty.

The Queen and the Queen Mother are laughing at the amusing account of the race given by Bryan Marshall after winning on the Queen Mother's *Devon Loch* at Hurst Park, February 1955. Mother and daughter enjoy close companionship.

The Queen and the Duke of Edinburgh travelled 1,133½ miles by train in September 1957 to take Prince Charles to his first boarding school, Cheam, Berkshire. They want to give their children a happy, normal upbringing away from public curiosity.

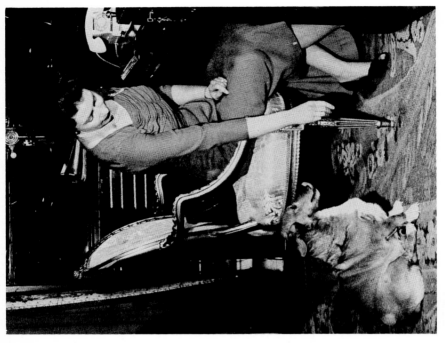

There have always been dogs in The Queen's home, including golden retrievers, a cocker, even a Tibetan lion dog. But for long The Queen has been faithful to Welsh corgis. Even when The Queen is working at her desk her dogs are with her.

The Queen's interest in horses is well-known; she is an acknowledged expert in horse-breeding and stable management. Here she leads in her first Classics winner, *Carozza*, trained by Noel Murless and ridden by Lester Piggott, after the 1957 Oaks.

THE QUEEN'S TOOLS

The Crown, the Sceptre, this Bodkin and this Hammer are The Queen's tools, used only by the Sovereign. The Queen wears the Imperial State Crown, most valuable of her Crowns at the Opening of Parliament at Westminster, although she was crowned with St. Edward's Crown. It contains the Black Prince's ruby or spinel (seen in front) worn by Henry V at Agincourt. Below it is the second part of the Cullinan diamond (the second largest cut diamond in the world, 309 carats). The largest cut diamond (530 carats) is the Star of Africa, the largest stone cut from the Cullinan diamond, which is set in the Sceptre with the Cross which The Queen carried in her right hand at her Coronation. The Bodkin, never before photographed, is used by The Queen every year when she pricks the Sheriff's Roll in Council. The Hammer, also never photographed before, was used for the only time in her reign, when The Queen "damasked" (defaced) the Great Seal of her father. But the tool which The Queen uses most frequently is her fountain pen.

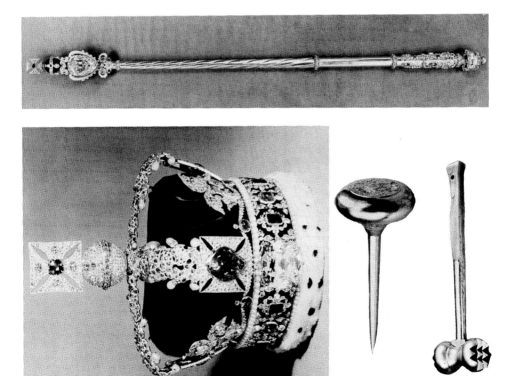

The Queen in the Irish State Coach with Princess Margaret for the Opening of Parliament in 1956, the only occasion on which the Sovereign has been accompanied by a sister.

The Queen opened Parliament in the Chamber of the House of Lords in the Palace of Westminster on October 28, 1958. This was the first occasion on which this impressive ceremony had been televised—or even photographed. The Duke is seated on her left. Grouped round The Queen were her Household, to her right the Earl of Home with the Cap of Maintenance, to her left Viscount Montgomery bearing the Sword of State, behind him the Lord Great Chamberlain (the Marquess of Cholmondeley). Facing her were the Judges on the Woolsacks. The diplomats were in the block of seats to her right, behind the Bishops, the royal ladies were behind the Dukes on her left, and behind them the Peeresses. The Peers, including for the first time Life Peeresses, occupied the foreground. Out of sight at the Bar of the House were Members of the Commons.

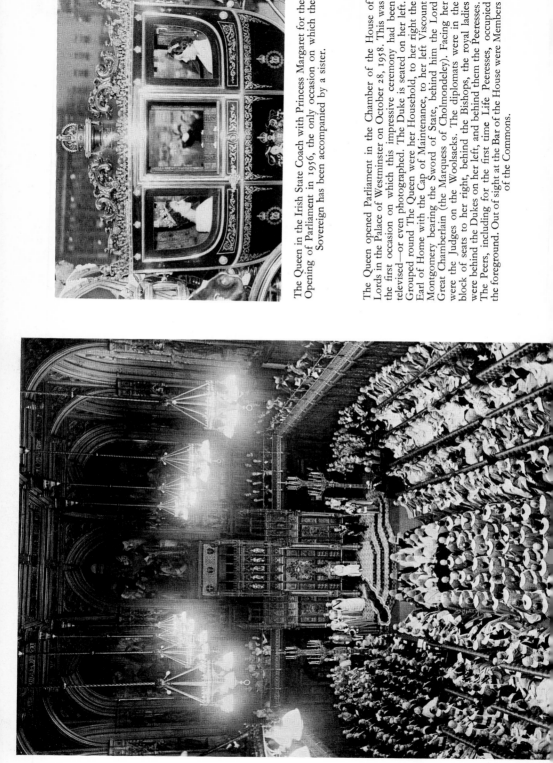

The Queen's first Prime Minister, Sir Winston Churchill, wearing court dress with the Garter, escorts her to her car after she dined at 10 Downing Street on April 4, 1955, shortly before he resigned the Premiership. The Queen's tiara was made for Queen Mary, her pearl ear-rings a wedding present from the Shaikh of Bahrain. Her white mink stole was given by the Hudson's Bay Company on her Accession.

The Queen with Members of the Privy Council, after holding her first overseas Privy Council of the United Kingdom in Wellington on January 13, 1954, which was also the first Privy Council meeting ever held in New Zealand. Left to right, Mr. T. J. Sherrard, Clerk of the New Zealand Executive Council who acted as Clerk; the Rt. Hon. K. J. Holyoake, Deputy Prime Minister of New Zealand; Sir William Jordan, former New Zealand High Commissioner in London, acting Lord President of the Council; S. G. Holland, New Zealand Prime Minister; The Queen; the Duke of Edinburgh; Walter Nash, Leader of the Opposition; Sir Michael Adeane, The Queen's Private Secretary; and Sir Harold Barrowclough, Chief Justice of New Zealand.

The Queen seating herself for the first time on the Throne of Canada before Opening the Canadian Parliament—the first Sovereign to do so—in Ottawa on October 14, 1957.

[8]

At St. Albans in 1957 The Queen was first Sovereign since Charles II to hold Royal Maundy outside London. She is with the Bishop (Dr. E. M. Gresford Jones) and the Dean ('The Very Rev. Kenneth Matthews). Behind is a Chapel Royal choirboy.

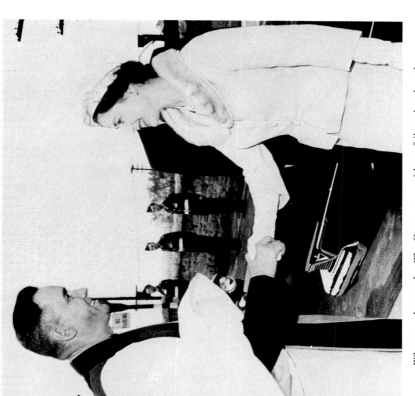

Wherever she may be, The Queen goes without fail to church each Sunday. Here she was greeted by the Very Rev. J. O. Anderson, Dean of Christ Church, Ottawa, as she arrived to attend morning service there during her stay in Canada in October 1957.

This beautiful portrait of Her Majesty, painted by Leonard Boden for the Royal Military Academy Sandhurst, is of particular interest because The Queen is the only one of our six Sovereign Queens to have worn the Mantle of the Order of the Bath. On November 15, 1956, she attended an installation service in Westminster Abbey of Knights Grand Cross of the Order of the Bath, presided over by the Duke of Gloucester, Great Master of the Order.

The Queen knighted Senid Bubakr Bin Sheikh
Al Kaf, Counsellor of the Kathiri state in Eastern
Aden, at a public investiture in Aden on April
27, 1954. The sword she was using is a Scots
Guards sword which belonged to her father,
and which is particularly light. The investiture
stool, seen here, has been used since the reign
of King George V and may well be older.

An historic picture, the first to be taken of the
Prince of Wales in Wales, when he landed at
Mackenzie Pier, Holyhead, on Saturday, August
9, 1958, only two weeks after The Queen had
created him Prince of Wales. The Prince of
Wales and Princess Anne were appropriately
passing under an arch lettered "WELCOME".

The Queen inspected the First Battalion of The Queen's Own Cameron Highlanders at Balmoral on May 30, 1955. The Duke of Edinburgh, who is their Colonel-in-Chief, was behind her. The Queen told them: "Your Regiment has strong links with Balmoral, for it was upon this lawn where you are drawn up to-day that Queen Victoria gave new colours to the Second Battalion in 1898."

The Queen walked round the ranks of holders of the Victoria Cross, at the centenary review in Hyde Park, on June 26, 1956. Here she was accompanied by Lieutenant-General Lord Freyberg, V.C. She is seen with Pakistani V.C.s. This is the highest decoration for valour, which takes precedence even over the Garter. The Queen said she was proud to take part in this parade.

In 1958 The Queen's Birthday Parade was held in heavy rain, when The Queen's Colour of the 1st Battalion, Scots Guards, was trooped. The Queen was riding the chestnut police horse *Imperial*, and appeared quite unconcerned, although her scarlet jacket gradually darkened with rain. The Queen is the first of our Sovereign Queens regularly to wear uniform and to ride in her Birthday Parade. This was the last Parade to be held on the traditional Thursday: in future, to lessen traffic troubles, The Birthday Parade will take place on a Saturday.

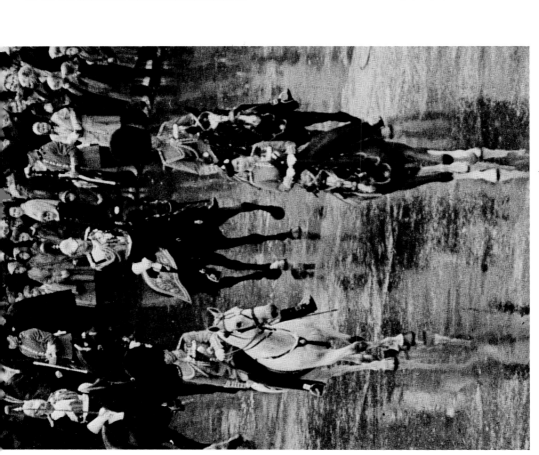

Miner 640, Her Majesty The Queen, at the coal-face 1,500 feet underground in Rothes Colliery, Thornton, Fife, on June 30, 1958. This was the first time a Queen has been underground in a coal-mine. Few women—or men either—have had such varied experiences as The Queen has had.

The Queen left her car to meet Mrs. Locke, 105-year-old widow, introduced by the Rev. J. H. Ransom, Rector of Great Bromley. It was at The Queen's wish that the old lady remained in the car—a typically thoughtful gesture.

The Queen is welcomed by some Scottish subjects on August 12, 1958. She is wearing a favourite sapphire and diamond brooch, a gift from builder and owner after she launched the *British Princess* on the Wear in 1946.

This picture of H.M.Y. *Britannia* off the Medway, returning with The Queen and the Duke of Edinburgh from their World Tour on May 15, 1954, is perhaps the finest of several paintings made by Norman Wilkinson of the royal yacht. She is wearing the Union Jack at the bow, the flag of the Lord High Admiral at the foremast, the Royal Standard at the mainmast, the Union flag at the mizzen and the White Ensign aft.

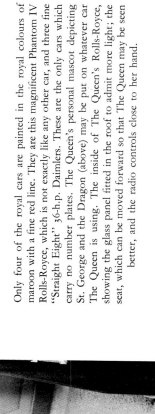

Only four of the royal cars are painted in the royal colours of maroon with a fine red line. They are this magnificent Phantom IV Rolls-Royce, which is not exactly like any other car, and three fine "Straight Eight" 36-h.p. Daimlers. These are the only cars which carry no number plates. The Queen's personal mascot depicting St. George and the Dragon (above) may be put on whatever car The Queen is using. The inside of The Queen's Rolls-Royce, showing the glass panel fitted in the roof to admit more light; the seat, which can be moved forward so that The Queen may be seen better, and the radio controls close to her hand.

At the Royal Show, Norwich, on July 3, 1957, The Queen admires Champion Hevingham Stonehenge, winning British White bull. British White Cattle, formerly called Park Cattle, are probably descended from our ancient wild cattle. The breed is popular in Norfolk.

The Queen examines the almost square ball only used in Harrow football when visiting the school on March 5, 1956. It is larger (31½ in. against 27 in.) and heavier (21 oz. against 16 oz.) than a "soccer" ball, which The Queen has kicked about with the Prince of Wales at Balmoral. The Queen is wearing the famous Williamson pink diamond brooch.

The Queen entertains the members of the American Bar Association at a Garden Party in the grounds of Buckingham Palace on July 29, 1957. The Earl of Scarbrough, Lord Chamberlain, grey top-hat in hand, can be seen just to the right of The Queen. The 40-acre grounds of Buckingham Palace, with their lawns, fine trees and pleasant lakes, lend themselves to the large-scale Garden Parties which are a feature of The Queen's entertaining.

The Queen entertains between 25,000 and 30,000 people in her homes each year. Here she is walking in the garden of Balmoral Castle with a group of the delegates attending the conference of Commonwealth nuclear scientists whom she invited to luncheon on September 20, 1958. Left to right, Shri M. R. Srinivasan, senior research officer, engineering division, Atomic Energy Establishment, Trombay, India; Dr. G. L. Miles, leader of chemistry section, Australian Atomic Energy Commission; and Dr. Nazir Ahmad, chairman, Pakistan Atomic Energy Commission.

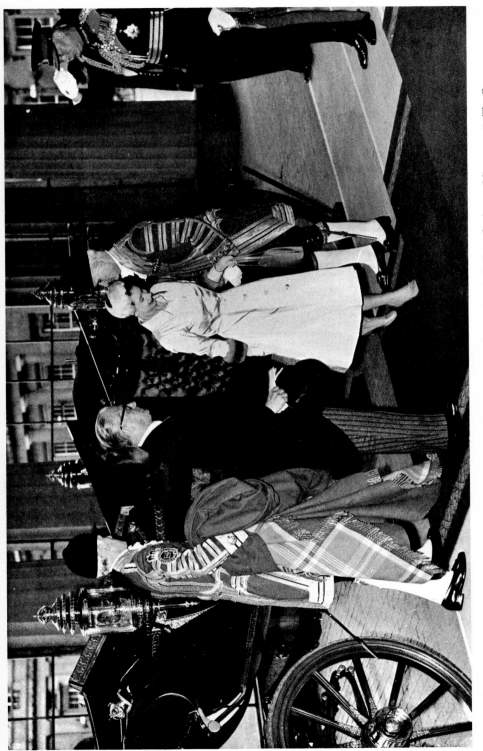

After welcoming Signor Gronchi, President of Italy, on his arrival in London at Victoria Railway Station on May 13, 1958, The Queen drove with him in an open State road landau to Buckingham Palace, where she is seen stepping down from the carriage at the commencement of the three-day State Visit. Footmen in State livery attend them. The Duke of Gloucester is on the right.

THE QUEEN AND HER PRIME MINISTERS

It is of vital importance that The Queen knows the leading personalities of the Commonwealth, foremost among them her Prime Ministers. She first entertained her Commonwealth Prime Ministers to dinner at Buckingham Palace on December 3, 1952. Those present were, left to right, Mr. Senanyake (Ceylon); Sir Godfrey Huggins (Southern Rhodesia); Mr. Holland (New Zealand); Mr. Churchill (United Kingdom); The Queen; Mr. Menzies (Australia); Mr. St. Laurent (Canada); Mr. Havenga (Minister of Finance, Union of South Africa); Mr. Nazimuddin (Pakistan); and Mr. Deshmukh (Minister of Finance, India.)

When The Queen entertained her Commonwealth Prime Ministers at Windsor Castle on June 26, 1957, only three of the Prime Ministers in office in 1952 were still holding that office. They were Mr. Menzies (Australia); Mr. Nehru (India), although he had not been able to be present in 1952; and Mr. Holland (New Zealand), who was ill and unable to be present in 1957. Left to right, Mr. Diefenbaker (Canada); Mr. Macmillan (United Kingdom); Mr. Menzies (Australia); Mr. Louw (Minister for External Affairs, Union of South Africa); The Queen; Mr. Suhrawardy (Pakistan); Mr. Nehru (India); Sir Roy Welensky (Federation of Rhodesia and Nyasaland); Dr. Nkrumah (Ghana); Mr. Macdonald (Minister for External Affairs, New Zealand); and Mr. de Silva (Minister of Justice, Ceylon).

The new gold Armills, a gift from members of the Commonwealth to The Queen and used at her Coronation. Armills were formerly a part of the Coronation regalia, but had not been used since Stuart times. The Coronation hallmark (by George Paulin), bearing The Queen's head, can just be distinguished.

The Queen is the first Sovereign in the world to circumnavigate the globe. She has travelled farther and more often than any previous King or Queen. The speed of modern transport creates difficulties as well as solving them. Immediately after a long air trip she is plunged into crowds, greetings, engagements. Here she is welcomed by the Rt. Hon. Vincent Massey, Governor-General of Canada, an old friend, on her arrival on October 12, 1957, at Ottawa by B.O.A.C. Douglas D.C.-7C airliner G-AOIE after a non-stop flight of $13\frac{1}{2}$ hours from London Airport. The Queen is wearing the diamond bow brooch which was a wedding present from Queen Mary.

The Queen steps ashore—first Sovereign to visit Australia—in Sydney on February 3, 1954. Every viewpoint was crowded with cheering people. A two-mile lane of yachts, dressed overall, lined her route from anchorage to Farm Cove. Her white chiffon dress was printed with wheatears and wattle.

m/v *Gothic* in magnificent Milford Sound, New Zealand, where Mitre Peak towers 5,560 feet sheer from the water, on January 31, 1954. This merchant ship had the honour of wearing the Royal Standard half-way round the world, from Jamaica, by way of the Panama Canal, the Pacific and Indian Oceans, to Aden. Her Master was, like Drake, knighted by his Queen on board his ship.

Against a seething background of Union Jacks, The Queen and the Duke of Edinburgh drive by Land Rover up and down lines of cheering schoolchildren assembled at Athletic Park, Wellington, on January 12, 1954. This is the best way of giving everyone a close-up view.

A father proudly holds up his sturdy son for the admiration of The Queen and the Duke of Edinburgh in a Fulani village in the Northern Region of Nigeria on February 6, 1956, fourth anniversary of The Queen's accession to the throne while in Africa.

Everywhere The Queen meets persons distinguished for their services in a multitude of fields. The Queen shakes hands with representatives from the Southern Cameroons at a reception at Government House, Lagos, during the highly successful tour of Nigeria in February 1956.

When The Queen attended a Women's Reception at Brisbane City Hall on March 17, 1954, women from the welfare services appropriately formed the guard of honour. On the left were V.A.D.s in their blue uniforms, on the right women of St. John Ambulance Brigade.

Visiting the sick. The Queen was the first Sovereign ever to visit a Leper Settlement when she went to the Oji River Settlement in Eastern Nigeria on February 9, 1956.

The factories and local industries The Queen visits throughout the Commonwealth add first-hand impressions to the economic facts she reads in official documents. Here she watches butter emerging from a giant churn in the Bell Block Co-operative factory at New Plymouth, in the rich Taranaki dairy district of New Zealand.

The Queen walks with President René Coty of France through the foyer of the Paris Opèra House, on April 8, 1957, first day of her State Visit to France. Members of the Republican Guard salute her. Her ivory satin evening dress had gold, pearl and topaz embroidery representing the flowers of the fields of France across a waving design of wheat representing the cornfields. Scattered here and there were small bees, the Napoleonic emblem of industry. It was made by Hartnell. The Queen wore an emerald and diamond tiara with emerald and diamond necklace, and the scarlet ribbon of the Légion d'Honneur.

The Queen was rowed ashore in the Swedish royal barge *Vasaorden* on arrival in Sweden for her State Visit on June 8, 1956. She is welcomed by King Gustaf VI Adolf and Queen Louise, aunt of the Duke of Edinburgh.

In Oporto, on February 21, 1957, during the State Visit to Portugal, The Queen and the Duke of Edinburgh commandeered an old green open bus which photographers had been using, so that the vast crowds could see them better. The photographers rode in the royal car!

The Queen and the Duke of Edinburgh with their host and hostess, President and Mrs. Eisenhower, during the State Visit to the United States in the autumn of 1957. The President was an old friend, who had been the guest of the Royal Family in the pleasant seclusion of Balmoral.

The West German Chancellor, Dr. Konrad Adenauer, dined with The Queen at Windsor Castle on April 16, 1958. It was not a State Occasion, so The Queen did not wear Orders or a tiara. Her necklace was the Jubilee offering to Queen Victoria from the women of the Empire, purchased with funds left after building the Albert Memorial in Hyde Park. The Queen has met Khruschev, Tito, and most other world leaders.

The "Dagmar" necklace, made by Diedrichsen and containing 2,000 diamonds and 118 pearls, before the pendant cross was removed. The cross is a replica of an eleventh century gold and enamel cross found in the grave of Queen Dagmar, wife of the thirteenth-century King Valdemar, Victor of Denmark.

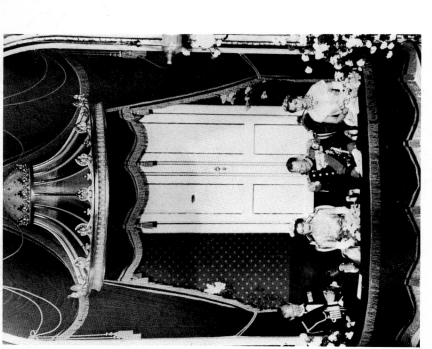

The Queen, at a gala performance in Copenhagen with King Fredrik IX and Queen Ingrid on May 22, 1957, is wearing the "Dagmar" necklace given to her Danish great-grandmother, afterwards Queen Alexandra, by King Fredrik VII of Denmark. The gesture went almost unobserved.

The Queen wore her most valuable brooch for the first time when she visited the Diamond Works of Messrs. Asscher in Amsterdam on March 25, 1958, because it was this firm which cut the famous 3,106 carat Cullinan Diamond (Star of Africa), of which this was a part. The Queen is admiring the Royal cipher laid out in diamonds set in wax. It contained 3,537 diamonds weighing 875·5 carats, of wholesale value £110,000. Left to right, Queen Juliana of the Netherlands, The Queen, Mr. Louis Asscher, Jnr., and Mr. J. Asscher, Jnr.

The Brooch, the third and fourth parts of the Cullinan Diamond. The square cushion-shaped diamond is of 62 carats, and the pear-shaped drop of 92 carats. The Queen referred laughingly to these fabulous jewels as "Grannie's chips".

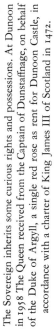

The Sovereign inherits some curious rights and possessions. At Dunoon in 1958 The Queen received from the Captain of Dunstaffnage, on behalf of the Duke of Argyll, a single red rose as rent for Dunoon Castle, in accordance with a charter of King James III of Scotland in 1472.

In Government House, Ottawa, The Queen examines a 330-lb. sturgeon caught off the Nova Scotian coast during her stay in Canada in 1957, and offered to and accepted by her. Sturgeon landed in the King's realm were declared a royal fish by Edward II over 600 years ago.

The Queen is in Council when she hands the Seals of Office to her Ministers. The new Member of the Cabinet takes his Oath of Office in The Queen's presence, kneeling on the floor, facing Her Majesty. He then steps forward and kneels on his right knee on a footstool, and "kisses hands". In fact he kisses only The Queen's right hand. Then he stands up and The Queen hands him his Seal of Office. The new Cabinet Minister bows and returns to his usual place. At no time does he shake hands.

When a Minister *not* in the Cabinet is taking an appointment with Seals, the Oath of Office is administered to the new Minister before the Lord President of the Council, the Lord Chancellor or one of the Secretaries of State. When he goes to The Queen to receive his Seals, he goes straight to the footstool, where he kneels, "kisses hands", rises, receives the Seals and returns to his place.

The one exception to this is the Chancellor of the Duchy of Lancaster, who always receives his Seals in private Audience.

The Queen's senior Privy Counsellor is the Rt. Hon. Sir Winston Churchill, who was sworn on May 7, 1907. The Clerk of the Council at that time, Sir Almeric Fitzroy, has left two rambling but extremely interesting volumes from his diaries, and recorded:

We had a Council in the morning at which Winston Churchill was sworn. Whether to mark his aloofness from ordinary restraints he came in a cut-away coat. [Frock coats were then worn: present-day dress is short black jacket and striped trousers.] The King kept us waiting for some time, and during the last ten minutes or so Winston paced up and down the far end of the room with rapid strides, his head bent upon his breast and his hands in his coat-tail pockets, a very curious figure. While explaining to him the nature of the ceremony, I found his hands straying up to my neck, and before I knew what he was about, he had put my tie straight for me, which I took to be another instance of a sedulous restlessness. The King treated him with marked distinction in retaining him for an audience after the Council.

Not long afterwards another distinguished and surviving Privy Counsellor, Lord Samuel, was sworn on November 21, 1908. Sir Almeric Fitzroy's diary recalls:

Council at Windsor. I went down with the Lord President and the new Privy Counsellors by special train at 12.15. Some variation in the ordinary procedure was necessitated by the presence of a Jew and a

Quaker. . . . Herbert Samuel was not only sworn on the Pentateuch but he took his hat into the Presence, and held it over his head as he kissed the book. Pease, the Chief Government Whip, made affirmation, which he read for himself in the usual form.

The only women who have been sworn members of the Privy Council have been Cabinet Ministers. The first was Miss Margaret Bondfield, who was sworn in 1929. The only two women at present Privy Counsellors of the United Kingdom are Dame Florence Horsbrugh, G.B.E., M.P., who was appointed in 1945, and Dr. Edith Summerskill, M.P., who was appointed in 1949.

The Queen was a member of the Privy Council before her accession. Her father introduced her, together with the Duke of Edinburgh, at a Council on December 4, 1951. Members of the Royal Family who are to be made Privy Counsellors are introduced into the Council and are not necessarily sworn. Princess Elizabeth was the first royal woman Counsellor for many years, possibly for all time. Queen Victoria, for instance, was not made a Privy Counsellor before her accession. The Queen Mother and Princess Margaret are not Privy Counsellors, although they have been appointed Counsellors of State during The Queen's absence abroad, and have then attended Privy Council meetings.

The royal Privy Counsellors are the Duke of Edinburgh, who was appointed in 1951, and the Duke of Gloucester, who was appointed by King George V in 1925.

The Members of the Privy Council are drawn from many different and distinguished walks of life. *Ipso facto* they always include all Cabinet Ministers, the Lord Chancellor, Lords of Appeal in Ordinary, the President of the Probate Division, the Lord President of the Court of Session in Scotland, the Lord Justice Clerk, the Lord Advocate of Scotland, and the two Archbishops. The Bishop of London is also a Privy Counsellor. Privy Counsellors include some senior Members of The Queen's Household such as the Duke of Beaufort, Master of the Horse; and her Private Secretary, Sir Michael Adeane. Distinguished members of the Commonwealth are also included, such as Mr. Vincent Massey and Mr. Diefenbaker of Canada, Mr. Robert G. Menzies of Australia, Mr. Sidney George Holland of New Zealand and Sir John Kotelawala of Ceylon.

Other well-known Privy Counsellors include Earl Mountbatten of Burma, the Duke of Buccleuch, the Earl of Rosebery and Lord Pethick-Lawrence.

Little is demanded of Privy Counsellors as such. There have been suggestions that more employment could be found for this distinguished company.

They have, however, a certain number of duties. Any Privy Counsellor can properly be summoned to give advice to The Queen at times of difficult decisions, as for example during the choice of a new Prime Minister. The members of certain important Committees are chosen from the distinguished ranks of the Privy Counsellors; for instance, Her Majesty's Commissioners in the House of Lords are peers who are also Privy Counsellors. The two peers who bear the Sword of Honour and the Cap of Maintenance at the Opening of Parliament are always Privy Counsellors.

Their rights are not many. They are entitled to the prefix "Right Honourable". Together with Scottish and Irish peers, the eldest sons of peers and the Dean of Westminster, they have the privilege of sitting on the steps of the Throne of the House of Lords to listen to the debates of that House.

In February 1957 The Queen appointed Mr. Herbert Morrison to a post open only to a Privy Counsellor, that of High Steward of Hull. This dignitary is appointed according to a Charter of 1661 which provides that when vacancies occur the Sovereign, on receipt of a humble petition from the Lord Mayor and Aldermen, "shall assign and constitute one other eminent and discreet man of our Privy Council to be High Steward . . . during his natural life unless in the meantime, for just and reasonable cause, he shall be removed from that office by us, our heirs or successors". The office had been vacant for twenty-six years.

In former times the High Steward was the town's advocate and representative with the Sovereign and in the Privy Council, and many instances are recorded of occasions when the High Steward defended and maintained the ancient rights and privileges of the town.

To-day the office has no particular privileges, but the High Steward enjoys precedence after the Lord Mayor on official occasions.

All Privy Counsellors have the right to be present at an Accession Council and on the occasion of a Council being held at which the Sovereign announces his or her engagement to be married. The last time this latter happened was when Queen Victoria in 1839 announced her engagement to Prince Albert of Saxe-Coburg-Gotha, to whom she wrote that evening:

The Council was held at two o'clock; more than a hundred persons were present, and there I had to read the Declaration. It was rather an awful moment, to be obliged to announce this to so many people, many of whom were quite strangers. . . .

A Privy Counsellor present wrote in a letter to a friend:

. . . her eye was bright and calm, neither bold nor downcast, but firm and soft. There was a blush on her cheek. . . .

Although it was not one of the prescribed occasions, King George VI summoned an unusually large number of Counsellors to be present at the Privy Council at which he announced his consent to the engagement of his daughter and heiress presumptive, Princess Elizabeth, to Lieutenant Philip Mountbatten, R.N.

What work does the Council do to-day?

"The Queen's Most Excellent Majesty in Council", which is the official and correct way of referring to the authority of the Privy Council, has a very large measure of duties. Some powers are The Queen's by prerogative, that is to say, the residue of royal powers which does not flow from Statute. War would be declared and treaties concluded by The Queen in Council. The Queen in Council mobilises the Armed Forces. The Queen in Council prorogues or dissolves Parliament, and summons Parliament. As we have already seen, the Queen in Council hands over the Seals of Office to Ministers. The Queen in Council fixes the value of money, of course a Government measure.

Another power vested in The Queen is the granting of Royal Charters to professional, legal, educational or charitable organisations and the like. During the early years of her reign, The Queen has granted Charters to the following bodies:

1952

Southampton University

School of Pharmacy, London University

St. Anne's College, Oxford
Royal Masonic Institution for Girls
Queen Elizabeth College
Royal Air Forces Association

1953
St. Antony's College, Oxford
Faculty of Radiologists

1954
The Australian Academy of Science
University of Hull
Royal Naval Association
Queen Elizabeth House, Oxford

1955
University College of Rhodesia and Nyasaland
Cuddesdon Theological College
Seafarers Education Service
Manchester College of Science and Technology
The Worshipful Company of Farmers
Australasian Institute of Mining and Metallurgy
University of Exeter

1956
Royal Ballet

1957
St. Edmund Hall, Oxford
Institution of Chemical Engineers
University of Leicester
City of London Solicitors Company
English Speaking Union

1958
British Institute of Radiology
Nuffield College, Oxford
National Institute for Research in Nuclear Science
Institute of Municipal Treasurers and Accountants

If a Body, in choosing its own title, wishes to include the prefix "Royal", that does not mean that it becomes a corporate body. An application for using the description "Royal" is made through the Home Office and is laid before The Queen, who gives permission personally, not in Council. It is also the Home Office which investigates misuse of the prefix "Royal".

Orders involving changes in the Constitutions of overseas territories are made in Council. The Queen in Council granted independence to Ghana and Malaya. The Commonwealth countries all came into being as the result of Orders in Council. Changes in the status of Colonies are brought into effect by Orders in Council, and there are many instances of this during The Queen's reign.

Orders in Council are also used for legislation in many international matters, including such very different subjects as diplomatic privilege, double taxation relief and matters affecting the safety of seamen.

Much ordinary Parliamentary business requires at some stage to be placed before the Privy Council. In one normal six-month period of The Queen's reign, no fewer than 173 Acts of Parliament were invoked in Orders in Council. Wherever possible, the Privy Council always tries to invoke a statutory power, but where this is not possible, the Order is made under the Prerogative.

There are always new matters being brought up in Council. Many powers are being conferred upon The Queen in Council through new Acts of Parliament, although a variety of safeguards are imposed against misuse. Sometimes the Order must be laid in draft before the House, as with measures of Double Taxation Relief, under section 57 of the Finance Act of 1945. Orders in Council under the Foreign Jurisdiction Act of 1890 must be laid before Parliament. Orders made under the Foreign Compensation Act of 1950 must be laid before Parliament, which has the power to annul them, in which case The Queen would revoke the original Order. And so on.

The reason for the increasing use of the Privy Council is that an Order in Council is more flexible than an Act of Parliament. It is also much quicker. Orders in Council are used where speed is essential. The Privy Council is also used to relieve Parliament, as more legislation is needed than there is time to devote to it in the House, where the overloading of the programme is causing considerable concern. It is also used to provide the Government with extra statutory powers in time of such crises as war.

The Queen in Council gives her consent to the marriage of British subjects who are in the direct line of Succession, under the Royal Marriages Act, 1772. This Act resulted from a series of scandals in the eighteenth century, involving the Duke of Cumberland, brother of King George III, who in October 1771 secretly married a widow, Mrs. Anne Horton of Catton in Derbyshire. Upon hearing the news King George III (who did not consider her suitable and was incensed by previous troubles) published a notice in the *London Gazette* to the effect that those who "waited on" the Duke and his wife would no longer be received at Court. In February 1772, the death occurred of the Princess Dowager, mother of King George III and the Duke of Cumberland, who had been greatly distressed by the marriage, although her illness was not connected with the event. Within a fortnight of his mother's death King George III instructed his Prime Minister, Lord North, to introduce legislation "from paternal affection to his own family and anxious for the future welfare of his people, and the honour and dignity of the Crown" which would make it illegal for "the descendants of his late Majesty King George II" to marry without the Sovereign's consent. The Act was keenly fought and passed only by a narrow majority, and then only after the addition of a clause stipulating that a member of the Royal Family, above the age of twenty-five, could give twelve months' notice of a marriage which had not been sanctioned by the Sovereign to the Privy Council, which, if there were no objection from Parliament, could sanction the marriage.

In this reign The Queen has given her consent to the marriage of several relatives, including Lord Carnegie, who is great-grandson of King Edward VII and eighteenth in the Succession, and, as already mentioned, to Captain Alexander Ramsay, great-great-grandson of Queen Victoria and considerably more remote in the Succession.

The Queen in Council annually appoints the Sheriffs of England and Wales, excepting those of the Duchy of Lancaster which she appoints privately and not in Council. She does this by pricking with a Bodkin the first in each of the groups of names written on the long Sheriffs' Roll, which is of parchment. More is said about this in the section about the Law.

Formerly, on the night before the Sheriff's Roll was pricked, the Lord President of the Council gave a fine dinner, called the Sheriffs' Dinner; but the last dinner was held in 1923 and thereafter luncheons were held until 1930, since which time the custom has lapsed.

A "volume of work and detail" as an official expressed it, is dealt with in connection with the Church of England by The Queen in Council. This includes such matters as:

1. Schemes for rearranging ecclesiastical units such as benefices, parishes, rural deaneries, etc., and transferring patronage of livings.
2. Orders providing new Constitutions and Statutes for Cathedrals.
3. Orders declaring vacant a Bishopric whose holder has resigned.
4. Orders creating new Suffragan Bishoprics.
5. Consent of The Queen in Council is also necessary for alterations of prayers for the Royal Family in the Prayer Book.

The Judicial Committee of the Privy Council is the final court of appeal from the Ecclesiastical Courts. This was strongly criticised in the Church Assembly held in February 1956, when a resolution was passed, by what the Archbishop of Canterbury described as "a majority against a very considerable minority", against retaining the Judicial Committee of the Privy Council as the court to which an accused clergyman in a reserved case (relating to doctrine, ritual or ceremonial) should have a right of appeal on a question of law. Dr. Fisher commented: "It is a very great thing to ask Parliament to surrender the total link of the State with the ecclesiastical courts and the Church." So far, no Parliamentary action has been taken to implement this resolution.

So it will be seen that The Queen in Council is far from a mere ceremonial residue of a former power. The Privy Council plays an increasingly important part in the legislative life of the country. Although its outer form remains unchanged through the centuries, yet, like most British institutions, it is constantly adapting itself to changing conditions.

The Queen's reign began with a new departure. The formal entry of the new Sovereign into his kingdom is through the meeting of the Accession Council of the Privy Council, which acknowledges and acclaims the new Sovereign as lawful successor to the Throne.

This Accession Council is, properly speaking, two different Councils, invariably—until this reign—held immediately after each other. The first part is a meeting of the great men of the land to acknowledge and proclaim their new Sovereign. It originates, of course, from the time when the King's heir might not be able to enter into undisputed possession of his kingdom. Even poor Lady Jane Grey, who ruled for a short fourteen days, was duly acknowledged by the Privy Council, which went further and sent a rude message to Mary Tudor, so soon to be Queen Mary I, "branding her in gross terms" (Strickland's *Queens of England*) "with illegitimacy and advising her to submit to her sovereign lady Queen Jane."

Some notable people who are not Privy Counsellors, including the Lord Mayor and Aldermen of the City of London and overseas representatives, are invited to attend the first part of the Accession Council, but withdraw before the second part is held.

Only Privy Counsellors are present at this second part of the Accession Council, and to them the new Sovereign enters and makes his or her Declaration.

As The Queen was in Africa when her father died, special arrangements had to be made. The first part of the Accession Council was held on the day of the King's death in the Picture Gallery at St. James's Palace.

But the second part of the Accession Council could not be held until February 8, 1952, two days later, at 10 o'clock on the morning after The Queen's return to London. The Queen had spent the previous night at Clarence House, which is a separate part of St. James's Palace, with which it has a connecting door.

Early that morning about 175 Privy Counsellors in mourning gradually assembled in the Entrée Room of St. James's Palace. This is the room which was the original "Cabinet" of King Charles II. The Accession Council included two women Counsellors, Dr. Summerskill and Miss Florence Horsbrugh. (The first woman Privy Counsellor to attend an Accession Council was Miss Bondfield, who attended the Accession Councils of both King Edward VIII and King George VI.) Among the last of the Privy Counsellors to arrive was The Queen's uncle, the Duke of Gloucester, who was followed, shortly afterwards, by the Duke of Edinburgh, who had come with The Queen from Clarence House.

It was just a few minutes after ten o'clock when the Lord Chamberlain, the Earl of Clarendon, who used a stick, limped slightly into the Entrée Room from the adjacent Throne Room, and intimated that The Queen was ready.

The Queen then received in the Throne Room a small deputation of leading Privy Counsellors, including the Duke of Gloucester, the Lord Chancellor (Lord Simonds), the Archbishop of York (Dr. Garbett—the Archbishop of Canterbury, Dr. Fisher, was ill), the Prime Minister (Mr. Winston Churchill) and the Leader of the Opposition (Mr. Clement Attlee). They were not with The Queen very long. Meanwhile the remaining Privy Counsellors waited in silence.

Then the doors of the Throne Room were thrown open.

The Queen entered. She was dressed in a black cloth coat over a black dress, and was wearing a close-fitting black felt hat. There was no one with her. She looked already—as all Sovereigns must be—very much alone. She was very serious, but completely composed and dignified. There was absolute silence. The Privy Counsellors made her a deep bow.

She walked up to the table and took up in her hand the copy of her Declaration, which had been mounted on a board. She looked over at the Lord President of the Council (Lord Woolton), who gave her a very slight nod. She then read in a clear voice, and without faltering, the words of her Declaration, which were:

"Your Royal Highnesses, My Lords, Ladies and Gentlemen:

"On the sudden death of my dear father I am called to fulfil the duties and responsibility of Sovereignty.

"At this time of deep sorrow it is a profound consolation to me to be assured of the sympathy which you and all my people feel towards me, to my mother, and my sister, and to the other members of my family.

"My father was our revered and beloved head as he was of the wider family of his subjects; the grief which his loss brings is shared among us all. My heart is too full for me to say more to you to-day than that I shall always work, as my father did throughout his reign, to uphold the constitutional Government and to advance the happiness and prosperity of my peoples, spread as they are all the world over.

"I know that in my resolve to follow his shining example of service and devotion, I shall be inspired by the loyalty and affection of those whose Queen I have been called to be, and by the counsel of their elected Parliaments. I pray that God will help me to discharge worthily this heavy task that has been laid upon me so early in my life."

The Queen then took her own pen—it had been sent over that morning from Clarence House by her Private Secretary—and with it signed two copies of the first official document of her reign, which was the Oath for the Security of the Church of Scotland. (One copy was for the Privy Council Register, the other for the Court of Session to be recorded in the books of sederunt.)

She then conducted a certain amount of customary Council business which had arisen as a result of her father's death.

About 10.30 a.m. she withdrew, again entirely alone, to the Throne Room, while all present bowed deeply. A few minutes later she was joined there by her husband and her uncle.

That it must have been a considerable ordeal is confirmed by the passage from the diary of her grandfather, King George V, which is quoted in *A Personal Memoir* by Gore, about that King's Accession Council some forty years earlier:

Made a short speech to all the Privy Counsellors standing around me; the most trying ordeal I have ever had to go through; they then all took the Oath of Allegiance and kissed my hand.

In old days appointments to the Privy Council ended with the Sovereign's death. In 1707 appointments were prolonged for six months into the new reign, and in 1910 the Judicial Committee of the Privy Council reported that it was unnecessary for Privy Counsellors who had taken the Oath of Allegiance and the Privy Counsellor's Oath to take either oath again on the Demise of the Crown. This report was approved by the King in Council on August 2, 1910.

There have been a number of interesting decisions taken by The Queen in Council during this reign.

An important personal decision made in Council was when The Queen, acting under the Prerogative and according to her own wishes, on April 9, 1952, fixed the name of her dynasty as *Windsor*. This name had been chosen for his dynasty by King George V, who had implemented it at a Privy Council meeting held at Windsor on July 17, 1917, at which he made a Declaration and signed a Proclamation. The Declaration ran:

My Lords, I think it proper to declare and ordain that from this day forth the name of "Windsor" shall be borne by my Royal House and Family, and to the same end I renounce and relinquish for Myself and my descendants the Foreign Titles and Arms of Duke of Saxony and Prince of Saxe-Coburg and Gotha, and on behalf of all descendants of Her late Majesty Queen Victoria, who are subjects of these realms, any German dignitaries, Titles, Honours or Appellations to them heretofore belonging, for the due promulgation whereof I hereby signify the intent to issue my Royal Proclamation.

This Declaration, by a strange combination of circumstances, affected both the Queen and her future husband. When her fiancé, then Prince Philip of Greece and Denmark, renounced these titles in order to take British nationality, he found himself in an unusual perplexity. The royal families of Greece and Denmark have, properly speaking, no surname. So he adopted the surname of his uncle, Lord Mountbatten of Burma. Lord Mountbatten's father was Prince Louis of Battenburg, grandson of Queen Victoria and a British subject. His German title being renounced, he changed his name to the English form of Mountbatten, which also happened to be the name of a small Naval fort in Plymouth Sound.

If the Queen had not made this Declaration in Council, the name of her successors upon the Throne would have been Mountbatten.

It was at a meeting of the Privy Council that The Queen signed a Proclamation approving the use of her new style and title in the United Kingdom, as follows:

Elizabeth the Second, by the Grace of God of the United Kingdom of Great Britain and Northern Ireland and of Her Other Realms and Territories Queen, Head of the Commonwealth, Defender of the Faith.

The Queen approved the design of the Great Seal in Council. It was at Balmoral on May 31, 1955, that The Queen in Council declared "a state of Emergency" as a result of the Railway Strike. This is the only occasion, up to the time of writing, that this power has been evoked in The Queen's reign.

The Queen has, at the time of writing, only once held two Councils on the one day, and that was on May 6, 1955, both at Buckingham Palace. The reason was the dissolution of Parliament. First, in the morning, The Queen made an Order in Council proroguing—putting into a state of suspension without dissolving —Parliament, with effect that day. Then, in the afternoon, she made an Order in Council dissolving Parliament, by making a Proclamation which she signed in Council. This is because it is the custom to dissolve Parliament only while it is in prorogation. Like most British customs, this is founded on sound common sense. In the old days there was sometimes an argument when the King went down to Westminster to dissolve Parliament. It was much quieter and easier to prorogue Parliament, and then, when the members were nicely dispersed, to dissolve it and present them with a *fait accompli*.

A great deal of the important work of the Privy Council is carried out by Committees of the Privy Council, and it is in connection with the work of one of these Committees that The Queen made one of the most far-reaching and unusual Orders in Council in March 1958. This will be described in connection with the work of that committee, the Judicial Committee of the Privy Council.

The Queen has, up to the time of writing, held four Privy Councils of the United Kingdom outside Britain.

The first United Kingdom Privy Council ever held outside Britain was that of King George V at Delhi in India on December 12, 1911.

On January 13, 1954, in Government House, Wellington, The Queen held the first Privy Council ever to be held by the Sovereign in New Zealand.

The Queen held a Council at 11.30 o'clock this forenoon at which the Duke of Edinburgh had been present.

The Right Honourable S. G. Holland, M.P. (Prime Minister and acting Lord President), the Right Honourable Walter Nash, M.P., The Right Honourable Sir William Jordan, the Right Honourable Sir Michael Adeane (Private Secretary to the Queen) were also present.

The Right Honourable K. J. Holyoake and the Right Honourable Sir Harold Barrowclough were sworn in Members of Her Majesty's Most Honourable Privy Council. Mr. T. J. Sherrard was in attendance as acting clerk of the Council.

On February 17, The Queen held a Privy Council at Government House, Canberra, which was the first ever to be held in Australia. Then, a week later, on February 25, she held a second Privy Council of the United Kingdom at Government House, Melbourne. The reason was that Mr. Edward James Holloway, the distinguished Australian Labour Party politician, had been unable to be present in Canberra, and The Queen was most anxious that all Australians who had been appointed Privy Counsellors but not sworn should be sworn in her presence during her visit to Australia.

When The Queen visited Colombo, a Privy Council was held at Queen's House, Colombo, on April 21, 1954, her twenty-eighth birthday. Possibly this may be the only meeting of the Privy Council of the United Kingdom ever to be held in Ceylon, which has indicated an intention eventually to become a Republic within the Commonwealth.

The Queen also held a Privy Council of the Canadian Privy Council when she visited Ottawa in 1957. This was the first occasion on which the Sovereign had met with the Canadian Privy Council, as King George VI did not hold a meeting of the Canadian Privy Council during his visit in 1939.

The meeting took place on October 14, 1957, in the dining-room of Rideau Hall, the Governor-General's official residence in Ottawa. The meeting really started as an informal meeting of Her Majesty with her Canadian Ministers. They then resolved themselves into a meeting of The Queen's Privy Council for Canada. The Queen approved and signed a Minute of the Council granting the Minister of Finance full powers to sign an agreement with Belgium for the prevention of double taxation and the avoidance of fiscal evasions with respect to taxes on income. This would be the first Minute of Council which The Queen has signed, as in the Privy Council of the United Kingdom this is done by the Clerk of the Council.

At the close of the meeting the Duke of Edinburgh was sworn of the Canadian Privy Council, the Oath being administered by the Clerk of the Privy Council. At this historic meeting there were present the Prime Minister of Canada (the Rt. Hon. J. G. Diefenbaker) and twenty-one of the twenty-two Ministers, including the Hon. Mrs. Ellen Louks Fairclough, Secretary of State, whose white linen dress and flame-coloured flower hat were in contrast to the sombre suits of the male Counsellors.

Only Canada, Northern Ireland and the United Kingdom have Privy Councils of their own. The Canadian Privy Council was provided for in Section 11 of the British North America Act. All Cabinet Ministers are sworn members and remain Privy Counsellors for life. In Canada the Privy Council exercises its legal functions as the Committee of Council, the membership of which has always been identical with that of the Cabinet, but basically their function differs in the same way in which the functions of the Westminster Cabinet differ from those of the Privy Council of the United Kingdom, although, as their membership is more nearly identical, they are frequently referred to indiscriminately.

There are only two statutory Committees of the Privy Council of Canada, one is "The Treasury Board", which is concerned with all matters relating to finance, and the other the Privy Council Committee on Scientific and Industrial Research, to whom the National Research Council reports.

The Committees of the Privy Council of the United Kingdom are active and important.

The Judicial Committee of the Privy Council of the United Kingdom is the Supreme Court of Appeal from the Commonwealth and Colonies to The Queen as "the Fountainhead of Justice". Many important matters come before them for final judgement, as in this reign, "the lion man murder" of Tanganyika; appeals by Mau Mau leaders against their sentences in Kenya; charges of obstructing the police in Singapore; reduction of the murder verdict brought in against a Hong Kong labourer to one of manslaughter; and so on.

During the years a certain number of Commonwealth countries have "opted out" and instead of using the Judicial Committee of the Privy Council, have set up their own Supreme Courts of Appeal. The right to appeal to the Judicial Committee has been abolished by Canada, South Africa, India and Pakistan.

There was, however, a significant development when Malaya

was given her independence. In the Federation of Malaya Independance Act 1957 (Section 3) there was a "completely new departure of tremendous constitutional importance", as it was described to me by one who understands the full meaning of this innovation. This section provides that "Her Majesty may by Order in Council confer on the Judicial Committee of the Privy Council such jurisdiction in respect of Appeals from the Supreme Court of the Federation as appears to her to be appropriate for giving effect to any arrangements made after the appointed day between Her Majesty and the Head of the Federation, for the reference of such Appeals to that Committee".

On March 14, 1958, this section was implemented in an Order in Council, when The Queen agreed that, in respect of Appeals from the Supreme Court of the Federation of Malaya, these can be made to the Head of the Federation (who is, at the time of writing, H.H. Tuanku Abdul Rahman Ibni Al-Marhun Tuanku Muhammed, ruler of Kedah).

The Queen, who is brilliantly and sympathetically adjusting her Queenship to being Head of a Commonwealth containing also two republics, thereby gave her blessing to a totally new approach to her own Privy Council, of which, for the past thousand years, the Sovereign of England has always been the direct head. Although the Malayans are not recognising her as "Fountainhead of Justice", she is willingly allowing them the benefits of her Judicial Committee, for the decision of Appeals from the Federation. This is an important example of the way in which The Queen stands upon the spirit and not the letter of her prerogative. It is possible that this may lead to an increased use of the Judicial Committee of the Privy Council as a Court of Appeal by countries which wish to be republics within the Commonwealth.

A number of Ministries were originally Committees of the Privy Council. They include the Ministry of Agriculture and Fisheries, and the Ministry—formerly the Board—of Education. The Board of Trade is still technically a Committee of the Privy Council.

There are Committees of the Privy Council to deal with the Channel Islands, the Scottish Universities and the Legislation of the Isle of Man.

Very important scientific matters are dealt with in the Department of Scientific and Industrial Research, the Medical Research Council, the Agricultural Research Council and the Nature Conservancy, all of which are responsible to Committees of the Privy Council.

Some of our most controversial problems are dealt with by Committees of the Privy Council, or by committees formed from Privy Counsellors. For instance, in the summer of 1957, the Government appointed a Committee of three Privy Counsellors to enquire into the exercise of the prerogative power of intercepting telephone and other communications. The recommendations of a Committee of Privy Counsellors on leakages from Government Departments and better means of obtaining security without affecting the liberty of the subject were set up in a White Paper, following the Burgess and Maclean case. The Medical Research Council studied the relationship between smoking and lung cancer.

Few people realise that the Privy Council is actively concerned in so many vital matters.

Many are also confused about the difference between Orders in Council and Orders of Council. An Order *in* Council is made when The Queen, by and with the advice of her Council, approves an Order. It is still an Order in Council if The Queen is represented by her Counsellors of State. An Order *of* Council is an Order made by the Privy Council without The Queen being present. The Queen is never present at the meeting of a Committee of the Privy Council. By virtue of power given them either by Her Majesty's authority or by Statute, the Privy Council are in many cases empowered to approve regulations or appointments on their own authority, and not in an advisory capacity. When they are thus acting on their own, their instructions are Orders of Council.

It seems that there is no tool so old, but that British ingenuity can shape it to modern tasks. Here is the Privy Council, dating back to the days a thousand years ago, when King Alfred sat taking counsel of his wise men; when William the Conqueror assembled his chief tenants at Westminster—although his son, William Rufus, had still to build Westminster Hall; and which has been used by every succeeding Sovereign, still playing a lively, important, useful and growing rôle in the middle of the twentieth century.

In the Orders of "The Queen's Most Excellent Majesty in Council" we have the oldest form of legislative assembly still functioning in our Government.

CHAPTER SIX

The Queen and the Church

"I, Elizabeth the Second, do solemnly and sincerely, in the presence of God, profess, testify and declare that I am a faithful Protestant, and that I will, according to the true intent of the enactments which secure the Protestant succession to the Throne of my Realm, uphold and maintain the said enactments to the best of my powers according to the law."

Declaration of Faith made by The Queen when opening The First Parliament of her Reign on November 4, 1952

"I want to ask you all, whatever your religion may be, to pray for me on that day—to pray that God may give me wisdom and strength to carry out the solemn promises I shall be making and that I may faithfully serve Him and you, all the days of my life."

Queen Elizabeth II speaking of her forthcoming Coronation, in her Christmas Broadcast, 1952

QUEEN ELIZABETH II is often called "Head of the Church, and Defender of the Faith."

Hardly any part of her position as Queen is found more puzzling by millions of her non-Church of England subjects and by foreigners as The Queen's connection with the Church of England. Indeed it is even imperfectly understood by some members of that Church. Is The Queen regarded as a religious authority? Is she responsible for the decisions of the Church of England? Who really chooses the Archbishop of Canterbury? What are the differences between the two established churches of her Commonwealth—both of which she is bound by law to maintain—the Church of England and the Church of Scotland? Must her husband be a Member of the Church of England? What is her position in relationship to the many millions of her subjects who are Roman Catholics or Jews, Moslems or Hindus? How does The Queen herself worship? In what way does The Queen's

147

position in relation to religion differ from that of her predecessors?

These are questions easier to ask than to answer.

The connection of The Queen with the Church is exemplified in an ancient ceremony. When a new Bishop of the Church of England is appointed, between his consecration and his enthronement he goes to The Queen to make his Homage.

The Homage may be made anywhere, but takes place usually in Buckingham Palace. The new Bishop is robed. He is accompanied by the Bishop who holds the office of the Clerk of the Closet, who is head of The Queen's Ecclesiastical Household, and who is also robed. The Master of the Household ushers them into The Queen's presence.

There the new Bishop kneels before The Queen (who is seated in a chair), with both hands together between the hands of the Sovereign as a sign of loyalty, and repeats, sentence by sentence, the words of his Homage, which are read aloud by the Secretary of State for Home Affairs.

The words of the Homage are:

"I acknowledge that I hold the said bishopric, as well the spiritualities as the temporalities thereof only of Your Majesty and for these temporalities I presently give my homage to Your Majesty."

The whole ceremony lasts only a few moments, and afterwards The Queen talks with the new Bishop, about his diocese and problems. At no time does the Bishop kiss The Queen's hand.

The Bishop who kneels before The Queen to do Homage is acknowledging that he derives his right to act as Bishop from The Queen, and to enter into his See and the incomes thereof—"for these temporalities I do homage".

The Queen is the Governor of the Church, but it is for the temporalities, not the spiritualities, that Bishops do homage. The Bishop owes his consecration (that which makes him a Bishop) to the Church, but his right to exercise his spiritual responsibilities in a particular diocese he owes to The Queen.

Archbishops do homage once more when they are translated to their higher office, as does a Bishop each time upon changing his See.

The Queen's nominal power towards the Church of England is certainly immense. The great officers of the Church of England are one and all appointed by the Crown. The final Court of Appeal for all ecclesiastical matters is the Judicial Committee of Her Majesty's Privy Council. Any considerable changes in the method of worship of the established Church of England must meet with the approval of "The Queen in Parliament". In fact, The Church carries out its duties according to its interpretation of its spiritual need.

It is an extraordinary position, only made workable by typical British compromise.

When Henry VIII broke with Rome in 1534, the Supremacy Act declared the King to be "the only supreme head in earth of the Church of England". Even then, this did not mean that Henry VIII claimed any spiritual powers, but that the Church came within his rule. His daughter, Queen Elizabeth I, changed the title from head to "Governor".

Parliamentary control became ever more rigid with the Restoration of Charles II, the succession of William and Mary, and the preferment of the Hanoverians over the Stuarts upon the death of Queen Anne. This control is defined in the Act of Settlement, 1701. Parliament meant to prevent utterly by law the reunion of the Church of England with the Church of Rome. Their fear, and the religious intolerance of those days, made them put their restrictions into very plain language indeed. The Queen's own position is thus laid down by law in The Act of Settlement:

That all and every Person and Persons that then were, or afterwards should be reconciled to, or should hold Communion with the See or Church of Rome, or should profess the Popish Religion, or marry a Papist, should be excluded, and are by that Act made for ever incapable to inherit, possess or enjoy the Crown and Government of this Realm and Ireland, and the Dominions thereunto belonging, or any part of the same, or to have, use, or exercise any Regal Power, Authority or Jurisdiction within the same; And in all and every such Case and Cases the People of these Realms shall be and are thereby absolved of their Allegiance: And that the said Crown and Government shall from time to time descend to and be enjoyed by such Person or Persons, being Protestants, as should have inherited and enjoyed the same, in case the said Person or Persons, so reconciled, holding Communion, professing, or marrying as aforesaid were naturally dead. . . .

II. Provided always, and it is hereby enacted, That all and every Person and Persons, who shall, or may take or inherit the said Crown, by virtue of the Limitation of this present Act, and is, or shall be reconciled to, or shall hold Communion with the See or Church of Rome; or shall profess the Popish Religion, or shall marry a Papist, shall be subject to such Incapacities, as in such Case or Cases are by the said recited Act provided, enacted, and established; and that every King and Queen of this Realm, who shall come to and succeed in the Imperial Crown of this Kingdom, by virtue of this Act, shall have the Coronation Oath administered to him, her or them, at their respective Coronations, according to the Act of Parliament made in the first Year of the Reign of His Majesty, and the said late Queen Mary, intituled, An Act for establishing the Coronation Oath, and shall make, subscribe, and repeat the Declaration in the Act first above recited, mentioned or referred to, in the Manner and Form thereby prescribed. . . .

That whosoever shall hereafter come to the Possession of this Crown, shall join in Communion with the Church of England as by Law established.

It is laid down only that The Queen must be a communicant member of the Church of England. Her Consort is proscribed from being a member of the Church of Rome but is not bound to be a member of the Church of England. The Duke of Edinburgh did, before his marriage to Princess Elizabeth, leave the Orthodox Church of Greece and join the Church of England.

With such solemn and all-embracing control of the religion of the Sovereign, it is not surprising to find that the official regulations controlling the elections of Bishops are equally unequivocally stated.

The officers of the Church of England who are appointed by the Crown are the Archbishops of Canterbury and York, the Diocesan and Suffragan Bishops, the Deans of all cathedrals of the Old and New Foundations and a number of Canons, as well as the incumbents of a number of livings. An appointment by the Crown means of course an appointment by The Queen on the advice of her Prime Minister, and once such advice has been tendered formally the Sovereign is supposedly bound to accept it or to precipitate a political crisis. Therefore the choice of the ecclesiastical leaders could supposedly be carried out by a Prime Minister who might, or might not, be a member of the Church of England or indeed a Christian.

In fact, the situation is by no means so cut and dried. The Prime

Minister consults with the Archbishop of Canterbury, and, for appointments in the Northern Province, with the Archbishop of Canterbury and the Archbishop of York. If the Prime Minister puts forward a name which the Sovereign does not approve, it is unthinkable that the Prime Minister would force through his choice, regardless of the Sovereign's wishes.

The viewpoint in favour of the present form of Establishment is that the position of the leaders of the Church of England is considered of such national importance, that the country as a whole—not only the members of the Church—is affected. In an erudite article, "Crown Appointments in Theory and Practice, with Special Reference to the English Episcopate" by R. H. Malden, Dean of Wells, published in *Theology* in September 1946, is stated:

> The Sovereign and the Prime Minister together represent the nation as no other men can pretend to do. They embody the two sources of authority . . . Hereditary Right and Power derived ultimately from the electorate.

There is no doubt that Prime Ministers have tried to fulfil fairly and reasonably this part of their duties, which often cause them much anxious thought.

Lady Salisbury, when her husband was Prime Minister, wrote to Sir Henry Ponsonby:

10 January, 1890.

> I always find that anything to do with appointing of Bishops has a special power of worrying and tiring him.

"I believe the Bishops die to vex me," exclaimed Lord Melbourne, when he had to fill an unusual number of bishoprics in a short space of time.

There is little doubt that however fairly and reasonably the Prime Minister approaches the subject of the Appointment of Bishops, the price of Establishment does weigh heavy with some members of the Church of England.

The actual procedure of creating a Bishop is:

1. The Chapter Clerk informs the Crown, through the Prime Minister, of the vacancy, and asks that licence be given to the Dean and Chapter to fill it.

2. The Queen, upon recommendation of the Prime Minister (who has consulted with the Archbishop of Canterbury and, when necessary, the Archbishop of York, although this is not laid down by law) nominates a candidate, and a licence is sent to the Dean and Chapter. This licence is called a *congé d'élire*, and is accompanied by the Letter Missive containing the all-important name.

3. The Dean and Chapter elect the candidate proposed. They have no alternative. Should they refuse to do so, they are exposed to the very severe penalties under the Statute of Praemunire, of the loss of all civil rights, with forfeiture of lands, goods and chattels and imprisonment "during Royal Pleasure".

In fact, of course, such penalties would never and could never be extracted. Nevertheless, when a Dean of Hereford once declared his intention of opposing the name put forward in the *congé d'élire*, Lord John Russell, who was then Prime Minister, sent him a nasty little letter, which read:

I have had the honour to receive your letter of the 22nd inst. in which you intimate your intention of violating the law. I have the honour to be . . . etc.

The disputed candidate was duly unanimously elected.

When it was once argued in front of Dr. Samuel Johnson that a *congé d'élire* had not the force of a command, but was to be considered only as a strong recommendation, Johnson replied:

"Sir, it is such a recommendation as if I should throw you out of a two pair of stairs window and recommend you to fall to the ground."

Indeed the *congé d'élire* has never been seriously opposed in recent memory.

4. The Bishop is then confirmed, a legal ceremony at which the Representatives of the Crown satisfy themselves that the election has been duly carried out, and that the correct candidate has been presented. It generally takes place in The Court of Arches. The Letters Patent are read out by the Dean of the Court, and The Queen's Seal is exhibited. After this ceremony the Bishop has really entered into his See and can undertake all his duties, even before the other ceremonies have taken place.

5. The Queen receives the Bishop's homage, in the ceremony already described.
6. The Bishop is enthroned.

The Crown has appointed the Bishop. Strangely enough, should the choice prove a bad one, the Crown cannot similarly dismiss the Bishop. The Crown's control over him has now gone, and when as a senior Bishop or Archbishop he takes his seat in the House of Lords, he is in no way bound by any other considerations than those of the Church of England.

The reason for this is that before the Reformation the power of dismissal lay with the Pope. After the Reformation this power was transferred to the King, but was made entirely unworkable by the Prohibition of 1641 against delegating any prerogatives of the Supremacy to the Commissioners. Should it ever (by some far-fetched supposition) be desirable to unseat an Archbishop or Bishop, supposedly this would have to be done by Parliament, possibly by impeachment but more likely by a Bill of Pains and Penalties, perhaps petitioned for by Convocation. An Archbishop can resign only to the Sovereign, as supreme Governor of the Church.

When Archbishop Davidson resigned in 1928, a form had to be evolved to meet the then extremely unusual circumstance of a Primate's retirement from office. The King, by Royal Warrant, appointed a Commission consisting of the Archbishop of York, the Bishop of London, the Bishop of Durham and the Bishop of Winchester, for the sole purpose of receiving the resignation.

In order to allow Archbishop Davidson to continue his seat in the House of Lords, King George V created him a Baron, and he took the title of Lord Davidson of Lambeth. This step—afterwards followed on the retirement of Archbishop Cosmo Gordon Lang—was to permit the benefit of the retired Archbishop's advice in the Upper House after he had lost his seat as a Spiritual Lord. (Law Lords, however, hold their seats for life, irrespective of Office.)

Occasionally a clergyman is created a Knight, especially when he has given personal services to the Sovereign, and is appointed a Knight of the Royal Victorian Order. He does not, however, receive the accolade, but is merely invested with the insignia of the Order. He does not use the prefix "Sir", nor does his wife style herself as "Lady Blank". The clergyman does, however, use the requisite letters after his name. Men in Holy Orders who have received the insignia of Knighthood at present include the Archbishop of Canterbury, the Most Rev. G. F. Fisher, G.C.V.O.; the Rt. Rev. Percy Mark Herbert, the Clerk of the Closet, the Bishop of Norwich; the Rt. Rev. Eric Hamilton, Dean of Windsor, who was created a Knight of the Royal Victorian Order by The Queen in 1953, and the Very Rev. Alan Don, Dean of Westminster Abbey. The Very Rev. Charles L. Warr, D.D., of the Church of Scotland, Dean of the Chapel Royal and of the Order of the Thistle, has also been invested with the K.C.V.O.

The Archbishop of Canterbury received the Royal Victorian Chain from King George VI in 1949, and the K.C.V.O. from The Queen at the time of her Coronation.

An important number of livings lie within the Patronage of the Crown, which is exercised in various ways.

In the time of Queen Victoria the number of church livings in the Patronage of the Lord Chamberlain's department was very large, and Lord Melbourne (Prime Minister) appealed to the young Queen Victoria for the transfer of some of these patronages to his own hands:

7th May, 1839.

The Patronage of the Lord Chamberlain's Department is of the greatest importance, and may be made to conduce at once to the beneficial influence of the Crown, and to the elevation and encouragement of the professions of the Church and of Medicine. This patronage, by being left to the uncontrolled exercise of successive Lord Chamberlains, has been administered not only wastefully but perniciously; the physicians to the late King were many of them men of little eminence; the chaplains were a sorry lot. Your Majesty should insist with the new Ministers that this patronage should be disposed of; not by the Lord Chamberlain, but as has hitherto been during your Majesty's reign, by your Majesty upon consulting with your Prime Minister.

To-day the Patronage of the Crown Livings is dispensed on behalf of The Queen by the First Lord of the Treasury, who need not necessarily be Prime Minister.

The Chancellor of the Duchy of Lancaster is responsible for

the patronage in the Duchy, the Home Secretary is responsible for the patronage in the Channel Islands and in the one Crown living (Kirk Andreas) in the Isle of Man. All other patronages in the Isle of Man are in the hands of the Lieutenant-Governor of the Isle of Man, subject to the Home Secretary.

The Duke of Cornwall has control of the patronages of the Duchy of Cornwall.

The distribution of the various patronages is as follows:

Crown: sole patronage	158	benefices
alternate	14	,,
alternate with Bishops of several dioceses	113	,,
Her Majesty The Queen	8	,,
The Duchy of Cornwall: sole	26	,,
alternate	2	,,
The Lord Chancellor: sole	558	,,
alternate	41	,,
The Home Secretary	41	,,
The Duchy of Lancaster	42	,,
Archbishop of Canterbury	204	,,
Archbishop of York	197	,,

The livings belonging to the Royal estates, such as Sandringham and Windsor Great Park, are filled by The Queen according to her personal choice.

Although The Queen has never attended this Church, she is Patron of the chaplaincy of St. George's Church, Cannes, in the diocese of the Bishop of Gibraltar. The Queen would be consulted if a permanent chaplain were appointed (the church is served at present from a rota of chaplains from Anglican Churches on the Riviera) or other important changes were contemplated. This church was built as a memorial to the Duke of Albany, youngest son of Queen Victoria, and Queen Victoria worshipped there occasionally.

The Queen has an Ecclesiastical Household, which comprises the College of Chaplains headed by the Clerk of the Closet (who is always a Bishop) and consisting of the Dean of the Chapels Royal, sub-deans and priests-in-ordinary, her Organist, Choir Master and Composer and her domestic chaplains.

The Clerk of the Closet is a very ancient office, which the

present holder, the Right Rev. Percy Mark Herbert, Bishop of Norwich, has discovered only recently was held by the first Bishop of Norwich who was Clerk of the Closet to Queen Matilda in the twelfth century. Though there are many references to the Clerk of the Closet from the thirteenth century onwards, there is no description of what the office entailed. There is, however, no necessary link between the bishopric of Norwich and the post of Clerk of the Closet; the Sovereign can choose whichever bishop he or she pleases to fulfil the post of head of the Sovereign's Ecclesiastical Household. The last Clerk of the Closet was the Rt. Rev. C. F. Garbett, Bishop of Winchester, who resigned when he was appointed Archbishop of York.

The Clerk of the Closet is Head of the Royal College of Chaplains and it is his duty to recommend appointments to the College when vacancies occur, although the over-riding authority in all Household appointments is the Lord Chamberlain.

It is also the Clerk of the Closet's duty to introduce new Bishops into The Queen's presence when they come to do Homage.

The Clerk of the Closet may also be asked to approve books containing religious references which the author wishes to present to The Queen—a relic, of course, of the days when the Sovereign's beliefs were of acute political, as well as spiritual, significance. There are no occasions on which the Clerk of the Closet, by virtue of his office, must accompany The Queen.

The College of Chaplains consists of the Clerk of the Closet, the Deputy Clerk of the Closet and thirty-six chaplains. The duties are mostly honorary, although members of the College are often invited to preach in the Chapels Royal.

Royal Peculiars is the strange and confusing name given to the churches which are directly linked with the Sovereign, and which are outside the province of the Archbishops and the dioceses of the Bishops. The Dean of the Collegiate Church of St. Peter— which is better known as Westminster Abbey—owes no authority to the Archbishop of Canterbury nor to the Bishop of London, who cannot by right come to the Abbey (although he is ex-officio Dean of the Chapels Royal). The Abbey is under the personal jurisdiction of The Queen, who is the Visitor. Although widely known as a "Royal Peculiar", Westminster Abbey is seldom so called in documents. Actually Royal Peculiars were quite common until the early years of Queen Victoria's reign, when most were suppressed by Sir Robert Peel.

The Queen's Free Chapel of St. George within her Castle of Windsor is also a Royal Peculiar, although it is not the property of the Crown but the freehold property of the Dean and Canons of Windsor.

There are also the Chapels Royal, which in theory are attached to the Court and should travel with it. Among the most beautiful is the chapel of St. John the Evangelist, the Norman chapel within the walls of the White Tower of the Tower of London, which, together with St. Peter ad Vincula (St. Peter in Chains), make up the traditional "A cure of Souls and The Queen's Donative" at the Tower of London. There are Chapels Royal at St. James's, Buckingham Palace, Windsor Castle, the Royal Chapel in Windsor Great Park where the Royal Family worships on most Sunday mornings and at Hampton Court. (Sandringham has not been and is not a Chapel Royal. It is the ancient Parish Church of Sandringham where The Queen worships.) The choir boys of the Chapels Royal wear scarlet tunics faced with gold and black braid, scarlet knee-breeches and black stockings and shoes, lace collar and bands. They sang at the christening of Prince Charles and of Princess Anne at Buckingham Palace, and gave a carol recital in the Palace in December 1954. They always sing at the Royal Maundy service.

The Royal Peculiars are not subject to the jurisdiction of the Bishop of their diocese, but the Bishop of London is at present Dean of the Chapels Royal and so, in that capacity, exercises supervisory authority over the Chapels Royal in London, from which he would otherwise be excluded.

The Queen's Chapel of the Savoy, which was annexed by Henry IV from the House of Lancaster to the Crown, together with all the other Lancaster land, is a private Chapel of The Queen in her right as Duke of Lancaster. The National Anthem, as sung in the Chapel of the Savoy, in the shadow of the great hotel which has taken the name and place of the ancient royal palace, is:

> God Save our Gracious Queen,
> Long Live Our Noble Duke,
> God Save The Queen.

It is administered through the Chancellor and Council of the Duchy of Lancaster, and its Chaplain is appointed by Letters Patent. Her Majesty The Queen is Lord of the Manor of the Savoy, on whose ground it stands. King George VI, at the time of his Coronation, appointed the Chapel of the Savoy to be placed at the disposal of the Royal Victorian Order, the personal Order of the Sovereign.

The Queen invariably attends Church each Sunday. When she is at Windsor she usually goes to the private chapel in Windsor Great Park. At Sandringham she worships in the small Sandringham Parish Church of St. Mary Magdalene. At Balmoral she goes to the Crathie Parish Church. When The Queen is overseas, she usually worships in the local Anglican church. The Anglican Churches in North Europe are the concern of the Bishop of Fulham, who is generally present when The Queen is attending one of them.

The Queen's faith gives her great strength personally, and also contributes to the stability of the country. She is a member of a devout family.

Queen Victoria took the greatest interest in every matter to do with the Church, and had a penetrating, commonsense knowledge of the requirements for ecclesiastical appointments, distinguishing clearly between the types of man needed for an industrial or a contemplative appointment. Although she never initiated the appointment of a Bishop, she exercised her veto on many occasions. Religion was a part of her every daily action. Isolated from the currents of ordinary life, she was extremely conservative in her church-going. In the private chapel at Windsor, clergymen—with the exception of Bishops, who preached in their robes—wore a black cassock without a surplice. It was a considerable time before she permitted *Hymns Ancient and Modern* to be used. Queen Victoria paid great attention to the sermons preached before her. She did not like allusion to large political affairs; but she liked reference to be made to those in her Household who were sick or who had recently died. A copy of the text of the sermon and the hymns to be sung was always placed in Queen Victoria's private pew.

A list of the hymns to be sung is still placed in Queen Elizabeth II's pew, but she does not ask for the text of the sermon.

King Edward VII was less interested in church affairs. When Cosmo Gordon Lang was made Archbishop of York, the King contented himself with charging him to keep the parties of the Church together—and to see that the clergy did not wear moustaches!

King George V, whose seafaring training had brought him into close contact with a much wider range of men, was deeply religious in a non-denominational way. He could not bear to offend the religious susceptibilities of others, and even before he came to the Throne had private conversations both with Ministers and the Archbishop, to find how the Parliamentary declaration, which had been compounded by a badly frightened Parliament in the days immediately following the "Popish Plot", could be better fitted to the more moderate and liberal feelings of the day. This declaration, which must be made by each Sovereign on succeeding to the Throne "on the day of the meeting of the first Parliament after his accession or at his Coronation", was laid down for members of Parliament in the Act of 1678 "for the more effectual preserving of the King's person and Government by disabling Papists from sitting in either House of Commons". In 1689 this restriction was extended to the Crown, after the accession of William and Mary, by the Act commonly known as the "Declaration of Rights". According to this form, the Sovereign must state:

"I, A. B., do solemnly and sincerely, in the presence of God, profess, testify and declare that I do believe that in the Sacrament of the Lord's Supper, there is not any Transubstantiation of the Elements of Bread and Wine into the Body and Blood of Christ, at or after the consecration thereof by any person whatsoever; and that the Invocation or Adoration of the Virgin Mary or any other Saint, and the Sacrifice of the Mass as they are now used in the Church of Rome, are superstitious and idolatrous. And I do solemnly in the presence of God, profess, testify and declare, that I do make this declaration and every part thereof in the plain and ordinary sense of the words read unto me, as they are commonly understood by English Protestants, without any Evasion, Equivocation or mental Reservation whatsoever, or without any dispensation already granted me for this purpose by the Pope, or any other person or authority whatsoever, or without thinking that I am or can be acquitted before God or man, or absolved of this declaration or any part thereof, although the Pope or any other

159

person or persons or power whatsoever should dispense with or annul the same or declare that it was null and void from the beginning."

When King George V succeeded to the Throne, he roundly told Mr. Asquith, who was then Prime Minister, that he would not consent to open Parliament until a more liberal formula had been devised. After some trouble from the more extreme Protestant quarters, a final form was suggested by the Archbishop of Canterbury, approved by the various authorities, passed through Parliament and received the Royal Assent on August 2, 1910.

This was the form of declaration used when, on November 4, 1952, Queen Elizabeth II entered the Chamber of the House of Lords as Sovereign for the first time, to open the first Parliament of her reign. As she had not been crowned, she wore on her head the diadem of King George IV, and the Imperial State Crown was borne before her on a cushion. She wore the crimson velvet Robe of State of her great-great-grandmother Queen Victoria over a gold lace evening dress. Her necklace was the "Jubilee Offering" necklace of diamonds and pearls, from which originally was suspended a diamond Crown, given to Queen Victoria by the ladies of her Empire. The Queen's earrings were a pair of beautifully matched drop pearls, which were a wedding present from the Shaikh of Bahrain. Queen Elizabeth II seated herself upon the Throne. Her Lord Chancellor, Lord Simonds, stepped forward and knelt before her, handing to her this amended Declaration of Faith, which she read in clear tones:

"I, Elizabeth the Second, do solemnly and sincerely, in the presence of God, profess, testify and declare that I am a faithful Protestant, and that I will, according to the true intent of the enactments which secure the Protestant succession to the Throne of my Realm, uphold and maintain the said enactments to the best of my powers according to the law."

King Edward VIII, during his brief reign, clashed with Cosmo Gordon Lang, Archbishop of Canterbury. When he abdicated, the Church found itself back on firmer ground. King George VI was throughout sustained by a deep and abiding faith, which shone through his Christmas broadcasts, and in particular deeply impressed those who were in close contact with him in the days when he knew that he must soon die.

Perhaps his own best epitaph was in the words from *Pilgrim's Progress* which he quoted in the Christmas broadcast of 1950:

"Whatever comes, or does not come, I will not be afraid."

Queen Elizabeth II was brought up in a sincerely Christian household. From the time she was very small she was taught the Christian religion in simple stories and prayers by her mother, and learnt from her, among much else, the Scottish metrical psalms. It was one of them, the 23rd Psalm, "The Lord's my Shepherd, I'll not want", which was included at her own request in her wedding service. Her first lesson every Monday morning was a Bible story, just as Prince Charles and Princess Anne, years later, began their lessons each morning. She always went to Church with her parents each Sunday. A thoughtful and serious child, the example of her parents' application to duty, the anxieties of war, the unusually long periods she spent with her sister and governess, when other girls of her age were lost in the hurly-burly of the schoolroom, early gave the future Queen a grave, thoughtful and conscientious realisation of the path of her duty. Her faith was, and is, always at the centre of her life.

Princess Elizabeth was confirmed on Saturday, March 28, 1942, at Windsor. It was the last act of the retiring Archbishop of Canterbury, Cosmo Gordon Lang, who wrote in his diary, quoted by Lockhart:

I had always hoped that I might have this privilege. The night before I had spent at the Castle and had a full talk with the little lady alone. She had been prepared by Stafford Crawley at Windsor, and though naturally not very communicative, she showed real intelligence and understanding. I thought much, but rightly said little of the responsibility which may be awaiting her in the future—this future more than ever unknown. The Confirmation itself was very simple—the ugly private Chapel at the Castle—only a few relatives and friends and the boys of St. George's choir present—My address was just what I have so often given in country churches.

Her First Communion was celebrated in private the next day.

Princess Elizabeth and the Duke of Edinburgh were married in Westminster Abbey on Thursday, November 20, 1947, at a ceremony which was as the Archbishop of York (the late Most Rev. Cyril Forster Garbett) emphasised in his Address:

"Notwithstanding the splendour and national significance of the service in this Abbey, it is all essentially the same as it would be for any cottager who might be married this afternoon in some small country church in a remote village in the dales.

"The same vows are taken, the same prayers are offered, and the same blessings are given."

Both the bridegroom and bride listened with marked and serious attention to the brief and kindly address which followed, and afterward the 23rd Psalm was sung, set to a descant which the bride herself asked for, in order that she could join in singing it.

The Queen gives evidence of the strength and sincerity of her belief on public occasions, in private worship and in talks with her advisers and intimate friends. Much of the impact of the Coronation, which was so closely followed by millions of people through television, was a result of her sincere faith.

In her Christmas broadcast before her Coronation, The Queen asked her people to pray for her:

"I want to ask you all, whatever your religion may be, to pray for me on that day—to pray that God may give me wisdom and strength to carry out the solemn promises I shall be making, and that I may faithfully serve Him and you, all the days of my life."

She prepared assiduously not only for the part she had to play, but for her great act of Dedication.

The Coronation of Queen Elizabeth II took place in Westminster Abbey on June 2, 1953. From my eyrie in the triforium high above the choir, I watched The Queen's procession appear below the choir screen, to the sung shouts of joy of the boys of Westminster School. I thought how young she looked and how vulnerable, how resolved and how steadfast. Her young, rounded arms were uncovered, in contrast to the formality of her magnificently embroidered dress and long-trained crimson velvet Robe of State.

The most moving moments were those in which the humility and the sincerity of Her Majesty shone out through all the magnificence with which she was surrounded. There was the instance when she had covered (all but a glimmer at the hem) her shimmering dress, with the plain white folds of the *colobium sindonis*, and her hands went up to her neck to assist her Mistress of the Robes to take off her diamond necklace. There was her slow and dignified walk, after the crowning with St. Edward's Crown, from the Coronation Chair to the throne chair up five steps covered with gold velvet of the exact shade but not texture of the royal robe or *pallium*, when the two sceptres swayed slightly in her hands, and the largest cut diamond in the world, of 530 carats, the first part of the Star of Africa, flashed multi-coloured fire from its position below the Cross in the sceptre carried in her right hand. Her husband's eyes followed her intently, as he leaned forward, with his hand cupping his chin. Her mother, the Queen Mother, wearing the circlet of her Crown, was bending down to answer the eager questions of The Queen's son, the Heir Apparent.

Perhaps the most moving of all that part of the ceremony was not the Recognition, not the Anointing, not the Investing, not the Crowning itself, but the part in which The Queen offered the sword upon the Altar, and which, above all, symbolised the offering of The Queen's life and work in the service of her people. In the words of the Service:

Then shall the Archbishop take the Sword from off the Altar, and (the Archbishop of York and the Bishops of London and Winchester and other Bishops assisting and going along with him) shall deliver it into The Queen's hands; and, The Queen holding it, the Archbishop shall say:—

"Receive this kingly Sword, brought now from the Altar of God and delivered to you by the hands of us the Bishops and servants of God, though unworthy. With this Sword do justice, stop the growth of iniquity, protect the holy Church of God, help and defend widows and orphans, restore the things that are gone to decay, maintain the things that are restored, punish and reform what is amiss, and confirm what is in good order; that doing these things you may be glorious in all virtue; and so faithfully serve our Lord Jesus Christ in this life, that you may reign for ever with Him in the life which is to come. Amen."

Then The Queen, rising up and going to the Altar, shall offer it there in the scabbard. . . .

The ceremony of her Coronation is undoubtedly the greatest religious service in which The Queen has taken or will take part.

Every year The Queen takes part in the ceremony of Royal

Maundy. The name comes from *mandatum* (commandment), and originated in the washing of the disciples' feet and the commandment of Jesus to love one another, and in consequence it is celebrated always on the Thursday in Holy Week.

In England it was instituted by Edward I in the late thirteenth century and was kept personally by all sovereigns until James II. Formerly it included the washing of the feet of the poor as a sign of humility and compassion. (In the days of the first Queen Elizabeth, the feet of the poor were washed by a series of ascendingly important officials before the Tudor Queen got to work on them with scented water and towel, a sufficient comment on contemporary personal hygiene.)

Beginning with James II there was a long break in royal participation in the Maundy. Then Princess Marie Louise, a granddaughter of Queen Victoria who was a great lover of tradition and history, suggested to King George V that he might care to renew the Sovereign's personal association with Royal Maundy, and this he did in 1932.

Formerly the gown worn by The Queen was given to the oldest woman, now this is redeemed by a cash gift to all recipients, who also receive the specially minted "Maundy money", which consists of silver coins—penny, half-groat or twopenny, threepenny and a groat or fourpenny pieces. Incidentally this is the *sterling*, the standard silver penny (so called from a small star on each coin) of Norman days, which gave its name to our currency. A pound sterling was originally the weight of 240 sterlings or silver pennies. The only sterlings now made are for the Maundy money.

The recipients are chosen from former householders and ratepayers, and number as many old men and as many old ladies as the Sovereign's age. When Queen Elizabeth celebrated her first Maundy in 1952, the old people had already been chosen to double the number of her father's age. Rather than disappoint any of them, she broke with tradition for that one year and presented the Royal Maundy to one hundred and twelve instead of the fifty recipients entitled to it by The Queen's age.

In recent years the ceremony has usually taken place at Westminster Abbey, but when the Abbey was closed for the immense preparations for the Coronation in 1953, it took place in St. Paul's Cathedral. Since then The Queen has from time to time varied the venue of Royal Maundy, the ceremony taking place in 1955 in Southwark Cathedral, which was then celebrating its diocesan jubilee, and in 1957 in St. Albans Cathedral (the diocese of the present Lord High Almoner). This was the first occasion that a Sovereign had personally distributed Royal Maundy outside London since the reign of Charles II. The old people were chosen locally.

At St. Albans a retired schoolmistress who was a beneficiary said afterwards, "Every recipient was given a special little smile. It went to her eyes—it was a real smile. She made everyone feel it was a personal thing."

At the Feast of the Epiphany (January 6) The Queen directs that the customary Sovereign's offering of gold (in the form of twenty-five sovereigns), frankincense and myrrh is made, symbolic of the gifts of the Kings to the infant Jesus. The ceremony takes place either at the Chapel Royal or Queen's Chapel of St. James's Palace, the gift being offered on gold salvers by two Gentlemen Ushers of The Queen's Household, wearing Court Dress, and the Yeoman of the Guard provide a guard of honour. This ceremony, too, was once carried out by the Sovereign himself, but since the reign of George II has been performed by deputies.

A very important gift to the Church by The Queen is the altar cloth, which is a part of her Coronation oblation. The gift of the cloth is an actual part of the ceremony.

Then the Queen, kneeling as before, shall make her oblation, offering a Pall or Altar Cloth, delivered by the Groom of the Robes to the Lord Great Chamberlain, and by him, kneeling to Her Majesty...

But the gift was of a token cloth only, the actual Altar Cloth presented by Her Majesty being made specially afterwards, to the design of Mr. Stephen Dykes Bower, Surveyor of the Fabric of Westminster Abbey. Its material is a specially woven blue silk damask richly embroidered in gold, with the royal cipher and eight panels or orphreys, beautifully worked with symbolic flowers. Among the flowers in one of these orphreys tiny gold spiders are sitting on their webs. The inscription on the superfrontal reads: "*Lactatus sum in his quae dicta sunt mihi; In domum Domini ibimus.*" The Frontal is used on the high altar of Westminster Abbey on special days associated with King Edward the Confessor, founder of the Abbey, and other special occasions. Unfortunately the altar frontal was damaged in a small fire in the Chapel Royal of St. Peter ad Vincula in the Tower of London in the summer of 1958. The damage was, however, quickly repaired.

The Queen (then Princess Elizabeth) and Prince Philip also gave to Westminster Abbey, in commemoration of their wedding there in 1947, two large silver gilt alms dishes, eighteen inches in diameter and inscribed accordingly. Gifts in kind made by The Queen are recorded—the lectern to the parish church in Windlesham where she worshipped during one summer when she and her husband rented a house in the neighbourhood. She sent a gift to the Treasure Sale in aid of the new Guildford Cathedral; she was the first subscriber to a fund for Lambeth Palace library; she gave a donation to a fund for the restoration of bells at All Saints', King's Langley, in which is housed the tomb of her ancestor, Edmund de Langley, first Duke of York. The silver chalice and patten used for Communion by the first settlers in Virginia, which was most generously presented to her during her visit to Jamestown in 1957, was by The Queen in turn presented to St. George's Chapel of Unity, Gravesend, within which is buried the Princess Pocahontas, the Red Indian Princess who, according to legend, saved the life of John Smith and who afterwards married a Jamestown settler and returned with him to England. The Queen gave an ancient Greek font to the Church at Sandringham. Made from a solid block of marble and at least 1,000 years old, it was brought from the island of Rhodes in 1886 and had been in the royal possession ever since.

The amount of a gift in money is never revealed, but is often recorded as "most generous".

The Church of England, as an established Church, is linked with almost all official occasions in which are incorporated a religious service. Among the most important is the Armistice Day ceremony, held at the Cenotaph, or empty tomb, in Whitehall on the Sunday nearest to November 11, the Armistice Day of the First World War, when The Queen lays a wreath on the memorial. A religious service also forms part of the British Legion Festival of Remembrance which takes place in the Royal Albert Hall on the preceding night. The Queen was the second sovereign in British history to visit Lambeth when she attended the service of the re-dedication of the Chapel there, which was destroyed by enemy action. She also attended the service of re-dedication of one of the beautiful Wren churches, St. Bride's, which had been gutted by fire during the blitz. She laid the foundation stone of the new Cathedral within the ruined walls of Coventry Cathedral; she has attended a service for seafarers inside St. Paul's Cathedral. She presented "a fair linen cloth" worked at her order by the Sisters of Bethany, a Church of England Order at Finsbury, in a design chosen by The Queen, at the consecration of the new High Altar, to the original Wren design, in St. Paul's Cathedral. The new cloth was the first to be placed upon the consecrated High Altar. She attended the re-dedication of the bombed Church of St. Clement Danes in the Strand on October 19, 1958, which is the famous "Oranges and Lemons" Church of the nursery rhyme, now restored to the glory conceived by Wren. She has attended many other religious services.

Although for centuries now the pre-eminence of Parliament over the Church has been established, there still remain corners of influence which are not fully explored. Even in this reign minor skirmishes for position have taken place. Such was the question of the use of Royal Arms in churches, which blew up when what the Church Information Board called "an over-cautious" intending donor of a representation of the Arms of The Queen to his parish church at Hanbury, Worcestershire, in order to commemorate the Coronation, made what a Church report called "a grievous mistake" in approaching the Home Office for permission to erect the Arms, instead of applying to the consistory court of his diocese.

The blow fell when the Home Office said that the Arms could not be displayed without their permission on behalf of The Queen, and the Home Secretary furthermore issued to the chancellors of the dioceses a total prohibition of the use of Royal Arms in any church without Governmental permission.

The Church of England view was that this was a "direct challenge to the authority of the Church courts", and to the long-established tradition of setting up the Arms to signify The Queen's position as Defender of the Faith and "Supreme over all Causes and Persons, as well Ecclesiastical as Civil, within her Realm".

Back to the records went diligent searchers after documents to prove either the Church or the State's authority, but without success. The original order to display the Royal Arms in churches, which must have been made either by Edward VI, or even perhaps by Henry VIII, has not been found.

Eventually, in 1954, after two years of correspondence between the Archbishop of Canterbury and the Secretary of State for Home Affairs, a typically English compromise was decided. In future the erection of Royal Arms painted on wood or canvas or carved, and hung on the church wall or in other customary position, is regarded as within the authority of the Church. But the reproduction of the Royal Arms in stained glass or in any non-traditional form requires Home Office permission on behalf of The Queen.

*   *   *   *

There is one other Church to which The Queen stands in a special position. That is the established Church of Scotland, which enjoys complete freedom from secular control, appointing its own leaders, formulating its own doctrines and carrying out its own policies in a way which the English Church sometimes envies. The first official signatures of the Sovereign's reign, and the only signatures required at the Accession Council of a new Sovereign, are when she signs two copies of her declaration to maintain the Presbyterian Government of the Church of Scotland.

The Church of Scotland states, in its fourth Declaratory Article:

The Church is part of the Universal Church wherein the Lord Jesus Christ has appointed a government in the hands of Church office-bearers. It receives from Him, its Divine King and Head, and from Him alone, the right and power, subject to no civil authority, to legislate and adjudicate finally in all matters of doctrine, worship, government and discipline in the Church.

The Queen is recognised by the Church of Scotland as the possessor of all secular authority, which the Church recognises and obeys. But she has no spiritual authority over the Church of Scotland.

At The Queen's Coronation, the Moderator of the General Assembly of the Church of Scotland (the Rt. Rev. Professor S. Pitt-Watson, D.D.) took part for the first time, when he presented the Bible to The Queen.

A unique connection between The Queen and Church is her appointment of a Lord High Commissioner to represent her each year at the General Assembly of Ministers and Elders of the Church of Scotland held annually in Edinburgh, at which all matters concerned with the Church of Scotland are thrashed out and decided. But the High Commissioner does not preside over the General Assembly.

The General Assembly is presided over by a Moderator, who is its one officer, elected each year. The Moderator is chosen by a committee of the General Assembly and then presented for election by the Assembly itself. The election is nearly always, but not invariably, unanimous. The Queen does not come into it at all, nor does the Government; it is entirely a matter for the Church.

The Lord High Commissioner occupies a position unique in Britain during his term of office at the General Assembly. He lives in the Palace of Holyroodhouse—the only occasion on which a royal palace is opened up for a Representative of The Queen—and he is accorded the same honours which would be given to Her Majesty.

The appointment is contained in a Royal Commission, under The Queen's own hand to her Trusty and Well Beloved Servant.

"The Lord High Commissioner is not a church officer, but the Sovereign's officer. He is there to guard The Queen's privileges, to see that the Church, whose spiritual authority she recognises, does not trespass on to her temporalities," was the explanation of the Office given to me by the late Mr. Walter Elliot, twice Lord High Commissioner, only three weeks before his death.

The Lord High Commissioner need not be, although he generally is, a member of the Church of Scotland. On the day of the Opening of the General Assembly, the Lord High Commissioner walks in the procession from St. Giles Cathedral to the Assembly Hall, accompanied by the Lord Lyon King-of-Arms in tabard with the Scottish quarterings, and the purse-bearer with mace. There he sits in a gallery, which is technically outside the Assembly, and from there notes and afterwards reports the proceedings of the General Assembly on the floor below to Her Majesty. The Lord High Commissioner is always charged with a letter from The Queen to the General Assembly, and this is read aloud to the Assembly, which stands in silence to receive it. A reply is returned on the following day. "Every General Assembly leaves the spectator in no doubt as to the deep affection in which Her Majesty is held and the unswerving loyalty of the Ministers and Elders of the Church of Scotland to Her Majesty's person and throne," said the Very Rev. Dr. Robert F. V. Scott, D.D., Moderator of the Church of Scotland in 1956–7.

In recent years a change of more than passing importance has taken place in the formalities which close the General Assembly, and which mean, in effect, that the General Assembly, unlike the Church Assembly in England, is self-summoning. Prior to Queen Anne, there was a constant and continual struggle between the Church of Scotland and the King, each claiming the right to summon and dissolve the General Assembly. But from 1704 onwards it was mutually agreed that the General Assembly should be twice dissolved—in the name of Jesus Christ by the Moderator, and in the name of the Magistrate by the Lord High Commissioner.

By an Act passed in 1921 the Articles Declaratory of the Constitution of the Church of Scotland in matters spiritual were declared lawful, and were enacted by the General Assembly of the Church Assembly of 1926. Up to and including the Assembly of 1926 the Lord High Commissioner used to take his part in dissolving the General Assembly with the words:

"In the virtue of the powers invested in me by His Majesty The King I now dissolve this Assembly in the King's Name, and appoint that the next Assembly shall meet on . . ."

although this was not recorded in the Minutes of the General Assembly.

This was not just a play of words. At the time of the General Strike it was proposed that the General Assembly should meet, but Government approval could not be obtained, and so the Sovereign's authority for summoning the General Assembly was withheld.

Without any public awareness, the form was quietly changed, and from the time of 1927 the Lord High Commissioner has used a new form of words. And so it is that the Lord High Commissioner now ends his part in the proceedings of the General Assembly with these words:

"I shall inform Her Majesty that, having concluded the business for which you were assembled, you have passed an Act appointing the next meeting of the General Assembly to be held at Edinburgh on [the date being named] and now, in The Queen's name, I bid you farewell."

The religious adherence of the Sovereign is determined by the Act of Settlement, which has already been quoted. As the Archbishop of Canterbury said at a recent session of the Church Assembly, while The Queen is the protector of both the Church of England and the Church of Scotland, she is a "member of one only".

The Queen worships in the national Church of Scotland when she is in Scotland, and she has her own Ecclesiastical establishment of Ministers of the Church of Scotland. It consists of the Dean of the Chapel Royal, who is also Dean of the Order of the Thistle, and eight other Chaplains-in-Ordinary, together at the moment with two Extra Chaplains. All are resident in Scotland. The Queen's domestic Chaplain at Balmoral, the Rev. John Lamb, C.V.O., D.D., is a Minister of the Church of Scotland.

In modern times the personal connection between the Sovereign and the Church of Scotland was founded by Queen Victoria, who first attended a service of the Church of Scotland in 1844, when she and the Prince Consort were the guests of the Duke and Duchess of Atholl at Blair Atholl. Queen Victoria was first present at a service of Holy Communion in 1871, and from 1873 regularly took Holy Communion in the Church of Scotland when in Scotland. No Sovereign since that time has joined in Communion in the Church of Scotland.

Each year the Minister at Crathie, the Parish Church of Balmoral (the Rev. John Lamb, C.V.O., D.D.), submits a list of names of Ministers of the Church of Scotland to The Queen, from which she selects those she desires to be asked to preach. The Minister then invites them to preach, and The Queen invites them to stay at Balmoral for the weekend.

She attends and sends gifts to the Crathie Church Sales of Work, and on a recent occasion, at a Fête organised by The Queen Mother to raise funds for the building of a vestry for Crathie Parish Church, she presided at a Royal Stall and, with all the members of the Royal Family, sold goods during the whole afternoon.

The Queen also gave a silver collection plate to St. Michael's Church, Linlithgow, in commemoration of her visit in 1955.

The Free Churches in England have—as their name implies—no official connection with the Sovereign, but The Queen has shown in conversation on many occasions her concern for the welfare of the Free Churches, and her considerable knowledge of their work. She invited Dr. Billy Graham to preach before her and to luncheon afterwards at Windsor, and invited also Dr. Leslie Weatherhead to one of the extremely interesting groups of thoughtful and influential people whom The Queen and the Duke of Edinburgh entertain to luncheon at Buckingham Palace from time to time. Another instance was the prominent position which was given to the Moderator of the Free Church Federal Council at the Commonwealth service in St. Paul's Cathedral immediately following the Coronation. This was not arranged by Her Majesty, but she must have known and approved the action.

With regard to the Roman Catholics The Queen's position is somewhat different, although the harsh partialities which led to the Act of Succession have become much modified by the centuries. The Queen never attends services in a Roman Catholic Church, nor do the dignitaries of that Church attend Church of England services, the Papal Delegate to the Coronation, for instance, taking a place on the stands outside Westminster Abbey, although the Coronation itself was in large measure excellently organised by the Earl Marshal, the Duke of Norfolk, who is a Roman Catholic.

The Queen, when Princess Elizabeth, was received in private audience by the Pope, visiting him as the Head of a State and not in his religious capacity. The Queen and other members of the Royal Family made private donations to the fund for rebuilding St. George's Roman Catholic Cathedral at Southwark, and at the reopening in July 1958 the Roman Catholic Bishop of Southwark, Dr. Cyril Cowderoy, in his address spoke gratefully of these gifts from the Royal Family, "good, generous people who are not of our faith". The Queen in June 1958 received at short notice in the grounds of Windsor Castle a large party of six hundred Australian Roman Catholic Pilgrims returning from Lourdes under the leadership of Cardinal Gilroy, Archbishop of

Sydney. "The Pilgrims were so delighted with the Audience," said the Cardinal afterwards, "that when The Queen was leaving, they spontaneously gave three cheers and then sang 'God Save The Queen'. The Queen paused, stood till the end of the anthem and then graciously waved good-bye as she entered the castle." When Her Majesty has any dealings whatever with the Roman Catholic Church there is an outcry from the extreme Protestant right wing, which is sometimes interpreted abroad as an indication of a high state of religious tension and intolerance within Great Britain. Such a protest was contained in a letter of thanks for a visit to the Island of Harris, from four Free Presbyterian ministers, which ended by praying that the Word of God "will ever remain the day-star of Your Majesty's illustrious Throne and its bulwark against the sinister encroachments of the false and blasphemous Papal system". In fact, such strongly expressed feelings are to-day confined to very limited groups and areas.

Although The Queen has not attended a Jewish religious service, the Duke of Edinburgh was present at a special service in the Spanish and Portuguese Synagogue in the City of London, which was held on December 19, 1951, to mark the 250th anniversary of the Synagogue.

The Queen is at one and the same time the Governor of the Church of England and the Head of the Commonwealth, which contains many millions of believers in other Faiths. A reverent and sincere Christian, The Queen has notwithstanding a very real appreciation of the faiths of other peoples. Uncompromising in her personal religious standards, she is understanding in her appreciation of the different ways in which her Commonwealth subjects and citizens reach up to God.

CHAPTER SEVEN

The Fount of Honour

"The object of giving medals, stars and ribbons is to give pride and pleasure to those who have deserved them."
Churchill, House of Commons, March 22, 1944

"The advantages of the British system is that The Queen is associated with the award, so that the person who receives an O.B.E. is shown to the world to be a person who has been thanked by The Queen for his services to the community."
Sir Ivor Jennings

THE Queen is the Fount of Honour.

Every form of organised society has found it necessary to institute some system of Honours, in order to distinguish and reward those who have particularly contributed to that society. An Honour is a token in which the prestige value far outweighs the money value. It has been gradually evolved in settled societies to take the place of the spontaneous rewards of money, jewels or land made by early absolute rulers. An Honour, to fulfil its purpose, must be kept in high repute, and must outweigh, in the eyes of both the recipient and the world at large, the meretricious rewards which may be gained in the more glamorous activities. As soon as an Honour is cheapened by being too easily gained, or tarnished by being acquired by dubious means or persons, its value has gone.

A monarchy lends itself particularly well to the dignified distribution of Honours. The monarchy is a stable and permanent office, the association of the monarch with the award lends lustre, and the actual presentation can be made in circumstances of the greatest possible ceremonial dignity.

The Queen personally approves all awards, even those which she does not personally present, and the knowledge that that is so gives them undoubted weight. An Honour received from the hands of The Queen gains a value that it could have in no other way.

An appreciable part of The Queen's time is spent in the approval and distribution of Honours. Such Honours emanate from The Queen as:

Peerages

Baronetcies

Knighthoods and membership of other classes of the Orders of Knighthood

Decorations and Medals for gallantry and meritorious service

Campaign Medals

Commemorative Medals.

The Honour of being appointed a Privy Counsellor has already been described. Certain appointments, which have now only residual duties, to The Queen's Household are also in the nature of formal Honours.

Apart from the Honours in her own bestowal, about which more is said later, all awards of the above-mentioned Honours are made by The Queen on the recommendation of one of her Ministers. The greatest number are submitted by the Prime Minister, whose list also embodies those from Government Departments such as the Foreign Office, Commonwealth Relations Office and the Colonial Office in respect of service overseas. The ultimate responsibility for the names it contains is, however, his and was placed fairly on his shoulders by the report of the Royal Commission under the chairmanship of Lord Dunedin in 1922, which reiterated that the Sovereign is the Fount of Honour but that, except in certain special cases, he or she can act only on the advice of the Prime Minister of the United Kingdom, or his counterpart of a Commonwealth country. The Commonwealth countries conferring Honours are notably Australia, New Zealand, Ghana and the Federation of Rhodesia and Nyasaland, and—for service awards and the George Cross and Medal only—Canada.

The Prime Minister has the power (which has been used in times of ill-will between Sovereign and Government) of enforcing the Sovereign, as a constitutional monarch, to give his formal Approval to names of which he disapproved most strongly. But such conditions would be almost unthinkable to-day when there is smooth and harmonious association between Queen and Government.

The number of each type of Honour awarded is approved by The Queen, because, as Churchill said in the House of Commons, "a distinction is something which everybody does not possess. If all have it, it is of less value", and the too easy distribution of an Honour immediately debases it. These quotas are held by the Central Chancery of the Orders of Knighthood, an office deriving from and still under the general control of the Lord Chamberlain. It would theoretically be possible for the Prime Minister of the day to overset such controls and indulge in unbridled distribution of Honours, or to go to the other extreme and present no list of recommendations at all. But that is not at all likely to happen.

So far, in the reign of Queen Elizabeth II, there has been no major change of policy in the type or number of Honours awarded compared with that of the reign of her father. The principles and custom underlying the awards of Honours have changed, however, several times even within the last century.

Always the two classes of Honours must be remembered: those in the Sovereign's own bestowal, and the larger part, which are recommended by the Prime Minister here or in the Commonwealth, and approved by the Sovereign, although the Honours in the Sovereign's own bestowal have varied with the years.

The attitude of recent Sovereigns in this important matter has been expressed either directly in their letters and memoranda, or indirectly through memoirs and biographies of their times.

Queen Victoria's statecraft and shrewd common sense guided her scrutiny of the Political Honours which came to her for approval. Take the pertinent comment on the gift of the Order of the Garter, then (though not now) a political Honour, to the King of Prussia, in her letter of January 19, 1861, to Lord Russell:

Has it ever occurred to Lord John Russell that, if Lord Clarendon were to go to Berlin carrying the highest compliment the Queen has to bestow, viz. the Order of the Garter to the new King of Prussia, and from thence to Vienna empty-handed to the Emperor of Austria for the purpose of giving good advice, the Emperor might look upon it as an offensive public proceeding towards him?

At the opening of her reign Queen Victoria had no personal Order in her own gift, such as the Guelph Order of the Kings of Hanover, to bestow upon those who rendered personal services to her. It was not until 1862 that she established the Victoria and Albert Order for Ladies, which has now fallen into disuse. Then in 1896, when she had reigned almost sixty years, she established the Royal Victorian Order, which is now the most generally awarded of the Honours in the Sovereign's bestowal. Queen Victoria herself awarded her new Order to very few people, and all such persons were very closely associated with her, or with the memory of her husband.

Queen Victoria's hand with the Honours in her bestowal was lavish to her relatives, but carefully selective to those who served her. She disliked to see those who were her servants wearing the decorations of foreign royalty, and kept to an absolute minimum her consent to the wearing of Foreign Orders by British subjects.

King Edward VII's attitude towards Honours was very different from that of his mother. He was a man who liked to give pleasure, and believed that nothing gave more pleasure than the bestowal of an Order. Indeed, he distributed the Royal Victorian Order so freely that it became somewhat ridiculed—an attitude which seems surprising to-day when it is one of the most desired of all decorations. King Edward VII also generously permitted his Household to accept all the Foreign Orders which were offered to them. At the same time, even at his most open-handed, his distribution of British decorations when overseas on State Visits was far more conservative than that of the rulers of many foreign countries. In consequence a British decoration was much sought after and valued.

King Edward VII had a strong feeling of the dignity of his Orders, particularly the Garter. During the Balfour ministry, there was a really first-class row when his Foreign Secretary, Lord Lansdowne, offered the Garter (without the King's consent) to the then Shah of Persia, the Shah Muzaffar-ad-Din. What was more, to make this fundamentally Christian Order more appropriate, Lansdowne took it upon himself to redesign the star without the Cross of St. George! King Edward eventually consented to bestow the Garter (with the Cross of St. George) upon the Shah, but only after it had become apparent that a political crisis would be the inevitable result of refusal.

King George V met the greatest modern crisis in the history of Political Honours. His personal bestowal of Honours was moderate and well-considered. It caused no comment.

But in the sphere of the Prime Minister's recommendations, the wholesale distribution of Honours for political reasons during the Prime Ministership of Mr. Lloyd George brought the whole system into discredit. No fewer than 25,000 Orders of the British Empire were given between 1917 and 1922. The Decoration was laughed at by the French as the "Ordre Britannique Embusquée", in Britain as the "Order of the Bad Egg". Some of the persons suggested even for the higher Honours, such as Peerages, had a somewhat questionable history.

King George V, with his strict code of honour and his constant guardianship of the dignity of the Crown and Country, was infuriated and distressed at the lack of respect with which his Honours were generally regarded. He criticised in the strongest terms some of the recommendations for high distinction made by the Prime Minister. The names were not withdrawn. With great reluctance the King, as a constitutional monarch, had no alternative but to "approve" the award of the disputed Honours.

The misuse of British Honours shocked and disgusted the public just as it did the King. Lord Halifax, in his memoirs *Fulness of Days*, comments:

The public conscience was gradually roused wide awake on this issue, and I do not suppose any single thing had more to say to Lloyd George's fall a few years later.

The most far-reaching consequence of the controversy over the unwise distribution of Honours was the appointment of the Royal Commission in 1922 under the chairmanship of Lord Duncdin, which resulted in what is commonly called the Dunedin Report. This advised that the suitability of candidates for Honours made in respect of political services should be investigated by an independent Committee, and that this Committee should consist of three Privy Counsellors, men of well-known character and position, who should not be members of the Government.

This Committee, called the Political Honours Scrutiny Committee, at the time of writing consists of Lord Templewood, Lord Pethick-Lawrence and Lord Thurso. They investigate the suitability of all candidates for Honours, who have been recommended on the grounds of political services. The Committee has no power to suggest names, only to investigate those names submitted to them. Should they refuse to pass a person, that name can still be submitted by the Prime Minister for the Sovereign's approval, but the fact that it has not been passed by the Political Honours Scrutiny Committee must be stated: in practice such a name would not be submitted.

The Dunedin Report also advised that Commonwealth citizens should be recommended by the Prime Minister of that Dominion, which is invariably the case to-day. The only persons resident in a Commonweaith country who might be recommended by the Prime Minister of another Commonwealth country would be, say, a Briton working for the United Kingdom in Australia, who would be included in the Commonwealth Relations Office list.

The constructive attitude of King George V to the distribution of Honours is shown in a memorandum prepared for Mr. Ramsay MacDonald's information when he became the country's first Socialist Prime Minister. Incidentally, it underlines the helpful guidance which the Government, of whatever party, receives from a wise Constitutional Sovereign. It is quoted as a footnote in Sir Harold Nicholson's invaluable biography *King George V, His Life and Reign* (Royal Archives K. 1917).

Honours and Appointments

It is hoped that a firm hand will be kept on the distribution of Honours. With the exception of the last Government, the bestowal has been extravagant. Especial care should be taken with regard to appointments to the Privy Council. Mr. Gladstone said that a Privy Councillorship used to be regarded as a greater honour than a Peerage.

Before any person is offered an Appointment under the Crown, or an Honour, the King's approval should be obtained, until which time the individual in question should not be approached on the subject.

All recommendations for Honours are submitted in conjunction with the Prime Minister, with the exception of the Order of Merit and the Royal Victorian Order (which are made on the King's initiative).

Except in very special cases, Submissions for Honours are only made twice a year, i.e. New Year's Day and the King's Birthday.

The number of names submitted on each occasion for Baronetcies and Knighthoods, other than those for the Dominions, should not respectively exceed 8 and 24.

The King deprecates the bestowal of Honours on Ministers while in Office.

The reign of King Edward VIII was too short to produce any marked effect upon the distribution of Honours.

The reign of King George VI contained the Second World War, and demanded from him, as the First World War had demanded from his father, officiation at many long and important Investitures, some conducted in the field.

The most important change which occurred during his reign was the return of the Orders of the Garter and of the Thistle to the Sovereign's bestowal. A notice was issued from Number 10 Downing Street on December 3, 1946, which ran:

The appointments announced to-day to the Most Noble Order of the Garter have been made under a procedure similar to that used for awards of the Order of Merit. The Order of Merit is awarded by the King without any formal submission by the Prime Minister or other responsible Minister of the Crown. This position was clearly established in 1902 when the Order was founded. Where appropriate the King is pleased to inform the Prime Minister of his intentions in regard to the award of this Order before conferring it and to consider any private and unofficial suggestions which the Prime Minister may make.

The Prime Minister and the Leader of the Opposition have both accepted the view that the same procedure should apply to appointments of the Most Noble Order of the Garter in future. The King has been pleased to approve.

Although the Garter had been officially in the Prime Minister's bestowal throughout at least most of the Hanoverian period and after, the Sovereign had always viewed with a specially jealous eye the bestowal of this, the highest of all his decorations. Queen Victoria was approached most circumspectly by her Prime Ministers with their suggestions for fitting recipients for the Garter. When Lord Derby resigned the premiership, Queen Victoria, without more ado, at once offered him the Garter, which he accepted.

The Most Ancient and Most Noble Order of the Thistle, Scotland's premier Order of Chivalry, was returned to the Sovereign's bestowal on June 17, 1947, when a similar announcement to that concerning the Garter was issued from 10 Downing Street.

When The Queen came to the Throne in 1952 she therefore had a greater number of Honours in her personal bestowal than any previous Sovereign upon accession since the days of the Stuarts. In The Queen's bestowal are the Garter, the Thistle, the Royal Victorian Chain, the Royal Victorian Order and the Order of Merit.

The Queen would not on her own initiative appoint a person to any Order or Distinction not within her own bestowal. Sir Harold Nicholson recalls that Lord Stamfordham, asked if the King had ever conferred an Order (beyond those in his undisputed bestowal, the Order of Merit and the Royal Victorian Order) except upon the advice of a responsible Minister, replied, "Never."

King George V once put forward the name of an inventor, whom he considered merited distinction, for a Knighthood in the Prime Minister's list. Mr. Lloyd George brushed aside the application and King George V minuted upon the correspondence, "As I so seldom ask for a knighthood, I really think that I might be treated with anyhow some consideration."

The Queen, as Fount of Honour, has a wide range of diverse duties.

The Queen creates all Peers, but again, as with all other Honours not in her personal bestowal, she does so on the advice of her Ministers, in this case the Prime Minister. This part of her duties is of great potential political importance. It controls the Upper House—as in the constitutional crisis where a deadlock in the House of Lords was resolved by Mr. Asquith's determination (to which King George V agreed most reluctantly) to swamp that House with specially created Peers, before which the Upper House gave way. Only the Sovereign can create a Peer; this power cannot be delegated to the Counsellors of State. Indeed, this applies to *all* Honours.

Peers are created by Letters Patent. After the announcement

of the conferment of a Peerage, the new Peer is remitted to Garter King-of-Arms to consult about his title, and if either the title or designation are to be Scottish, the Lord Lyon King-of-Arms is likewise consulted. This is submitted to The Queen for her approval, when The Queen signs the Letters Patent, to which are afterwards affixed the Great Seal in green wax. (The Great Seal is otherwise used in red wax.)

The five degrees of the Peerage are Duke, Marquess, Earl, Viscount and Baron. Apart from royal Dukes, no Dukedom has been created in the present century. Again excepting the Royal Family, only a few men have been created Marquesses in this century; nearly all were Viceroys of India. There have been over twenty Earls created, such as Earl Mountbatten of Burma, and Earl Attlee; they have all been men of considerable prominence in public life. Since the Second World War, Viscounts have included such notable men as Lord Monckton, who had a very prominent public career, and Lord Cherwell, who was promoted to the rank of Viscountcy some years after receiving his Barony, as he had continued to deserve well of his country. By far the greatest number of men promoted to the House of Lords are made Barons.

The Queen is the first Sovereign to create women life peeresses with a seat in the House of Lords, under the Life Peerages Act, 1958. This has already been dealt with in the chapter about Parliament.

In the few cases where a title can be inherited by a woman, and where there are co-heiresses (as the law of primogeniture does not hold good in this case), if all but one of the co-heiresses agree to relinquish their claims, The Queen may declare the remaining co-heiress to be the holder of the title. Such an instance took place in 1958, when The Queen declared Georgina Angela Maxwell, wife of Lieutenant John David Maxwell, R.N., to be Baroness De Ros. The new Baroness is the elder granddaughter of Una Mary, Baroness De Ros, who died in 1956. Baroness De Ros is the twenty-seventh holder of the title, the premier barony of England, which was created in 1264.

When the heir to a title dies before the holder, The Queen sometimes bestows upon his widow and family the same honours which would have been theirs if the holder of the title had died first. For instance, in August 1958 The Queen declared that Alice Mary Clifford, widow of the late Captain G. G. J. Clifford, 8th King's Royal Irish Hussars, "shall have, hold and enjoy the same style, title, place and precedence to which she would have been entitled had her husband survived his uncle, the late Sir Walter Clifford, baronet."

Baronets, like Peers, are created by Letters Patent. A Baronet does not receive the accolade unless or until he is created a Knight. As is well known, a baronetcy is also an Honour which is inherited by the Holder's male heirs.

The Queen is Sovereign of all nine British Orders of Knighthood, which are:

The Most Noble Order of the Garter
The Most Ancient and Most Noble Order of the Thistle
The Most Illustrious Order of St. Patrick
The Most Honourable Order of the Bath
The Most Exalted Order of the Star of India
The Most Distinguished Order of St. Michael and St. George
The Most Eminent Order of the Indian Empire
The Royal Victorian Order
The Most Excellent Order of the British Empire

Three of these Orders of Knighthood are in The Queen's personal bestowal—the Garter, the Thistle (already mentioned) and the Royal Victorian Orders. Three are made in recommendation of the Prime Minister or the Ministerial Head of Department: the Bath (which has both a military and a civil membership); the St. Michael and St. George, which is generally given to those who have given distinguished service to the Foreign Office, the Commonwealth Relations Office or the Colonial Office; and the Order of the British Empire, which is awarded for many varied types of services to the British Empire, and is entirely redeemed from the low repute in which it was held some thirty to forty years ago. There have been appointments to all six of these Orders during The Queen's reign. The awards to the Military Division of the Order of the Bath are made on the recommendation of the First Lord of the Admiralty, or the Secretary of State for War or Air.

The remaining three Orders of Knighthood are either concerned with Ireland or with India, and no awards have been made to any of them during this reign, although there are recipients still living.

The Knights Bachelor are not a constituted Order.

The Most Noble Order of the Garter is the premier Order of Knighthood in the world. It was founded by Edward III in 1348. It has never been enlarged, and has therefore retained its prestige. There are only twenty-six Knights, although an additional number of Kings and Princes may be installed. The Royal Dukes of Edinburgh, Gloucester and Windsor are Knights of the Garter, as are King Leopold III of the Belgians, King Fredrik IX of Denmark, King Gustaf VI Adolf of Sweden, the Emperor of Ethiopia and Prince Paul of Yugoslavia.

The Sovereign is always Sovereign of the Order, and The Queen as Princess Elizabeth was previously installed as Lady of the Garter by her father in 1947. The first Ladies of the Garter were the daughters of King Henry VII. The custom then lapsed for centuries until King Edward VII installed Queen Alexandra as the first Queen Consort ever to be a Lady of the Garter. At present the Queen Mother and Princess Wilhelmina of the Netherlands and the Queen of the Netherlands are Ladies of the Garter. The Queen has not so far installed a Lady of the Garter.

With the first installation of her reign The Queen to some extent broke with general practice. She made Sir Winston Churchill a Knight of the Garter shortly before her Coronation. The Garter was not specifically reserved for peers, but few commoners have been Knights of the Garter in its 500 years of history. Those who were created while commoners were often raised to the peerage shortly afterwards. Pepys records the creation of his patron, Sir Edward Montagu (soon afterwards the Earl of Sandwich), as Knight of the Garter while still a commoner, by King Charles II shortly after the Restoration.

the King . . . do send him this George and Garter to wear as a Knight of the Order, with a dispensation for the other ceremonies of the habit of the Order, and other things, till hereafter, when it can be done. So the herald putting the ribbon about his neck, and the Garter on his left leg, he saluted him with joy as a Knight of the Garter.

General Monck, afterwards Duke of Albemarle, was also made a Knight of the Garter before he was ennobled.

In this century four commoners had previously been created Knights of the Order, Sir Edward Grey in 1912, Mr. A. J. Balfour in 1922 and Mr. Stanley Baldwin, who was later in the same day created a Peer. Only one, Mr. Austen Chamberlain, who received the Garter after concluding the Locarno Pact in 1925, has so far died a commoner and a Knight of the Garter.

The Queen in 1954 created Mr. Anthony Eden a Knight of the Garter. These were breaks with tradition also in that the recipients were actively engaged in politics at the time of their appointment. The Queen has also appointed the Earl of Iveagh, the Earl Attlee, Lord Ismay and Lord Middleton to be Knights of the Garter.

Sometimes investitures to the senior Orders of Knighthood take place in private, as when The Queen invested King Gustaf VI Adolf of Sweden and the Emperor Hailé Selassié of Ethiopia at Buckingham Palace, on the first day of their respective State Visits. Sometimes investiture takes place in a ceremony of the Order.

The ceremony of investiture is one of the most impressive in English history. It takes place in the presence of the Royal Family and Knights of the Garter and their wives in the Throne Room of Windsor Castle. Members of the public who have applied and received tickets have the privilege of seeing the procession of the Knights of the Garter made afterwards from the Castle through the Middle and Lower Wards to the Chapel of St. George's, which is the Chapel of the Order, for the Installation.

Queen Elizabeth I wore the Mantle and Collar on the Feast Day of St. George, but Queen Anne appears to be the first Queen Regnant often to wear the George and riband. Queen Victoria often wore the riband of the Garter, and Queen Elizabeth II habitually wears it in full evening dress, except when she is in Scotland, when she wears the riband of the Thistle. Unusual among Orders, both Garter and Thistle are worn over the left shoulder.

When The Queen presides at a Garter ceremony she wears the magnificent Sovereign's mantle of the Order, which is velvet of a wonderful dark blue shade, entirely lined with white silk. It has a considerable train, lined with white satin, which is carried by a Page of Honour.

The hood of the Garter mantle is of crimson velvet, lined with white silk. (The only other British Order with a hood is the Royal Victorian Order.) On the left breast is worn the Sovereign's badge. The Sovereign's badge is of metal and jewelled, and is slightly smaller than the Knights' badges, which are embroidered. In other respects the Sovereign's Mantle is similar to that of the Knights. It is a garment linked to history. On the right shoulder is the shoulder tie, whose use is to gather up and tie on the shoulder the folds of the cloak, gaining freedom for the sword arm. It also holds on the hood of the Order. The white bows on the shoulders hold on the collar of the Order, while a curious oval white loop is the residual remains of the rolled back face of the hood, as worn in medieval days.

All mantles are gathered at the neck by long cords called the Cordons, which are finished with heavy tassels roughly twelve inches long, formed over hollowed pieces of wood an inch and a half in diameter (they knock awkwardly on the wearer's knees when walking). These cordons are woven of the colour or colours of the Order, together with gold thread. They are, in fact, the only means of fastening the mantle.

The Queen wears the mantle which formerly belonged to her father.

Under the Garter robe The Queen usually wears evening dress. The collar of the Order, from which is suspended the George—a jewelled and enamelled ornament depicting St. George on a white horse with his lance in his hand, slaying the dragon—is worn over the shoulders outside the mantle.

The bonnet or hat—which is extremely large—is made of dark-blue, almost black velvet, considerably darker than the mantle. The bonnets of all three senior Orders of Knighthood are of the same colour, although different shapes. The bonnet should be worn with badge to the left, and with three ostrich feathers to that side, but ostrich feathers have a will of their own and assume their individual set.

At the ceremony of Investiture of Knights of the Garter, The Queen, attended by the Officers of the Order, proceeds between her mantled Knights to the dais on which her chair is placed. The new Knight to be invested is summoned to this dais where The Queen, assisted by his two sponsors, buckles the blue and gold embroidered garter on his left leg, puts on the riband and the star, and places over his shoulders the mantle and collar, after which the new Knight takes the oath.

Afterwards, the Knights walk in procession—a magnificent sight—attended by the pursuivants, heralds and kings-of-arms, the Military Knights of Windsor in uniform dating from the Napoleonic period, between ranks of dismounted Household Cavalry, for the Installation in the Chapel of St. George.

The corresponding Scottish Order is The Most Ancient and Most Noble Order of the Thistle. This Order is stated to have been founded by James II, King of the Scots (c. 1452), which may be so; certainly it was in existence in the reign of James III and prior to 1480. Its institution, development or period importance in this century was probably around 1470. It lapsed and was re-established under Royal Warrants and Statutes by King James VII of Scotland (King James II of England) in 1687 and by his daughter, Queen Anne, in 1703.

This is the smallest of all the British Orders of Knighthood, and exclusive of members of the Royal Family, has only sixteen Knights. Personal choice in the bestowal of the Thistle, like that of the Garter, has recently returned to the Sovereign. The Queen nominated the Duke of Edinburgh to this Order in the year of her accession, and has since nominated the Earl of Crawford and Balcarres, Lord Bilsland, Lord Mathers, Sir John Stirling of Fairburn, Lord Kinnaird of Inchture and Lord Rowallan to be Knights of the Order.

After the roof of the Abbey Church of Holyroodhouse fell in, there was no chapel of the Order until the present Thistle Chapel of St. Giles' Cathedral was built in 1911, so for many years no services of the Order took place. The Queen is the first Queen Regnant to take part in the Thistle ceremonies as Sovereign of the Order.

When the ceremony of Installation of new Knights of the Thistle takes place in the chapel of the Order of the Thistle in St. Giles' Cathedral, Edinburgh, the Scottish Pursuivants and Heralds lead a procession into the chapel, together with the Officers of the Order and the Knights of the Order, of whom the newly nominated Knights to be installed walk first. When the Knights Brethren have taken their places within the

187

chapel, the officers of the Order (attended by the Heralds and Pursuivants) proceed to the foot of the steps of the entrance to the west door of the cathedral. There the Queen and the Duke of Edinburgh are received by the Chancellor and the Dean accompanied by the King-of-Arms and Green Rod, who, preceded by the Heralds and Pursuivants, conduct the Queen and the Duke of Edinburgh into the chapel.

When the Sovereign and Knights have occupied their stalls and all others taken up their positions, the new Knight or Knights stand before The Queen.

The service of the Order then takes place. When it is held on a Sunday, the Queen and the Knights move in procession from the chapel into the Cathedral, where they occupy the royal pew during the morning service.

The mantle of the Order of the Thistle is dark or "thistle" green, with a hood of purplish-blue velvet lined with white silk. The badge, which consists of St. Andrew and Cross on an eight-pointed elongated Star, is rather smaller and made of enamel for the Sovereign, and embroidered for the Knights. The bonnet is in dark-blue velvet turned up in front, with a gold cord. Like all the bonnets of the Orders, it is no mean size—measuring one foot to fourteen inches in diameter across the brim. The bonnet badge is in gold wire embroidery for both Sovereign and Knights.

The only other Order whose ceremonies The Queen has attended as Sovereign is the Most Honourable Order of the Bath, which was founded by Henry IV in 1399. When she attended the Service of the Knights of the Order of the Bath in the King Henry VII Chapel in Westminster Abbey on November 15, 1956, while the Duke of Gloucester, as Great Master of the Order, installed eight Knights Grand Cross, she was believed to be the first Queen Regnant to take part in such a ceremony.

The History of the Order of the Garter etc. by Sir Nicholas Harris Nicolas, Chancellor of the Order of St. Michael and St. George, which was published in 1842, makes the following reference to the Order of the Bath:

The Sovereign's Habit

The Habit provided for Her Majesty the present Sovereign is a mantle and Surcoat (or Kirtle) in rich crimson satin with white ducape

silk lining, worn over a petticoat of very rich silver tissue, or white
and silver, or white and gold. The star on the mantle, which is silver,
chipped and enamelled, is that of a Military Knight Grand Cross. On
her head Her Majesty usually wears a tiara.

The Queen wore the cerise silk mantle of the Bath over a white
evening dress occasionally embroidered with pink roses, which
she also wore when she was painted in the mantle by Mr. Leonard
Boden for the Royal Military Academy Sandhurst. At the
ceremony the Queen wore the hard velvet hat of the Order,
which is turned back in the front with a gorgeous gold wire
ornament containing three buttons, technically known as a "hat
loop", and decorated with three white ostrich feathers. The hat
of the Bath, until King George IV commanded that it should
be of black velvet, was of white satin. It is now of the same very
dark-blue velvet as are the hats of the other senior Orders.

The Queen was depicted wearing the Sovereign's Badge of the
Order of the Bath in her effigy on her Coronation medal.

The Bath is not in The Queen's bestowal. It is a large Order,
having both military and civil Knights, limited to 82 G.C.B.s and
294 K.C.B.s. Its title is supposed to have originated in the vigil
and preparation of a Knight on the eve of his Installation.

The Queen has not yet worn the Robes of the Royal Victorian
Order, which consist of a dark-blue satin mantle, edged with
two-inch red satin, with a hood in the reverse colours of red satin
edged with blue, all lined with white, nor the Robes of the Order
of the British Empire.

The Queen approved a recommendation that St. Paul's Cathedral should be the church of the Order of the British Empire,
and that a chapel of the Order should be created at the east end
of the crypt, but she has not, in the first seven years of her reign,
taken part in any ceremony of that Order of Knighthood of which
she is Sovereign.

There remain a number of Orders, not of Knighthood.

The most intimate Order of all is the Family Order, of which
no record is kept. It is found in many monarchies, not only in
the British. It consists of a painted miniature portrait of the
Sovereign given by him or her to certain female relatives and
usually designed to be worn on the shoulder. In this country, the
history of the Family Order can be traced back continuously to the

reign of George I. Up to and including the reign of Queen Victoria, it consisted of a cameo set in brilliants, but since then has been a miniature painted on ivory, set in diamonds, and worn on the left shoulder on a piece of watered silk.

The Queen wears the Family Order of King George V on blue watered silk, and of King George VI on pink watered silk. The Elizabeth II Family Order consists of a painted miniature portrait of The Queen within a border of brilliants and baguette diamonds. It is surmounted by a diamond-set Tudor Crown and three-stone diamond loop, resting on a velvet cushion of red enamel. The whole is set in platinum. The miniature depicts The Queen wearing evening dress with the riband and Star of the Order of the Garter, wearing pearl drop earrings, which are family jewels, and the necklace of diamonds which was part of a wedding present from the Nizam of Hyderabad. The reverse of the Order has a ray design with the Royal Cypher and St. Edward's Crown in gold and enamel, and it is suspended from a two-inch-wide bow of chartreuse yellow watered silk. Although her gift of her Family Order is nowhere publicly recorded, the following wear it: the Queen Mother, Princess Margaret, the Princess Royal, the Duchess of Gloucester, the Duchess of Kent and Princess Alexandra.

The Queen has in her bestowal the Order of Merit. It has been in the Sovereign's bestowal since its creation by King Edward VII. It is a special distinction for men and women, but does not confer knighthood upon them. It is confined to a membership of twenty-four. The Queen has awarded the Order of Merit to Mr. Wilder Graves Penfield, Lord Hailey, Sir John Cockcroft, the late Viscount Waverley and Sir M. Burnet (Australia). She has made Dr. Albert Schweitzer an Honorary Member.

The Queen has also in her bestowal—and has used rather more generously than her predecessors—the Royal Victorian Chain which, like the Order of Merit, was founded in the Coronation year of King Edward VII, and which confers no precedence upon its holders. It is awarded as a pre-eminent mark of the Sovereign's esteem and affection towards such persons as the Sovereign specially desires to honour. The Queen first gave this chain to the late Earl of Clarendon, who was Lord Chamberlain in the last and the beginning of this reign; to her second cousin

Crown Prince Olav—now King Olav V—of Norway; to the President of Portugal; the late King Feisal of Iraq; and to King Fredrik of Denmark. King Fredrik wore this high British Decoration during The Queen's State Visit to Denmark, when it was generally wrongly identified as the insignia of the Order of the Garter, which King Fredrik also holds.

The Order of the Companions of Honour carries no title. It is limited to sixty-five and its recipients are recommended by the Prime Minister. The Distinguished Service Order is an Order having one class only, that of Companions, and is an award of the Armed Forces. The Imperial Service Order is an Order which may be granted in the Civil Services of the Crown.

Pre-eminent among Decorations and Medals is the Victoria Cross, the centenary of whose founding has fallen within Queen Elizabeth II's reign. The Victoria Cross takes precedence in the order of wear before all other Orders and Decorations, including even the Garter.

The Victoria Cross was founded by Queen Victoria. The Cross itself was designedly made of little value, and is always of bronze cast from one of the guns captured in the Crimea. The inscription "For Valour" was suggested by Queen Victoria, who pointed out that the original suggestion "For the Brave" might imply that only those were brave who had been awarded the Victoria Cross.

The Queen herself specially distinguished the Victoria Cross, the supreme acknowledgement of gallantry in the face of the enemy. The Review by Queen Victoria's great-great-grand-daughter of three hundred of the 1,344 men who had at that time been awarded the Victoria Cross took place in Hyde Park, where Queen Victoria had reviewed the original holders on June 26, 1857. The sight was unforgettable and moving. The Queen and the Duke of Edinburgh were conveyed in an open landau, drawn by four greys and escorted by Household Cavalry, to a royal dais guarded by Yeomen of the Guard and Ghurka orderly officers. There followed a march-past of the holders of the Victoria Cross, ended by a wheel-past in wheel-chairs of a few unable to march.

The Queen was obviously moved as she spoke to holders of the Victoria Cross saying:

". . . its plain ribbon with its simple cross rightly takes precedence over the symbols of all other honours bestowed upon the brave or upon the distinguished. . . . To-day I am proud to stand here, with men and women from all parts of the Commonwealth, to do honour to the successors of that first gallant band, to the 300 brave men who are present, and to those others who can be with us only in spirit, or in the memory of family and friends."

Because the Victoria Cross can be won only in the face of the enemy, King George VI instituted the George Cross for deeds of equal gallantry wherever they might be done. The George Cross has precedence in the order of wear immediately after the Victoria Cross and before the Garter. Queen Elizabeth II linked the George Medal more closely with its Founder, and directed that the box containing the medal should be inscribed "Instituted by King George VI" since it would not have been practicable to add these words to the medal itself without spoiling the design.

Decorations and Medals for Members of the Armed Forces are recommended to The Queen through the First Lord of the Admiralty, or the Secretary of State of the Service concerned. The Imperial Service Order, which is usually awarded only once a year, in the Birthday Honours, is approved by The Queen on the recommendation of the Prime Minister of the appropriate Minister of State of other Member Countries of the Commonwealth, the governments whereof shall desire to submit recommendations.

Recipients of the Police and Fire Service Medals, if from the United Kingdom, are recommended by the Home Office, or the authority concerned; if from overseas, by the Colonial Office. Recommendations for medals for Saving Life at Sea are made by the Minister of Transport.

In this reign civilians given gallantry awards generally receive the George Cross, the George Medal, awards in the Order of the British Empire including the British Empire Medal, or a Queen's Commendation for brave conduct. The Albert Medal and the Edward Medal are now awarded only posthumously.

The Queen has approved a number of new awards during her reign. Entirely new awards have to be instituted by Royal Warrant, which The Queen signs, but no Royal Warrant is required for new awards in the existing series of Badges of Honour. The following are The Queen's Awards in the first years of her reign:

June 1952

The Queen gave orders that on the insignia of certain Decorations and Medals, the effigy of King George VI should be changed to her effigy, the Royal Title changed and the new Royal Cypher displayed. St. Edward's Crown was to supersede the Tudor Crown, but these changes were to take place only when the redesigning of any particular award might become necessary for some other reason.

The Korea Medal, instituted by King George VI, would have borne the King's Head, crowned. As it would have been contrary to precedent to show a medal bearing the Queen's crowned head before the Coronation, the Queen commanded that her Classical Effigy (that is, the portrait without the Crown) should be used.

The same decision was made about the *Royal Observer Corps Medal*.

November 17, 1952

The Queen by Royal Warrant instituted the *Army Emergency Reserve Decoration*, granted for twelve years' continuous efficient commissioned service in the Army Emergency Reserve or in the former Supplementary Reserve of Officers.

January 26, 1953

The Queen by Royal Warrant instituted *The Queen Elizabeth II Long and Faithful Service Medal* granted to the servants of the Royal Household for twenty years' service. This is a silver medal surmounted by the royal cypher and crown, on the obverse the Royal effigy and on the reverse, "For Long and Faithful Service." The ribbon is an inch wide, dark blue with three vertical red stripes. When worn by a woman, it may be suspended from a similar ribbon fashioned into a bow. The name of the recipient is engraved on the rim.

March 1953

The Queen approved the wearing of the *Queen's Medals for Chiefs* in reduced size on the left breast. They had previously

193

only been worn suspended round the neck from a ribbon, and were no less than 2½ inches in height and nearly two inches in breadth.

The Queen also approved the wearing in reduced size on the left side in European dress of the Badges of Honour awarded in Colonies and Protectorates and previously worn only by a ribbon round the neck. These are of two types, worn in African and non-African territories respectively, with different reverse designs.

June 1953

Shortly after her Accession The Queen gave Commands that a *Coronation Medal* be designed, and this she subsequently instituted. The Medal showed the Queen crowned wearing an ermine cloak, the Collar of the Order of the Garter and the Badge of the Order of the Bath. The reverse bears the official Royal Cypher "E.R.II" surmounted by the Crown, and surrounded by the inscription "Queen Elizabeth II crowned 2nd June 1953".

The ribbon is cardinal red with two Garter blue stripes near the centre and a narrow white stripe at each side.

Thirty-seven of these medals were presented by Her Majesty to members of the Mount Everest Expedition and to Sherpa porters employed by the Expedition and by The Queen's special Command were inscribed on the edge, "Mount Everest Expedition".

June 12, 1953

The Queen by Royal Warrant instituted a new Medal designated *The Queen's Medal for Champion Shots of the Air Forces*. One Medal is granted annually in each of the Air Forces of the Commonwealth, the Government whereof may desire to take part in the award.

September 1, 1953

The Queen by Royal Warrant made special provision for a new ribbon and a new subsidiary title for the *Efficiency Medal* when awarded to a Warrant Officer, Non-Commissioned Officer or man of the Army Emergency Reserve. (The dark-blue ribbon bears three vertical yellow stripes near the centre.)

January 27, 1954

The Queen instituted the *Coast Life Saving Corps Long Service Medal*, which supersedes the medal for long service with the Rocket Life Saving Apparatus Companies or Brigades, instituted in 1911. Members of the Coast Life Saving Corps are awarded the medal for twenty years' satisfactory service as Life Saving Apparatus men or Watchers.

May 18, 1954

The Queen by Royal Warrants instituted four new Medals in place of the two King's Police and Fire Service medals, namely:

The Queen's Police Medal for Gallantry
The Queen's Fire Service Medal for Gallantry
The Queen's Police Medal for Distinguished Service
The Queen's Fire Service Medal for Distinguished Service

June 1, 1954

The Queen by Royal Warrant instituted the *Fire Brigade Long Service and Good Conduct Medal*, granted for twenty years' whole-time or part-time service with fire brigades at home.

February 1955

The Queen approved the award of the *African General Service Medal* for operational service in specified areas in Kenya after October 21, 1952, until November 17, 1956.

July 25, 1955

The Queen approved informally the institution of a *Queen's Medal for Champion Shots of the New Zealand Naval Forces*. Her Majesty subsequently instituted the award formally by Royal Warrant.

October 28, 1955

The Queen by Royal Warrant instituted the *Colonial Prison Service Medal*, granted for eighteen years' exemplary service in the rank of Assistant Superintendent or below.

March 21, 1956

The Queen by Royal Warrants instituted two separate awards, a *Colonial Police Long Service Medal* and a *Colonial Fire Brigades Long Service Medal* in place of the former Colonial Police and Fire Brigades Long Service Medal, granted to subordinate members of the Police Service and properly organised Fire Brigades who have completed eighteen years' whole-time service.

April 1956

The Queen approved the extension of the award of the *Queen's Medal for Chiefs* to Southern Rhodesia.

May 1956

The Queen approved the extension of the award of the *Naval General Service Medal for Bomb and Mine Clearance* in the Mediterranean as from January 1, 1955.

February 1957

The Queen approved the design for the new *Badge of Honour for the Federation of Rhodesia and Nyasaland*. (The design for several other Badges of Honour had from time to time also been approved.)

April 1, 1957

The Queen by Royal Warrant instituted the *Colonial Special Constabulary Medal*, granted for nine years' unpaid service or fifteen years' paid service.

June 1957

The Queen approved the award of the *Naval General Service Medal* and the *General Service Medal* (Army and Royal Air Force) for service in Cyprus since April 1, 1955, and in the operations in the Near East, October 31 to December 22, 1956.

Most Honours, including new peerages, are announced in two long Honours Lists issued at the New Year and at the time of the

Sovereign's official birthday in June. Each list contains round about 4,000 names.

Special lists are sometimes announced at a change of Government, or on such occasions as a Coronation or Jubilee, Commonwealth Tour or State Visit, or in connection with operations of war. Because The Queen has travelled so widely, there have been more of these short, extra lists this reign than recently in peacetime. Occasional individual Honours are announced between these times; perhaps a statesman retires on the grounds of ill health and is given a Peerage, a new Knight is appointed to the Order of the Garter to take the place of one who has died, or a gallantry award may be made to a Police Officer in Kenya or a soldier in Malaya.

The Queen can make whatever arrangements she wishes for Investitures. She may decide to knight a man at a private Audience —when the sword and the investiture stool will be left ready for her—and she invests many, although not all, of the recipients of the Royal Victorian Order in private. Occasionally, she receives at a special "Next of Kin Ceremony" the relatives of a man who has been awarded a gallantry award posthumously, or who has died since the gallantry award was made to him, speaking to them alone before the Investiture. She holds Investitures when in Commonwealth or Colonial countries, and has at least twice knighted a man on board ship, including Sir David Aitchison, Master of the Shaw Savill *Gothic* which was chartered to take The Queen on the World Tour, just before leaving the ship at Aden, thereby following the example of Queen Elizabeth I, who knighted Drake on board the *Golden Hind* at Deptford.

There are few more historic ceremonies than knighting, when the recipient drops to one knee, is touched lightly on both shoulders with the flat of the sword, at the same time being enjoined to "Rise Sir . . ." (These words are not used at a public Investiture.) Immediately afterwards, The Queen shakes hands.

In the early days of her reign The Queen used a naval sword when bestowing the accolade. It was an ordinary service pattern naval sword, belonging to King George VI, and which is now in Westminster Abbey. Since then she has used her father's Scots Guards sword, which happens to be a particularly light sword. It is taken along when The Queen travels and is likely to require it. No actual date can be traced for the construction of the present investiture stool (which is its correct name). It is, however, known that it has been used since the early days of the reign of King George V, and it is more than probable that it was in use before that.

A man cannot call himself "Sir . . ." when he is gazetted in the Honours List; he must wait until he has received the accolade. Ladies who are appointed Dames Grand Cross or Dames Commanders in Orders of Chivalry can, however, immediately assume the prefix "Dame" after gazetting. If the new knight is to be long absent from the country, he may apply for a Dispensation Warrant, which enables him to make use of the title until it is convenient for the accolade to be given. No Dispensation Warrants are given for Knights Bachelor. If he is perhaps in very bad health, or permanently resident abroad, the knighthood may occasionally be conferred on him by Letters Patent. Some exceptional cases have arisen in which Knighthood without accolade was conferred by Special Warrant. But in those cases the Knights will in no circumstances afterwards receive the accolade.

The Queen may by Royal Warrant depute her Governor-General or some other distinguished person to give the accolade to Knights Bachelor on her behalf, and to invest the members of the different classes of the Order of the British Empire. Investiture in the senior Orders of Chivalry is seldom delegated to Governors-General in this way.

The power to hold an Investiture is withheld from Counsellors of State, who can neither hold an Investiture nor sign a Royal Warrant authorising an Investiture.

No man can be knighted twice. (It is believed the only time a slip-up occurred was with Sir John Herschel, the astronomer in Queen Victoria's reign, who was knighted both on receiving the K.C.B. and later when receiving the G.C.B.)

As mentioned in the previous chapter, when a member of the Church of England is gazetted as receiving a Knighthood, he is invested with the insignia only, and does not receive the accolade. He does not call himself "Sir . . ." but uses the letters K.C.V.O., or whatever they may be, after his name. His wife remains plain "Mrs." This is because a clergyman in the Church of England may not receive a temporal distinction. There have, however, been many holders of hereditary titles among members of the Church of England. It is, in fact, impossible for the holder of a hereditary title to divest himself of it—to the embarrassment of some young peers, who feel that the road to the highest political honours is closed to them as members of the Upper House, as Prime Ministers are now almost inevitably men of the House of Commons.

The descent of a Peerage has, however, been altered by Act of Parliament (Dukedom of Atholl by Statute I, George I, cap. 34, and also again by VI, George II, cap. 16), and Scottish Peerages used frequently to have their lines of succession and descent altered by Crown Charters of confirmation or resettlement.

By far the greater number of presentations of awards are made in the series of Investitures which The Queen holds after every Honours List, and which number not less than twelve in each year. Investitures for the New Year Honours are held in February and March, for the June Birthday Honours in July and November, all at Buckingham Palace and usually at 11 o'clock on Tuesday mornings.

The Investitures take place in the Ballroom of the Palace, the largest of the State Rooms, added by James Pennethorne in Queen Victoria's reign to Nash's range of State Rooms. It is a large room with silk-covered benches round the sides and a musicians' gallery in which the string orchestra of one of the Household Regiments is playing. It has no visible windows, and is lit by six large pink lustre chandeliers. The parquet floor is almost completely covered by rows of gilt chairs, for, since King George V introduced the custom during the First World War, each recipient is permitted to bring two relatives or friends.

About two hundred and ten persons are commanded to attend each Investiture, which allowing for those unavoidably unable to be present, means that on each occasion The Queen invests about two hundred men and women, a yearly total for the Buckingham Palace Investiture alone of 2,400 British subjects who annually receive their Honours from the hands of their Queen. An Investiture is considered by The Queen's Household to be one of the most tiring of her duties. It lasts for upwards of an hour and a quarter, and demands unceasing concentration, and a grave dignity. One woman whose husband was invested and to whom Her Majesty spoke expressed disappointment afterwards that The Queen did not come over afterwards and talk to the relatives who were watching the ceremony, but she had not realised that she was watching a ceremony and not an informal gathering in The Queen's home. Another spoke to me of the straightened back and head held high of a badly crippled man with whom The Queen had spoken. My own impression was of the vulnerability, the dignity and the sympathy of the young, bare-headed woman who looked slight and small under the glowing crimson drapery or *Shamiana* from the Durbar of 1911, and of the infinite variety of bearing, feature and expression of those who have served her and her Commonwealth well.

The Queen has had from childhood, and particularly from a girlhood passed in the shadow of war and death among her relatives and in her circle, a great admiration for bravery, physical and moral. An Investiture is no idle ceremony for her, but her thanks to those who deserve well of their country.

The Queen distributes many awards, but as one would expect from her innate modesty, she is extremely sparing in those which she permits herself to wear. The insignia on the tunic of Her Majesty Queen Elizabeth II, on the occasion in the year when she wears uniform, The Queen's Birthday Parade, are as follows:

The Imperial Order of the Crown of India
Defence Medal
War Medal 1939/45
Jubilee Medal of King George V
Coronation Medal of King George VI
The Canadian Forces Decoration (Silver)

with which she wears the riband and Star of the Order of the Garter.

The most important title which The Queen can confer is that of Prince of Wales upon her eldest son and Heir Apparent. This, unlike the titles of Duke of Cornwall, Duke of Rothesay, Earl of Carrick, Baron Renfrew, Lord of the Isles and Great Steward of Scotland, which are his by right as Heir Apparent, is in her bestowal. The Queen decided to confer the title upon Prince Charles in Wales, at the concluding ceremony of the sixth

Commonwealth and Empire Games at Cardiff on July 26, 1958. She had intended to do this in person, but she was suffering from a severe attack of sinusitis and confined to Buckingham Palace. Nevertheless she found a way. The message was recorded on a tape-recorder at Buckingham Palace and taken to Cardiff. It was a splendidly-kept secret, and no one suspected what was about to happen when the Duke of Edinburgh introduced a message from The Queen in which she would close the meeting.

The message began:

"By a cruel stroke of fate I have been prevented from visiting North and South Wales and seeing something of the British Empire and Commonwealth Games. I regret particularly not being with you in Cardiff to-day for the closing ceremonies of this great meeting of Commonwealth athletes.

"I am glad to say that I have been able to watch many of the competitions on television. . . ."

(As, indeed, The Queen was even then watching and listening on television, waiting, no doubt with suspense and rising excitement, for what the next few minutes would bring.)

". . . I want to take this opportunity of speaking to all Welsh people, not only in this arena, but wherever they may be.

"The British Empire and Commonwealth Games in the capital, together with all the activities of the Festival of Wales, have made this a memorable year for the Principality.

"I have, therefore, decided to mark it further by an act which will, I hope, give as much pleasure to all Welshmen as it does to me.

"I intend to create my son Charles, Prince of Wales today. . . ."

The Queen's words were drowned in a roar of cheering. Hats flew in the air. Excited Welshmen hugged each other and danced on the terraces. Even for those at their television sets at home, whether they were Welsh or not, it was a moment of great emotion. Fortunately the engineers stopped the tape. Even minutes later, when The Queen's voice began to speak again, thousands of those present could not hear her voice for the sustained cheering.

"When he is grown up I will present him to you at Caernarvon."

CHAPTER EIGHT

The Queen has Approved . . .

". . . all jurisdiction of the courts is either directly or immediately derived from the Crown."   Blackstone's *Commentaries*

"A soldier serves his Queen, not the Government."
A Regular Army Officer

WHEREVER there is important work being done in the
Commonwealth, there will be found a link—direct or
tenuous—with the Sovereign. A very considerable
number of these fields of activity really deserve lengthy treatment,
which there is not always the space to give them. In this chapter
will be grouped the law, the armed forces, The Queen's special
association with youth, her encouragement of the arts and
sciences, and many besides. If this seems overcrowded, then the
excuse must be—so is the life of The Queen!

The Queen is traditionally the Fount of Justice. In early
years Justice was dispensed by the King's Court, where the King
discussed what to do in important matters with the great men of
the land (this eventually became Parliament); rewarded bravery
and good service (now done at investitures); received notables
(Audiences, garden parties and so on). With the growth and
complication of the Kingdom, these parts of the work of the
King's Courts split off and set up as separate entities. Yet each is
still linked to the Sovereign.

So the Courts of Justice share with the Courts at which
débutantes were presented the same name and the same derivation.
Queen's Counsel, appointed by Letters Patent through the Lord
Chancellor, are another link with the royal derivation.

Through the centuries both Parliament and the Courts of
Justice have established their independence. The Queen to-day

has little direct link with the administration of the law. But she is always its titular head. All Justice is dispensed in The Queen's name.

One annual link does remain. This is the pricking of the Sheriff's Roll each year in March. The Roll is pricked by The Queen in Council. It is presented to The Queen in the shape of a long vellum roll, on a wooden roller, tied with green ribbons. It is unrolled before her by the Clerk of the Council. On it are written in black ink, in a graceful copperplate, the names of those who have been nominated for the office of Sheriff. The man to be selected as Sheriff for each county is usually the top name of the three who have been nominated to the Roll by Great Officers at the Nomination during the previous November. The Queen takes up a Bodkin and pierces the vellum roll through the name of the Sheriff designate. This Bodkin has a brass handle, like that of a small doorknob, on which is engraved the Privy Council Arms. The steel spike is some three inches long, and in all it is a formidable weapon, unlike the usual sewing implement from which it is derived. Tradition has it that Queen Elizabeth I was sitting sewing in the garden when the annual Sheriffs' Roll was brought to her for marking. Having no pen with her, she pricked it with her bodkin. The legend gains likelihood because earlier Rolls are marked with a small black dot, and all subsequent Rolls are marked by piercing.

The Roll for the Duchy of Lancaster is never pricked in Privy Council, but always at a private Audience given afterwards by The Queen to the Chancellor of the Duchy of Lancaster.

The Queen makes a number of high judicial appointments on the recommendation of the Prime Minister. This is the way in which the Lords of Appeal in Ordinary, the Lord Chief Justice of England, the Master of the Rolls, the President of the Probate, Divorce and Admiralty Division and the Lords Justices of Appeal are appointed. The Queen appoints the rest of the judiciary in England and Wales on the recommendation of the Lord Chancellor.

In Scotland there are only two higher legal appointments, which are made on the Prime Minister's recommendation, namely, those of Lord Justice General (who is also Lord President of the Court of Session) and of Lord Justice Clerk. The rest of the judiciary in Scotland is appointed on the recommendation of the Secretary of State for Scotland.

The Queen approves all high legal appointments in the Colonies, such as Chief Justices, Appeal Judges and Puisne Judges, on the advice of the Prime Minister, in consultation with the Lord Chancellor. She approves the appointment of the Attorney-General and Solicitor-General of the County Palatine of Durham.

In Scotland, The Queen has approved, on the recommendation of the Secretary of State for Scotland, the appointment of a Scottish Judge (Senator of Her Majesty's College of Justice in Scotland). She has approved the appointment of Sheriffs and Sheriff-Substitutes (who bear a greater share of legal responsibility in Scotland than they now do in England). On the recommendation of her Secretary of State for Scotland, to whom names were submitted by the Lord Justice General, she has approved the appointment of Queen's Counsel in Scotland.

In the Isle of Man too, The Queen has approved the appointment of Second Deemster and Attorney-General.

(Up till the time of King James II, the Sovereign could set aside the law in certain cases. But in the Bill of Rights of 1689 it was set out:

That the pretending power of suspending the laws or the execution of laws without the consent of Parliament is illegal.)

The Prerogative of Mercy is now exercised by the Sovereign on the advice of her Ministers. Queen Victoria possibly felt that she could exercise the Prerogative without the advice of her Ministers. There is an interesting little anecdote in Lady Frederick Cavendish's diary:

OSBORNE. Saturday, January 16th, 1864: [Lady Frederick is in waiting as a Maid of Honour]. Cold wind, but fine. At Parkhurst, the poor women convicts found out it was the Queen and numbers fell on their knees begging for mercy and pardon, so as quite to upset those who heard them, and the Queen said she was sure, if one had managed to fall down at her feet, she must have forgiven her!

Mr. Herbert Morrison in his book, *Government and Parliament*, published in 1954, said, however, with regard to modern use of the Prerogative of Mercy:

It is perfectly legitimate for the Sovereign to discuss any matter with the Minister or Ministers concerned, and naturally this is particularly so where the Royal Prerogative is involved, as, for example, in the mitigation of sentences of the Law Courts. George VI twice discussed particular death sentences with me when I was Home Secretary. He expressed his views ably and reasonably, and naturally I gave them every consideration. However, I did not feel able to accept His Majesty's view in either case, and when I respectfully told him so, he accepted my decision with every good grace.

In the rare instances when Justice has miscarried, the Court's decision is set aside by means of a Free Pardon.

When the Home Secretary has decided that there are grounds for exercising the Royal Prerogative of Mercy either to set aside the conviction of a court by a Free Pardon or to commute or reduce the sentence imposed for an offence, the act of clemency is, by ancient practice, signified by the Royal Sign Manual—that is, by The Queen's personal signature on a Royal Warrant.

This document, reciting that: "We in consideration of some circumstances humbly represented to Us are graciously pleased to extend our Grace and Mercy" is signed by The Queen at the top and afterwards at the bottom by the Home Secretary, as the Minister who advised her.

People often ask why a "Pardon" should be granted when no offence has been committed. The reason for this is that the word "Pardon" is here used in a special sense: it does not mean forgiveness of the offence—which an innocent person does not need —but the removal (or "pardoning") of the conviction and all its consequences.

Persons who have been found guilty of committing an offence, and who are found to be insane, are confined "during The Queen's pleasure", a form of wording which is sometimes misunderstood. This is the last thing in the world to give The Queen "pleasure" in the ordinary, everyday sense of the word to-day, but the term is used in what was once a common but now is only a legal sense, meaning "discretion". Persons are therefore confined "during The Queen's discretion".

In fact it is the Home Secretary who decides where and for how long such persons are detained.

The Queen has a connection with the officers who implement

the Law. She approves, on the recommendation of the Home Secretary, the Chief of the Metropolitan Police and his immediate subordinates.

The Queen, again on the recommendation of the Home Secretary, approves the appointments of Prison Commissioners.

All the orderly processes of law derive from and must be approved by The Queen. But there are occasions, in these days chiefly of external origin, when the power of the law must be backed by force. The Queen's link with the Navy, the Army and the Air Force is more direct and personal than that with the law, which is impartial and depends upon the dignity, but not upon the sentiment, which it gains from its association with the Crown.

"A soldier serves his Queen, not the Government," a regular officer said to me. This is a very real feeling of loyalty centred upon the Sovereign and not upon the political party in power. One of the greatest gains of a constitutional monarch at the head of government is that there is no difficulty in separating patriotism from party. This loyalty to the Sovereign is an encouraged part of military discipline.

If you look up the Royal Navy in a book of reference, you will find The Queen at the head of the list. She has not, however, taken any rank connected with the Senior Service, although she is Master of the Merchant Navy and Fishing Fleets in succession to her father. The Queen is the source from which the Lord High Admiral's powers are derived, and when she is afloat she flies the crimson flag with a yellow anchor, now known as the Admiralty flag, which is the symbol of the authority of the Lord High Admiral.

The routine work of the Royal Navy comes before her, and means more than routine to the wife of a Naval officer, who enjoyed perhaps her only period as almost an ordinary citizen when she was the wife of the First Lieutenant of the destroyer H.M.S. *Chequers* and the Commanding Officer of the frigate H.M.S. *Magpie*, based at Malta. The Queen often wears her Naval Crown brooch on private as well as public occasions.

She approves many of the senior Royal Naval appointments, such as the Commanders-in-Chief and the Lords Commissioners of the Admiralty. She has approved new titles for ratings in the Engineering and Electrical branches of the Royal Navy. She appoints Naval aides-de-camp (as she does officers from the other services). They are Captains R.N. (or corresponding rank in the other services) and serve as aides-de-camp for a period of six months, or until they are promoted or retired, and their duties consist mainly of attending The Queen at Naval ceremonies, and acting as Ushers at garden parties and on similar occasions.

The Queen has had a great deal to do with all the Armed Forces, and the Navy, in which both her father and her husband saw active service, cannot fail to be of very real interest to her.

Among the greatest of the naval occasions of her reign with which she has been personally connected was the Coronation Review at Spithead; dinner with the Board of Admiralty at Greenwich on the 150th anniversary of the Battle of Trafalgar (this was the occasion on which she referred to "an ocean of Admirals"); the Jubilee Review of the Royal Naval Volunteer Reserve on a pouring wet afternoon on Horseguards Parade in June 1954; the inspection of the Home Fleet off Invergordon in May 1957, when Sea Hawks and Wyverns from the *Ark Royal* formed her cipher "E II R" in the fly-past; and unveiling the Merchant Navy War Memorial on Tower Hill in November 1955.

The Queen has shown marked interest in the Fleet Air Arm. She presented a Queen's Colour for the first time to the Fleet Air Arm at Lee-on-Solent in July 1956, "in recognition of the size and status of the Fleet Air Arm". On the occasion of the fly-past of aircraft from the *Ark Royal* at Invergordon, she sent them a message which said: "I was particularly interested to witness the air operations from the *Ark Royal* this morning, which were carried out with so much skill and dash", ending it traditionally "Splice the main-brace."

The Queen has associated herself actively with the Army. After all, she served in the A.T.S., and the almost passionate partisanship which, as a young girl, she held for "her" Regiment, the Grenadier Guards, is well known among her acquaintances of those days.

She is the Head of the Army, just as she is the Head of the Royal Navy. She is also:

Captain-General of the Royal Regiment of Artillery
Captain-General of the Honourable Artillery Company

Colonel-in-Chief of
  The Life Guards
  Royal Horse Guards (The Blues)
  The Royal Scots Greys (2nd Dragoons)
  16th/5th The Queen's Royal Lancers
  Royal Tank Regiment
  Corps of Royal Engineers
  Grenadier Guards
  Coldstream Guards
  Scots Guards
  Irish Guards
  Welsh Guards
  Royal Welch Fusiliers
  Loyal Regiment (North Lancashire)
  The Second Green Jackets (The King's Royal Rifle Corps)
  The Argyll and Sutherland Highlanders (Princess Louise's)
  Royal Malta Artillery
  Royal Army Ordnance Corps
  The Duke of Lancaster's Own Yeomanry (T.A.)
Honorary Colonel of
  The Queen's Own Warwickshire and Worcestershire
    Yeomanry (assumed 1957)
Captain-General of
  Combined Cadet Force (British Regiment and Corps)
  Royal Canadian Artillery
Colonel-in-Chief of
  Regiment of Canadian Guards
  The Corps of Royal Canadian Engineers
  King's Own Calgary Regiment
  Royal 22e Régiment
  Governor-General's Foot Guards
  Canadian Grenadier Guards
  Royal New Brunswick Regiment of Canada
  Le Régiment de la Chaudière
  48th Highlanders of Canada
  The Argyll and Sutherland Highlanders of Canada (Princess
    Louise's)
  Royal Australian Artillery
  Royal Australian Engineers

Royal Australian Infantry Corps
The Royal Australian Army Ordnance Corps
Royal Australian Army Nursing Corps
Ghana Regiment of Infantry
Captain-General of the
Royal New Zealand Artillery
Royal New Zealand Armoured Corps
Colonel-in-Chief of the
Royal New Zealand Engineers
Auckland Regiment (Countess of Ranfurly's Own)
Wellington Regiment (City of Wellington's Own)
Royal Natal Carabiniers
Imperial Light Horse
Royal Durban Light Infantry
Railways and Harbours Brigade
The Kaffrarian Rifles
Royal Rhodesia Regiment
Royal West African Frontier Force
King's African Rifles
Northern Rhodesia Regiment

The appointment of a Colonel-in-Chief, or when a unit of the Territorial Army, a Royal Honorary Colonel, is entirely within The Queen's Prerogative. Very occasionally, in exceptional circumstances, the Secretary of State for War considers it his duty to advise the Sovereign. But the usual procedure is that The Queen expresses the wish to make one or a number of appointments, and it is then customary for the Secretary of State to recommend Regiments or Corps for the honour.

The Queen's own service in the A.T.S. has already been mentioned. This was a formative experience of far more importance than its comparatively short duration. Queen Elizabeth II is not the first Queen to feel herself in particular sympathy with her troops. The bond of personal loyalty between a Sovereign Queen and her serving forces is a particular strength of a Queen, *vide* Queen Elizabeth I and Queen Victoria. But Queen Elizabeth II is the first to have served in the Forces, the first to take part in uniform in a regular parade.

This is, of course, The Queen's Birthday Parade, which takes place each year on the "Official Birthday", not The Queen's actual birthday. Up to 1958 this was usually held on the second Thursday in June, but will in future be held on a Saturday.

It was at the wish of her father that Princess Elizabeth first rode in the Birthday Parade in 1947, not as Heiress Presumptive, but as Colonel of the Grenadier Guards. This first Trooping after the war was done in khaki. Princess Elizabeth wore a blue habit, with medal ribbons and military type hat. She rode a big bay horse called Tommy, belonging to the Duchess of Beaufort. The Princess rode side-saddle, which, as she generally rides astride, involved special instruction and practice for some weeks before. In 1948 Princess Elizabeth did not ride. In 1949 she rode again wearing a blue uniform, but this time riding Winston, the chestnut police horse which became so well known, beside her father's carriage, as his health did not enable him to ride. Princess Elizabeth watched in 1950, and rode alone in 1951, wearing scarlet for the first time, when she deputised for her father who was ill.

In 1952 she was Queen, and for the first time a Sovereign Queen took part in her Birthday Parade. It was a brilliant occasion, the more so because it took place in a period of mourning. She has since ridden in all but one year between her accession and to-day. Until 1956 she rode Winston, and since then she has ridden another chestnut, Imperial, also a police horse but with a lot more white on his legs.

The Queen wears the tunic of the Regiment of Guards whose Colour is being trooped that year, with a dark-blue habit skirt, and black tricorne hat. The buttons are grouped according to the seniority of the Regiment, from single-spacings for the senior Grenadiers to groups of five for the junior Welsh Guards.

The only previous occasions on which it is known that a Sovereign Queen has worn uniform is once or twice during the reign of Queen Victoria.

The troops which take part in the Birthday Parade are in a special relationship to The Queen. They are her Household Brigade, which is formed of the Household Cavalry consisting of the Life Guards and the Royal Horse Guards, and the five Regiments of Foot Guards. These troops form the Sovereign's personal troops. They stand guard over the Royal Palaces. They form the Sovereign's escort on State occasions. In normal times they are not sent overseas except in time of war, but have been serving overseas since the Second World War, although a Battalion of Guards was stationed at Gibraltar and Egypt for many years before the Second World War. The First Company of the First Battalion of the Grenadier Guards is The Queen's Company, consisting of specially picked men of six feet and over whose given duty it is to provide the Sovereign's pallbearers.

The Queen's orders are passed through the Lord Chamberlain, in the case of the Household Cavalry, to a high officer, Gold Stick, or in his absence Silver Stick in Waiting, who used in Restoration days to be responsible for the Sovereign's safety, and to carry a Stick to show his authority. In the case of the Foot Guards, the Lord Chamberlain communicates with the Field Officer in Brigade Waiting.

In Canada, a Regiment of Canadian Guards was formed in Coronation year. The Queen assumed the rank of their Colonel-in-Chief, and herself suggested that a replica of the cap-badge, a ten-pointed star for the ten provinces of Canada, should be used in place of the stars to show an officer's rank.

The Queen's very real interest in the Army lightens the considerable amount of paper work, much of it of a routine character, with which she has to deal. The routine appointments which receive her approval are all those which appear in the *London Gazette* (Military Supplement)—a formidable number. These include Appointments to Commissions; Substantive Promotions; all appointments in the ranks of Field Marshal, General, Lieutenant-General and Major-General; appointments of Colonels and Colonels Commandant of Regiments and Corps; appointments of Honorary Colonels of the Territorial Army and Army Emergency Reserve units; and the appointments of Governor and Lieutenant-Governor of the Royal Hospital, Chelsea; the Constable, the Lieutenant, the Major and Resident Governor of the Tower of London; and Aides-de-Camp to The Queen.

The Queen also approves all Honours and Awards; the Territorial Army Efficiency Decoration; the Army Emergency Reserve Decoration; Retirements; Resignations and Transfers between Regiments and Corps.

In addition there are numbers of special decisions and approvals of which space does not permit a full record. It has been her sad duty to cut down the Army, in accordance with the Defence White Paper announcing a reduction from 373,000 in 1957 to about 165,000 in 1962. She called Mr. Hare, Secretary of State for War and Field Marshal Sir Gerald Templer, C.I.G.S., to Buckingham Palace for an Audience on July 8, 1957, and while realising the necessity for the change, The Queen keenly felt the blow to many of her soldiers, who would be called upon to serve under another cap badge.

In the amalgamation of the units, she had many hard decisions to make with regard to re-apportioning the appointments of Colonel-in-Chief, a level at which redundancy was also to be equally found. In the case of two Regiments amalgamating, which had Royal Colonels-in-Chief—The Buffs of which King Fredrik IX was Colonel-in-Chief, and the Royal West Kents whose Colonel-in-Chief was the Duchess of Kent—The Queen solved the problem by appointing King Fredrik Colonel-in-Chief of the new Kent Regiment, and the Duchess of Kent Colonel of the new Regiment. This is the first time for many years that a member of the Royal Family has been appointed Colonel of a line regiment. The Queen left significantly vacant a new appointment of Colonel-in-Chief to the regiment formed by the amalgamation of The Somerset Light Infantry and The Duke of Cornwall's Light Infantry.

The Queen has granted all the 1939/45 battle honours which have been awarded, with one exception. In 1950 her father, the late King, presented Colours to the Parachute Regiment. He then granted temporarily, since they had no battle honours on their Colours, the honour "2nd World War 1939/45" pending the award of their full honours. The temporary honour has now been removed from their Colours, and has been replaced by their proper honours.

The Queen's personal share of duties with the Army includes the inspection of guards of honour, taking the Salute at special parades, and the Presentation of Colours and Guidons. On each of these occasions The Queen has to play her part in association and comparison with highly-trained troops. It is not the easiest of duties to present new Colours before a Regiment on parade in ordinary day clothes, with a high wind blowing. Yet The Queen has always accomplished her part at all military ceremonies with great dignity and fine sense of occasion.

The Princess Elizabeth sent her bridal bouquet to be laid on the tomb of the Unknown Warrior. The Queen—who quoted a letter from a private soldier to his Colonel, after he had been posted to another Regiment:

They have taken my cap away and with it the great love of my life. The traditions of my county regiment are in my blood, and to be known as a Forester was an estate of which I was deeply proud.

—is a woman who takes great pride in her soldiers. (I had just written that, when, reading further in the speech at the Army Council dinner at the Royal Hospital in Chelsea on November 27, 1956, from which the above was quoted, I found The Queen had used almost the same words, "I take great pride in my Army.")

The Royal Air Force, which was in 1918 deliberately moulded in the same personal relationship to the Sovereign as the older services, is by no means "behind the door" in The Queen's interest and affections. The Queen's father, her uncles and her husband are or were pilots. The Battle of Britain is one of the first outside events which seared itself into her consciousness. It has been said elsewhere but I can truly repeat that The Queen, who herself can know and conquer fear, has a deep respect for courage, wherever it is found whether in the face of physical danger or moral criticism. The Queen never takes courage for granted.

Her personal commands in the Royal Air Force, in addition to being the Head, as she is of the other two services, are:

Air Commodore-in-Chief of the
    Royal Australian Air Force
    R.A.F. Regiment
    Royal Observer Corps
    Royal Canadian Air Force Auxiliary
    Australian Citizen Air Force

She takes the same part with regard to the R.A.F. as she does to the other Services, approving senior appointments, reading reports, inspecting guards of honour and visiting airfields. She has seen the latest guided missiles and secret bombs.

The Queen has been present at some most interesting R.A.F. occasions during her reign. She has presented two Standards to the R.A.F. On July 23, 1956, at Marham, she presented the Squadron Standard to No. 107 Squadron, which is equipped with Vickers Valiant aircraft, and on June 4, 1957, she presented a similar Standard to No. 43 (Fighter) Squadron, during her visit to the R.A.F. at Leuchars in Fife.

The latter was the occasion on which she flew in the new Comet, boarding an R.A.F. Comet at Marham in Norfolk and flying to Leuchars, returning direct to London Airport in the evening.

At the Coronation Review of the R.A.F., which was held on July 15, 1953, she inspected 300 aircraft and 3,000 officers and men on the airfield, and watched a fly-past of 643 aircraft, both jet and pistoned. There is always a fly-past on the occasion of her Birthday Parade in June each year.

The Queen, with nearly all members of the Royal Family, attended the Dinner given by the Air Council at Fighter Command Headquarters, Stanmore, to mark the fortieth anniversary of the Royal Air Force on April 1, 1948.

The Queen, said then, in her televised Speech which millions will remember:

"Forty years ago to-day my grandfather created the Third Fighting Service of the Crown—the Royal Air Force, to which I and my family are here to do honour to-night . . . around this table to-night are men who . . . have seen history made in those forty years."

Speaking of the Battle of Britain, The Queen went on, "I and the rest of my generation will always remember with pride that we lived through those weeks of courage which have become an epic . . . when we looked up to see the summer sky criss-crossed with the vapour trails of fighter aircraft."

Yet even with regard to the R.A.F., The Queen has had to participate in disbandment. The Queen gave a farewell party at Buckingham Palace in 1957, at which she received more than eighty senior officers of the Royal Auxiliary Air Force and the Air Divisions of the Royal Naval Volunteer Reserve, to mark their disbandment. Each officer present received a signed copy of a message from The Queen, recalling their proud history. The Queen wrote:

It is a sad day when it is necessary to tell so many that it is no longer possible to use their services on the duties they have assumed so willingly. I wish them to know that they can look back with pride and satisfaction to service well done.

The Queen has always carried out her father's wishes as far as she possibly could, and she endorsed King George VI's decision, made shortly before his death, to present a new Sovereign's Colour to the R.A.F. Regiment, and this she presented personally at Buckingham Palace in March 1953.

The Queen has always taken a natural interest in the wives of serving men. As the wife of a serving Naval Officer in Malta she came into personal contact with the individual problems of a small group of wives—the difficulties of constantly changing housing; schooling; transport; and the possible return to civilian life of a husband highly trained in a skill no longer particularly appropriate. This has helped her to appreciate the whole problem of Service wives. In The Queen, the woman is never submerged in the official figure. For instance, when she was being shown over R.A.F. married quarters at Leuchars, Fife, she spotted, just as she left the sitting-room to see the bedrooms, that everyone grown-up was following after her, and the two-year-old toddler would be left alone. "Do you think that's safe?" she asked. A senior R.A.F. officer detached himself to act as nursemaid.

The Queen sometimes takes an interest in an unexpected side of things. For instance, in 1953 she contributed to a fund to help eighteen-year-old Leading Aircraftsman James Sexton of the R.A.F. to fly home from the Middle East to represent Britain in the world solo piano-accordion championship in Holland that September. She sent a message saying that she well remembered hearing the band in which this young man played when she was in Nairobi.

Certain critics have attacked The Queen's association—or alleged *lack* of association—with the Arts. This sometimes boils down to their own particular and unappreciated aspects of the Arts, which would derive much benefit from royal recognition. There are two distinct aspects of this: The Queen's own personal enjoyment of the Arts, and the benefits she can confer by her patronage. To take The Queen's personal tastes first, she plays the piano and derives great pleasure from it, although she has little enough time to spare for it now. To listen to music in public is not, for her, a complete relaxation as it is for many people, because she knows that she is always being stared at, and even when the lights are down, her faintly-seen face, her silhouette, are being studied.

The Queen, like her mother, is very fond of dancing, and is an excellent Scottish country dancer. There are many impromptu dances held at Windsor, Sandringham or Balmoral.

The Queen enjoys paintings far more than is generally realised. Here again, as with people, the more she knows and looks at a painting, the more she appreciates it. Unlike the rest of us, she can see the works of Rembrandt and Leonardo da Vinci without leaving her home, and she can and does spend considerable time with her paintings.

With regard to the theatre, The Queen enjoys good acting in a good play without being particularly fond of costume plays. She goes quite frequently to the theatre privately—not so much as her sister, Princess Margaret, but then The Queen does not have as much time. An actress tells me that The Queen is always in her place before the time for the curtain to rise and is always appreciative and understanding in her comments afterwards.

Although not a balletomane, The Queen certainly enjoys ballet, and she enjoys fine singing, without having the same encyclopaedic knowledge as her cousin, the Earl of Harewood, whose life interest it is. The Queen enjoys those arts she can appreciate in her own home. Like King George V, King George VI and Sir Winston Churchill, an hour-long film at the end of a tiring day is a relaxation and a fresh interest. She enjoys, as has already been said, television when it shows her, without the interest of the public being directed upon her, the lives of other people. Plays, which require uninterrupted application for a given period, are sometimes too demanding of her most precious commodity—time.

Now to her public recognition of the Arts, and how she gives it. The Queen is Patron, Protector and Supporter of the Royal Academy of Arts, which was founded by King George III and started life in the then royal Palace of Somerset House, London. She invests the President with his Chain and Medal of Office at a private audience, in the presence only of the Secretary of the Royal Academy, who has previously handed over the Insignia to The Queen, as well as a document, which she signs, confirming the President's election. The Queen assents to any changes in the Royal Academy laws before they can come into force. No announcement of a newly-elected President is made to the Press, nor are the Academicians who have made the election allowed to leave the meeting, until the Secretary of the Royal Academy has obtained The Queen's consent to the election. This he does by telephone through the Keeper of the Privy Purse, whose office is the traditional link between the Royal Academy and the Crown. No Royal portraits are included in the Summer Exhibition without the consent of The Queen. The Queen has made many visits to the Royal Academy, perhaps especially to see the loan exhibitions. Many other Societies of Art have a connection, but a more distant one, with the Sovereign. For instance, The Royal Society of British Artists was permitted the prefix "Royal" in 1886, and The Queen has visited one of its Exhibitions, as she has so many exhibitions throughout the country. An official of the Royal Household remarked to me dryly, in connection with the criticism that The Queen has too little to do with Art, that he had abstracted a long list of The Queen's visits to various exhibitions of art and other cultural pursuits for a few months only, and it had covered more than a page.

The Queen lends pictures, which are of great value and subject to damage, with considerable generosity. Paintings and objects of art from the royal collections have been seen in this reign in Canada and Belgium, in the Antique Dealers Fair and Holland Park. Besides this, many great works of art and curiosities of every kind are on permanent loan to Museums throughout the country.

Perhaps most important of all, The Queen has generously given her time to the living artists of to-day, sitting indefatigably, conscientiously and punctually to a formidable series of artists. She has bought several paintings of herself to give to bodies close to her, such as the town of Windsor, to whom she presented a portrait by Dennis Fildes.

Although The Queen's Household in England has no corresponding rank, The Queen has in her Scottish Household both a Painter and Limner (Stanley Cursiter, C.B.E., R.S.A.), and a Sculptor (Sir William Reid Dick, K.C.V.O., R.A.). There are, however, quite a number of Household Appointments in England connected with the Arts, the Master of The Queen's Music—the final, archaic "k" was quietly dropped in this reign— Sir Arthur Bliss, Mus.D., LL.D.; the Librarian, Mr. R. C. Mackworth-Young, who in 1958 succeeded Sir Owen Morshead, now Librarian Emeritus; the Surveyor of The Queen's Pictures, Professor Sir Anthony Blunt, K.C.V.O.; the Surveyor of The Queen's Works of Art, Sir James Gow Mann, K.C.V.O., F.S.A.; the Keeper of the Prints and Drawings, Miss A. Scott-Elliot, M.V.O., and others.

Probably nothing The Queen has done in the world of music is more important than her gift to the Trustees of the British Museum of the Royal Music Library, which has been on loan to the Museum since 1911. She presented the Music Library to mark the bi-centenary of the gift of the Old Royal Library by King George II to the British Museum. In money alone, the Music Library is worth several hundreds of thousands of pounds, but it is really priceless. The library contains some 7,000 pieces of music, including a contemporary copy of a *motet* composed by King Henry VIII, and ninety-seven volumes of autograph works by Handel, constituting the most extensive collection anywhere of works in the hand of a major composer.

Incidentally, the Sovereign appoints a representative as Trustee, and also the Director of the British Museum, although The Queen has not had to make such appointments in her reign so far.

The Queen approved a Royal Charter for the Covent Garden Ballet, the Sadler's Wells Ballet Theatre and Sadler's Wells Ballet School, so that it should be known as the Royal Ballet. She attended a special centenary gala performance of opera and ballet at the Royal Covent Garden Opera House. She attended too the 25th gala performance of the Sadler's Wells Ballet. She has been present at many memorable occasions at Covent Garden, including the Gala Performance which is staged there on the occasion of each State Visit. There she has heard Callas sing, has watched Ulanova, Fonteyn and Shearer dance. "You have given a most beautiful performance I shall always remember," The Queen told Ulanova after she had seen her dance *Giselle*.

The Queen has been to far too many stage performances for it to be possible or fair to single out special occasions. Nearly every year she has attended the Royal Variety Performance in aid of charity, and in 1958 she attended a Scottish Variety Performance and also a gala performance of *My Fair Lady* at the Theatre Royal, Drury Lane, in aid of King George's Fund for Actors and Actresses. In 1956 she attended a French play in connection with the French Festival.

One theatrical practice in which she follows her father is in going to some of the well-acted shows at the Windsor Royal Theatre to support the local "Rep", an action which might well be copied by more lovers of the theatre. The Queen has sometimes taken her house guests, and everyone has obviously enjoyed the entertainment.

The Queen goes most years to the Royal Film Performance in aid of charity, and has been to an Italian film festival, but I do not know of an unofficial occasion on which she has attended a public cinema since her accession. She sees the films that interest her in the cinema of her various homes. Even in the royal yacht *Britannia*, films are shown in the dining-room, and attended by as many as possible of all ranks. The Queen has not confined her patronage to the major Arts. A searchlight tattoo, the circus, a masque in Gray's Inn Hall last performed before Queen Elizabeth I, visits to television studios—The Queen has been to all these since her accession.

In the scientific field The Queen quite frankly relies heavily on the Duke of Edinburgh. Although one would never guess it from her interested expression, it is possible that one turbine or mechanical what-not is very much like another to The Queen. Here she benefits greatly from The Duke's enthusiasm, his ability to point out clearly the significance of the new scientific endeavours, to bring distinguished and promising scientists to her notice, and generally to illuminate the world of scientific progress in the particularly pleasant and clear way which is so much his own. The result is that The Queen knows more about the progress of things scientific than most women.

The Queen has some official connections with the scientific world. For example, she is Patron of the Royal Society, founded by King Charles II (how many of our more worthwhile institutions have royal origin) and she awards the Royal Medals annually, upon the recommendation of the Council, for the two most important contributions to the advancement of natural knowledge published originally in Her Majesty's Dominions within a period of not more than ten years and not less than one year of the date of the award. These medals have been awarded by the Sovereign since 1825. On January 30, 1947, The Queen, when Princess Elizabeth, was elected a Royal Fellow, and she attended the Society's rooms for formal admission on July 3, 1947.

While the Duke of Edinburgh is more absorbed in science than The Queen, an interest which they share deeply is everything to do with youth.

The Queen and the Duke of Edinburgh are not mere theorists or idealists about children. They have two sturdy, individual, and no doubt at times distinctly trying children of their own. They know the joys, the hopes, the trials and successes of bringing up two very healthy and happy and intelligent children. They are interested in children not just as the future of the Commonwealth—which they are—but as individuals.

The Queen's connections with youth have been so numerous that it would possibly give more idea of the sincerity and depth of her interest to go into some details about her connections with one or two youth organisations, rather than merely to list the names of those in which she is interested. The Boy Scouts Association is an excellent example. The Queen is Patron—which might be, but is not, a purely formal relationship. Take the matter of changing the name of King's Scouts to Queen's Scouts. There had never previously been a Queen's Scout. The King's Scout was initiated at the suggestion of King Edward VII, who proposed privately to Lord Baden-Powell, who was staying at Balmoral, that Scouts who attained a certain standard should be given the title of "King's Scout" and wear the Royal Crown on their arm. In 1946 the standard for King's Scouts was raised, with the consent of King George VI, who then approved a certificate to be given to each King's Scout. When The Queen gave permission for the title to be changed, she also made a number of suggestions regarding details of the Certificate, such as a slightly larger certificate, and the use of facsimile ink for her signature, in place of the black printer's ink for her father's signature.

Similarly since 1934—and Princess Elizabeth, then aged eight, was present at that first parade—the King's Scouts or Queen's Scouts have annually had the Sovereign's permission to hold a service in St. George's Chapel and a parade on St. George's Day each year. The Sovereign has always, when at all possible, taken the Salute.

This parade in 1952 was the first public engagement of Queen Elizabeth II's reign. In 1953 when the Chief Scout, Lord Rowallan, again approached The Queen for permission to hold this Parade at Windsor Castle, he purposely refrained from asking The Queen to take the Salute because of her heavy commitments during the Coronation Year—a consideration not often shown. In her reply, The Queen said that she had noticed that she had not been asked to take the Salute, adding that if the Chief Scout had no one else in mind, she would be very pleased to do so. Consequently The Queen has taken the salute of Queen's Scouts on St. George's Day at Windsor on all but two years of her reign. These were 1954, when she was absent on the World Tour, and 1958, when she had to cancel her presence because of illness and the Duke of Edinburgh deputised for her.

When the World Jamboree of Scouts was held at Sutton Cold-field in 1957, The Queen and the Duke of Edinburgh made a five-hour tour which obviously gave them both "very real pleasure", and the letter of thanks from her Assistant Private Secretary to the Chief Scout showed clearly the real interest The Queen and the Duke of Edinburgh took in the Jamboree.

The Queen provided the site in Windsor Great Park for the Girl Guides' World Camp, which was also held in August 1957. When visiting it she wore the trefoil Guide badge presented to her by the Guides of the British Commonwealth on her twenty-first birthday. She remarked that the cooking stoves—shades of her own Sea Ranger days?—were the right height for stirring without stooping.

Apart from organisations for youth, The Queen has certain contacts with individual schools, through presenting prizes or appointing Governors. For instance, she approves the recommendation for the award of The Queen's French and German prizes at Eton College.

She also presents in person a Bible to the pupil in Dersingham Secondary Modern School, near Sandringham, who is most proficient in religious knowledge. In 1958 it was a boy, Bruce Annison, son of the head plumber on the Sandringham Estate, whose mother had received a Bible for the same reason from King George V some thirty years before.

A public school which has a particularly close connection with royalty is Wellington College, which celebrated its centenary in 1959. It was founded as a memorial to the great Duke of Wellington, by public subscription headed generously by Queen Victoria and the Prince Consort. The Prince Consort was first President, and the school carries out his educational ideas. It was granted a Charter of Incorporation by Queen Victoria who expressly stated:

That we reserve to Ourselves, Our Heirs and Successors, to be the Visitor of the said College.

The Queen is therefore Visitor of Wellington College. In this capacity she has to approve all Governors, and in 1958 she approved the appointments of four distinguished Governors, who included her Private Secretary, Sir Michael Adeane.

In The Queen's crowded life there are a considerable number of occasions, duties, approvals, appointments which are hard to classify. Some are historical remnants. Some have come up now, and may never require a decision again. Some occur only once in a reign. Some are recurrent but of minor importance. Some are interesting, more are dull. But each of them has at some time taken up The Queen's attention. There are enough of these oddments to fill a very long chapter, but if there is one thing any account of The Queen's life and work does not need, it is padding. Therefore it is possible only to skim through these accumulated details, to give a very brief glimpse of their diversity.

When The Queen came to the Throne she had to decide which of the very large number of societies and organisations of which her father was Patron she would take on herself, and which might be more suitably filled by her husband or some other member of the Royal Family. The Queen will not undertake the Patronage of any Society or Organisation in which she cannot feel a real and personal interest. No list of Patronages is officially prepared, each is individually decided and announced, and they range widely over many fields. For instance, The Queen is Patron of the Friends of the Clergy Corporation, in succession to Queen Mary, and Patron of the Thames Nautical Training College. She was Patron-in-Chief of the 1956 Olympic Games in Melbourne and the Festival of Wales in 1958. She is Patron of the Star and Garter Home for Disabled Sailors, Soldiers and Airmen and of the Family Welfare Association.

The Queen has a mass of decisions to make and approvals to give, other than those noted already or later in this book. She chose the design on her stamps—the design of the Coronation stamp was chosen from seventy-five designs submitted to her; the design on her coins; she chose her cypher—and plenty of trouble that caused in Scotland at the time; she chose the design for the Great Seal, the obverse of which shows her mounted in the uniform of Colonel-in-Chief of the Grenadier Guards; she chose the design for the Seal of the Duchy of Lancaster, which incorporates one of her favourite corgi dogs. The Queen approved the Coronation year hallmark, and even found time to give a sitting to the artist. The Queen gave permission for some regional stamps to be introduced for the first time in the United Kingdom in 1958, in which, in addition to The Queen's head, appear the appropriate symbols of Scotland, Wales, Northern Ireland, the Channel Islands and the Isle of Man.

The Queen sends messages of sympathy, both officially and unofficially, to a wide range of persons and organisations, such as the King of the Hellenes following a tragic earthquake in Greece, and to Sir William Lyons, chairman and managing director of the Jaguar Works, after an extensive fire there.

Because of the disruption of traffic which is liable to follow the Trooping the Colour ceremony, The Queen decided to change the day on which her official birthday is celebrated to a Saturday, beginning with Saturday, June 12, 1959. The Queen also decides on which date Armistice Day, now held on a Sunday, shall be held each year.

There are many appointments which The Queen must approve which have not yet been noted, such as the appointments of the

Regius Professors; of the Lord Mayor of London (through the Lord Chancellor at the House of Lords); she approves the re-appointment of the Court of the Bank of England; The Queen approved, after the post had been vacant for some years, of the appointment of the Duke of Wellington as Governor of the Isle of Wight; she approves the appointments of the Astronomers Royal; of the Royal Commissioners on Ancient and Historic Monuments both in England and Scotland, of the Royal Fine Art Commission for Scotland. The Queen approved re-naming the *Tiger* class cruiser *Lion*, in order to keep alive one of the oldest ship names in the Navy.

The Queen (through the Home Secretary) consented to the continued usage of the description "Royal County of Berkshire", which has been in use for many years, but for which there was no record of a grant of the title. Berkshire has many royal associations, dating back to the birth of Alfred the Great at Wantage. Windsor lies in it, and at one time, during the reign of Henry III in the thirteenth century, Windsor Great Park was so large that it incorporated the whole of present-day Berkshire.

The Queen laid down that the Queen Mother should receive from the Lord Mayor of London the same privileges as those accorded to a Head of State. To greet the Queen Mother, the Lord Mayor therefore wears his crimson and gold reception robe which he otherwise wears only to greet The Queen or the visiting Head of a Foreign State.

The Queen decided to present a banner to the Royal Military College at Duntroon in Australia, and she also approved its design, and she gave this banner to the Queen Mother to present during her 1958 visit to Australia. This banner will be carried on all ceremonial occasions at the College.

The Queen took the deepest interest in the King George VI Foundation, in the working out of all the plans and approving them all, by means of which large sums were allocated to encouraging the youth of the Commonwealth and in providing club facilities for the old people.

To end on a lighter note, The Queen, through the Duke of Beaufort, Lord High Steward of the City of Gloucester, accepted the proposed traditional gift of a lamprey pie for her Coronation, which was duly presented to her at Windsor Castle by the daughter and son-in-law of the Sheriff of Gloucester (Mr. Howard A. Gibson) in the year of the Coronation. Lampreys, a rather horrid-looking sucker fish, were greatly in demand in royal circles during the fast of Lent and the feast of Christmas, and early English kings laid great store upon a good service of Severn lampreys to their castles. Henry I died of a surfeit of *French* lampreys (Gloucester is firm upon this point). Presents of Severn lampreys from Gloucester were made to successive kings. In the last years of her reign Queen Victoria had an annual pie, taken to whichever residence she happened to be occupying at the time.

Queen Elizabeth II's pie weighed forty-two pounds and contained eight fine lampreys. It was decorated with the Royal coat of arms and the coat of arms of the City of Gloucester in colour, and it was baked by No. 2 School of Cookery of the Royal Air Force at Innsworth, Gloucester.

CHAPTER NINE

The Queen's Public Duties in Britain

"The use of The Queen, in a dignified capacity, is incalculable."   *The English Constitution*, Bagehot

"She is very, very easy to work with—even when she was
tired, she was completely co-operative."
                                        A B.B.C. official, concerned with The
                                                Queen's television appearances

HERE we come to the public duties in Britain—the public
duties which are sometimes considered to be almost the
only duties of The Queen. They certainly are among The
Queen's most important tasks, and they are legion. Some are
exactly the same as those carried out by her forefathers. Some
were introduced by her father or grandfather and she is continuing
them. Some are being discarded or reduced. Others are completely new. The pattern, which may seem so fixed to the casual
eye, is constantly being adapted to the changing concept of
monarchy.

How does The Queen prepare for this public work? How are
the duties chosen? How are they carried out?

Instead of listing the public duties The Queen has carried out
—which would in any case run us out through the back cover of
this book—it seems a better idea to choose one particular duty
that The Queen has undertaken, and to show how she prepared
herself for it. Moreover, it seems best to choose something entirely new—something which The Queen has introduced, and
where she herself is founding a new tradition.

The first television of The Queen's Christmas broadcast from
Sandringham, which took place in 1957, seems the best possible
example.

A Member of The Queen's Household emphasised to me that
the reason why The Queen was the first to use television for her

Coronation inside the Abbey, for the Christmas broadcast and for the Opening of Parliament in Ottawa and Westminster was that "television was by that time technically advanced enough to be used". But this does not take away from the fact that The Queen was ready to turn this new device to the service of her ancient office.

The Christmas broadcast was begun by her grandfather, King George V, in 1932. He, too, was making an early use of a new scientific wonder. The overseas service of the B.B.C. had been in operation for only six days.

The B.B.C. approached The Queen early in 1957 to request her to permit the Christmas broadcast to be televised. In the spring The Queen agreed, and plans were under way between the Palace and the B.B.C. by early summer.

The problems to be solved were many. It was not just a question of placing a camera in front of The Queen while she was making a radio broadcast. Nor was it televising The Queen— as she has so often been televised—while she was doing something else. It is a far more difficult thing to face an inanimate object like the lens of a camera and to talk to it as a friend. This is quite as hard for The Queen, to whom this kind of public appearance does not come naturally, as it would be for you. But—being convinced that the television of her Christmas broadcast was a good, and indeed almost inevitable step—The Queen quietly set to work to do it as well as she possibly could.

In July the B.B.C. made a special film for The Queen, showing the various methods by which her talk could be televised. In each, the experienced announcer, Miss Sylvia Peters, interpreted the part of The Queen, talking while sitting at a desk. The various methods were as follows:

1. The eavesdropping angle, as though the camera just happened to be there when The Queen was making her radio broadcast.
2. The Queen frankly reading the speech in front of her.
3. The Queen reading the speech, but looking up occasionally.
4. The Queen looking straight at the camera and the script prompter, but using the speech in front of her from time to time.

5. The Queen looking almost all the time at the lens and the prompter, with little reference to the script on the desk.

The film, together with a script-prompting machine, was sent to her at Balmoral at the beginning of August. The Duke had already used one, and was entirely competent to show The Queen how it worked. This script prompter (the "Teleprompter") is fitted on the front of the camera and, by means of mirrors, the script is seen in large black capital letters right across the front of the lens.

Although it is the most difficult, the B.B.C. experts hoped that The Queen would choose the last method, that of looking directly into the lens with almost no reference to the script, as it is by far the most natural. The Queen chose it without hesitation.

When The Queen returned to London from Balmoral on October 3, she was plunged into preparations for her forthcoming stay in Canada and State Visit to the United States. In Canada she was to be televised while broadcasting her speech to the Canadian people. Partly in preparation for this, partly with the Christmas television in mind, the B.B.C. team, headed by the producer, Mr. Antony Craxton, who would be responsible for the Christmas television from Sandringham, were asked to go to Buckingham Palace on Tuesday, October 8. They took their bulky equipment with them—two television cameras and a prompting machine— and it was all set up in the State Dining Room on the first floor of the Palace, overlooking the gardens.

About 3 o'clock The Queen came in for her first television rehearsals. She was obviously a little nervous. "Almost as much as I was," remarked her producer afterwards.

First The Queen sat down in front of the cameras and read a bit of the script for the Canadian broadcast, without the teleprompter, just to get the feel of things. Then she went through her speech with the teleprompter. She made two recordings, neither of which—frankly—were very good, although the second was slightly better. The Queen was obviously nervous of this exacting new medium, she was unrelaxed and tensed up. For the shy person, television is a tremendous ordeal, and there are only a few—a very few—television "naturals" like the Duke of Edinburgh, who took to the medium like a duck to water.

The Duke of Edinburgh was there, and contributed enormously to the progress of the rehearsal, especially as he was at school with the producer, and had worked with him over three important and strikingly successful television appearances.

On the following day The Queen and the Duke of Edinburgh, together with the producer, went to the billiard room at Buckingham Palace where the telerecording was run through. The Queen's tension had been caught by the relentless eye of the camera, and her voice—which in private is delightful and low-pitched—had become strained and high through nervousness. The Queen has a great gift of making those with her feel at ease. Her sincere desire to do her best is obvious, so the producer's task of pointing out her beginner's mistakes to her was made easy for him.

But The Queen had got to "jump into the deep end" with this extremely important televised speech in Ottawa in exactly one week. What was to be done?

The Queen decided, at the Duke of Edinburgh's suggestion, to do the whole thing over again.

Her programme was crammed with engagements and duties and papers and Audiences, clothes to be seen to and hair to be done in that short time between her return from Scotland and her tour overseas. But somehow time was found in the crowded programme, and on the following day again the camera teams went to Buckingham Palace, and again The Queen went twice through her speech, the script of which had been lightened.

This time there was a decided improvement. The Queen was gaining experience of the medium and more confidence, therefore she was less nervous and her voice was lower pitched.

For a fourth time the producer went to Buckingham Palace to discuss this second effort with The Queen and the Duke of Edinburgh, who had just returned from the memorial service to King Haakon of Norway in the Chapel Royal, St. James's Palace.

The film was then sent to Canada as a help to the Canadian producer there. And on the day appointed The Queen captured Canada with her first televised speech—part of which was in French—to her Canadian people.

Meanwhile preparations continued for the Christmas television from Sandringham. Cables were laid underground through the park; from there two separate vision circuits led all the way from Sandringham to London. Three cameras were used in the actual broadcast, two of them on the principal circuit, one on a reserve circuit in case of breakdown.

Towards Christmas time Mrs. Tommy Manderson, one of the B.B.C. television senior make-up experts, went to The Queen to advise her about the special problems of television. (The make-up technique employed by the B.B.C. is lighter than that used in Canada.)

Then, on December 17, the same television team again went to Buckingham Palace, this time to the Drawing Room of the Belgian suite on the ground floor. Here the surroundings of the Christmas television talk were simulated with the actual Sandringham curtains and a similar desk set out in the way intended.

The trouble this time was with the script, which requires a different form of words from a radio broadcast, and here the Duke of Edinburgh—always helpful, always stimulating—gave valuable advice. There were three visits to Buckingham Palace, each marking a distinct step forward, before The Queen went to Sandringham for Christmas.

On the afternoon of December 23 The Queen held her first television rehearsal at Sandringham. Here in her country home she was noticeably relaxed and at ease. The little study, where every Christmas broadcast except one has been made by three Sovereigns, proved too small for all the television equipment. The library—originally an American bowling alley installed by King Edward VII—was used instead. The Queen and the Duke of Edinburgh and the royal children came quite informally in and out of the room.

Each rehearsal was better, but The Queen—perfectly relaxed thirty seconds before—still found it difficult to be entirely at ease before the prying glassy stare of the lens. On Christmas Eve there were further rehearsals and discussions, culminating with The Queen working alone with the producer in a long session over the script. This Christmas message was to be seen and heard by millions in Britain, to be heard alone by many millions more throughout the Commonwealth. Television—as The Queen was quick to understand—requires a different technique from sound radio: here both had to be combined, a difficult task even for a veteran.

The Queen has always the additional difficulty that her speech is a talk not only from a young woman from the heart of her family, but from the Sovereign to her peoples. She must conform to the policy of her Governments.

The Queen always shows the script of her Christmas talk to her Prime Minister before she makes it. This does not necessarily mean the Prime Minister of the United Kingdom. In 1953 Her Majesty spent Christmas in New Zealand; on that occasion she showed her speech to Mr. Holland before delivery, and she could do likewise in any other Commonwealth country, if she were there at Christmas.

While the producer was having his forty-five-minute talk with The Queen, the door opened and in came Prince Charles. He sat down quietly on a chair and listened without interruption. It did not disturb The Queen at all to have her son in the room while she was working out the final details of this formidable duty.

There were no further rehearsals. The Queen was willing to rehearse as often, as much and as long as the experts considered necessary, but the producer felt that any further work at that stage might induce staleness.

On Christmas Day the talk was timed to begin exactly at 3 p.m. The Queen had decided to go to the library fifteen minutes before that. But make-up took longer than was anticipated, and there was only four minutes to go when she entered the room. She was looking very pretty in a gold lamé afternoon dress, and one who was present remembers she seemed only the least degree nervous. She took her place at the desk, and almost at once the television broadcast opened with a long-distance shot.

"Happy Christmas," said The Queen.

It was her own suggestion for beginning her Christmas talk.

Her first paragraph was partially read from the script, and partially memorised; then, as the cameras tracked in, she looked straight at the lens, able to prompt herself—although she knew the speech practically by heart—from the teleprompter, which was operated by remote control, keeping time to The Queen's own pace. Of the half-dozen technicians needed in the room, only four were visible to her. (The same team of technicians were used throughout.) The producer was in the television van in the courtyard outside.

The Duke of Edinburgh was in the room all the time, and watched the broadcast through the spare camera on the reserve circuit. At the end of the broadcast The Queen intended to smile, to avoid that stiff expression (known colloquially at the B.B.C. as "stuck pig") of staring solemnly at the camera during the fade-out. The Duke of Edinburgh had moved in close to the camera, and it was to him that The Queen gave her brilliant and spontaneous smile of relief at the end of her talk.

That televised Christmas talk, as the many millions who saw it know, was a great success. Her people had the sense of joining her in her own home. Although a slight nervousness was still apparent, so was the sincerity and desire to do her very best which The Queen had shown at every moment of her long preparations.

As one of those who worked with her on this broadcast said, "After you have met The Queen for the first time, you feel completely relaxed and natural with her. She is very, very easy to work with. She is always willing to do whatever is wanted. Even when she was tired, she was completely co-operative and left no stone unturned to make a success of what would be a difficult task for anyone, and was particularly so to one of her shy and reserved nature. Once she made up her mind to do the television talk, she was determined that it must be as good as it possibly could be."

Now this is a very long and detailed description of just one duty of The Queen's—a public duty, although it took place within her own home. Television is still, and perhaps always will be a tremendous strain to her. But by Christmas 1958, she was already more confident and relaxed.

The reason for this account is to show the person behind the task; the trouble which The Queen considers is part of her job to undertake to fulfil her rôle as Sovereign. The Queen prepares carefully and conscientiously for her public occasions. She would think it an insult to us not to do so. Her sincerity, in an age remarkable for eyewash and bally-hoo, gives a special lustre to the ceremonial and official occasions of which she is the centre.

We have already seen that The Queen's public duties are very carefully planned.

The functions which The Queen attends are chosen because they are worthy of distinction. Great numbers of authorities and public bodies, arts and industries ask The Queen to visit them. The choice is difficult. But the principle is that The Queen should attend occasions of *national* importance, and occasions always of good repute. For this reason, the Home Secretary or relevant Secretary of State or Minister is always consulted before The Queen makes a public engagement in the United Kingdom, to make sure that she is not unwittingly embarrassing her Government, or connecting herself with an unworthy object.

Many of The Queen's engagements mark the start or the completion of a great new enterprise. Others take place because the centenary or other anniversary occurs of a great man or a great work. Some places are visited because they have been plugging along the right road for a long time, and it seems time notice is taken of them. Others are noteworthy and admirable examples of local industry or good work.

In other words, The Queen goes because it is A Good Thing, and because this occasion has been associated with The Queen, everyone knows that it is A Good Thing.

The exception to this is in the time of national disaster or calamity, when The Queen shows her personal and the national sympathy by visiting a district devastated by flood or by sending messages of condolence to the victims of a train disaster. Even here, she must be guided by her Government. Messages of sympathy to the Overseas Commonwealth countries, for instance, are not sent unless in the opinion of the Governor-General the scale and range of the disaster warrants The Queen's message.

Apart from her public messages of sympathy, The Queen makes many private enquiries about those who are ill or afflicted. Like her mother, she has a very real sympathy with suffering.

She arranged that an aircraft of The Queen's Flight should meet Sir Anthony Eden at Liverpool, on his return after illness in North America, and fly him to the nearest airfield to his Wiltshire home.

As has already been indicated in writing about The Queen's Christmas broadcasts, The Queen's speeches are not her carefree utterances. She must remember that she *always* speaks as Sovereign and therefore must never run across Government policy, nor must she offend the reasonable beliefs and ideals of sections of her people.

This is a difficult—no, it is an impossible task. The Queen is naturally extremely careful of people's feelings, and would do nothing willingly to offend any person's susceptibilities. But we should all like The Queen to pay particular attention to our own hobby-horses, and most of us would not much mind if The Queen paid little attention to the things in which we personally are not interested. Furthermore, we should like The Queen to take an active stand in opposing whatever it is of which we disapprove.

A lover of modern music bewails that The Queen has not "given a lead" to his favourite undiscovered composer. A Town Clerk of a Yorkshire borough complains that The Queen will spend only half an hour in his town. A believer in the strictest keeping of the Sabbath forgets that she invariably attends Church every Sunday and remembers only that she sometimes watches polo on Sunday afternoons. The wonder is not that The Queen has not listened to a particular concert or has only once visited a particular English town, but that she has been so far and done so much. Take down *Whitaker's Almanack* or a similar work of reference, and look at the list of prominent British societies and institutes, look at the number of counties and towns in Britain alone—how can *one* person get round them all?

In each year there are a number of events which are hardy perennials, included in each year's royal programme. Wherever possible, and unless such an event as a World or Overseas Commonwealth Tour intervenes, The Queen tries to undertake them each year. Some have been mentioned in other chapters, but it would seem clearest to summon them together briefly here:

INVESTITURES: of which about a dozen are held each year, six after the New Year and six after the Birthday Honours (see "The Fount of Honour".)

MAUNDY THURSDAY (see "The Queen and the Church")

QUEEN'S SCOUT PARADE AT WINDSOR ON EASTER SUNDAY

CUP FINAL (FOOTBALL ASSOCIATION)

QUEEN'S BIRTHDAY PARADE (Trooping the Colour)

THE DERBY AT EPSOM

ROYAL ASCOT

VISIT TO HOLYROODHOUSE WITH SCOTTISH GARDEN PARTY, ETC. (about two years in three)

INSTALLATION OR SERVICE OF THE ORDER OF THE GARTER (most
   years—see "The Fount of Honour")
INSTALLATION OR SERVICE OF THE ORDER OF THE THISTLE (most
   years—see "The Fount of Honour")
GARDEN PARTIES (see "The Queen, Our Hostess")
GOODWOOD
BRAEMAR GATHERING
OPENING OF PARLIAMENT (see "The Queen and Parliament")
BRITISH LEGION FESTIVAL OF REMEMBRANCE
ARMISTICE DAY SERVICE, THE CENOTAPH
DIPLOMATIC PRESENTATION PARTY
CHRISTMAS BROADCAST

There have been a number of other frequently recurring public
engagements, which had by force of habit become regarded as
annual. These The Queen has been sifting, and in some cases
reducing, for the reason that she must somehow find time for the
ever-increasing duties of each year, for more travel, for a changing
and closer contact with the people. That must mean some readjustment of the basic programme.

Among the sufferers are the Presentation Parties, cut out after
1958 for reasons given in the chapter "The Queen, Our Hostess",
and the Royal Film Performance and the Royal Variety Performance. These are often incorrectly referred to as "Command"
performances, but this applies only to an occasion on which The
Queen is hostess to the entire gathering. The Ideal Home
Exhibition is also being visited less frequently. None of these
will be entirely cut out from future programmes; they will
simply recur at longer intervals, so that there will be more time
available for more public engagements drawn from a wider
range. For instance, in 1958 The Queen did not attend a Royal
Film Performance although she agreed to attend a Royal Variety
Performance, and she also attended—for the first time ever—
a Scottish Royal Variety Performance in Glasgow on July 3.

Many other events, although not quite frequent enough to be
listed as "annuals", have been attended by The Queen on several
occasions already during her reign. For instance, she has watched
many games of rugby football, she has been once to Wimbledon
and gone to a number of Test Matches. In most years she sees

the final of the Football Association Cup; she has seen American football, watched athletics, goes regularly to the Highland Games at Braemar, and has watched most kinds of equestrian sports from trotting (in Perth, Western Australia) to Badminton Horse Trials and the Derby.

The Queen's reign opened with the traditional visits to Scotland, Wales and Northern Ireland, which had their special features and ceremonies. This continues a tradition begun by King George IV, who visited Ireland in 1821 and Scotland in 1822.

The Queen is also systematically visiting every one of the forty-three counties of England, thirty-three counties of Scotland and thirteen counties of Wales. By the time she had been six and a half years on the throne she had been to all but four or five of the eighty-nine counties of Britain.

The Regional Tour is of more modern origin. In his biography of Archbishop Cosmo Gordon Lang, Lockhart recalls the part he played in instituting the Regional Tours. He originally suggested them to King George V in the autumn of 1911, when staying at Balmoral.

I urged the importance of his (the King's) coming into contact with the masses of his people, that it was not enough that they should assemble in the streets on ceremonial occasions to see him, but that he might, so to say, go to see them—move about with as little ceremony as possible through their own towns, villages and workshops.

The Archbishop was afterwards asked to submit a memorandum on paper, and when the first Regional Tour took place in 1912 it was to the South Riding of Yorkshire, which lay within the province of Archbishop Lang, who was then Archbishop of York.

It was a great success, although at that time a bold experiment. Possibly for the first time King George V was able to overhear the spontaneous comments of his people upon him, and although he was a little taken aback by their frankness, he thoroughly appreciated the genuine warmth of his welcome.

During the Tour a mining disaster took place in Cadeby Pit, a South Yorkshire coalpit, just the day before the King was scheduled to make the first descent of a coalpit ever made by a Sovereign. Some pressure was put upon the King to cancel his visit to the mine, but Lord Halifax and the Archbishop sided with the King, and he went down the pit, with a profound effect upon the mining population.

The King and Queen Mary also visited the tragic pit, and showed great sympathy with those who had lost their men in the disaster. The second occasion when a Sovereign went down a coal mine was on June 30, 1958, when The Queen went down the Rothes mine in Fife.

Regional Tours have grown to be a considerable part of the Sovereign's duties. Generally The Queen and the Duke of Edinburgh travel through a district, which may be only a part of one of the largest counties, or many Tours incorporate two separate counties for two or perhaps three days. Such visits usually induce long drives through crowds—this is most tiring; receptions at the Town Halls, where considerable numbers of local notabilities meet The Queen and the Duke and talk to them; inspections of Guards of Honour drawn from the County Regiment; and visits to local industries, schools and welfare organisations and so on.

A typical Regional Tour, chosen at random, was that paid by the Queen and the Duke of Edinburgh to Lincolnshire in June 1958. Here is the formal *Court Circular* account of that day, in which places are shown in small capitals and persons in italics, to give emphasis, and to which a few comments have been added:

The Queen and the *Duke of Edinburgh* arrived at LINCOLN this morning and were received by the *Earl of Ancaster* (Her Majesty's Lieutenant for Lincolnshire), *Sir Denis Le Marchant* (High Sheriff) and the Mayor (*Councillor L. H. Priestley*), who presented to *The Queen* the King Richard II Sword which *Her Majesty* was pleased to return.

Her Majesty and *His Royal Highness* drove to the USHER ART GALLERY where presentations were made. *The Queen* and the *Duke of Edinburgh* then drove to the LINCOLN CITY FOOTBALL GROUND where the school children were assembled.

[Note: It was pouring with rain, so community singing was substituted for morris dancing.]

Her Majesty and *His Royal Highness* subsequently drove to the PELHAM BRIDGE where *The Queen* unveiled a commemorative tablet and declared the Bridge open.

[This Bridge had been built to eliminate one of Lincoln's worst level crossings.]

Her Majesty and the *Duke of Edinburgh* then drove to the CATHEDRAL and were received by the Bishop of Lincoln (*the Right Reverend Kenneth Riches, D.D.*) and the Dean of Lincoln (*the Right Reverend Colin Dunlop*). *Her Majesty*, with *His Royal Highness*, toured the CATHEDRAL and unveiled a Window in the Airmen's Chapel.

[The Window commemorated R.A.F. Flying Training Command personnel who died during the war while stationed in Lincolnshire.

In the Chapter House The Queen sat in the chair occupied by King Edward I when he opened Parliament in Lincoln in 1301.]

The Queen and the *Duke of Edinburgh* then visited the CASTLE and subsequently left Lincoln in the Royal Train for SCUNTHORPE.

Upon arrival at SCUNTHORPE this afternoon *Her Majesty* and *His Royal Highness* were received by the Mayor (*Councillor Mrs. Violet Wilmshurst*).

The Queen and the *Duke of Edinburgh* drove to the CIVIC THEATRE and visited the OLD PEOPLE'S RECREATIONAL CENTRE.

[They spoke to many old people, and planted trees in THE FESTIVAL GARDENS.]

Her Majesty opened the new MODEL TRAFFIC AREA and later, with *His Royal Highness*, drove to the TECHNICAL COLLEGE.

The Queen and the *Duke of Edinburgh* were received by *Sir Weston Cracrofts-Amcotts* (Chairman of the County Council) and toured the COLLEGE.

Her Majesty and *His Royal Highness* subsequently drove to the APPELBY-FRODINGHAM STEEL WORKS and were received by *Sir Walter Benton-Jones* (the Chairman).

The Queen and the *Duke of Edinburgh* toured the WORKS and proceeded to the ROYAL LAWN where presentations were made.

Her Majesty and *His Royal Highness* then drove to the REDBOURN WORKS of Messrs. Richard Thomas and Baldwins Limited and proceeded to IMMINGHAM DOCKS.

The Queen and the *Duke of Edinburgh* were received by *General Sir Brian Robertson, Bt.* (Chairman, British Transport Commission), and embarked in H.M. YACHT "BRITANNIA".

The Countess of Euston, Sir Edward Ford, Captain the Lord Plunket and *Mr. Esmond Butler* were in attendance.

The Queen and the *Duke of Edinburgh* gave a dinner party on board the ROYAL YACHT this evening. The following had the honour of being invited:

The Earl of Ancaster, the Earl and Countess of Yarborough, the Viscount Crookshank, the Bishop of Lincoln and Mrs. Riches, and Wing Commander and Mrs. Beresford Horsley.

For the regional journeys, many journeys are carried out by royal train. In the days when there were separate railway companies, several of them kept special coaches for royal use. The Great Western prided itself on the honour of the first train journey made by the Sovereign, when Queen Victoria travelled from Slough to Paddington on June 13, 1842. It took only twenty-five minutes and was a great success. Queen Victoria wrote:

free from dust and crowd and heat, and I am quite charmed with it.

Early royal carriages were designed as coaches on wheels. Queen Adelaide, widow of King William IV, had a royal railway carriage which still survives. It had no corridor.

The Southern Railway on occasion even whitewashed the coal in the tenders for royal journeys. There used to be a royal "pilot" engine which ran fifteen minutes ahead of the royal train, to see that all was well. Even to-day special precautions are taken in regard to the signalling of the royal train, and tunnels are inspected before it passes through them.

The royal train at present in use was built in 1941 for King George VI's many wartime train journeys, and in those days was lent by the L.M.S. to the other companies when required. It is painted royal purple with black and scarlet edging to the panels, and has specially wide doors. The Queen's day coach is a pleasantly furnished room with big easy chairs covered in oatmeal coloured material, her bedroom is in worcester blue with a mulberry red carpet, and her adjoining bathroom is primrose yellow. The Duke of Edinburgh's sitting-room has plain folk-weave curtains and plaid chair covers. Prominent are the telephones—white for The Queen, deep red for the Duke of Edinburgh. There is a 28-line switchboard on the royal train.

During this reign a plain but comfortable coach has been built for the royal children, and this is attached to the royal train for the journeys to and from Balmoral and whenever else it is required. There is nothing particularly juvenile about the fittings.

When The Queen and the Duke of Edinburgh are making an overnight stay away, a suitably secluded siding is selected and the train is shunted in there. A special generator is a part of the train so that heating can be maintained. In this way The Queen can stay overnight without fuss or extra expense, almost anywhere within Britain.

Nor is The Queen's experience of trains confined to the coaches. When Princess Elizabeth, she has been at the controls of a railway engine on three occasions and in three countries, the Union of South Africa, Canada and, most recently, in England, when at Swindon in 1950 she drove the engine named *Princess Elizabeth* from the engine sheds to the platform.

The Queen's cars, on the other hand, are her personal property, and are a charge upon the Privy Purse. They are the responsibility of the Crown Equerry. Four principal cars are finished in the royal colours of maroon with a fine red line. The other cars are in all sorts of colours. It is well-known that the Sovereign's car is the only motor vehicle on the public roads of Britain which is not registered and does not carry a number-plate. (King Edward VII's car was stopped and his chauffeur arrested in Paris for failure to comply with this regulation.) Only the four principal cars bear no plates. The station wagons and estate cars The Queen owns, and often drives, carry number-plates.

The Queen's principal car carries a silver mascot of St. George and the Dragon. This was her mascot when she was Princess Elizabeth, and she has preferred to retain it rather than use the figure of Britannia on top of a globe used by King George VI. The mascot is usually carried by The Queen's principal car, but sometimes transferred to whichever car she is using. Her principal car is a magnificent Rolls-Royce Phantom IV, which was specially built for her. There is no other car exactly like it. It has large windows and a glass panel let into the top of the roof at the rear, also a seat which can be moved forward so that The Queen may more easily be seen. The built-in radio has special controls built into the arm-rest in the rear compartment.

The royal cars 2, 3 and 4 are "Straight Eight" 36-h.p. Daimler cars, and incidentally the first of all British royal cars was a Daimler, ordered by King Edward VII in June 1900.

When The Queen is on ceremonial duty, her car flies the Royal Standard and carries a Shield bearing the Royal Coat of Arms. The Duke of Edinburgh, the Queen Mother and Princess Margaret, when driving on official occasions, also fly their own standard on their cars. When on public duty, those members of the Royal Family who do not fly standards drive in cars bearing a Shield, showing a royal Crown on the roof to help the traffic police to identify them. At night, the Shield with the Royal Arms on The Queen's car is illuminated when she is on official duty. Cars used at night by other members of the Royal Family show a blue light. When The Queen or any other member of the Royal Family is off duty, the cars carry no distinguishing mark.

The Queen, of course, has passed the full A.T.S. training in driving and maintaining vehicles, specifically a saloon car, a utility truck and an ambulance. She is knowledgeable and interested in what goes on under the bonnet of her car. While The Queen (as Princess Elizabeth) was training, an A.T.S. high official made careful enquiry of the Queen Mother as to whether The Queen ever mentioned her training experiences at home. "Well," replied the Queen Mother, "last night we had sparking plugs during the whole of dinner!"

When The Queen goes on a Regional Tour, her car and the cars for the Household are driven ahead, to await her arrival. The Queen's car is even taken overseas, and is used by The Queen when she is visiting her subjects in that country, is at the Embassy, or going to worship in the Church of England there, or to the receptions she gives for British Commonwealth subjects and citizens. On other occasions, she rides in her host's car. The royal yacht *Britannia*, skilfully designed for her double job of royal yacht and hospital ship, even has a garage hidden in her super-structure, in which the royal Rolls-Royce can make the sea passage! At other times it houses a launch.

The royal yacht *Britannia* is partly the reason why The Queen, in addition to carrying out the most concentrated and numerous regional visits on the mainland of Britain of any Sovereign, has also been able to visit the more remote parts of the British Isles. Unexpected though it may be to the inhabitants of the more far-flung Dominions and Territories beyond the Seas—parts of the British Isles can be surprisingly remote.

A new royal yacht was planned before the war, but was cancelled. The present *Britannia*, much smaller than the pre-war ship, was announced by the Admiralty in the autumn of 1951, and it was intended to complete her as soon as possible, so that she could be used by King George VI for health cruises. But the King died before the yacht was ready.

A royal yacht is the handiest method by which The Queen can visit Overseas Commonwealth countries and Colonies and make State Visits. Air travel is much swifter, but an aircraft cannot be used as headquarters, or for entertaining, while, although the air is certainly the swiftest, it is not yet the most restful form of transport.

The new royal yacht, to be useful, was required to be big enough to cross any ocean, yet small and handy enough to get into as many harbours as possible. She had to be at once manoeuvrable and comfortable, sufficiently speedy and with a long range of operation. Her accommodation needed to be of three types:

(1) pleasant and secluded apartments for The Queen and her family,

(2) a suite of State apartments sufficiently large to be a convenient and dignified setting for official entertaining,

(3) accommodation for The Queen's suite.

It was decided that the yacht would have dual uses, and be constructed for quick conversion in wartime into a hospital carrier ship; that is, a hospital ship to go forward into advanced areas and bring back sick and wounded to base. She has therefore been built with many special fittings such as lifts large enough to take stretchers, and stabiliser fins to enable operations to be carried out in rough weather.

The present royal yacht is the successor of a line of royal yachts which, although it has been traced back to Saxon days, began in its present sense with King Charles II. The royal sailing yacht *Royal George*, with Queen Victoria aboard, was *towed* from London to Leith in 1842, an experience she did not enjoy, and she forthwith ordered the first of the three royal steam yachts all named *Victoria and Albert*. The third *Victoria and Albert*, which had become unseaworthy, was recently broken up and many of her furnishings are now aboard *Britannia*.

The royal yacht *Britannia* was built by John Brown of Clydebank, and launched by The Queen on a day of heavy rain in April 1953. The occasion is commemorated by Norman Wilkinson's painting of the scene which is hung above the staircase in the Royal Apartments. *Britannia* is of 4,715 tons load displacement, has a maximum speed of 22 knots and a range of about 3,000 miles, and can also be refuelled at sea. She is painted blue with a thin gold line round the hull, white upperworks, red boot-topping and a buff funnel. When The Queen is on board, the yacht flies the flag of the Lord High Admiral (red with a gold anchor) from the foremast, the Royal Standard from the main-mast and the Union flag from the mizzenmast, with the White Ensign from the stern.

Britannia is beautifully designed for the job. Although her reception rooms are not high, they appear so because of clever decoration close to the ceiling, and the very shallow chandeliers. There is room to sit fifty-six persons at the long mahogany table in the dining-room, the largest in the ship, which runs the full width of the superstructure. Yet The Queen's and the Duke of Edinburgh's own apartments are almost on a doll's-house scale. The Queen's sitting-room is furnished in moss-green and pink roses chintz, with a green carpet. The Duke of Edinburgh's sitting-room is panelled, with folk-weave cushions and hangings, and a model of his first command, H.M.S. *Magpie*, is displayed in a case let into panelling. The verandah room has low chairs and cupboards decorated with plans of sailing ships. The current chart is displayed in a case. Outside, on the royal games deck, stands the binnacle, ornamented with flamboyant dolphins, which has been preserved from the Prince Regent's *Royal George*, and which is now fitted with a repeater reading of the ship's gyro-compass.

Britannia has proved one of the most useful ships on the Navy List, and has been used for Commonwealth tours, including visits to the West Indies, the Indian Ocean and the eastern sea-board of Canada, for State Visits and on visits round the coast of Britain. She has maintained the efficiency of her crew by taking part in Naval manoeuvres. Her longest voyage so far was her first circumnavigation of the world, with Princess Margaret in the Indian Ocean, and then with the Duke of Edinburgh to Australia, the Antarctic and the Atlantic islands.

In *Britannia* The Queen has almost circumnavigated Great Britain at one time or another—only small distances of the Eastern coastline remain to be sailed round from the Thames estuary to Harwich, where she embarked for the Dutch State

Visit; and from Harwich to Grimsby, where she embarked for her visit up the East Coast to Holy Isle in Northumberland. The Queen was the first Sovereign for many hundreds of years to set foot there when she landed on June 29, 1958.

The Queen has visited islands of both the Inner and the Outer Hebrides, sailed through the stormy Pentland Firth (landing to visit the Queen Mother's Castle of Mey), and come by sea to Milford Haven, Dundee, Leith and to the Pool of London, where I saw the unforgettable welcome she received on her return home from the World Tour of 1953-4.

Some of the places which The Queen has visited by the royal yacht *Britannia*, being remote, have retained extremely interesting constitutions, and provide a direct link with very distant days.

The Queen has a small number of aircraft, known as The Queen's Flight, at her disposal. The Queen's Flight is employed for air journeys of moderate length, arrangements being made through the Private Secretary. It is manned and maintained by the R.A.F., and its cost is included in Air Estimates.

First royal interest in aircraft was early. In 1909 at Pau, King Edward VII saw Wilbur Wright make a flight—landing not on wheels, but on skids! The King's Flight was instituted by King Edward VIII on his accession, and consisted at first of his private aircraft, with his personal pilot as Captain of The King's Flight. Captain of The Queen's Flight to-day is the same man, Air Commodore Sir Edward Fielden, K.C.V.O., C.B., D.F.C., A.F.C., who has, in this country of long traditions, the unique distinction of being the sole occupant of an important post so closely associated with the Sovereign.

For a considerable time Vickers Vikings were used with great success in The Queen's Flight, but these became obsolete and have now been replaced by three four-engined de Havilland Herons. Helicopters, which the Duke of Edinburgh pioneered with great success for royal use on short journeys, especially in congested areas, were originally borrowed from the Services when required, but two Westland Whirlwind six-seater helicopters are now being acquired for The Queen's Flight.

Aircraft of The Queen's Flight bear a special Badge under the pilot's window. This is the Crown, in natural colours, over the cipher E II R in red. Underneath is a blue scroll on which is lettered in white "The Queen's Flight".

They have backward-facing seats for greater safety.

The Queen's Flight is stationed at Benson airfield in Oxfordshire.

Aircraft of The Queen's Flight are used on many royal flights to and from the Continent, are frequently used for journeys across Britain, and enable members of the Royal Family to undertake many engagements which it would otherwise be difficult or impossible to fit into the timetable.

For longer journeys aircraft are chartered from B.E.A. or B.O.A.C.

The Queen has flown by at least ten different types of aircraft—Dakota, Heron, Argonaut, Stratocruiser, Comet, Douglas DC7, Douglas C5, Constellation, The Queen's Flight Vikings and Viscount.

When The Queen or any other member of the Royal Family is on board an aircraft on the ground, the appropriate Standard is flown, but this is, of course, withdrawn during flight.

There are special safety regulations in force when The Queen or any other member of the Royal Family is in the air. The areas through which the royal aircraft will pass are known as "*Purple Airways*", which means that aircraft coming within five nautical miles of the royal route within half an hour of the estimated time of the royal aircraft passing, are subjected to strict control from the ground. In fact, these regulations involve little restriction upon the civil or military aircraft in the area. There are three *Purple Airways* permanently listed, so that they can be put into operation at once; these are from London to Marham in Norfolk for Sandringham, from London to Aberdeen for Balmoral, and from London to Caithness for Castle of Mey. Other *Purple Airways* are worked out for each occasion. On ocean passages, ships are stationed at intervals along the royal route, and a constant wireless watch is kept.

From the newest to the oldest existing form of royal transport—the coaches and carriage horses, now all kept in the mews at Buckingham Palace. These are a charge upon the Privy Purse. They, like the cars, are in the charge of the Crown Equerry.

There are at present thirty carriage horses in the royal stables, of which ten are greys and the remainder bays. Many of the grey horses are bought in Ireland. Some of the bays come from Holland, the remainder are of the fine Yorkshire breed of Cleveland Bay carriage horses, although to-day they may not always come from Yorkshire. Grey horses always draw The Queen's carriage. Only on occasions are the greys used for other purposes, in order to let young horses see the crowds. The horses are only sent to Windsor (where the grey horses used to be stabled, hence the familiar but obsolete description "Windsor greys") for Ascot.

However, The Queen's personal riding horses are stabled at Windsor, and one or two are moved from there to Sandringham or Balmoral when required. The Duke of Edinburgh also keeps his polo ponies at Windsor.

The carriages at Buckingham Palace are of three groups. There is the State Coach—a magnificent, lumbering, gilded vehicle built in 1761 and weighing four tons. It was formerly used for the Opening of Parliament each year, drawn by four pairs of greys, postillion ridden. In this reign it has been used once only, for the Coronation of The Queen. Originally driven by a coachman, the box has been removed to allow a better view for the occupants, and the brakeman walks behind. Eight walking footmen walk beside the carriage, one by each horse.

For the Opening of Parliament the Irish State Coach is now used. It used to be driven from the box and drawn by four grey horses. The addition in 1958 of a leading pair of horses, ridden by a postillion, was not for extra show, but to strengthen the coachman's control, as the Irish State Coach, which is driven at a trot and weighs two tons, has no brakes. The Coachman driving The Queen on a State occasion, such as the Opening of Parliament, wears a dark-blue velvet cap and white wig (known as "cap and curls"), state livery of scarlet heavily laced in gold, scarlet kneebreeches and flesh-coloured stockings, and buckled shoes. Four footmen stand on the step behind.

At a State Visit, after The Queen has met the visiting Head of State at the London terminus, whether it is the riverside or a railway station, she drives with the Head of State in a State Road Landau, drawn by six greys, ridden by postillions. The carriages used for the State Drive at Ascot are kept at Windsor and known as Ascot carriages. State Landaus, driven off the box by a pair of horses, are used when an Ambassador is driven to Buckingham Palace to present his credentials to The Queen. All landaus open up, but the Road Landaus are always closed for this occasion, whatever the weather, as it is otherwise difficult for the two footmen to stand on the rumble. A State Landau also takes the Crown from the Lord Chamberlain's office to the Palace of Westminster before the Opening of Parliament. Another carriage in regular annual use is the barouche (which looks, when closed, rather like an old-fashioned pram), in which the Queen Mother, accompanied often by Princess Margaret and Princess Anne (the Prince of Wales now being at boarding school) drive to The Queen's Birthday Parade on Horseguards Parade. A second barouche follows with the ladies and gentlemen in attendance.

A royal brougham is often seen in Whitehall, where it is used daily to distribute official documents, and is found as convenient as a car. Ladies-in-Waiting used often to drive out in a royal brougham or a clarence, but the last lady to use a brougham for this purpose was Lady Kavanagh, wife of the previous Crown Equerry.

For the Coronation procession, the number of royal carriages in the Mews was not adequate, and the procession would have had to be half in carriages and half in cars, if it had not been for the generosity of private owners in England, who lent their own clarences (many of which had been sold out of the Royal Mews), their horses and in some cases themselves as Coachmen, donning the royal livery for the day.

There are also a number of most interesting royal carriages, formerly at Windsor, in the Carriage Museum The Queen has formed at Buckingham Palace in one of the coach houses.

It is as Lord of Man, as The Queen is always known and regarded in the Isle of Man, that she was welcomed there on Tuesday, August 9, 1955, when she visited the Island with the Duke of Edinburgh and the royal children in *Britannia*. When The Queen's health is drunk in the Island it is as "The Queen, Lord of Man", and The Queen herself, to the deep contentment of the Island people, described herself as Lord of Man in her reply to the Tynwald address of welcome.

The Isle of Man, which is about thirty miles long, lies in the

Irish Sea about equidistant from England, Scotland and Northern Ireland. Through the centuries it has been successfully under the sway of the Celts, the Norse, the Scots and the English; taking from the Celts (or perhaps the Scots) its ancient language, now almost in complete disuse; and from the Norse its Tynwald and House of Keys, the ancient Parliamentary system, the oldest in the whole Commonwealth.

England acquired the Isle of Man from the Scots by Treaty or *force majeure* on the part of Edward I; and the English Kings handed over the kingship of the Isle of Man, subject to tribute, to great lords of their own, finishing in 1405 with the Stanley family (later the Earls of Derby), who remained Kings of Man and later Lords of Man for over three hundred years. The succession then passed through the female line to the Dukes of Atholl. Eventually the island was such a stronghold of smugglers and such a thorn in the flesh of the English Revenue Department that in 1765 the United Kingdom Government stepped in, and took the lordship back to the Crown. Thus the Sovereign, in the person of George III, became Lord of Man.

The Queen appoints the Lieutenant-Governor of the Isle of Man, and the Island affairs are dealt with in Privy Council. The Island to-day looks after most of its own affairs by Island legislature, with the exception of such major subjects as Defence, Foreign Policy and Currency, and subject to the United Kingdom's overriding right of paramountcy.

King George VI visited the Island and presided over the annual open-air meeting of the Tynwald or Parliament at St. John's, but The Queen was the first Sovereign to preside over a meeting of the Tynwald, her oldest Court, in the famous beamed Chamber of the Tynwald in Douglas. There she was seated with her Lieutenant-Governor, her Deemsters and Council, and attended by the Sword-Bearer of the fine thirteenth century Manx Sword of State, together with the Members of the House of Keys (which approximates to the House of Commons) to listen to an address of welcome read by the Speaker, which began:

"We, the Lieutenant-Governor, Council, Deemsters and Keys in Tynwald assembled . . ."

The Queen, in her reply, said:

"I am specially proud to preside at this gathering of Tynwald, which has had a continuous history of more than a thousand years and is the oldest Parliament in all the countries of which I am Queen."

She ended by saying a few words in Manx "As nish, moghrey mie as aigh vie." ("And now good morning and good luck.") As the local paper afterwards commented:

She knew how to pronounce them too!

The Channel Islands are not a part of Britain, but I hope Channel Islanders will forgive me for including them in this chapter.

The history and background of the Channel Islands is Norman French, more remotely Scandinavian and Celtic. The Queen, as Princess Elizabeth, had visited the islands in 1949. In July 1957, together with the Duke of Edinburgh, she visited them as Queen, visiting Jersey, Guernsey, Sark and Alderney. On the last day of her tour, owing to bad weather springing up, The Queen had to make use of six forms of transport in order to fulfil her programme and not disappoint the people of Alderney. In the prevailing weather, the royal yacht *Britannia* could not safely enter the Alderney harbour of Braye. So from Sark, which The Queen had visited in the morning, she returned to Guernsey, and flew to Alderney in a Heron of The Queen's Flight, which had been standing by for such a contingency. In Sark she had conducted her short tour in a one-horse carriage. During that one day The Queen employed royal yacht, royal barge, horse-drawn carriage, car, foot and aircraft.

In the Channel Islands The Queen of course, as she does everywhere, saw evidence both of the particular industries and skills of the place, and the services—both armed and social—by which the level of life is held secure and advanced. She saw Jersey and Guernsey cattle, inspected guards of honour, and laid the foundation stone of a new hospital—a tightly packed schedule of engagements throughout the three days of her visit.

The Channel Islands are a remainder of the Duchy of Normandy, and were an integral part of the duchy when William the Conqueror, Duke of Normandy, made himself King of England. When the Kings of England lost their possessions in France, the islands remained the last part of the lost lands of the Duchy and were regarded, as they are to-day, as possessions of the Crown which have never been incorporated into the kingdom of England. The island Governments, which have a very large measure of autonomy, are responsible to The Queen in Council (who is advised by the Home Secretary) and not to Parliament.

The official proceedings in the Channel Islands were therefore quite unlike the usual civic welcome for The Queen, and that in Guernsey on July 26, 1957, may well serve as an example. The Queen presided over a meeting of the States of Deliberation, which is the "House of Parliament" of Guernsey, held in the Royal Court. "This meeting of the Legislature of one of my most ancient Possessions", as Her Majesty called it in her reply to the Address of Welcome made by the Bailiff (Sir Ambrose Sherwill, C.B.E., M.C.).

Later in the day The Queen and the Duke of Edinburgh went to St. George's Hall, where The Queen presided over an Extraordinary sitting of the Court of Chief Pleas. This is the most solemn and full session of the Royal Court of Guernsey, which is normally held three times a year, and is attended by all the officers of the Court (Bailiff, constables, jurats, law officers, prevot, greffier and, in the Middle Ages, a bedel and a hangman as well—the Bailiff acting as "president"), together with those holders of fiefs or "free tenements", who owed suit of court as part of the service due on the property they hold, and the Senior Constables of the Island's ten parishes. The earliest record of such a court dates from about 1180, but the judicial administration in the Channel Islands was thoroughly re-organised in the thirteenth century, when the Court of Chief Pleas probably took shape. Gradually it lost power, and the legislative powers of the Court of Chief Pleas were transferred to the States by the Reform (Guernsey) Law of 1948. Now the Court of Chief Pleas does principally routine business. When The Queen presided at the Guernsey Court of Chief Pleas it was, so far as is known, the first occasion on which an English Sovereign had ever presided over the Islands' Court of Chief Pleas. "Whether, before 1066, Dukes of Normandy had done so, I, of course," said Sir Ambrose Sherwill, "would not know." King George V and Queen Mary attended a similar assembly in 1921, but the King did not preside over the Court of Chief Pleas.

The Royal Court in general (of which the Court of Chief Pleas is the full session) in its various divisions deals with all criminal and civil proceedings arising in the Island.

When The Queen was in the Chief Court of Pleas in Guernsey, she received homage from the Seigneurs and Dames of Fiefs holding in Chief from Her Majesty, but, according to so great an authority as Dr. J. Le Patourel, the Professor of Medieval History at Leeds University and Archiviste of Guernsey, this took place at this time "not . . . because it was the Court of Chief Pleas, but because it was the convenient and natural opportunity during Her Majesty's first visit to the island since her accession". The ceremony of "Foi et Hommage" was enacted when Mr. Cecil de Sausmarez, M.B.E., Seigneur of Le Fief Sausmarez de Saint Martin, on behalf of the Seigneurs and Dames of Fiefs holding in Chief from Her Majesty, did homage in conformity with ancient custom. He bowed, knelt before The Queen, and placing his hands together between her hands, pronounced the following words:

"Souveraine Dame, je demeure votre homme lige à vous porter Foy et Hommage contre tous."

to which The Queen replied:

"Nous vous acceptons, advouant tous vos légitimes droits et possessions releveant de cette teneore de nous, sauf pareillement à tous nos droits de Régalité."

As the Seigneur of Le Fief Sausmarez de Saint Martin placed his hands together, the other Seigneurs and Dames, all standing, did likewise, and softly repeated the words of their homage.

Following the ceremony of "Foi et Hommage", the Seigneur of Le Fief des Eperons advanced and, on bended knee, presented to Her Majesty the pair of silver-gilt spurs owing by his Fief on the occasion of a visit by the reigning Sovereign, saying, as he did so:

"Souveraine Dame, je désire m'acquitter de mon service et offrir à Votre Majesté les éperons dorés que je Vous dois à cause de mon fief."

Her Majesty touched the spurs in token of Royal acceptance.

During the sitting of the Chief Pleas, Her Majesty carried a posy of sweet-smelling flowers and herbs grown in the little garden at Castle Cornet which was tended by General John Lambert, one of Cromwell's principal generals, during his imprisonment there for a number of years from 1661.

One place which is not remote, but which is "special", is the Duchy of Lancaster, of which The Queen is the hereditary Duke of Lancaster—note, she is not Duchess but Duke of Lancaster, just as she is not Lady but Lord of Man.

Apart from annual and regional visits, The Queen makes many special visits throughout the country and in London to one special place for one special occasion. All in all, her visits and her consequent knowledge of her country mount steadily. Although the framework of the visits may be similar, The Queen is looking at the differences, not the resemblances, and she sees and learns much from even a formal occasion.

To give an idea of how these separate visits mount up, here are lists which have been abstracted from The Queen's diaries, and which I am privileged to quote:

Hospitals visited by The Queen in Great Britain from the time of her Accession until the late autumn, 1958:

Hospital for Sick Children, Great Ormond Street (Princess Anne had her tonsils out here in 1958)
London Hospital
Moorfields, Westminster and Central Eye Hospital
Gloucester Royal Hospital
Hammersmith Hospital
Dundee Royal Infirmary
Aberdeen Hospital for Sick Children
Royal London Homeopathic Hospital
King Edward VII Sanatorium, Midhurst
Hull Royal Infirmary
Bute Hospital, Daliburgh, South Uist
Queen Elizabeth's Hospital for Children, Banstead
Royal Surrey County Hospital
Norfolk and Norwich Hospital (Opened new Operating Theatre)
Royal Infirmary, Chester
Royal Dental Hospital of London

During the same period, she visited the following industries:

British Industries Fair (on four occasions)

Duchy Land, Gillingham, Dorset (Went over a brush factory)

Opened Claerwen Dam

Harrisons and Sons Limited, Printers (Factory at High Wycombe)

Attended Dress Show of the Incorporated Society of London Fashion Designers

John Brown and Company (Clydebank) Limited (Launched H.M.Y. *Britannia*)

Burroughs Adding Machine Company Limited

Shaw Savill and Albion Company Limited (Launched *Southern Cross*)

Tour of Lilac Mill, Shaw, near Rochdale, Lancs. (Saw nursery where fifty children between the ages of two and five stay while their mothers are at work)

English Steel Corporation Works, Sheffield

Cawthra and Company Perseverance Mills, Bradford (Textile Mill)

British Petroleum Company (Kent Oil Refinery)

Walter Pollard Limited (Textile Mill)

Nelson and Malvern Mill

Mullard (Blackburn) Works Limited

Gloucester Railway Carriage and Wagon Company

Fairfield Shipbuilding and Engineering Company Limited (Launched Canadian Pacific Railway Company's *Empress of Britain*)

James Templeton and Company Limited (Carpet Factory)

Jute Industries Limited (Camperdown Works)

James Keiller and Sons Limited, Dundee Works (Marmalade and Confectionery Works)

Imperial Chemical Industries Limited, Grangemouth

Birkin and Company Limited, Nottingham (Lace Factory)

Inauguration of Usk Reservoir, Swansea

Richards Limited, Aberdeen (Linen Makers)

Josiah Wedgwood and Sons Limited (China and Earthenware)

Johnson Brothers (Hanley) Limited (China)

Joseph Lucas Limited (Electrical Works)

Jaguar Cars Limited, Coventry

Bristol Waterworks Company (Inauguration of Chew Stoke Reservoir)

Charles Hill and Sons Limited, Bristol (Shipbuilders)

Imperial Chemical Industries Limited, Wilton Works, Middlesbrough

Dorman Long and Company Limited, Middlesbrough (Steel Works)

Kenneth Mackenzie Limited, Stornoway (Tweed Works)

Inauguration of Daer Reservoir

United Steel Companies Limited (Works at Workington)

Opened Nuclear Power Station of United Kingdom Atomic Energy Authority—Calder Hall

English Steel Corporation Works, Sheffield

Harwell Atomic Energy Research Establishment

Walter Somers Limited (Heavy Engineers), Halesowen

Stevens and Williams Glass Works, Brierley Hill

Royal Radar Research Establishment, Malvern

Lever Brothers (Port Sunlight), Lancs.

Hydraulic Research Station, Howbery Park

Building Exhibition

Harlow Metal Company Factory

N. Corah (St. Margaret) Limited, Leicester

Appleby-Frodingham Steel Company, Scunthorpe

West Market, Grimsby Fish Docks

Rothes Colliery, Fife

Linburn Workshops and Training Centre of the Scottish National Institute for the War Blinded

India Tyre Works, Inchinnan

R. W. Crabtree and Sons Limited, Leeds (Toured Machine Shops and Assembly Bays)

Montague Burton Limited, Leeds

Textiles Exhibition in the Central Court of the Parkinson Buildings, Leeds

How many of you have visited over fifty industrial plants and mills within the United Kingdom alone in the last six years? Only those, I am sure, who are engaged in industry in some way. A number of highly important events have fallen within the Queen's reign. Perhaps the most far-reaching, one which created world-wide interest, was the opening at Calder Hall in Cumberland, of the first large-scale nuclear power station in use for peaceful purposes in the world (October 17, 1956).

There have already been many specially important events in The Queen's reign, events which do not happen in every reign, and some of these should be recorded here.

First of all, there is the unhappy aftermath of war. Although the war ended in 1945, it is in The Queen's reign that many memorials have been completed. The Queen unveiled at Runnymede the memorial to 20,000 airmen of the Commonwealth Forces who have no known grave (October 17, 1953); she unveiled on Tower Hill the Merchant Navy Memorial to 24,000 members lost at sea in the war (November 5, 1956); in connection with the rebuilding of war damage The Queen opened the rebuilt Trinity House on Tower Hill, London (October 21, 1953); she laid the foundation stone of the new Coventry Cathedral (March 23, 1956); she opened Bristol's new Council House (April 15, 1956).

The Queen unveiled the monument to her father, King George VI, in Carlton Gardens, and spoke most movingly on a dark, rainy day, of his fortitude and sense of duty.

The Queen has marked many anniversaries and centenaries by her presence. For instance, she held a Jubilee Review of 2,000 officers and men of the Royal Naval Volunteer Reserve on Horseguards Parade (May 2, 1954)—and barely suppressed her amusement when a wet flag, too low above the dais, slapped her husband across the face at a solemn moment of the ceremony (July 14, 1954); she attended the Thanksgiving Service in Westminster Abbey for the third jubilee of the Bible Society. The Queen and the Duke flew to Gloucester on the 800th anniversary of the granting of its royal charter and took part in a service in the Cathedral (May 3, 1956): The Queen and the Duke of Edinburgh attended dinner at the Royal College, Greenwich, in commemoration of the 150th anniversary of Trafalgar (October 21, 1956). The Queen reviewed 300 holders of the Victoria Cross at a moving ceremony in Hyde Park, to mark the centenary of the award of the decoration. She attended a reception to mark the 60th anniversary of the Royal Automobile Club (October 17, 1956); and on the one day (November 2, 1956), she visited Abingdon, which was celebrating the 400th anniversary of its incorporation, and Wallingford, which was celebrating the 800th anniversary of the granting of its charter.

Many of The Queen's official duties of this kind mark great material, technical or educational advances. For instance what a considerable number of new water supplies she has opened, while in the field of education, she has already personally presented the royal charter founding the University of Exeter (May 6, 1956); opened the New Library of the National Library of Scotland (July 4, 1956); and opened the new Faculty of Letters building at Reading University (March 22, 1957).

The Queen has attended a luncheon in Westminster Hall at which Ministers and Members of Parliament from fifty-two Commonwealth legislatures were present (April 27, 1953). She broke her summer holiday, and travelled from Balmoral—a distance of nearly 600 miles—to open the annual conference of the Inter-Parliamentary Union when it was held in London (September 12, 1957). She laid the foundation stone of the new building for Lloyds (November 6, 1952).

And this is by no means a full list.

Yet it is the little, human incident which is often remembered when the grand occasions have passed into history.

There is a famous architect who remembers the moment when The Queen, being shown round an exhibition, asked him a question, and then, seeing he did not know the answer, smiled and said, "I am sorry I asked that one."

There is a rector in Essex who had a parishioner, Mrs. Locke, who had reached the grand age of 105 without ever seeing a member of the Royal Family. Encouraged by a particularly cordial telegram to the old lady on her latest birthday, he wrote to Buckingham Palace to ask whether, when The Queen passed through her native village of Great Bromley on her way to Harwich to embark for the State Visit, it would be at all possible for The Queen to stop long enough for the old lady to be presented to her. The Queen's Assistant Private Secretary replied very hopefully. The Rector told me:

"At first we thought that Mrs. Locke would get out of my car and meet Her Majesty in the road between the two cars, and we had a special message that if it was raining, Mrs. Locke was not to get out of the car but that The Queen would do so, despite the rain, and come over to my car. Later on we received word that whether fine or wet, Mrs. Locke was to stay in my car, as it was thought that the excitement of the presentation to The Queen might make it too risky for her to do otherwise than sit still.

"When the royal car arrived, The Queen got out, I and my wife were presented to her and she then walked a few steps to my car where she spoke to Mrs. Locke through the open door. I had told her that she was now very deaf, so The Queen took great care to speak into her best ear. . . . Mrs. Locke was full of pleasure at meeting The Queen and thought her so kind and sweet. My chief feeling was utter admiration of her absolute graciousness and kindness."

Or there is the instance of the Mayoress who was lying ill in hospital when The Queen was to visit her Borough. Some days before The Queen was to visit the town, the Mayor told the Clerk to the Lieutenancy of the County that his wife the Mayoress was gravely ill. The Queen was informed of this, through her Assistant Private Secretary, and that the Mayoress was in a hospital which was close to the route on The Queen's drive. When The Queen arrived she told the Mayor that she would like to visit the Mayoress in hospital. After the official luncheon, the necessary rearrangements being made in the tightly-timed schedule, The Queen, taking a gift of roses, went to the hospital to visit the sick Mayoress. The visit was quite private, and apart from the Mayor's immediate family, only the Head Physician and the Matron were present.

There is the gardener Councillor who wrote to The Queen when he could not afford to buy a new dark suit for his presentation to The Queen, and who received the reply, signed by The Queen's Assistant Secretary:

The Queen never stipulates the colour of clothes to be worn, and any instructions issued locally should be regarded merely in the nature of guidance.

Her Majesty never wishes people to be put to extra expense on account of her visits, and would certainly not wish you specially to acquire for this occasion a suit of darker colour than the one you already possess.

CHAPTER TEN

The Queen, Our Hostess

"We found Her Majesty a most engaging, pleasant and vivacious personage and person, warm, human, interested and interesting. Our brief visit was engaging in its simplicity and lack of pomp and circumstance, and gave us the feeling that the concerns, interests and problems of the Royal Family were not so very different—except in extent and importance—from our own."

An American army officer, who was one of a small group
received in Audience by The Queen

"After the first few moments The Queen put me completely at ease. It was the happiest party, gay and serious by turns, and everyone was drawn into the conversation."

A guest at luncheon at Buckingham Palace

THE Queen is the hostess of the Commonwealth. The guests she entertains in her own home every year must, even in normal years, number between 25,000 and 30,000.

Some are entertained at magnificent State Banquets, some at the numerously attended, pleasant Garden Parties, some are Heads of State, some are distinguished statesmen and ambassadors who "dine and sleep" at Windsor. Many are from the Commonwealth overseas. Interesting personalities from every kind of life in Britain to-day come to lunch or dinner so that The Queen and the Duke of Edinburgh can get to know them better. Personal friends stay at Windsor for Ascot week, or at Sandringham or Balmoral for the shooting. The Queen's guests represent a range of race and background, interest and varied occupation, which it would be hard to match throughout the modern world.

The Queen's task as hostess of the Commonwealth is a tremendous one. In itself, this one part of the Sovereign's duties would constitute a full life. It is a part of the duties of the Head of

State particularly happily filled by a Sovereign, and perhaps most happily of all by a Sovereign Queen. Official hospitality gains dignity and value which it would be hard to reproduce in any setting where the Head of State was a temporary incumbent.

The British have long realised that antagonisms, rivalries, shyness and other barriers to communication can be most easily dissolved in the atmosphere of a home. The Queen's home is impartial; she has not been linked with one side or the other in violent political argument. All may equally easily be invited there. To each it is an honour. The Queen's guests, sitting side by side at table, strolling together through a picture gallery or a garden, discussing chance topics in a friendly atmosphere, may have a better opportunity to form new friendships or to strengthen old ones than in many hours round a conference table.

The Queen's hospitality has a further advantage. The Queen can select or change the conversation, should any topic be embarrassing or tedious. However, in general circumstances, I am told by guests, The Queen directs the conversation no more and no less than any other skilled young hostess, eager to secure the pleasure of her guests.

The Queen has so many people to entertain.

When The Queen entertains a Head of State on a State Visit, he is generally given the Belgian suite at Buckingham Palace. This suite, in the north-west corner on the ground floor, was originally designed for King George IV, who was too infirm to climb stairs. He never occupied it, but it was used by King Edward VIII, and by The Queen and the Duke of Edinburgh after the death of King George VI and before the Queen Mother moved to Clarence House. King Haakon VII of Norway lived here in the early days of his exile in 1940.

The principal rooms of the suite were redecorated in 1958, being completed just before the State Visit of the President of the West German Republic, Dr. Heuss, in October.

The Drawing Room, a large room with two windows overlooking the gardens, now has walls hung with a cream damask-patterned wallpaper. The curtains and upholstery are of French embroidered silk. Some exceptionally fine pieces of English eighteenth-century furniture have been placed in the room, including Vile and Cobb's celebrated mahogany cabinet with

Corinthian columns and glass doors, behind which are displayed Sèvres and Chelsea porcelain. The paintings are by Allan Ramsay, Samuel Scott and James Ward. The carpet, of floral design, is an early nineteenth-century Axminster.

The principal bedroom, known as the Orleans Bedroom, which adjoins the Drawing Room, has been redecorated. It has wallpaper of similar design, and curtains of blue silk taffeta. The carpet and chairs are in matching shades of pale grey-green. On the walls are paintings of Queen Victoria, her family and friends, by Winterhalter and Westall. On the marble chimney piece stands a Louis XV ormolu clock mounted with a group of Chinese figures in white Vincennes porcelain—said to be the largest and most important group of its kind in the world. The fine chandelier is of English eighteenth-century crystal.

The State Banquet, held during a State Visit, is, in the opinion of many, the most magnificent and splendid of all royal occasions. It is held in the largest room in Buckingham Palace, the Ballroom, which is 123 feet long, 60 feet wide and 45 feet high, and was built for Queen Victoria in 1853, to designs by James Pennethorne. Even by day no direct daylight falls into the great room, of which the main decoration is a throne dais in front of a recess enclosed by Corinthian columns. The room is lit by six fine pink-lustre chandeliers.

The Queen usually sits in the centre of the table. She wears a magnificent evening dress, with tiara and other splendid jewellery. When a foreign guest is present who has presented her with a High Order of his country, naturally The Queen wears this, in preference to the Garter, which otherwise she always wears on great ceremonial evening occasions in England.

In front of her there is always a fine *low* floral decoration, so that The Queen can see and be seen by her guests. This centrepiece consists of various round dishes placed on a $27\frac{1}{2}$-inch round plateau with Roman scroll, laurel borders, and basket and grape pedestal ornaments. It was presented to George IV by his mother, Queen Charlotte, about 1819.

The gold plate makes a splendid and glittering show. The tables are decorated with silver-gilt vases of various designs, many incorporating classical themes, which are filled with flowers. On the tables stand also silver-gilt candelabra of various designs, made by Paul Storr around 1816 and John Bridges in 1828. One such candelabrum, designed by Flaxman and executed by Storr, has three piping fauns round the base, from which springs a central stem and six single branches for candles. Above, grouped round a tree trunk, Mercury presents Bacchus to the Nymphs.

The Royal Plate is extremely valuable. With the exception of plate for the Coronation Banquet, which is with the Regalia in the Tower of London, and the plate in use in the Chapels Royal, it is divided between Buckingham Palace and Windsor Castle. The Royal Plate belongs to the Crown. In addition, there is the fine Private Plate, the personal property of the Royal Family, which is also in the Palaces.

None of the plate is earlier in royal ownership than Charles II, but much dates from Frederick, Prince of Wales, son of George II and father of George III, who ordered what is now a unique collection of the work of Nicholas Sprimont, who founded the Chelsea porcelain factory. King George IV collected antique plate, including a beautiful Nautilus cup and cover, originally attributed to the master of all goldsmiths, Benvenuto Cellini.

The plate also contains one piece which may properly be described unique: a silver-gilt table centre thirty inches high, to the design of the Prince Consort. It displays the favourite dogs of Queen Victoria in active pursuit of rats. One rodent (dead) is lying deserted on the steps, while another (alive) in a trap, rivets the attention of Queen Victoria's famous terrier Islay and dachshund Waldmann. Not, one would have imagined, conducive to the royal appetite!

The whole meal is eaten with gold cutlery and served on silver-gilt plates, with the exception of the dessert, which is served on china. The china is chosen from the following services:

(a) William IV Garter Service in Bleu-du-Roi, emblazoned with the Royal Arms and the supports surrounded by six medallions of the Insignia of the Orders of Knighthood. It was made for William IV on his accession in 1830 and is of Worcester porcelain.

(b) Louis XV French Sèvres Dessert Service in Turquoise with detached bouquets and rare birds, 1760.

(c) Louis XV French Sèvres Dessert Service in apple green with detached bouquets by Chappuis, 1759–63.

(*d*) Victoria Minton Service in turquoise with Royal Monogram "VR 1859".

(*e*) The Royal Rockingham Dessert Service made for William IV, *circa* 1830.

The table glass at State Banquets is English cut crystal in a fluted style, hand-engraved with the cypher E II R. It was made for the Coronation in 1953 by the Stourbridge Glass Company.

The menu is carefully thought out, and the names of the dishes are often graceful compliments to the guests.

The tables used always to be set out in a gigantic horseshoe, and the guests were always seated in order of Precedence. On the occasion of the Banquet in honour of Signor Gronchi, President of the Italian Republic, during his State Visit in the summer of 1958, The Queen introduced an informal touch which added to the enjoyment of those present. The enormous horseshoe table was replaced by one large top table, and a number of small, round tables, each seating ten people. The only previous occasion on which these round tables had been used for a State Banquet was at the Coronation Banquet.

The footmen wear powdered hair, scarlet livery decorated with gold braid, scarlet plush knee breeches, pink stockings and black buckled shoes. The senior servants wear black and gold braid livery with fine white wool cloth breeches, white stockings and black buckled shoes. The reason is supposed to be that before the Prince Consort's death all the servants wore scarlet, but that Queen Victoria put them all in black and although ultimately the footmen were put into scarlet again, black for the senior servants was maintained and still remains.

Scarlet livery is the exclusive usage of Royalty, and at Coronations the pages to those Peers whose family livery incorporates scarlet have to change this for the darker shade known heraldically as "murrey", a late-medieval word derived from mulberry.

The guests, naturally, are dressed in their finest, with all Orders and decorations and, as one woman who has attended many such occasions said to me smilingly, "Every woman who owns, or can beg or borrow a tiara, is of course wearing one."

Such State Banquets have been held comparatively frequently during The Queen's reign. There were two State Banquets, on successive evenings, for official guests at the Coronation. State

Banquets were also held during the State Visits of King Gustaf VI Adolf of Sweden, the Emperor Hailé Selassi of Ethiopia, the Portuguese President and Mme Craveiro Lopes, the ill-fated King Feisal of Iraq, the President of Italy and Mme Gronchi, and the President of West Germany, Herr Heuss.

At these Banquets, The Queen makes a Speech, welcoming her guest, to which he replies.

Of equal importance are the Banquets held for the Commonwealth Prime Ministers, of which three (and one luncheon) have been held at Buckingham Palace, and one in the Waterloo Chamber at Windsor Castle in 1957. On such occasions The Queen likes to show prominently the magnificent Commonwealth Vase, which was made for her in commemoration of her Coronation by the British Pottery Manufacturers Federation in "fine china", to the design of J. Wadsworth.

The vase is twenty-four inches high and weighs twenty-nine pounds. It is ten-sided and the lid is surmounted with a crown. In the centre panel is the Royal Coat of Arms. In the panels on either side are the Tudor Rose and the Scotch Thistle in one, and the Welsh Leek and the Irish Shamrock in the other. On each of the remaining seven panels is an emblem of the other Commonwealth countries, commemorating the Commonwealth countries at the time of The Queen's Coronation. At the base of the vase are ten alcoves which house The Queen's Beasts.

To these great Banquets The Queen asks, as well as the Commonwealth Prime Ministers, the High Commissioners of the countries concerned, some senior Members of the Commonwealth Prime Ministers' staffs and some members of her own Household. On these most formal occasions the places are naturally filled almost entirely from those of highest office.

Perhaps the most unusual feature in this country is that the Leaders of the Opposition parties are always included. This is an appreciated courtesy, but it is far more important than that. It means that the visiting notability, whether it be a Commonwealth Prime Minister or a foreign Head of State, during his stay in this country is meeting and re-meeting all the important political leaders. Should the political party in power change, he is still able to deal with men known to him personally.

As early as the fourteenth century, protocol was laid down by which the Sovereign was definitely established as the head of Society. (Yet up to 250 years ago, it was quite an informal thing for people to go to Court and see the King. Pepys recounts going to Whitehall to see King Charles II at dinner. But as the population of Britain increased, so formality around the Court had to increase too.) The concept of the Sovereign as the leader of Society has persisted through the centuries, but The Queen is not anxious to avail herself of it. She undertakes fully the duties of hostess of the Commonwealth. But Society, in the former narrow and restricted sense, has little place in her crowded and useful life.

One restriction remains, and that is with regard to divorced persons. In 1957 an official of the Lord Chamberlain's office explained the position as follows:

Guilty parties in divorces cannot be invited to functions held by The Queen within her royal palaces. The royal yacht, *Britannia*, would come within this category.

Innocent parties in divorces can be invited.

Persons in public office are received on account of the office.

Characteristic of The Queen's attitude has been her decision to discontinue Presentation Parties.

Queen Anne introduced the Levée, at which gentlemen were received; and its complement, the Drawing Room, to which ladies whose husbands had attended the Levées brought their daughters to be presented to the Sovereign.

In the Prince Regent's time the headdress of three ostrich feathers, in complimentary imitation of the three feathers of his crest, became part of the Court dress. In Queen Victoria's reign, Drawing Rooms were a kind of social birth, by means of which the presented schoolgirl burst from the chrysalis into the marriageable young lady.

King Edward VII found the Drawing Room intensely dull. Instead, he substituted the gayer Evening Court, at which wine suppers were served after the presentations. These functions were very beautiful, although more crowded than the exclusive State Banquet. Evening Courts continued, with a break for the First World War, right up to the outbreak of the Second World War in 1939, during which there were no presentations. In 1947 King George VI reintroduced an austerity Presentation Party, at which attendance counted as presentation. However, the débutantes themselves—a word which came into the English language only at the time of the accession of Queen Victoria to the Throne—were delighted when individual curtseys to Sovereign and Consort were reintroduced in 1951.

When Elizabeth II succeeded to the Throne she made no immediate changes in this procedure, and that is typical of her. Her reign has been remarkable for the way in which her changes— which have been considerable—have never been precipitate but always considered and deliberate, and done in such a way as to cause the least possible heart-burning.

Through the years the Presentation Party had become a formally organised ceremony, with strict rules to prevent misuse, although these rules, as regards dress for instance, had been sensibly modified to accord with the time.

Late each year the regulations for next season's Presentation Parties were announced, and as they may soon be as dead as the originator of the first Drawing Rooms, it may not be without interest to give them here. The regulations are for the 1956 Presentation Parties, but they varied little from year to year.

The Lord Chamberlain announces that The Queen, with the Duke of Edinburgh, will hold afternoon parties for the presentation of ladies at Buckingham Palace next year.

Ladies whose applications include the names of *débutantes* will be summoned to make their presentations at one of the parties to be held on March 21 and 22. Ladies whose applications do not include the name of a *débutante* will be summoned to attend one of the garden parties in July. The regulations are as follows:

Ladies, who have already been presented in their present name and style, wishing to make presentations, should forward the names as soon as possible to the Lord Chamberlain, St. James's Palace, London, S.W.1.

Any lady who has attended, or been presented at a presentation party in 1954 or 1955 is not eligible to attend in 1956, except for the purpose of presenting an unmarried daughter.

No applications can be accepted from ladies wishing to be presented; their names must be forwarded by the ladies who wish to present them.

Unmarried ladies are ineligible to make presentations even though they themselves have been presented.

No applications can be accepted for attendance only.

A lady eligible to make a presentation who wishes to present her daughters and/or daughters-in-law may, in addition, present one other lady. Otherwise ladies are limited to one presentation only.

On the occasion of their own presentation, ladies may only present their daughters and/or daughters-in-law.

Invitations will be extended to the husbands of ladies making presentations or being presented, only if their names are submitted in the original application. It is emphasised that the attendance of gentlemen at these presentation parties will not count as presentation at Court.

Ladies domiciled in the Commonwealth countries and colonies wishing to be presented, must make application to the High Commissioner, or Secretary of State, concerned, for presentation by his wife.

Ladies of foreign nationality, either by birth or by marriage, can only be presented through the diplomatic representative of the country concerned, except when they are in possession of British passports.

But the Presentation Party, at which only about 200 débutantes could be presented and only 750 persons could be present, was a wasteful manner of using The Queen's time in present-day circumstances. If the number of girls being brought forward for presentation had been falling off naturally, then the function might have been permitted to continue or to atrophy gradually. On the contrary, each year more and still more applications were being received by the Lord Chamberlain. They came not only from all parts of the United Kingdom, not only in greatly increasing numbers from the Commonwealth countries overseas, but also from foreign countries. The wife of the United States Ambassador, for example, was besieged by requests to present young American girls to The Queen.

It became obvious that either The Queen would have to give considerably more time to the Presentation Parties, or some form of rationing or selection of the débutantes would have to be introduced, or they would have to cease. To give more time from The Queen's vastly over-burdened calendar would be unrealistic; to introduce some form of rationing would be unfair; and so, on November 14, 1957, the Lord Chamberlain issued the following announcement from St. James's Palace:

The Lord Chamberlain gives notice that there will be no Presentation Parties after 1958. The Queen proposes to hold additional Garden Parties in order that larger numbers may be invited to Buckingham Palace.

Immediately there was a rush by mothers to have their daughters included among the last débutantes. So many applications were received that The Queen decided, in spite of heavy commitments, to hold an extra Presentation Party to accommodate them all. In March three Presentation Parties, in place of the customary two, took place at Buckingham Palace. A Presentation Party was held in Scotland, at the Palace of Holyroodhouse, on July 3, 1958. Two further Presentation Parties for Commonwealth débutantes were to be held by The Queen after her return to Buckingham Palace, before the Garden Parties on July 10 and July 17. But the plans, even of a Queen, can "gang a-gley". The Queen became ill with sinusitis. Although the Royal Standard flew over the roof of Buckingham Palace as a sign that The Queen was in residence, she was confined to her room, and it was Queen Elizabeth The Queen Mother, deputising for The Queen, to whom the last Presentations of all were made.

Although she did not know it at the time, the last débutante to make her curtsey to the Sovereign was Miss Fiona Macrae, daughter of Mr. and Mrs. Kenneth Macrae of Edinburgh, a tall, pretty girl in a short white-and-grey flowered dress and a small hat of violet petals, who was presented by the wife of Mr. D. L. Mackintyre, V.C., Under-Secretary to the Ministry of Works in Scotland, in the brilliantly lit, oak-panelled Throne Room of the Palace of Holyroodhouse. The Queen, in primrose-yellow lace with a yellow hat to match, sat on a crimson chair with the Duke of Edinburgh seated on her left. The Hereditary High Constable of Scotland, the Countess of Erroll, carried her baton of office. The Lord Chamberlain, the Earl of Scarbrough, read out the names. The Queen was attended by the Mistress of the Robes (Mary, Duchess of Devonshire) and a Lady-in-Waiting (Mrs. Abel Smith). One after the other, eight every minute, the débutantes came forward and made their curtseys to The Queen and the Duke, until, with the second curtsey of Miss Macrae, a ceremony 250 years old had ended.

The best device for entertaining the largest possible numbers in The Queen's home is the Garden Party. Each year The Queen has held two Garden Parties at Buckingham Palace, and generally one also at Holyroodhouse. It is more than likely that this number may be increased. Very large numbers of people are commanded to be present, as many as 8,000 to a Buckingham Palace Party. In spite of the numbers, these are extremely pleasant affairs when the weather is kind. There is ample room for such guests as may have a liking for comparative solitude to wander through the beautiful wooded grounds of the thirty-nine-acre garden. (One clergyman guest is reputed to have secreted a collapsible butterfly net, and to have used it to good purpose to collect some notable specimens at one such Garden Party. When an account of his prowess appeared subsequently in a learned journal and was brought to the notice of his host, King George VI, the King's comment is said to have been "Sensible man!")

To these Garden Parties are asked people prominent in all forms of society, politicians, civic leaders, the heads of Institutions, Welfare organisations and Museums, doctors, nurses, scientists, professors, clerics, soldiers, headmasters and athletes, not only from the United Kingdom but also from all parts of the Commonwealth and indeed, in lesser numbers, from foreign countries as well.

At a Garden Party, The Queen comes out from the garden entrance on the north side of the Palace and, at a signal, one of the military bands present strikes up "God Save The Queen".

The Queen comes forward, accompanied by other members of the Royal Family, towards the packed ranks of her guests. First presented to her are her tenants from the Duchies of Lancaster and Cornwall. The royal party splits up. Each group walks very slowly and by a circuitous route through a line of guests towards the royal tea tent. On the way the Gentlemen Ushers bring forward a number of people, who are individually presented to The Queen. Many of these are on lists which have been prepared beforehand, others are brought forward spontaneously. The Queen chats to each, and although this presentation is repeated again and again throughout the afternoon, she gives the impression of real and genuine interest in each person. The tea tent at last reached, The Queen has tea with a number of persons and then, with the Duke of Edinburgh, goes forward to stand under a scarlet and gold awning. Formerly the *Shamiana*, which was made for the Delhi Durbar of King George V and Queen Mary, and which usually hangs over the dais of the Palace Ballroom, was used. There The Queen and the Duke meet a continual stream of often exotically arrayed Colonial guests, to each of whom they chat with friendly interest. When each short audience is over, The Queen dismisses them with a smile and a half-step backwards. The art of disengaging oneself gracefully and politely from a conversation is a difficult one which The Queen has mastered to perfection. After a most strenuous two hours, during which The Queen may have met individually as many as two hundred people and has given ample opportunity for everyone of her eight thousand guests to see her at close quarters, she again withdraws slowly, smiling and speaking to those close to her, to the Palace.

The catering for these great Garden Parties is done by an outside firm of purveyors. For many years the royal kitchens themselves coped with this occasion, but it was obviously un-economic to retain all the year round the very large staffs necessary to deal with the entertainment of many thousands of guests on only a few occasions in each year. By good teamwork and organisation the whole Garden Party is extremely well arranged.

Apart from these large Garden Parties, The Queen gives Garden Parties or Sherry Parties for special groups of people. The largest of these was probably the Afternoon Party which she gave for the members of the American Bar Association when they were in London in the summer of 1957 and which I heard, from an enthusiastic group of guests, was enormously appreci-ated by those who attended it. Incidentally it was the only recep-tion of their visit to this country at which all members of this very large party were entertained together by one host. Quite a lot was written at the time about the Queen's friendly gesture by ordering "hot dogs". Some people went so far as to say that the Americans present would not have served such homely fare, any more than we would have had fish and chips at a formal occasion. But The Queen had good grounds for her gesture, as her mother and father had eaten "hot dogs", and greatly en-joyed them, when guests of President Roosevelt in 1939.

The Queen and the Duke of Edinburgh have liked to entertain small groups of distinguished people such as the Everest climbers and the Transantarctic explorers; the staffs of Commonwealth conferences, and the French delegation to the Entente Cordiale celebrations. Both before and after her principal Tours, she has generally invited Government and Opposition leaders to the

Palace to a Sherry Party. In September 1958 The Queen invited forty nuclear scientists from the Commonwealth to luncheon at Balmoral. In March 1959 The Queen arranged an Afternoon Party for members of the W.V.S.

In 1958 The Queen had arranged to hold a special Garden Party for the Bishops of the Anglican Church, assembled in London for their ten-yearly Conference. Unfortunately, at the end of a strenuous visit to Scotland, which held a particularly official programme, The Queen became ill. When her illness failed to clear up as soon as was hoped, The Queen was disappointed and distressed that she could not entertain the Bishops as planned. Whenever her doctors could permit it, The Queen quickly arranged another day on which she could entertain the Bishops, who came to Buckingham Palace on August 5, the first day on which The Queen undertook any public engagements after her illness. More than 300 Archbishops and Bishops of the Anglican Communion attended. Their wives assembled in the Picture Gallery, through which The Queen passed on her way to the Ballroom, where all the 300 delegates were individually presented to The Queen. The Bishops were delighted by the charming way in which The Queen welcomed them, and by her obvious pleasure in meeting them after two postponements.

The Queen sometimes asks those who have had the last Audience of the morning to stay to luncheon, although it would appear from studying the *Court Circular* that she has recently rather reduced this form of hospitality. Royalties visiting London often go to lunch. The Queen entertained Governor-Generals, and senior Commonwealth Ministers. Over the excellent, but simple and quickly served meal, The Queen and the Duke have a fine opportunity to discuss outstanding problems with their guests. Foreign leaders she has entertained include the Crown Prince of Iraq (murdered with his nephew, King Feisal), Prince Himalaya Bir Bikram Shan and Princess Griha Rahya Laxmi Shah of Nepal, and the Prince and Princess of Monaco. Among other distinguished foreigners have been Mr. and Mrs. Harry Truman, Mrs. Eleanor Roosevelt and Maréschal de France Alphonse Juin. Commonwealth luncheon guests have included the Rt. Hon. Vincent Massey of Canada, the President of Pakistan and Begum Iskander Mirza, and Dr. Ernest G. Jansen, Governor-General of the Union of South Africa, and Mrs. Jansen. The Queen likes to talk over lunch with those going to fill important posts overseas, for instance the Earl and Countess of Dalhousie, when he was appointed Governor-General to the Federation of Rhodesia and Nyasaland, and Lord and Lady Hailes, when he was appointed Governor-General of the West Indies.

A most interesting development has been the lunches and dinners which The Queen and the Duke of Edinburgh have instituted in order to get to know the leading people in the country—from such spheres as Commerce, Politics, the Church, the Social Services, Sport, the Theatre, Industry and Letters. These lunches began, or rather were first made public, on May 11, 1956, and have continued ever since. While The Queen is in London, about two such lunches have been held every month; dinners, to which wives or husbands are also invited, are less frequent. There is no specially favoured day for either these luncheon or dinner parties, although rather more lunches have been held on Thursday than on any other day. Monday has several times been the day chosen for a dinner party.

The guests on these occasions are an extremely interesting and lively section, including some of the most stimulating people in the country. The Queen has continued to give them when the Duke of Edinburgh has been overseas, having the Queen Mother, or Princess Margaret or, on one occasion, the Duke and Duchess of Gloucester to support her. Quite apart from the honour and privilege of being The Queen's guest, these parties would in any circumstances be notable, as they are made up of not only distinguished people, but stimulating personalities. They are cleverly mixed with the sure hand of an expert hostess; not too many persons in the same "line of business", but subtly and interestingly blended. Generally there are eight guests at a luncheon and about twenty guests at dinner. Two lists of guests are quoted at random, to give an idea of the richness of composition:

Luncheon Party at Buckingham Palace on November 21, 1957.
  The Queen and the Duke of Edinburgh.
  Dame Myra Hess, the distinguished pianist.
  Chief Superintendent Elizabeth Bather of the Metropolitan Women's Police.

Mr. James Callaghan, Labour M.P. for Cardiff, S.E.

Professor J. G. Edwards, Professor of History, University of London.

Mr. F. A. Perkins, Chief and Managing Director of F. Perkins Ltd., Diesel Engines.

Mr. George L. Schwartz, Deputy City Editor of *The Sunday Times*.

Mr. Christopher Brasher, athlete.

Dinner Party at Buckingham Palace on November 13, 1957.

The Queen and the Duke of Edinburgh.

United States Ambassador and Mrs. Whitney.

Doreen, Marchioness of Linlithgow (widow of the former Viceroy of India).

Colonel the Hon. Angus McDonnell, a former Conservative M.P. for Dartford.

Sir Bryan Sharwood-Smith, Governor of Northern Region of Nigeria, and Lady Sharwood-Smith.

Sir Leslie Farrer, The Queen's Solicitor, and the Hon. Lady Farrer.

Sir Michael Balcon, film producer, and Lady Balcon.

Sir Geoffrey Crowther, Editor of *The Economist*, and Lady Crowther.

Vice-Admiral D. E. Holland-Martin, Second Sea Lord, and Mrs. Holland-Martin.

Mr. Aidan Crawley, political commentator, and Mrs. Crawley.

Mr. John Betjeman, author, and the Hon. Mrs. Betjeman.

Mr. and Mrs. Reginald Grenfell (Joyce Grenfell the actress).

Who else would have the opportunity to bring together just such wide varieties of interesting people?

A guest at one of these lunches, who happened to be the only woman other than The Queen present, told me how easy and simple everything had been. The Queen had led her guests into lunch and immediately the conversation had ranged widely, wisely and wittily, adroitly directed by The Queen and the Duke, and bringing in everyone at the table.

On that occasion the menu consisted of poached egg in pastry with asparagus, roast beef and new potatoes, crepe suzettes, fruit, and cheese. Everyone had what they wanted to drink. The Queen drank a glass of Moselle, the Duke took beer. Often the food chosen by The Queen for her guests consists of a plain first course, followed by a roast, grill or bird prepared and served with tender young vegetables, followed by perhaps an unusual ice. Both The Queen and the Duke dislike over-elaborate drawn-out meals.

Another traditional way in which The Queen and the Duke of Edinburgh entertain people are the invitations to "dine and sleep" at Windsor, which were in full swing in Queen Victoria's day and which continue. Outwardly these visits have changed little, but they have been modernised in tune with The Queen and the Duke's progressive attitude to life.

"Dine and Sleep" guests are generally invited to Windsor at Easter, when The Queen is in residence there for some weeks. Generally three or four couples are asked at the same time which, together with the house party, makes a dinner party of twenty or twenty-two people. The Queen entertains many eminent states-men and other official personages in this way. They have included High Commissioners from the Dominions, The Speaker, Cabinet Ministers, Ambassadors, distinguished soldiers, Judges, and the Chaplain to the Forces. Wives are always invited too.

Here is the account given to me by one of The Queen's recent guests at Windsor. She and her husband were invited some three or four weeks beforehand by letter from the Master of the House-hold. They were told "Dinner jackets will be worn". It was indicated that they should arrive between six and seven.

On arrival they were greeted by Members of the Household and shown to their rooms.

After changing for dinner they came down to the Green Draw-ing Room where the other guests were assembling. It is interesting here to note that the quickness with which The Queen changes, and the little time she allows herself, are commented upon (some-times more in sorrow than in praise) by all those in contact with her. I was astonished at the speed with which The Queen changed in Stockholm, during the Swedish State Visit, at the end of a long and tiring round of duties which had dragged about forty minutes after its specified time, so that she had only about half an hour to change into full evening dress with tiara before dining with the Swedish Royal Family and going to a gala performance at the Opera. Yet she reappeared as radiant and composed as though she had had all the afternoon in which to prepare.

In the Green Drawing Room are displayed in cabinets round the wall the lovely blue Sèvres porcelain of the period of Louis XVI, which was bought by King George IV.

Dinner was at eight-thirty. They went in to dinner without much formality. The Queen went first with the guest senior in precedence and the others followed in no particular order. The dining-room is in the north-east corner of Windsor Castle, at the junction of the State and private apartments. The walls are panelled in white and gold and there are large equestrian paintings on the walls.

It was a lovely spring evening and the curtains had been left undrawn, so that everyone could look out through the big windows on to the beautiful Berkshire countryside—a happy break with tradition.

There was no music during dinner, although in former days the string orchestra of one of the Regiments of Guards played in a small room—described by the Duke of Windsor as almost a Black Hole of Calcutta—separated from the dining-room by a grille.

After dinner much of the evening was spent as it is often spent when there are guests at Windsor. The Queen, knowing how much her guests would like to see something of the treasures of the historic castle, takes her guests round and shows them, with obvious affection and pride, the treasures of her home. More than one of these fortunate guests has told me how interestingly The Queen recounts the history of the fabulous pictures and magnificent furniture, and how much she knows about it. The Queen shows her guests not only the State rooms, but some of the older rooms which have now been modernised to make them useful and comfortable living spaces to-day. This tour of inspection generally occupies a considerable time.

When The Queen and her guests came back to the drawing-room, there were drinks and fruit juices laid out. After some further talk, The Queen and the Duke of Edinburgh withdrew a few minutes before midnight, and shortly afterwards her guests also went to bed.

On the following morning the guests had breakfast in their rooms, having been asked the night before what they would like.

The Visitors' book at Windsor is brought to the room for the guests to sign. (There are Visitor's books in each of The Queen's Residences and these are signed by guests at the end of their stay. There is, however, a Visitors' book at Buckingham Palace which is there for anyone to sign who wishes to pay their respects or who know the Royal Family personally. You can see a constant stream of guests who have been to a garden party returning to sign the Visitors' book at Buckingham Palace.) They leave at whatever time suits them. They do not see The Queen in the morning, having said "Good-bye" the night before.

Such a visit is in considerable contrast from the etiquette surrounding even informal entertaining by Queen Victoria. Cosmo Gordon Lang, afterwards Archbishop of Canterbury, recorded revealingly, after dining with Queen Victoria at Osborne in January, 1898:

> The dinner was exactly like any other private family party, except that of course the Queen did not actually speak except to the royalties next to her.

The Queen's hospitality is distinguished by its extreme thoughtfulness. A Moslem member of the Commonwealth, who is a great admirer of Her Majesty, has told me how tactfully their religious restrictions of diet have been managed by The Queen. Whenever wine is served, he and his wife were always served interesting-looking fruit drinks. When pork was served, which again is forbidden on religious grounds, another dish was unobtrusively served to them.

When The Queen is at Windsor for Ascot, she also has guests, but these are generally in residence for the whole week and include a number of her young friends. The Queen and her friends go to Ascot races each afternoon, and in the evening other friends may be asked in for a drink or to dinner, and sometimes there is informal dancing in the evening.

Two other, and more formal, entertainments which take place at Windsor are the luncheons held on the day of the installation of new Knights of the Garter, and the Waterloo Dinners. The Waterloo Dinner is held on June 18 each year, to commemorate the victory over the French at Waterloo in 1815. Appropriately the Duke of Wellington is guest of honour, and that day presents to The Queen a small silken tricolour flag, the prescribed rent for the estate of Stratfield Saye. This is displayed in the Guard Chamber at Windsor, together with the white "standard or colours, with flower-de-luces painted thereupon", sent to Windsor Castle annually by the present Duke of Marlborough on the anniversary of the Battle of Blenheim, as the quit-rent for the Blenheim estate, which was presented to the great Duke of Marlborough for his victories in the War of the Spanish Succession in the eighteenth century.

The Waterloo Dinner is held in the Waterloo Chamber, the largest room in Windsor Castle, which was formerly the Horn Court and was roofed by George IV to house his collection of Lawrence portraits. The tables are always decorated with blue and yellow flowers, the colours of the great Duke.

When The Queen resides in the Palace of Holyroodhouse she has around her those who are pre-eminent in Scottish life, such as the Moderator of the Church of Scotland, the Lord Provost of Edinburgh and also sometimes the Lord Provost of Glasgow and the other Cities of Scotland, the Sheriff of the Lothians and Peebles, the Lord Justice General, the Lord Advocate and various Members of The Queen's Scottish Household. In addition, The Queen entertains a cross-section of those active in the professional, intellectual and industrial life of Scotland. Often, guests from the Commonwealth are also entertained.

Dinners for small numbers, up to a maximum of from twenty-five to thirty, are held in the Household Dining Room. Larger Dinners, often for about sixty guests, are held in the Long Gallery (or Banqueting Hall) which contains the industrious but not very reliable portraits of all the Scottish Kings and of Mary, Queen of Scots painted by De Wet.

At the end of dinner, the Pipers play round the table, two at the smaller dinners, but in the Banqueting Hall usually no fewer than twelve Pipers march round the table.

Queen Mary, The Queen's Grandmother, took a great interest in the decoration and furnishing of Holyroodhouse, and a fine portrait of her by Jagger hangs above the mantelpiece in one of the anterooms.

The silver used at Holyroodhouse is kept there. It consists of a very comprehensive service of over two thousand pieces, which was given by Sir Alexander Grant, Bt., to King George V in 1935, His Majesty's Jubilee year. The silver bears the Scottish Heraldic insignia, that is, the Crest with the Scottish Lion. The larger pieces are engraved with the Scottish Royal Arms and the smaller pieces with the Scottish Royal Crest. All pieces bear the Silver Jubilee and Edinburgh hallmarks. At the same time Sir Alexander Grant gave a complete set of table and household linen, amounting to over seven thousand pieces, the table linen being woven in Dunfermline. He also gave china and crystal.

Among the plate on the table at the Holyroodhouse Royal Dinners are some pieces of special interest, such as the Monteith Punch Bowl, dating from the late seventeenth century, and two tankards of James VII period.

During The Queen's residence in Holyroodhouse she also holds such functions as Garden Parties, for which large tubs of thistles much higher than a man are placed just outside the Palace. Presentation Parties came to an end in 1958, but Evening Receptions are also held, and an impressive Sunset Ceremony.

In Scotland The Queen is attended by the Royal Company of Archers, The Queen's Scottish Bodyguard. The Company consists of a large number of Scottish gentlemen drawn from the whole of Scotland, although the Company's principal duties are naturally centred in Edinburgh. Their Border green uniform, is worn with a black Kilmarnock bonnet in which eagles' feathers denote rank. They carry bows and have three arrows stuck through their belts.

At all these functions there are present the High Constables of Holyroodhouse, who are the Palace Police Force, and have made the claim that they are the oldest Police Force in the world. They spring from a system of law and order (which included also a Court) dating from the days when the Church owned the land on which the Palace is built. Some sources trace its origin back to about 1130, in the time of David I. Its members are leading Edinburgh citizens and its duties are complementary to those of the Archers, who are the Sovereign's Bodyguard, while the duties of the High Constables are to keep law and order within the precincts of the Palace and the Abbey Sanctuary. (There was sanctuary for debtors at Holyrood right up to the year 1880.) The uniform of the High Constables includes plumed top-hats and batons.

While the Archers can only come on duty when The Queen is present in person, the Constables function in the Palace of Holyroodhouse on all official occasions.

The Sunset Ceremony is a new custom which began in 1946 with King George VI and his Scottish Queen, but which has continued every year that The Queen has visited Holyroodhouse. It developed spontaneously out of the fact that the people in Edinburgh gathered in the forecourt of the Palace on the eve of the departure of the King and Queen, to bid them farewell, singing "The Lord's my Shepherd" to the Scottish Psalm tune "Crimond", and "Will Ye No' Come Back Again?".

Now this has become a regular custom, when the people of Edinburgh gather for this informal leavetaking, and a display of piping and dancing is combined with community singing. The Queen and the Duke of Edinburgh watch from the windows of the Household Dining Room, and later usually go out on to the stage erected in front of the main entrance of the Palace, where the dancers are presented to them. At the close of the evening's entertainment they wave farewell to the crowd from the Palace roof.

One of the great advantages of the royal yacht *Britannia* is that, wherever The Queen travels in her, she is ready and equipped to act as The Queen's home. This cuts out the expensive preparation of an Embassy or Governor's House up to the standard suitable for giving a Sovereign's dinner party or reception.

In seven years The Queen has already entertained on board her royal yacht *Britannia* King Haakon VII of Norway and his son, now King Olav V of Norway, King Gustaf VI Adolf of Sweden, King Fredrik IX of Denmark, Queen Juliana of the Netherlands, the President of Portugal, and many other distinguished guests.

The Queen's visits to Sandringham and Balmoral are regarded as private and the names of her guests are not usually published.

Christmas at Sandringham is a family affair. The habit of assembling at Sandringham at Christmas dates from its earliest years. Both King Edward VII and Queen Alexandra (then Prince and Princess of Wales) loved to entertain and to give presents, and Queen Alexandra had a truly Danish delight in the festivity of Christmas. The Queen Mother and Princess Margaret are always at Sandringham for Christmas. Often the Duke and Duchess of Gloucester and their sons, and the Duchess of Kent and her family, are there. The Princess Royal generally spends her Christmas at Harewood House with her sons and grandsons.

In the beginning of the year The Queen and the Duke of Edinburgh generally ask a series of friends to stay for a few days for the shooting. The men go out shooting in the morning and The Queen and the other ladies join them for lunch, which is a substantial picnic lunch, taken indoors in a village hall, a schoolroom or even on occasion the Royal Waiting Room of Wolferton Station. Whatever the weather, the Royal Family are always out and about. Not only The Queen, but also Princess Margaret and the other royal ladies, quite unconcernedly go out walking in the most atrocious weather.

The principal holiday of the year is the late summer stay at Balmoral on Deeside. It is not of course a complete rest, because The Queen's Constitutional duties follow her everywhere, but it is the time above all others when The Queen can feel untrammelled and free with the wide range of hillside and valley on which to wander undisturbed. By that time of the year The Queen is pretty tired, and for the first ten days it is the custom to have no friends at all to stay. Princess Margaret generally stays with The Queen at Balmoral while The Queen Mother is seven miles away at Birkhall. There is much coming and going between the two houses. The Queen is out of doors every possible moment.

After the first days of relaxation, a few close friends of The Queen are asked to stay. Customarily there is a weekend visit from the Prime Minister, and from time to time other statesmen and prominent people come to stay for one or two days. The Minister of the Church of Scotland, who is invited to preach at Crathie Church, is usually asked by The Queen to stay on the Saturday and Sunday nights.

The Royal Family lives a happy wholesome outdoor life. There is shooting, deer stalking and fishing. The horses are sent up from Windsor, and the children also have bicycles. The Duke of Edinburgh has his speed-boat on Loch Muick. Above all, there are picnics, a great favourite with the Royal Family. Customarily The Queen and her family go off by themselves to picnic on their own and enjoy freedom from that surveillance which must be the greatest trial of royalty.

In the evening entertainment is self-made. There are games, some of them home-made, charades, Scottish dancing, cards, talk and a great deal of laughter. It is the most intimate of all the Royal Family homes, and there are comparatively few who have been privileged to be The Queen's guest there.

All guests of The Queen, whether in the stately formality of a banquet or in the delightful intimacy of a royal home, may be sure of one thing, they will be regarded by The Queen and all around her as a person who matters, a guest for whose pleasure and well-being The Queen exerts herself.

As a guest of The Queen said afterwards to me:

"The whole atmosphere was happy and friendly. Not only the family and the Household, but the servants were so friendly and nice."

Another guest said:

"Obviously it was an honour to be a guest of the Sovereign's—something one would always remember—but it was so enjoyable too. The Queen is a wonderful hostess."

CHAPTER ELEVEN

The Queen and the Commonwealth

"The Commonwealth bears no resemblance to the empires of the past. It is an entirely new concept—built on the highest qualities of the spirit of man: friendship, loyalty, and the desire for freedom and peace. To that new conception of an equal partnership of nations and races I shall give myself heart and soul every day of my life."

The Queen in her Christmas broadcast
from New Zealand, 1952

"The unfolding of your love has been bounteous, O Queen,
'Tis now outspread and shared by all the tribes."

New Zealand Maoris at Hamilton, in a "Song of Love".

WHEN Queen Elizabeth II came to the throne in February 1952, she became Queen of Great Britain and Northern Ireland, the Channel Islands and the Isle of Man, Queen of Canada, Australia, New Zealand, the Union of South Africa, Pakistan and Ceylon. India had become a republic during her father's reign, but acknowledged her as Head of the Commonwealth. Southern Rhodesia, a self-governing colony, many dependent territories, some colonies, some protectorates, some protected states, some in United Kingdom trusteeship, all looked to The Queen as their Head. The principal among them were Aden; the Bahama Islands; Barbados; Bermuda; British Guiana; British Honduras; Brunei; Cyprus; the Falkland Islands and its dependencies South Georgia, South Orkney, South Sandwich, South Shetland and Graham Land; Fiji; Gambia; Gibraltar; the Gold Coast, including the Trust territory of Togoland; Hong Kong; Jamaica, with its dependencies the Cayman Islands and the Turks and Caicos Islands; Kenya; the Leeward islands, including Antigua, Montserrat, St. Christopher-Nevis and Anguilla, and the Virgin Islands with their dependencies; the

Federation of Malaya, consisting of the nine Malay states of Johore, Pahang, Negri Sembilan, Selangor, Perak, Kedah, Perlis, Kelantin, Trengganu and the two British settlements of Penang and Malacca; Malta; Mauritius; Nigeria, including the Cameroons, under U.K. trusteeship; North Borneo; Northern Rhodesia; Nyasaland; St. Helena and its dependencies, including Ascension Island and Tristan da Cunha; Sarawak; the Seychelles islands; Sierre Leone; Singapore and its dependencies of Christmas Island and the Cocos-Keeling islands; Somaliland protectorate; Tanganyika; Trinidad and Tobago; Uganda; the Western Pacific islands, consisting of the Gilbert and Ellice Islands colony, the British Solomon Islands protectorate, the protected state of Tonga, the New Hebrides condominium and Pitcairn Island; the Windward islands, comprising the colonies of Granada, Dominica, St. Lucia and St. Vincent, with their dependencies; and the protectorate of Zanzibar.

No part of Queen Elizabeth II's life of service is more important than her rôle as Head of the Commonwealth. Yet no part of the Sovereign's duties is changing more.

Queen Elizabeth I was Queen of England. She was ruler, leader, schemer and national emblem of a small, vigorous and enterprising little country. Scotland, Ireland or France were to her far-flung and foreign, and she never set foot in any of them.

Some three hundred years later a great and powerful Empire grew up round Queen Victoria. At the suggestion of Disraeli, Queen Victoria was declared Empress of India. Queen Victoria envisaged her Empire bringing the benefits of fair British rule to the most distant parts of the world. She was the kindly, strict head of an Empire as though it were her Household, and her prestige was enormous. Such was the power of her personality and her belief in her people and that she had the right to speak for them, that politicians who were aggressive in other company, and who had the weight of constitutional practice on their side, were often known to acquiesce obediently to her dictates. At this distance of time, we can see that Queen Victoria was remarkably often right! Yet Queen Victoria knew her great Empire only through the Governors and Generals who brought her reports and gifts, through a small number of high-born inhabitants of those distant lands who had Audience of her, and through her

Indian servant Abdul Karim, who stood behind her chair. Queen Victoria never visited the Empire. Her foreign travelling was confined to a very occasional State Visit, to sojourns with her royal kin in Germany, and to mildly incognito holidays in the South of France and Italy.

King Edward VII was principally interested in Europe rather than the Empire. A man never engrossed by the contents of his Red Boxes, it was notoriously difficult to get him to take an interest in places as physically remote as Australia.

All this was changed when King George V, King Edward VIII and King George VI were on the throne. Each was a man who knew the Empire personally and intimately. Each regarded himself not only King of the United Kingdom, with its long, remarkably stable history, but King also of the long, blue distances of the Outback of Australia, the sharp, snowy crests of the New Zealand mountains rising from dark native bush or rolling green sheep-country, of the plains and ancient cities of India, of remote Colonies, isolated jungle riversides steaming in tropical heat or a lonely island set among thousands of miles of cool, windswept seas. Each of our last three kings was, in his different way, immensely Empire-minded. All were deeply proud of the British Colonial administrators who identified themselves so deeply and passionately with their protegés, of whom Sir Arthur Grimble, who wrote the minor classic *A Pattern of Islands*, may well stand as a worthy example. These kings were proud of and touched by the fine soldiers who came from Australia, Canada, India and other parts of the Empire. They knew the lives they led, and the countries they were building. They liked meeting their overseas subjects and travelling among them. They never forgot the Empire point of view. King George V's last rational words were "How is the Empire?"

But times, for King George V in particular, were different. Perhaps he saw the Empire as a place where the Englishman—so implying all his subjects of European stock—for some time to come would almost automatically hold by far the largest balance of power, and who must take the consequent responsibility. The Empire was, in large part, held in trusteeship by the man of British stock, for the many millions of subjects of other races. King George VI, with understanding and his unfailing integrity and sense of duty, set the pattern of new Kingship in his relations with India.

Queen Elizabeth II is Head of the Commonwealth at the most challenging period of our history. There is nothing new in an Empire. But never before has the controlling nation voluntarily passed full government to the former dependent parts, with full goodwill and much material help. The new Commonwealth countries have been welcomed by the Mother country as equal partners, the former Colonies have accepted her without rancour. With mutual generosity of spirit they take their equal places at the conference table. The wonder is not that some friction remains, but that such a profound change can take place with so much concord and affection, even in these early and most difficult stages of independence.

The part the Sovereign has to play in the new Commonwealth was clearly stated, as only he can put it, by Sir Winston Churchill in a speech at the time of the Queen's accession.

"There is no doubt that of all the institutions which have grown up among us over the centuries or sprung into being in our lifetime the Constitutional Monarchy is the most deeply founded and dearly cherished by the whole association of our peoples.

"In the present generation it has acquired a meaning incomparably more powerful than anyone had dreamed possible in former times. The Crown has become the mysterious link, may I say the magic link, which unites our loosely bound but strongly interwoven Commonwealth of Nations, states and races. Peoples who would never tolerate the assertions of a written Constitution which implies any diminution of their independence are the foremost to be proud of their loyalty to the Crown."

In a conversation with Mr. H. S. Suhrawardy, then Prime Minister of Pakistan, in July 1957, he described to me The Queen's value to a Republican member of the Commonwealth as follows:

"The Queen plays no practical part in the Commonwealth, she plays a psychological part. It is owing to The Queen, or the Crown, that Commonwealth countries can get together. The Queen's part is not practical but psychological, so that countries which had links with the British historically can get together.

"Other countries which had no links with the British cannot get together in the same way. France or Germany or Italy could not become members of the Commonwealth.

"This Commonwealth, as a conglomeration of countries, getting together with a view to exchanging ideas, and having a certain sense of inter-dependence and loyalty to each other, is a very good institution. These various countries form a substantial group. And all are equally independent. The question of considering the position of The Queen can be better appreciated against the background of the possibility of any other similar combination.

"I visualised, for instance, a number of countries in the Middle East getting together in some form of co-operative and consultative body. But the practical difficulty was that there was no symbolic Head round which they could revolve, no cementing force, no force which can bring them together on one platform."

The change in The Queen's position is emphasised by the change in her titles from those of her father. He was "His Most Excellent Majesty George the Sixth, by the Grace of God of Great Britain, Ireland and of the British Dominions beyond the Seas, King, Defender of the Faith."

At the time of the Commonwealth Economic Conference in December 1952, the first meeting of the Commonwealth Prime Ministers of The Queen's reign, the delegates agreed upon the changes in the form of the royal title. Each Commonwealth country agreed to incorporate the phrase "Head of the Commonwealth", now common to The Queen's title in all Commonwealth countries. In addition, the United Kingdom agreed that reference to "Dominions" would be replaced by "other Realms and Territories". The Queen's title in the United Kingdom is therefore now:

"Her Most Excellent Majesty Elizabeth The Second by the Grace of God, of the United Kingdom of Great Britain and Northern Ireland and of Her Other Realms and Territories, Queen, Head of the Commonwealth, Defender of the Faith."

At that first meeting of Commonwealth Prime Ministers, nine representatives were present from Ceylon, Southern Rhodesia (not a full Commonwealth member, but regularly attending the meetings of Commonwealth Prime Ministers), New Zealand, the United Kingdom, Australia, Canada, the Union of South Africa, Pakistan and India. The representatives were Mr. Senanayake for Ceylon; Sir Godfrey Huggins for Southern Rhodesia;

Mr. Holland for New Zealand; Mr. Churchill for the United Kingdom; Mr. Menzies for Australia; Mr. St. Laurent for Canada; Mr. Havenga, the Minister of Finance, for the Union of South Africa; and Khwaja Nazimuddin for Pakistan. Mr. C. D. Deshmukh, Minister of Finance for India, represented Mr. Nehru, Prime Minister of India.

On June 26, 1957, The Queen entertained her Commonwealth Prime Ministers to dinner at Windsor Castle. The one new Commonwealth country represented was Ghana, while Southern Rhodesia was now incorporated in the Federation of Rhodesia and Nyasaland. Only Mr. Menzies of Australia had been present at that first meeting just five years before (although Mr. Nehru of India had been Prime Minister on both dates)—an example of how people at the top change continually. At the second meeting Mr. Diefenbaker came from Canada; Mr. Macmillan from Great Britain; Mr. Menzies once more from Australia; Mr. Louw, Minister for External Affairs, from South Africa; Mr. Suhrawardy from Pakistan; Mr. Nehru from India; Sir Roy Welensky from the Federation of Rhodesia and Nyasaland; Dr. Nkrumah from Ghana; Mr. Macdonald, Minister of External Affairs, from New Zealand; and Mr. de Silva, Minister of Justice, from Ceylon.

At the next meeting of Commonwealth Prime Ministers, Malaya and the British West Indies will also be represented. The Commonwealth is the only really strong bond between East and West in the world to-day.

It was significant that Commonwealth representation at The Queen's Coronation was just double what it had been at her father's Coronation in 1937. At her Coronation The Queen wore a special gift from Members of the Commonwealth, a pair of gold armills or bracelets, which are ancient royal emblems, but had probably not been used at a Coronation since that of King Edward VI in 1547. In February 1959 in "a generous and imaginative gesture," as Mr. Macmillan described it, The Queen placed the royal palace of Marlborough House at the disposal of the Government for use as a Commonwealth meeting place in London.

The Queen has to know the problems and understand the aspirations of a wide range of different peoples, united only by her. Mr. Suhrawardy spoke for many Commonwealth members with whom I have talked, when he said—"The Queen undoubtedly keeps herself extremely well informed of the conditions of countries in the Commonwealth, the political problems as well as the economic, and also the international problems."

The Queen has a deep love for her peoples, which suffuses all her contacts with them. She is truly concerned with their troubles, their triumphs, their quarrels, their setbacks and their achievements. She cares and she knows. Again, one voice must speak for many, and Lady Foot has given me permission to quote her words on going to tragic Cyprus on her husband's appointment there as Governor. In an interview with the *News Chronicle* on November 29, 1957, she said:

"In all sincerity I must tell you that I am terribly apprehensive about going to Cyprus.

"But I've just come back from seeing The Queen and twenty minutes at a private audience restored my heart. For the last eight days since my husband and I arrived in London from Jamaica we have been on the go all the time, preparing for our take-off for Cyprus next Monday.

"And those twenty minutes we had with The Queen—so calm and serene—put everything into perspective somehow. The force of her presence is amazing. She is so authoritative and well informed about Cyprus, too. Not just about the main issues but all the minor ones as well. She did the job she is expected to do—restoring people's hopes and hearts."

The Queen has to be the emblem for a great range of different aims and ideals. She has to, and she does, understand and sympathise with the different and equally sincere views held by a Colonial Administrator, recently severed from his life-work and the people he regarded as his trust and his friends, and by the politician of a newly autonomous state, eager to do everything for himself, even if he may encounter difficulties.

The Islamic republic of Pakistan was inaugurated on March 23, 1956, and in accordance with the declaration made by the Commonwealth Prime Ministers at their meeting in London in February 1955, Pakistan, like India, continued to be a Member of the Commonwealth and, while ceasing to owe allegiance to the Crown, recognised The Queen as Head of the Commonwealth.

A prominent Pakistani, who has immense respect and affection for The Queen, explained the decision in these terms:

"The establishment of the Islamic Republic of Pakistan was largely for sentimental and religious reasons. The Muslims of Pakistan are an Islamic people. They wanted to have an Islamic State and therefore we had to be a Republic as no non-Muslim can be Head of an Islamic State. On the other hand, large sections of the population were anxious to remain within the Commonwealth. As The Queen is greatly liked and respected throughout Pakistan, there was no difficulty in Pakistan, after becoming an Islamic Republic, joining the Commonwealth and recognising The Queen as the Head of the Commonwealth."

The reason for the change of status in countries newly acquiring Commonwealth status is that there is a basic urge in these countries to *show* themselves to be free of all outside control. For that reason they wish to put up a form of Government which shows quite clearly that the link with the country which once ruled them is completely voluntary.

Unfortunately, in former days, a certain number of United Kingdom subjects laid claim to the Crown and the Sovereign as though they alone constituted the Sovereign's true subjects. Even to-day there is an unfortunate aspect of fierce insular pride which makes some United Kingdom Britishers regard The Queen as their Queen, and occasionally indicate that they consider her overseas subjects—Australians, West Indians, Canadians or whoever they happen to be—as in some degree "second-class passengers". Because the United Kingdom had claimed to itself the attributes of the Sovereign, some of the Sovereign's attributes are regarded overseas as pertaining as much to the United Kingdom as to The Queen. Countries wishing to prove their independence from the United Kingdom are apt to discard or limit the use of these symbols, without meaning a slight to The Queen herself. This The Queen knows and understands better than many of her subjects. Take one such measure as an example.

In Accra, capital of Ghana, on June 27, 1957, Mr. Kofi Baako, Minister without Portfolio, explained in the National Assembly that "God Save The Queen" would no longer be played in Ghana even if The Queen or her representative were present. "God Save The Queen", he said, was the National Anthem of the United Kingdom, and until it became the Commonwealth National Anthem it would not be allowed in Ghana, where the Ghana National Anthem would be played. Lord Listowel, answering a question about this at his Press Conference in London, before he went to Ghana as Governor-General, said:

"I do not think the fact that our national anthem is not played in Ghana shows any less respect for The Queen than the fact that we do not play the Ghana national anthem when The Queen is honoured in public here. The Queen is Queen of Ghana as well as Queen of the United Kingdom, and the Ghana national anthem is just as much her anthem as 'God Save The Queen'. I think the very fact that I, as The Queen's representative, am being treated with so much cordiality and respect, shows the real warmth of feeling in Ghana towards Her Majesty."

Both sides of the Commonwealth have, on the whole, and considering the limitations of all human beings, coped astonishingly well with the difficulties of completely readjusting the balance of a great conclave of peoples. As the Commonwealth emerges into full partnership, only Burma and Eire have chosen to leave the family. Indeed, would Burma have left the Commonwealth if at that time the formula had been fully evolved and found workable by which a Commonwealth country could be a republic and yet remain a member of the Commonwealth?

The Royal Family has never taken the narrower view of the Commonwealth. Our Royal Family is completely, enthusiastically and loyally Commonwealth-minded. That is why The Queen and the Duke of Edinburgh, widely travelled, with broad horizons and immense interest in everything that happens in the Commonwealth, have found it so much easier to understand the feelings of people who have newly acquired Commonwealth status than some of the stay-at-homes. But it must never be forgotten that the altruism and integrity of United Kingdom statesmen, civil servants and many others of United Kingdom origin made possible this miracle of readjustment within the Commonwealth.

The Queen is engaged always in the slow process of healing. Always she is smoothing out our difficulties. Daily she meets an infinity of problems. No sooner is one crisis over than at least one other has taken its place, while the pinpricks of minor disagreement are continuously evident in the papers that pass before her. In many of the problems The Queen must surely recognise the same faults of the human race—the desire to be the upper dog, to take offence at unthinking slights, to ditch the less pleasing parts of responsibility, to "forget" a promise which has become inconvenient, the same suspicion of neighbours, the same desire to put one over on the other fellow. Alas, they are to be found in all of us, and in every assembly of human beings, whether we constitute a youth organisation or an executive council. I wonder if The Queen ever wants to knock our heads together? But, of course, she would never do it. That would be unthinkable in the tradition of the British Royal Family.

And she meets other things too, pleasanter, more heart-warming, hopeful things. She meets consideration, self-sacrifice, far-sightedness, loyal devotion to duty even in circumstances more difficult than those first imagined. She meets friendships persisting in bad times, loyalty, love, affection, trust where there was fear, health where there was sickness, tolerance where there had been tyranny. Much of The Queen's greatest work is not dramatic, and it is not spectacular. The Queen summons, develops and uses always in our service her loyalty, courage of principle, self-sacrifice, generosity of spirit, compassion and self-abnegating patriotism. She is not only a symbol, but an example to her millions of Commonwealth subjects and citizens of all that is good in love of country.

The senior Commonwealth countries, the United Kingdom, Canada, Australia and New Zealand, have inherited a great affection for the Sovereign. With these Commonwealth countries The Queen has in every way fostered the relationship so soundly founded by her predecessors. Unlike her grandfather, uncle and father, she had done comparatively little Commonwealth travelling before her accession at the age of twenty-five. Her only fulfilled long tours were to South Africa and to Canada. The disadvantage of youth at accession is balanced by the vitality and energy of a young Sovereign. The Queen, in the first decade of her reign, has already travelled much farther than any King or Queen in our history.

The Queen is the first Sovereign to open Parliament in person in New Zealand, in Australia, in Ceylon and in Canada. She has in a great number of ways shown that she regards herself as much Queen of these countries as Queen of the United Kingdom. She gave certain proof of it when she spoke of herself, on her visit to the United States, as "Queen of Canada". She insisted on her "stay" in Canada, not "visit" to Canada, as she knew herself at home there.

The Queen identified herself specifically as Queen of Canada when she broadcast to the Canadian nation on Sunday, October 13, 1957, and said:

"Next week I have another important and pleasant duty to perform. When I go to the United States I shall be going as the Head of the Canadian Nation to pay a State Visit to the Head of our great neighbouring country. I shall be going in other capacities as well, but when you hear or read about the events in Washington, and other places, I want you to reflect that it is The Queen of Canada and her husband who are concerned in them."

In The Queen's speech from the Throne at the opening of the First Session of the Twenty-third Parliament of Canada on October 14, 1957, she said:

"I greet you as your Queen. Together we constitute the Parliament of Canada. For the first time the representatives of the people of Canada and their Sovereign are here assembled on the occasion of the opening of Parliament. This is for all of us a moment to remember."

The Queen, in her capacity as Queen of New Zealand, performed a number of duties while in that country, in 1953–4. The principal of these were as follows:

1. The reading of the "Speech from the Throne" in the old Legislative Council Chamber in relation to a special session of Parliament, and accepting the Address-in-Reply.
2. Assenting to an Act intituled the "Judicature Amendment Act" specially passed for the occasion in 1954. (This was No. 1 1954, as there was a similar Act passed later in the year.)
3. A meeting of the Executive Council.
4. A meeting of the Privy Counsellors.
5. Three investitures.
6. Presentation of colours to Royal New Zealand Navy and Royal New Zealand Air Force.
7. Reception for Heads of Diplomatic Missions.
8. Laying the foundation stone of the Wellington Cathedral.

To enable The Queen to perform some of the constitutional functions a special Act, known as the Royal Powers Act, was passed in 1953 declaring that Her Majesty herself might exercise any power conferred on the Governor-General by any enactment in New Zealand.

On a day-to-day basis The Queen exercises in relation to New Zealand, just as in the United Kingdom, her prerogatives connected with honours and awards, the appointment of New Zealand diplomatic representatives overseas and the receiving of ambassadors and ministers in New Zealand.

The greatest changes that have taken place within the Commonwealth during The Queen's first years of reign have been the continued process, begun in her father's reign, of Asian, and now African territories becoming full members of the Commonwealth. When The Queen came to the throne, there were already three Asian Commonwealth countries, India, Pakistan and Ceylon. India had become independent immediately after the Indian Independence Act, 1947, had received the Royal Assent on July 18, 1947, but did not formally become a republic until January 1950.

Pakistan remained a dominion for several years more, but eventually decided to follow the example of India and become a republic, while acknowledging The Queen as Head of the Commonwealth. The reason for this was to have a structure similar to that of India, and to have a President who would be Head of the country in a way completely Pakistani in character. The Queen was and is regarded with immense respect and affection by the vast majority of Pakistani citizens, and some touching references to her character and charm have been made in the debates in the Pakistani parliament. It was also a factor, as has been recounted, that an Islamic state found some discrepancy in accepting as its head a Queen who is officially head of a Church of another faith.

Ceylon also contemplates altering its Constitution from dominion to republic. Ghana and South Africa have made similar declarations.

The change in status in India and Pakistan means that The Queen no longer appoints Governors-General, and that legislation is no longer carried out in her name. But paradoxically enough her symbolic importance is not lessened. Whereas all their official ties are cut, The Queen, as Head of the Commonwealth, becomes the one remaining emblem of co-operation, between the Republican Commonwealth countries and peoples of the Commonwealth family of nations. During The Queen's reign two new territories moved from colonial to full Commonwealth status and decided to remain within the circle of the Commonwealth.

The changed position of the Commonwealth is shown by the considerably increased number of occasions on which The Queen has appointed one of her family to act as her representative overseas. In former reigns this was a fairly unusual event, generally confined to the coronations or funerals of the kings of friendly foreign countries. Members of the Royal Family undertake most of their public duties in their own right, although the Duke of Edinburgh has acted on behalf of The Queen on a number of occasions, such as the Welsh Tour and visit to the Scilly Isles in the summer of 1958, when The Queen was ill. When a Member of the Royal Family presents Colours to a Regiment, it is always on behalf of The Queen. But the specific occasions on which the Sovereign has appointed a member of his or her family to represent him or her on a great occasion have always been fairly rare. Yet in the opening years of this reign The Queen has already appointed Princess Margaret to represent her at the inauguration of the Federation of the West Indies; the Duchess of Kent at the celebration of the independence of Ghana; the Duke of Gloucester at the independence celebrations of Malaya; and the Princess Royal to deliver messages to the Eastern and Western Houses of Assembly in Nigeria, to mark the attainment of self-government in these regions.

Ghana came first. In September 1956 it was announced in the House of Commons that, subject to Parliamentary approval, the Gold Coast would become the first African state to achieve independence within the British Commonwealth, and that this would take place on March 6, 1957. The Queen in her Constitutional capacity came into this process at several stages. First of all, the Ghana Independence Bill passed through all its stages. There were certain difficulties, but to the credit of the British Government they were not in any way connected with the main purpose of giving independence to Ghana, but only with safeguarding the minorities. It was stated, during the second reading,

"Whether Ghana would be a full member of the Commonwealth was a matter for all the members, and at the request of the Gold Coast government, the United Kingdom government was approaching other members on the subject. They had, however, hoped that Ghana would become a full member on the same day that she became independent." The House cheered lustily. The Queen gave her Royal Assent to the Bill which, making the necessary formal alterations in the Constitution, provided her with authority to make an Order in Council so that Ghana became fully independent. (The name "Ghana", incidentally, was taken from an ancient West African kingdom which flourished in that part of Africa for about eight centuries from round about A.D. 300–1100.) This immensely important step was obviously not without its difficulty, but The Queen and her Governments, both in the United Kingdom and Ghana, did everything in their power to make the transfer of authority as smooth and as easy as possible.

It was suggested in some places that The Queen should go to Ghana to preside over the Independence celebrations, but it was felt that such celebrations, although they should be given every possible attribute of dignity, were for the *independence* of Ghana, and that The Queen's visit could much more suitably take place as a sign of interest, affection and union with the Commonwealth when the new State was established on its own feet. Dr. Nkrumah asked The Queen to visit Ghana during the meeting of Commonwealth Prime Ministers—he was the first African to attend—in London in June and July of 1957. This invitation has the unanimous support of the people of Ghana. The invitation was cordially accepted, and The Queen's visit to Ghana was afterwards arranged for the end of 1959. This visit of The Queen of Ghana to her African self-governing territory will be without precedent, and of the greatest significance.

The Independence of Ghana was celebrated on March 6, 1957, as planned. It took the typically Commonwealth form of a Parliamentary ceremony. The Legislative Assembly building was crowded with members, each in his national costume, providing, as *The Times* correspondent put it, "the general effect of a sea of gold". First the Governor-General, Sir Charles Arden-Clarke, who as Governor had done so much to smooth the transfer of power, was sworn in as Governor-General. After he withdrew, the Speaker's procession, headed as in Westminster by the mace, entered, and the Governor-General returned. The doors were closed. There was the traditional knocking on them and they were reopened to admit the Royal procession in which the tall, graceful Duchess of Kent was The Queen's representative. A most dignified and moving ceremony followed and high tribute was paid by those present to the Speaker, Sir Emmanuel Quist, for his great sense of dignity. The Duchess of Kent first read out the Speech from the Throne in which the Ghana Government had, with a fitting sense of history, presented their statement of policy in broad and idealistic terms. The Duchess of Kent then read the historic message from The Queen to the people of Ghana. No sovereign of England, or indeed of any other country, had ever made such a pronouncement to an African people:

"I have entrusted to my aunt (the Duchess of Kent) the duty of opening on my behalf the first session of the Parliament of Ghana. My thoughts are with you on this great day, as you take up the full responsibilities of independent nationhood, and I rejoice to welcome another new member of our growing Commonwealth family of nations.

"The hopes of many, especially in Africa, hang on your endeavours. It is my earnest and confident belief that my people in Ghana will go forward in freedom and justice, in unity among themselves and in brotherhood with all the peoples of the Commonwealth. May God bless you all."

From that moment Queen Elizabeth II became Queen of Ghana.

The Independence of the Federation of Malaya within the Commonwealth followed in the same year. This time The Queen sent her uncle, the Duke of Gloucester, as her representative at the Independence celebrations, which took a different form.

One of the final stages in Malaya's progress towards independence was reached when The Queen made an Order in Council giving the force of law to the new Constitution for the Federation of Malaya. Arrangements to welcome the Federation of Malaya to membership of the Commonwealth had already been made at the conference of Commonwealth Prime Ministers in June and July. The ceremony of Independence took place in the open air early on the morning of September 1, 1957, in the new Merdeka (freedom) Stadium in Kuala Lumpur. The Queen's message of goodwill was read by the Duke of Gloucester, who said also: "A jewel is beautiful in itself, but far more beautiful when it is set and mounted in gold. To-day not only does Malaya wear the jewel of Independence, but that jewel is mounted in the unrivalled setting of the Commonwealth." He handed to the Tuanku Abdul Rahman, who would become Prime Minister of the new State, the bound copy of the Constitution. (Although the United Kingdom has no written Constitution herself, she has been, as Sir Ivor Jennings has reminded us, one of the most prolific makers of Constitutions in history!)

On the following day a very different ceremony took place at which was installed the Head of State of the new Independent Commonwealth country of Malaya, with the official title of King. Chosen from the rulers of the nine former British protected states which, with the former settlements of Penang and Malacca, make up the Federation of Malaya, he will rule for five years as first King and ruler of the Federation of Malaya, with the title and style of His Majesty Yang-di-Pertuan Agong. First King of the new Federation is the Tuanku Abdul Rahman Ibni Al-Marhun Tuanku Muhammad, the ruler of Kedah.

The ceremony of his installation must be unique even in the widely varied experience of the Commonwealth. It took place in a building, open on two sides, in the grounds of his Palace, and was attended by the Duke and Duchess of Gloucester, who was wearing the gown she wore at Her Majesty's Coronation, and was attended by several Malayan rulers and their consorts. The Head of State and his consort arrived in procession. Preceded by two maces representing temporal and spiritual power, they walked between two Lords of Attendance in red and black Malayan costume who were bearing spears and open yellow umbrellas, which is the colour of Royalty. The Grand Chamberlain and his priests and warriors in attendance brought to the King a gold bound copy of the Koran, and the Kris of State, whose blade had been fashioned from the blades of eleven Krises collected from the States and Settlements which make up the Commonwealth of Malaya. The newly installed King accepted the Kris, unsheathed it, kissed the blade, then sheathed it and placed it in his gold belt, thus publicly entering into the power of his office.

The Yang-di-Pertuan Agong is the King of Malaya. When

the Malayan regiment was granted the prefix "Royal" in April 1958, it was granted by the Yang-di-Pertuan Agong.

As has already been noted in the chapter about the Privy Council, the Yang-di-Pertuan Agong now shares the right, which until then had been The Queen's alone, to permit appeals from his Courts to the Judicial Committee of the Privy Council, a far-reaching decision which permits Malaya, without in any way surrendering a part of her Sovereignty, to make use of the accumulated wisdom of the Judicial Committee.

Other countries have progressed towards independence in the Commonwealth within The Queen's reign. Among these are the Federation of Nigeria, the Federation of Rhodesia and Nyasaland, the Federation of The West Indies and Cyprus.

There are many problems. It is all very well to give people "freedom", but what constitutes freedom and to which people should it be given? The troubles of Cyprus and the difficulties of Malta—an island The Queen knows so well and loves so dearly—illustrate the appalling difficulties which lie in the confused tangle of different races and religions, and changing strategic and economic importances. But what has been achieved should not be underestimated.

It would be hard to sum up The Queen's changing position to the Commonwealth more happily than in the calypso written by Mr. Henry Bowman, one of the British Honduras delegation to London in 1958:

> Joy and Happiness to our heart she brings.
> She is known to us in the Commonwealth as the
> Queen of Independence and freedom felt.
>
> During the past five years or so
> A great change has come about wherever we go.
> With Ghana, Malaya and Burma free
> And the British West Indies for all to see.
>
> Her smile and dignity hold the Key
> That ties us together across the sea.

These constitutional changes that have taken place already in The Queen's physical contacts with the Commonwealth are almost unprecedented in history and of immense importance. The reason for the survival of the Head of the Commonwealth is the same as the reason for the long survival of the Commonwealth itself. It is not a set thing laid down by law, but a living and changing concept which adds to all the visible qualities and assets the imponderable of emotion. You do not weigh atmosphere (except in a barometer), and yet it is atmosphere which gives light and shade, emotion and feeling to the landscape. We do not love a well-remembered view in our homeland for its sticks and stones alone, but for the light and shade of cloud shadows chasing each other over the hillside or for the changing glow of sunset fading into twilight. Similarly we cannot weigh what the emblem of The Queen means in shaping our thoughts of patriotism—not the thoughts of English and Scottish and Welsh alone, but of many millions of people of many creeds and races and backgrounds, for whom she symbolises freedom, independence and liberty for the individual.

Queen Elizabeth II has travelled further, faster, more frequently than any previous sovereign—*already* in the seven years of her reign. The Queen's Commonwealth travels have been:

1. From Kenya by way of Uganda and Libya to England upon her succession, 1952.
2. Round the world—the first of our Sovereigns to circum-navigate the globe—in 1953—from England by way of Gander, Bermuda, Jamaica, the Panama Canal, Fiji, Tonga, New Zealand, Australia, the Cocos Islands, Ceylon, Aden, Uganda, Libya, Malta, Gibraltar to London.
3. Nigeria in 1956 by way of Libya.
4. Canada (and the United States) 1957.

In 1959 The Queen has planned to visit Canada, Ghana (the first visit of the Sovereign to an Independent African State) and Sierra Leone and the Gambia. (In addition The Queen has under-taken more State Visits than any sovereign previously in our history, but this aspect will be detailed in the chapter, "The Queen and Foreign Powers".)

Complementary to these great Commonwealth tours are the Commonwealth trips of the Duke of Edinburgh. He can move with less formality and more speed than The Queen. He is a sailor by profession, and by nature is enormously interested in the other fellow. His swift fact-finding expeditions have been a wonderful asset to the Sovereign's knowledge. The Duke of Edinburgh crossed Canada in 1954 (the objective being the Empire Games in Vancouver) and managed also to get a very fair impression of the pioneering industries and potentialities of Canada's great North. In 1956 he circled the world for the second time in The Queen's reign, this time eastward-bound round the world, and, in addition to opening the Sixteenth Olympic Games at Melbourne, which was his initial reason for the expedition, he saw a considerable number of great projects of the future. Although the danger of being shut in by ice, with consequent embarrassment to the authorities, made him reluctantly cut out a visit to the mainland of Antarctica, he saw quite a number of seldom-visited spots ranging from whaling settlements in the South Shetlands to the lonely settlement of Edinburgh on the isolated South Atlantic island of Tristan da Cunha.

1959 is scheduled as the Duke of Edinburgh's most travelled year of all. It opened with his third circumnavigation, first India and Pakistan (the first member of the Royal Family to visit these countries since they became republics), and then by way of Singapore, Sarawak, Brunei, North Borneo, Hong Kong, the Solomon Islands, the Gilbert and Ellice Islands, Christmas Island, the Bahamas and Bermuda. He accompanies The Queen on his fifth visit to Canada in June and July. Toward the end of the year he will accompany The Queen to Ghana and Sierra Leone and the Gambia.

In addition, the Queen Mother, in most successful tours, has herself flown round the world—the first member of the Royal Family to complete the whole circumnavigation by air—has visited Canada and the United States, and has twice visited the Rhodesias and Nyasaland, and also Kenya and Uganda.

Princess Margaret, who went on the first of the Queen Mother's visits to the Rhodesias and Nyasaland, visited East Africa in 1956 when she went to Zanzibar, the distant island of Mauritius, Tanganyika, and Kenya (flying out by way of Kano in Nigeria, because of strained relations in the Middle East). Princess Margaret has also twice visited The West Indies, first in 1955 when she visited eight islands and then the Bahamas and Bermuda; and again to inaugurate the Federation of The West Indies in 1958, when she was the third member (not the first as was suggested by some newspapers) of the British Royal Family to visit British Guiana, and the first member of the British Royal Family to visit British Honduras. Later that year she crossed Canada to take part in the centenary celebrations of British Columbia. The Duke of Gloucester visited Malaya for the Independence, taking with him the Duchess and their elder son, Prince William. In 1958 the Duke and Duchess visited Aden and the Somaliland Protectorate. In 1959 they go to Nigeria. The Duke of Kent accompanied his mother the Duchess of Kent to Singapore and Malaya in 1952, going also to Sarawak, North Borneo, Brunei and Hong Kong. The Duchess of Kent, this time accompanied by Princess Alexandra, visited Canada. The Princess Royal has been to The West Indies, and British Guiana, to Canada and to Nigeria. Indeed, every member of the British Royal Family has played his or her part in the increasingly important representational journeys of The Queen and her family to distant parts of the Commonwealth. The Sovereign requires and receives the unstinted assistance of other members of the Royal Family in the fulfilment of her duties.

The Queen has not yet visited one of the republican countries of the Commonwealth, but the possibility of such a visit has already been raised from time to time in the countries concerned, and such visits will most probably take place within her reign.

Commonwealth Tours are not casual, easily-arranged jumps into space, like random holidays. Even a holiday may involve one in plenty of planning and work, so one may well reflect how infinitely more complicated and complex are the plans which involve the Sovereign.

The planning of a Commonwealth tour may begin a year or more before the actual journey. Indeed, the probability of The Queen visiting a Commonwealth country may be anticipated several years in advance, when it is known that some great enterprise will be completed, or an important anniversary will fall in a particular year. Such is the opening of the St. Lawrence Seaway, an achievement which turns lakeside cities many hundreds of miles inland into great seaports, and with which Canadians have long been anxious that The Queen should be associated.

The first informal approach that The Queen should visit an overseas part of the Commonwealth comes from the host country.

It is informal and generally verbal. If it is favourably received and The Queen sees that she will be able to spare the time, tentative dates are agreed. A formal invitation is then issued, and is accepted. There are simultaneous announcements from Buckingham Palace and from the host country that The Queen and the Duke of Edinburgh will be visiting that country and at what time of the year. Generally this preliminary announcement gives only the fact and the season.

After that, things get moving at great speed behind the scenes. A series of plans, at first tentative and full of alternatives, is submitted by the host country to The Queen. As time goes on these become fixed, until eventually they are so detailed that—as one Member of the Household who was going on a Tour illustrated to me several weeks beforehand—"I know that at 3 p.m. on Tuesday the 19th I shall be standing on the steps of the Town Hall at——waiting to take my place in car No. 3 on our way to a rally of schoolchildren."

The Queen goes through these plans with the greatest care and she makes many suggestions. She reads a programme as an architect reads plans or a musician an orchestral score. The Queen has always had an excellent sense of time. She knows very well the numbers of people who are put out if a royal visit "over-runs", with the subsequent dislocation of traffic arrangements. It is therefore easy for organisers to fill The Queen's programme very full, sometimes distinctly over-full—because they know that she will always allow sufficient time for the last engagement as well as for the first.

The object of Queen Elizabeth's visits to the Commonwealth are that The Queen shall be seen by as many of the people as possible. Everything is arranged with that in view. The Queen visits as many large centres of population as possible, she drives through the streets, she attends huge outdoor rallies of children, she inspects troops. At garden parties, receptions, luncheons and dinners she meets as many as possible of the representatives of the people. It is as well to remember that people do not cease to be people because they represent something. The fairest way of spreading The Queen's influence is to ask people in their official capacity from widely spread organisations and societies, working for civic, educational and social welfare advancement. Always the children are specially considered, because these children hold the future of the Commonwealth.

There are many important engagements common to the Commonwealth pattern of life and liberty, which have been transplanted from the Mother country and taken root in many different soils. In opening Parliament in the different Commonwealth countries The Queen takes part in a ceremony entirely familiar in its pattern, however unusual its setting. When she presides at meetings of her Privy Council of Canada, or holds meetings of her Privy Council of the United Kingdom in Australia, New Zealand or Ceylon, the pattern is much the same as when The Queen holds a Council at Buckingham Palace.

What The Queen herself sees of the countries she visits must, especially on a first visit, be a secondary consideration. But of course her hosts want her to have as good a time and to enjoy her visit to their country as much as possible. They want her to see their scenery, their achievements, their history and their potentialities. The people of Katoomba in the blue mountains of New South Wales acted with self-sacrifice when they suggested that The Queen should spend the few minutes which could be allocated in the crowded programme to their township, looking out over the sheer-sided valley of the Blue Mountains, rather than shaking the Municipal party by the hand. That was a very much appreciated gesture. The Queen and the Duke of Edinburgh can never forget that magnificent view. But it is not necessary for other civic communities to feel that they must follow Katoomba's example, and give up their own brief meeting with The Queen, so that she may enjoy their scenery. The Queen goes out to meet her people. She wants to meet them, she wants to be seen by them and through her person to be the instrument of gathering a deeper loyalty and unity for the future.

Before The Queen goes on a Commonwealth Tour—or indeed on any Tour—she spends a great deal of time in "mugging up" the background. She knows a very great deal about every Commonwealth country whether she has been there or not, but when the visit is definitely planned everything becomes more actual. She will drive along that road, sleep in this house, meet all these people. Naturally she discusses it all with her husband and with the Members of the Household who have been there

before. There are few places in the Commonwealth where one
or more of the Royal Household have not stayed, and, moreover,
relatives and friends have their own personal reminiscences and
advice to offer. The hosts, the United Kingdom representatives
stationed in that country, give basic and valuable information
and advice. Every possible aspect of the life of the country is
made familiar before The Queen leaves these shores. The political,
legislative, judicial and economic background are already part of
her daily working life. The season, the climate, the type of clothing usual, the way of life are all gone into thoroughly. Her wardrobe has to be planned well in advance, and of course the types
of materials suitable to the very hot or the very damp or the very
cold climate concerned have to be carefully chosen. The style and
type of dress for the country, the range of day and night tempera-
tures at the season of the year, everything to do with The Queen's
clothes has to be thought out. How much time will be allowed for
changing? Will changes have to be made in an aeroplane or train?

Presents have to be remembered for the people who will
serve The Queen during her Tour. There are the Orders and
Medals which are distributed with a considered hand, photographs signed—generally a pose which has not been released for
public use. Then there are small presents to take, such as tiepins,
cuff-links and brooches engraved with the Royal monogram.

The Queen chooses the jewellery which she will take with her
to wear, ranging from the most important tiaras and necklaces
and earrings she will wear on formal evening occasions, to the
brooches which she will wear during the day. The Queen
remembers to take and wear on the appropriate occasion those
pieces of jewellery which have a special association with the
country she is visiting, whether it has been a wedding present, a
Coronation present, a regimental brooch presented by a corps or
regiment of which the Queen is Colonel-in-Chief, or a gift made
on some previous Tour. Sometimes she takes furs which have
been presented to her by the people of the country concerned.
The Queen will almost certainly take to Canada some of the
beautiful furs she has received as gifts. It will probably be too
warm for her to wear her wedding present of a calf-length coat
of Canadian wild mink, but she will probably bring some of her
evening furs from Canada, including the winter ermine wrap

which she received from the women of Canada and which she so often wears in Britain. Another Canadian gift which she has often worn is the cape of breath-of-spring Silver Blu mink which she received from the Hudson's Bay Company in lieu of the black beaver skin traditionally due to the Sovereign, on her first visit to Canada as Princess Elizabeth. Another favourite is the white mink stole, an Accession present from the Hudson's Bay Company.

Often in her dresses there are neat compliments to the national emblem of the Commonwealth country. During her 1954 visit to Australia, for instance, she wore a yellow evening gown trimmed with wattle (mimosa), which was obviously a favourite, as she often wore the dress after her return to Britain. She wore an evening dress decorated with maple leaves in Canada in 1957.

The Queen stocks up with a good library of reference books and general reading about the country she is visiting—I noticed what an interesting library had been gathered in *Britannia*, when I was visiting the royal yacht immediately after the World Tour.

Much of the expense of Commonwealth Tours is always paid for by the host country. This principle was decided by King George V in 1927 when there was some ill-judged criticism of the expense of the Duke of York's visit to attend the first Federal Parliament of Australia in Canberra. King George V then ruled that the Sovereign would refuse permission for any other member of the Royal Family to pay an official visit to a Dominion, unless that Dominion defrayed expenses. When a member of the Royal Family visits Colonial Territories, it is the U.K. Government which is financially responsible for their journeys.

Transport to and from the country being visited is not generally paid by the host country, but is usually defrayed by the U.K. Government.

A Commonwealth Tour involves extremely hard work for The Queen, and also for the small, picked, highly efficient Household who accompany her. When The Queen is away, even when Counsellors of State have been appointed to undertake some of The Queen's routine duties, many other duties still remain The Queen's concern. Particularly she must always be informed about changing events throughout the world. Moreover, she receives many messages of good wishes everywhere she goes. These must all be acknowledged. When The Queen spent the first Christmas of her life outside the United Kingdom, in Auckland, New Zealand, a tremendous number of telegrams, letters and cards of good wishes were received. It was three o'clock the next morning before the small staff "packed it in", but it was with the satisfactory knowledge that every single message of good wishes had been acknowledged.

Behind the scenes during a Royal Tour there are all the problems of packing and moving, which require the most skilled co-operation and efficiency. So particularly well was this organised in New Zealand during that Tour, that The Queen specially sent for the New Zealand officer who was in charge of the baggage, to thank him for the way in which he had made everyone's journey a little easier. The more permanent presents which The Queen receives must be safely packed for transport home. The question of space is not difficult where ocean travelling is involved, but with air transport, weight is a very pressing consideration, and special arrangements may have to be made for gifts to follow The Queen home.

Then there are the inevitable bouquets with which The Queen is presented, often several times a day. When The Queen is based at one of her homes in the United Kingdom, or when she is staying for some time in the same place overseas, these bouquets are unfastened and used as much appreciated flower decorations in The Queen's room. When The Queen is spending some days in one place, this can be done on Tour. But often, when The Queen is travelling, there is no chance for her to enjoy the beauty of the bouquets. Then arrangements are always made to rush the flowers to the most convenient hospital or other suitable institution. The same holds good for gifts of fruit or other perishables. "And of course kind people seldom give The Queen just three or four pears," remarked a Member of the Household. "They generally send a crate. So there is often a surplus to dispose of." Sometimes The Queen gives the excess of her gifts to those round her on the Tour. For instance, every seaman in *Britannia* was given a stick of rock from a handsome present to Prince Charles when the royal visit to the Isle of Man took place in August 1955.

Although The Queen primarily undertakes her Tours to the Commonwealth so that the people of the Commonwealth may see her, she herself gains enormously from them. No place one has visited, however briefly, can ever again be a dot on the map. The Queen gains in experience, in confidence, and in sheer enjoyment from her tours. She meets many interesting people. She sees many fascinating things. She is young and vigorous and, naturally, she is immensely stimulated by her experiences. Although the framework of the various royal visits is very similar, whether she is in Australia or Canada or Fiji, the picture framed is widely different. Even the bouquets which she receives from the hands of pretty little girls of every Commonwealth race are so different. She has had bouquets of wattle and Queensland orchids in Australia, white heather in Scotland, of roses, carnations and every possible flower.

The triumphal arches under which she has driven are worth a chapter by themselves. There was the arch at Tonga, orthodoxly lettered, and adorned by wildly waved, welcoming brown arms thrust through the spaces; archways of dark green fern across the beautiful roads of the South Island of New Zealand, and archways of palm leaves from which hung baskets of fragrant frangipani at Lautoka in the Fijis, nearly a mile of arches, Crowns and trees festooned with lights in Melbourne and a thousand more examples of ingenuity and forethought. She may have recognised old acquaintances in some of the decorations—those in front of Government House, Canberra, for instance, and at Manly, New South Wales, had been used at the Coronation in London.

The Queen has inspected guards of honour throughout the Commonwealth—and strange guards of honour formed of such unusual subjects as the seventy-five merino rams and ewes lined up at Dubbo in New South Wales.

Often The Queen has commemorated her visit by planting a tree, a sessile oak at Windsor to mark the Coronation, a pine yew in Bermuda, a yoke wood tree in Jamaica, an ash by a volcanic lake in Victoria, Australia. The Queen planted trees at both ends of the 200-mile-long memorial avenue from Sydney to Canberra.

She has planted a whole botanical garden of different trees, in this permanent record of her far-flung progress.

She bravely swallowed in one draught, as etiquette demands, the soapy-tasting Yaqona (known elsewhere as Kava) of Fiji— something that the Queen Mother, for all her natural courtesy, has not managed to do in her two visits to the island. She has eaten the exotic foods of half the world.

The Queen has had some memorable and some very beautiful experiences. She was particularly struck by the two-mile line of small boats, all gay with flags, through which the Royal Party passed on its way from the *Gothic* to Farm Cove, Sydney, when she first landed in Australia. Even more effective was a similar escort of boats, this time yachts under sail, every yachtswoman and yachtsman dressed in black and white, which escorted her into Hobart. There were the magnificent sailing war canoes which skimmed with such speed and daring over the water as she approached Fiji. She remembers the overcast morning when the *Gothic* entered Milford Sound in New Zealand, and a few minutes afterwards the sun blazed through to reveal Mitre Peak rising sheer from the fjord.

The Queen was the first of our Sovereigns to visit a leper settlement—which she did partly to emphasise that leprosy is not the appallingly highly contagious disease that it is traditionally supposed to be, and partly because The Queen has long had a compassionate sympathy with the sufferers from this disease. She has adopted several leper children, one after the other, paying for all their medical and other needs. At present The Queen's charge is a small boy of about Prince Charles's age, called Edau, who is receiving medical care at the Kumi Leprosy Settlement in Uganda.

The Queen with the Duke of Edinburgh (who has also adopted a child suffering from leprosy) went to the Oji River Settlement on February 9, 1956, where she saw and was seen by nearly 1,000 patients, many well on the way to recovery through new forms of treatment, but some in a sad and advanced condition of the disease.

I am privileged to take extracts partly from an account written by one of the devoted helpers stationed in the Settlement, with whom I was put into touch by the British Leprosy Relief Association.

As you can guess we were very busy for weeks before the great day; everything had to be spick and span, although we were very careful not to change anything from the way it usually is,

she wrote. The Queen and the Duke first met most of the officials in the office, then drove through the hospital compound and round to the girls' compound.

Among those whom The Queen saw at the Oji River Settlement is the little girl in a checked dress whom the Queen Mother had adopted, and whose name is not given because many of the patients do not wish to reveal to their friends that they are undergoing treatment for leprosy. This little girl, now about twelve years of age, is an Ibo from Eastern Nigeria, and although she is still in the Settlement, at the time of writing I was told "she is making very good progress and it should not be long before she goes home. She is a very nice-looking girl and should not be left with any trace of leprosy at all."

The Queen walked through the Girl Guide Guard of Honour past the other girls into the centre of the compound "and all the time Her Majesty was asking questions about the children".

The Queen asked how many children were in the Settlement— about 200; where they came from—a radius of about fifty miles; how many Guides there were—usually between twenty and twenty-five; and was told how the children improve with the good feeding of the Settlement, and how their treatment now takes the form of taking Depsone tablets on two afternoons a week, in place of the former painful and nauseating hydno-carpus injections.

The Oji River Settlement houses approximately 600 patients, and treats about 8,000 patients in outside clinics and segregation villages.

During this time the Duke of Edinburgh had been following behind and deviated to go into one of the sleeping-houses ("I hope it was all neat and tidy as I had not had time to look and see earlier in the morning").

In the infirmary square an aged blind leper, John Aguh, said movingly, "We cannot express our joy and happiness to see your Majesty and the Duke of Edinburgh in this country, more especially now that we are enjoying your shade and protection in both food and medical matters. Remember, O Queen, the infirm and blind group of this settlement."

The Queen went on to see the boys' compound and the Church, decorated with blue jacaranda, branches of flame tree and many Harmatten lilies, gathered in spite of the drought. She went to the Technical School and saw the girls weaving and the boys doing carpentry; outside again to see the blacksmith's smithy, shoemaker's and palm oil press, and past the primary schools to the exhibition of Arts and Crafts, where she was interested in a group of leper women with their hair done in elaborate native styles, some of which had taken hours to prepare. "After passing through a Guard of Honour of six Scouts and six Girl Guides, The Queen went into her car and drove very slowly out of the settlement.

"All the patients are thrilled to think that they have really met The Queen, and all thought that she looked very beautiful."

The Queen sees the advances in medical care in many parts of the Commonwealth, from the Karitane child welfare homes of New Zealand to hospitals for wounded ex-Servicemen in Australia and other places.

She also sees relics of old customs, which have perhaps been revived for the first time for many years in her honour, and which the ordinary traveller is seldom privileged to encounter.

The Queen will remember the serenade of nose flutes which woke her in the dawn in Tonga and the droning of the *didjeredu* and the music sticks of the Australian Aborigines at Toowomba.

Always she particularly looks forward to agricultural occasions of whatever kind. Country people always feel especially at home in the country, whatever country. She was delighted by the expert teams of axe men who chopped wood in competition before her in New Zealand, and by the Bowen brothers, also in New Zealand, who sheared sheep in unison in front of her, ending with exactly the same stroke in precisely the same time of two minutes twelve seconds per sheep.

The Queen always snatches such opportunities as she can to see the bloodstock in other countries, and it is noticeable how relaxed and refreshed she is after even a few minutes in this congenial atmosphere. The problem of relaxation within the framework of a Commonwealth Tour is an acute one.

The strain of such Commonwealth Tours cannot properly be understood by those who have not endured them. They are exciting, they are stimulating, they are immensely worth while, but they cannot fail to be exhausting. Even the logistics involved are impressive.

I have been given the privilege of quoting the following figures, compiled after the Overseas Tours.

The total mileage and transport involved in the 1953–4 Commonwealth Tour round the world were:

Means of Conveyance	Number of Trips	Distance (Miles)
Car, Land Rover, Jeep, etc.	702	4,006
Ship, Boat, Ferry, etc.	75	19,644
Aircraft	51	18,106
Train	44	1,857
Carriages, Rail Trollies	6	5
TOTALS	878	43,618

The details of such a tour from which these figures are compiled would be extremely tiring even to read, and they would take a great deal of space. I have, however, included as an Appendix complete mileage details for a much shorter tour, that to Nigeria in 1956, which involved only one-fifth of the distances covered in the World Tour, although it was compressed within one-eighth of the time.

The changing pattern of the Commonwealth undoubtedly means that The Queen will have to spend—and wants to spend—more of her time on the affairs of the Commonwealth countries than any previous Sovereign. The Queen is Head of her Commonwealth. She is not just Queen of the United Kingdom, she must constantly keep all Commonwealth viewpoints in mind. Increasingly often it is suggested that The Queen should regularly live for some weeks or months in one or other of the overseas Commonwealth countries.

(Queen Victoria once considered, if not very seriously, emigrating to Australia! She wrote to the Princess Royal in Germany in an undated letter in April 1859, which is preserved in the Kronberg archives, and was quoted in *The English Empress* by Egon Caesar Conte Corti: "I am sick of all this horrid business of politics, and Europe in general, and think you will hear of me going with the children to live in Australia, and to think of Europe as the moon").

Queen Elizabeth looks forward to revisiting the Commonwealth as eagerly, perhaps even more eagerly, than she looked forward to her first visit. She told Mrs. Richard Casey, wife of the Australian Minister for External Affairs, that she would like to visit Australia again, but with a less exhausting programme, when perhaps she could stay in one place with the children. She is always most particular to make clear that she regards her visits to the Dominions not as going to a strange place, but as going to stay in another of her homes.

The proposal that The Queen should devote her time more equally between the United Kingdom and the overseas Commonwealth countries was put with vigour and sincerity by Sir Keith Officer, the former Australian Ambassador to France, speaking in London in May 1957.

"As an Australian, I can say that there is a very strong inclination here to regard The Queen as your private property. She is not. She is our Queen of Australia, just as much as your Queen, and we rather resent the suggestion that her right place is at Buckingham Palace, Balmoral or Sandringham.

"Many of us would like to see the day when she can come out for two months a year to live in her residence in Canberra and carry on her duties there as Queen of Australia, just as she carries them on here as Queen of the United Kingdom."

The idea is at first tempting and attractive. But on looking into it, it presents almost insuperable difficulties. The first is that The Queen has ten (and may soon have more) Commonwealth countries which regard her as either Queen or Head. It would obviously be impossible to have any kind of coherent life if it were divided between them all. The second is the undoubted fact that a great deal of The Queen's Constitutional work still centres upon her in London. Added to this there is of course the personal side of it, the necessity that The Queen should be a balanced and stable person, with her roots down, both for her own sake and for that of her children, and this would be difficult to achieve if she became a peripatetic "walk-about". This is understood by those throughout the Commonwealth who work with The Queen on an official level and who understand what she has to do.

"The Queen, like anyone else, likes to know where she can find her hair-brush," said a Member of the Household.

Mr. Menzies, Prime Minister of Australia, commented on Sir Keith Officer's statement as follows:

"Proposals for the Queen to live regularly in Australia are quite impracticable. The proposal has been advanced from time to time. Naturally it was given the closest examination and the warmest consideration, but almost from the outset the difficulties became manifest."

Mr. S. G. Holland, the Prime Minister of New Zealand, said that:

"Royal residence in New Zealand would be a great event for us, but I am sure we would not want it at the expense of Her Majesty's personal life."

There were great practical difficulties in any scheme for the Queen to move from one Commonwealth country to another at regular intervals.

"If Her Majesty were to reside in turn in each Commonwealth country, her time would be very finely divided up. It is no secret that periodic royal tours must be a great strain on Her Majesty and represent sacrifices of family life on her part."

The Royal Family is known to favour less formal tours, said Mr. Holland,

"which would enable advantage to be taken of the speed of modern communications."

The Queen's duties and responsibilities have multiplied and are still constantly increasing. Yet she has no more hours in her day than had Queen Victoria or any of her predecessors. In order that she may fulfil, as she is so willing to do, her greatly increased contact with other Commonwealth countries, The Queen must necessarily prune and adjust her commitments in the United Kingdom. As has been discussed in the chapter about "The Queen's Public Duties in Britain", she does not want to be bound by annually recurring public commitments which are not a part of her Constitutional or ceremonial duties. Obviously, whenever possible, she will open the Parliament of the United Kingdom every year: that is a great occasion of deep constitutional significance. But she can no longer always spare the time to undertake annual commitments which have no direct and deep reason for The Queen's regularly recurring presence. Similarly she has pruned social commitments to leave more time for meeting a wider range of her peoples.

We of the United Kingdom in some measure deserve Sir Keith Officer's strictures. We *are* inclined to accept The Queen as our personal property, whom we are kind enough to let our cousins in the Commonwealth glimpse from time to time. Nothing can be more detrimental to the Commonwealth as a whole. Every time we try, from whatever motive, to tie The Queen to a purely United Kingdom outlook, we are doing her and the Commonwealth a great disservice.

The Queen belongs to us all equally. We have an *equal*, but not a *greater*, right than the Australian or the Ghanian or the Fijian to admire The Queen and to be inspired by her. A sense of superiority, for no better reason than that we live in the United Kingdom, is one of the most irritating and least useful attributes of the British character. The Queen is truly Commonwealth-minded—thank goodness. Her width and range of vision, and that of the Duke of Edinburgh, far exceeds that of most of her millions of citizens—and of course a parochial outlook is not confined to the United Kingdom, but can also be found in Australia, or in Ghana or in Fiji, or indeed in any other Commonwealth country or colony. The Queen is our emblem of unity. As a great conductor can lift every member of his orchestra to play above himself, so a great sovereign can raise our efforts for the common good above our known best. At the most trying time in the history of the Commonwealth we are led by a Queen who really understands its conception.

In her words, from her Christmas broadcast from Auckland, quoted at the beginning of this chapter:

"The Commonwealth bears no resemblance to the empires of the past. It is an entirely new concept—built on the highest qualities of the spirit of man: friendship, loyalty, and the desire for freedom and peace. To that new conception of an equal partnership of nations and races I shall give myself heart and soul every day of my life."

313

CHAPTER TWELVE

The Queen and Foreign Powers

"In law, the Sovereign is the only person with authority to represent any part of her dominions in intercourse with a foreign State, and to contract international obligations. Constitutionally, these and other acts of Government requiring the participation of the Sovereign are performed on the advice of the Commonwealth Government concerned."

The Monarch and The Commonwealth, issued by The Central Office of Information—February 1955

"It is, we think, a deeply felt sense of common interests in the world-wide community of free men which leads so many Americans to pay homage to this young woman and the evolving tradition which she represents. Canadians steer their own course in the world but call her Queen. Independent India pays her honor as Head of the Commonwealth. In many lands she reigns in one capacity or another as the symbol of their devotion to freedom, although it may be expressed in diverse ways.

"This country accords Her Majesty no title, but it offers her, we think, its heart."

Washington Post: October 17, 1957, on the Eve of The Queen's State Visit

THE most momentous step which can be taken by a nation—that of declaring war—would be made by The Queen in Council. Fortunately this solemn and terrible step has not so far fallen to The Queen's lot. Although not personally responsible for such a decision, the Sovereign could not but feel a deep sense of responsibility upon taking such an irrevocable step.

We know from the diary of King George V, quoted in Sir Harold Nicolson's invaluable *King George V: His Life and Reign*, the deep feelings of emotion and unhappiness with which he felt the declaration of war on Germany in 1914:

Tuesday, August 4th. I held a Council at 10.45 to declare war with Germany. It is a terrible catastrophe, but it is not our fault. An enormous crowd collected outside the Palace; we went on the balcony both before and after dinner. When they heard that war had been declared, the excitement increased and May and I with David went on to the balcony; the cheering was terrific. Please God it may soon be over and that He will protect dear Bertie's life. Bed at 12.00.

The Queen in Council would also make peace. In fact, The Queen conducts all the most important, all the binding agreements, between those Commonwealth countries of which she is Queen and foreign powers, either in person or through her representatives, such as Governors-General, or Ambassadors.

This is most clearly put in *The Monarch and the Commonwealth*, issued by the Central Office of Information in February 1955, with which this chapter opens:

In law the Sovereign is the only person with authority to represent any part of her dominions in intercourse with a foreign State, and to contract international obligations.

This statement is immediately modified.

Constitutionally, these and other acts of Government requiring the participation of the Sovereign are performed on the advice of the Commonwealth Government concerned.

Of course The Queen has these powers in a constitutional sense only; she could not take any of these drastic steps except on the advice of her Government.

In the old days, a considerable amount of foreign policy was conducted—just as all processes of Government were conducted—through discussion and arrangement among friends and relatives. Then it was possible for the Sovereign to enter into private agreements with the rulers of foreign countries. But these could not be made binding upon the Government. Queen Elizabeth I initiated foreign policy. Even Charles II, it may be remembered, entered into private agreements with the King of France, although these were not implemented. Queen Victoria, as we know from her letters and those of her relatives, took a very personal interest in the conduct of foreign affairs, which was only natural when she was so closely connected with almost every member of every Royal House in Europe.

The Queen's active participation in Foreign Affairs is a thing of the past, but her dignity plays a supreme part in the relationships between the countries of the Commonwealth and foreign states.

From earliest times, formal connections with friendly countries have been maintained by accrediting envoys between the Heads of the countries concerned. Diplomatic envoys to this country are formally accredited to The Queen and are referred to as residing at the Court of St. James's. This continues, although The Queen lives in Buckingham Palace, and though the office of the Marshal of the Diplomatic Corps has been situated, not in St. James's Palace, but in Buckingham Palace, for over twenty years, since King Edward VIII brought it there with him. "One just takes it for granted," I was told. "It just has not been changed since the days when the Sovereign used to live in St. James's Palace."

King Henry VIII acquired the land on which St. James's Palace stands from Eton College, in exchange for lands at Chattisham in Suffolk. Built on the ground was "a spittle for mayden lepers", which was called St. James's Hospital. King Henry VIII demolished the priory and dispersed the lepers, but retained the name for his new Palace.

Thereafter St. James's Palace was the principal London Palace of the Sovereigns, and was naturally the venue for most official functions. Even when King George III built his "Queen's Palace" where the greatly altered Buckingham Palace stands to-day, it was a private residence, and all official occasions continued to be held at St. James's Palace.

Queen Victoria moved into the new Buckingham Palace immediately after her Accession, and was the first occupant of the grand palace conceived by King George IV and his architect, Nash. But she continued to hold her Drawing Rooms at St. James's Palace until 1865, and her Levées there throughout her reign. Indeed Levées continued to be held at St. James's Palace till they came to an end with the outbreak of the Second World War.

The Presentation of Letters of Credence to the Sovereign by a new Ambassador or Minister is a dignified ceremony of ancient origin. There are many descriptions of it in Tudor, Stuart and Hanoverian times, but little is known about the ceremony to-day.

What happens is this. New Ambassadors, their wives and certain of their Staffs are presented to The Queen when the Ambassador is first appointed. Ambassadors used to be exchanged only between the Great Powers. But now, there is a world-wide inflation in the number of Ambassadors. Before the war there were about fifteen Ambassadors and from forty to fifty Ministers appointed at the Court of St. James's. To-day, there are sixty-four Ambassadors and only five Ministers, to whom must be added a dozen High Commissioners from Commonwealth Countries, who rank with Ambassadors, a total of around eighty Heads of Missions in London.

When an Ambassador is to present his Letters of Credence, the Marshal of the Diplomatic Corps (Major-General Sir Guy Salisbury-Jones, K.C.V.O., C.M.G., C.B.E., M.C.) goes to fetch him in a State landau. Two other State landaus are available for his Staff. Each of these landaus will seat four, which effectively limits to eight the number of Ambassador's Staff who can be presented to The Queen on this occasion.

Ministers and the wives both of Ambassadors and Ministers make their own way to the Palace, but otherwise there is little difference in the procedure for an Ambassador or a Minister.

At Buckingham Palace the landaus drive into the courtyard and pull up outside the Grand Entrance. There the Ambassador and his Staff alight—thankfully if they are bad sailors, as the State landaus are very lightly sprung and have a rocking action—and are met there by the Vice-Marshal of the Diplomatic Corps and the Equerry-in-Waiting.

Inside the Grand Entrance the Master of the Household is waiting, and the Marshal of the Diplomatic Corps introduces the new Ambassador to him. The Master of the Household then conducts the Ambassador to the Bow Room, where he will meet either the Foreign Secretary or the Permanent Under-Secretary for Foreign Affairs. The Bow Room is the centre room on the lower floor, through which the Garden Party guests pass on their way to the Gardens. It adjoins the 1844 Room, in which The Queen generally receives Ambassadors, and in which Privy Councils are also held.

When The Queen is ready to receive the Ambassador, he is conducted into the Presence with the Marshal of the Diplomatic Corps on his right and the Master of the Household on his left.

With The Queen will be the Foreign Secretary or the Permanent Under-Secretary of State for Foreign Affairs. When they enter the room they all take one pace forward and bow together. After taking a second pace forward and again bowing, the Marshal announces the Ambassador to The Queen. The Master of the Household and he then withdraw, and the Ambassador goes forward and makes a third bow as he reaches The Queen and shakes hands with Her Majesty. He then presents his credentials and Letters of Recall of his predecessor, which are in an envelope addressed to The Queen. The Letters of Credence are in essence a request from the Head of one State to the Head of another State, asking (in the words of The Queen's Letters of Credence), "We therefore request that you will give entire Credence to all that he will communicate to you in Our name." The language of such documents, which used to be highly ornate, has now given place to a more simple address. These Letters may be in French or the language of the country concerned and are sometimes, especially with countries employing the Arabic script, beautifully prepared and attractive in appearance.

The Queen then converses with the Ambassadors privately either in English or French while they remain standing. Her Majesty's own extensive travelling and that of other members of the Royal Family, combined with the knowledge acquired from the reading of official documents, greatly facilitates such conversation.

The Queen then asks the Ambassador to present his Staff, and they then enter the Presence, in order of their seniority, and are presented individually to the Queen. When the last member of the Staff has withdrawn, the Marshal of the Diplomatic Corps conducts the Ambassador's wife into the Presence, announces her to The Queen and withdraws. She then goes forward to The Queen and either curtseys or uses the form of salutation of her own country.

The Ambassador wears diplomatic uniform if it is the custom of his country to do so; otherwise he wears evening dress with decorations. The wife wears day dress or national costume.

When the Audience is over, the Ambassador bows and his wife curtseys to The Queen. They then turn round (in the old days they had to back out, as it was against protocol to turn one's back on the Sovereign) and go to the doorway, where they again face The Queen and bow and curtsey respectively before withdrawing.

The Queen meets the Ambassadors and the Ministers accredited to her Court on many subsequent occasions.

The Heads of Missions are always asked to the annual Garden Parties at Buckingham Palace, half of them to each Party.

The Queen has also continued the Annual Diplomatic Party, begun by her father, King George VI, in 1950, to which some distinguished British people are also invited. There The Queen passes through the State Rooms, shaking hands and talking to the Heads of every Mission—and remember that including High Commissioners they number about eighty—with their wives, and with some of their Staffs. "In itself," said a Member of her Household, who is closely concerned, "that is a very big proposition. But The Queen, like the rest of her family, has a very good memory, and she is really interested."

The Queen also, of course, meets Ambassadors at many of the great or more intimate occasions she attends. On occasion—but only in exceptional circumstances—she may informally visit an Ambassador in his London Embassy. Such occasions have occurred when there has been a special Ballet or Film festival involving that country's nationals, when she has made or is making a visit to that country. When, however, The Queen is entertaining the Head of a foreign State on a State Visit to this country it is customary for Her Majesty to dine with him in his country's Embassy as one of the items in the programme of the visit.

"The Queen follows the welfare of an Ambassador and his wife with real interest," I was told. "If an Ambassador or his wife is ill, The Queen will always enquire."

An Ambassador who has been here for a long time generally requests a farewell Audience of The Queen, which she grants him whenever possible. When the Head of any Mission leaves, The Queen always instructs the Marshal of the Diplomatic Corps to see him off at the railway station or airport, with a farewell message of good wishes.

It is through the Ambassador or Minister concerned that every foreigner is invited to Court. No foreigner can be invited otherwise, so that The Queen may only entertain persons of good standing in his or her own country.

Incidentally, although on all Commonwealth occasions, such as the Opening of Parliament, all High Commissioners are grouped together, in diplomatic precedence they take chronological order with the Ambassadors, according to the date upon which they presented their Letters of Credence. But the doyen of the Diplomatic Corps must always be a foreigner.

Diplomatic immunity is enjoyed by an Ambassador, and is extended to all who assist him in the performance of his duties. These include members of the diplomatic staff (Counsellors, Secretaries, Attachés) who are engaged in the political economic work of the Embassy; Chancery staff (archivists, clerks, typists) and also the domestic staff employed in the Ambassador's household (cook, butler, housemaid, etc.) or in the Embassy offices (commissionaire, messengers, drivers, etc.). United Kingdom practice is the most generous in the world, and diplomatic immunity can be claimed for all members of an Embassy. No officer of the law can enter an Embassy without consent of the Head of the Mission (although to say an Embassy is "a piece of France", or whatever the case may be, is just nonsense). No person on the diplomatic list can be arrested or sued in the Courts. This creates an immune community, which consists at present of somewhere over two thousand persons, who cannot be arrested or sued for any crime or misdemeanour whatsoever unless the Ambassador waives immunity in this specific connection. In practice it is expected by Her Majesty's Government that immunity will be waived by the Ambassador in cases of car accidents or similar non-political offences. Certainly a car driven by a diplomat cannot be sued for damages *unless* diplomatic immunity is waived, but, as has just been said, this is almost always done.

In addition to diplomatic immunity, diplomats enjoy a number of privileges, on a strict basis of reciprocity. Diplomats are exempt from our taxation (but pay their own). They are relieved from paying Customs Duties on articles for personal consumption, and have partial relief from local rates. There are absolutely no regulations regarding the flying of any flag in this country. All immunity and privilege stems from the Ambassador who has presented his Letters of Credence to The Queen, and it is the

Ambassador alone who can waive immunity, subject always to the overriding authority of his Government.

British subjects employed in a foreign Embassy or Legation in this country, however, have neither immunity nor privilege. No subject of Her Majesty can be removed without the jurisdiction of Her Majesty's Courts.

The Queen's custom in connection with awarding decorations to foreigners and her permission to her own subjects to wear foreign decorations has already been discussed in the chapter "The Fount of Honour".

The Queen has herself received a considerable number of Foreign Orders, and will no doubt be invested with more, as her reign lengthens. Her Foreign Orders are at present as follows:

Order of the Elephant	Denmark
Order of El Kamal	Egypt
Grand Cordon of the Legion of Honour	France
The Most Glorious Order of Ojaswi Ranjanya	Nepal
Order of The Netherlands Lion	Holland
Order of the Seraphim	Sweden
Order of Manuel Amador Guerreor	Panama
Order of Qeladet El-Hussein Ibn Ali	Jordan
Grand Collar of the Order of Idris I	Libya
Order of the Seal of Solomon	Ethiopia
Order of St. Olaf	Norway
Grand Cross of the Three Orders of Christ, Aviz and Santiago	Portugal
Grand Order of the Hashmi with Chain	Iraq
Grand Cross with Grand Collar of the Order of Merit of the Republic	Italy
Special Grand Cross, with Star, of the Order of Merit	Federal Republic of Germany

Now we come to The Queen's own visits abroad.

Queen Elizabeth II had been less than twenty-four hours on the throne, she had not even met her Accession Council, when for the first time she landed on foreign soil. The visit was purely fortuitous and was when her aircraft from Entebbe in Uganda touched down at the El Adem airport near Tobruk to refuel on the passage home to London.

The first time The Queen set foot on foreign soil after her Accession was in Panama on Sunday, November 29, 1953, when the liner *Gothic* was passing through the Panama Canal on her way to the Pacific, the Fijis, Tonga, New Zealand and Australia.

The Queen landed at Panama, where she was received by the American Governor of the zone and the President of Panama, Colonel José Ramon. Then she had an exciting and crowd-beset drive through Colon and drove swiftly across the Isthmus to the Miraflores Lock on the Panama Canal, where The Queen helped to work a banana boat through the lock by manipulating some of the lock machinery. She joined the *Gothic* in Balboa, where The Queen (but not the Duke) had her first view of the Pacific. That evening The Queen and the Duke attended a banquet given for them by the President and Señora de Ramon.

The Queen's next visit to a foreign country was her second to Libya, at the end of the World Tour. Above all it will be remembered by The Queen because it was on board *Britannia* in Tobruk Harbour that her reunion with her children took place after a separation of five and a half months. But only after The Queen had meticulously undertaken four hours of public duties in Tobruk!

Since then The Queen has been abroad only once unofficially, and that was when, after the exhausting tour to Nigeria, she flew south from England to join the royal yacht *Britannia*, which was in the Mediterranean for Fleet exercises, in search of winter sunshine. The Queen spent six days on board *Britannia* while she cruised round the shores of Corsica, but alas, the sun went A.W.O.L. and The Queen had to make the best of her holiday without the sunshine.

The Queen *travels* far more than her predecessors, but she holidays abroad much less than they did. The Hanoverians naturally enough liked to go to Hanover. Queen Victoria travelled to visit her relatives in Germany and liked to stay on the Riviera "incognito", when she used the title of Countess of Balmoral.

King Edward VII much liked to holiday in France, and visited the United States "incognito" in 1860, as Prince of Wales, using the name of Baron Renfrew, which was one of his minor titles, as it is of Charles, Prince of Wales, to-day.

King Edward VII was even, surprisingly enough, "incognito" when he arrived in Naples on the start of his State Visit to Italy in 1903, with an escort of eight battleships, four cruisers, four destroyers and a dispatch vessel. King Edward VII frequently visited Denmark, the homeland of Queen Alexandra, and in 1908 he went also to Sweden and to Norway, a threefold tour facetiously referred to as "the Hennessey tour" by the Suite, each of whom received three Stars!

King Edward VIII also much enjoyed his holiday visits to the Continent. But The Queen resembles her father and grandfather in preferring to take her holidays among the familiar and well-loved scenery of her Scottish or Norfolk homes, or like her great-great-grandmother, to cruise among the many scattered islands and round the more remote coasts of Great Britain.

State Visits are quite a different matter. The Queen has made more State Visits already in her reign than any of our previous Sovereigns. The Queen has made the following State Visits:

Year	Month	Country	Host
1955	June	Norway	King Haakon VII
1956	June	Sweden	King Gustaf VI Adolf
1957	February	Portugal	President, General Francisco Higino Creveira Lopes
1957	April	France	President René Coty
1957	May	Denmark	King Fredrik IX
1957	October	United States of America	President, General Eisenhower
1958	March	The Netherlands	Queen Juliana

What is a State Visit? When is it undertaken? When did we start making them? What is their purpose? These are questions one often hears asked.

A State Visit is basically the visit of a *new* Head of State to a friendly country. A Sovereign only pays one *State* (as opposed to official or private) visit to any country. It is returned wherever practicable.

In other words, although King Olav V, the new King of

Norway, might pay a State Visit over here, The Queen will not pay one to Norway, where she has already been in State to visit King Haakon VII. Queen Victoria paid two State Visits to France, but this is regarded as exceptional.

As a State Visit is formal, the visiting Head of State always brings, in attendance, a Minister of the Government, normally the Minister for Foreign Affairs.

Another State Visit between the two countries can take place only should one of the Heads of State die or be superseded.

The Queen's first State Visit was to King Haakon of Norway. King Haakon was then eighty-two years old and unfortunately, only a few days after The Queen's visit, this stalwart old man, who had been such a symbol of courage and freedom to his people, slipped and broke a thigh, an injury from which he made only a partial recovery and which necessitated passing the business of Sovereign to his son, Crown Prince Olav, as Regent. King Haakon VII died on September 21, 1957, and was succeeded by the Crown Prince, who became King Olav V.

On the other hand it is not likely that there will be another State Visit between this country and Holland, where Queen Juliana is a comparatively young woman, for many years.

The most famous of all State Visits took place most probably at the Field of the Cloth of Gold, near Guines, between King Henry VIII and King Francis I of France in the summer of 1520. It was a scene of unparalleled magnificence. There King Henry VIII in cloth of gold jousted on a horse trapped in cloth of gold and russet velvet, while the French King's horse was trapped in purple satin, brocaded with gold and embroidered with raven's wings in black. Artificial bushes had been set up, a hawthorn for the English king, a raspberry for Francis, made of cloth of gold with silver flowers and fruit.

The first visit of a British Sovereign in modern times, which corresponds with the State Visits of to-day, was by Queen Victoria in the late summer of 1843, to stay with King Louis Philippe of France at his Chateau D'Eu near Tréport; this was the first voyage Queen Victoria and Prince Albert made on board their new yacht the first *Victoria and Albert*, and was arranged by Queen Victoria herself, without consulting the Government.

The Duke of Wellington, who was Leader of the House of

Lords in Sir Robert Peel's Government at the time, is said to have observed to Raikes, who published the account in his Journal:

I was never let into the secret, nor did I believe the report then in circulation, till at last they sent to consult my opinion as to forming a Regency during The Queen's absence. I immediately referred to precedents as the only proper guide. I told them that George I, George II (George III never went abroad) and George IV had all been obliged to appoint Councils of Regency; that Henry VIII, when he met Francis I at Ardres, was then master of Calais, as also when he met Charles V at Gravelines; so that, in these instances, Calais being a part of his dominions, he hardly did more than pass his frontier—not much more than going from one country to the next. Upon this I decided that The Queen could not quit this country without an Act of Regency. But she consulted the Crown lawyers, who decided that it was not necessary.

When Queen Elizabeth II goes abroad for a few days only, no Counsellors of State are appointed. When her absence will be longer, Counsellors of State (*not* Council of State) are appointed to conduct routine business.

Many years later, in 1858, Queen Victoria paid a second State Visit to France, where she was lavishly entertained by the Emperor and Empress of France. Queen Victoria always remembered with poignancy the contrast between the pomp and magnificence with which she was entertained in France on these occasions, and the very changed circumstances in which the Empress Eugénie found herself as an exile in England. Queen Victoria showed great compassion and understanding in the markedly dignified way in which she always surrounded the exiled Empress's visits to her.

King Edward VII really understood the art of human relationship. He had nothing like the interest or knowledge which The Queen has in the Commonwealth, but he travelled widely on the Continent and did a great deal to improve British relationship with our traditional enemies, the French. His initial visit to France in 1903 was not notably successful in a country which had strongly opposed our policy in the Boer War until, at a luncheon given in his honour at the Hotel de Ville, he said:

"Je n'oublierai jamais ma visite à votre charmante ville, et je puis vous assurer que c'est avec le plus grand plaisir que je reviens à Paris, où je me trouve toujours comme si j'étais chez moi."

After which the Parisians accepted him to their hearts.

The reigns of King George V and King George VI were disrupted by war. The reign of King Edward VIII was extremely short, so it has been left to Queen Elizabeth II to undertake the present revival of State Visits.

"A State Visit always does good," an experienced and responsible Member of The Queen's Household said to me. International friendships do not flourish by themselves. They are often disrupted by misunderstandings, which may be mere pin-pricks—and how irritating a pin-prick can be—by conflicting interests, commercial or political, or different political points of view, even when there is harmony on the main issues. It is an axiom that all friendships require to be kept in repair in order to endure, and this is by no means less true of international friendships.

A State Visit is a splendid occasion on which to review the things we already share in common, the admirable qualities we find in each other, and to recall occasions of friendship and mutual help in the past. They focus attention upon the achievements of both countries. Displays of British goods in the shops boost export sales. A State Visit—as The Queen is always accompanied by a Minister of State—is often the occasion for the exchange of commercial, welfare or cultural advantages. It has, moreover, a considerable and beneficial effect upon the political climate.

Some of The Queen's most vivid and unusual memories must come from her State Visits. Although their pattern is apparently cast in a similar mould, the setting is so very different. Mr. Godfrey Talbot, the skilled and experienced radio commentator, said to me in this connection:

"When you look only at the central figures of the ceremonies there is of course a repeating pattern—for every place wishes to salute The Queen for itself, just as if she had never been saluted before—but what I try to do is to look also, as it were, over Her Majesty's shoulder. For then the scenes are immensely different. What The Queen sees is always changing, especially on overseas tours."

The Queen's most memorable arrivals have been by water. The first State Visit of all took place on the morning of Midsummer Day, and all the previous evening The Queen had sailed in *Britannia* along the south Norwegian coast, which was studded

with the fire of the myriad bonfires with which every good
Norwegian celebrates "St. Hans Aften". The landing from the
Royal Barge was enlivened by the serio-comic incident of a seaman
in Crown Prince Olav's launch taking a toss into the water, from
which he was assisted by the Crown Prince himself.

There were sea-landings also at Stockholm, at Lisbon, at
Copenhagen, at Amsterdam, and the first two were particularly
memorable because Royal Barges were used. In Lisbon it was an
eighteenth-century green and gold barge, with forty oars rowed
by eighty oarsmen in red.

The barge in Stockholm was of eighteenth-century design also,
but a perfect replica, used then for the fifth time only, of the
original 1774 royal barge *Vasaorden*, which was destroyed by fire
in 1921. The new barge is even equipped with the first *Vasaorden*'s
blue velvet cushions, blue silk curtains and original oars for
eighteen rowers, as these had been salved from the fire. What a
magnificent sight it was when, in brilliant sunshine which had
succeeded fog, the white and gold barge *Vasaorden*, with enormous silken Royal Standard in the bow, and a great Swedish blue
and gold three-tailed ensign in the stern, slowly rowed The
Queen to land!

Then The Queen seated herself beside King Gustaf VI Adolf
in the State Carriage drawn by four horses à la Daumont, with
postillions in uniforms and caps heavily fringed with silver, and
the King's servant, standing behind him with a cap topped with a
magnificent three-foot ostrich feather. The escort, in their bright
blue uniforms on their chestnut horses, were carrying exceedingly
business-like automatic weapons.

Each State Visit brings its particular memories of great beauty,
vitality and interest. We know The Queen remembered the wonderful moment in her journey down river under the twenty-one
bridges of Paris, when two hundred small boys in white, the
Petits Chanteurs à la Croix de Bois, chanting a medieval hymn,
came down the steps of the Pont au Double. Then, from nearby
Notre Dame, the music of Handel thundered out, and the rose
windows of the transept were suddenly illuminated. The Queen
specially mentioned that memory in her letter of thanks to the
President, Monsieur Coty.

In Portugal she was intrigued, amused and touched when the

students flung their black cloaks into the roadway for her car to drive over or for her feet to touch. So gaily did she enter into the spirit of her riotous welcome in Oporto that The Queen and the Duke spontaneously decided to ride back to the airport in the back of an open bus, while the royal Rolls transported two incredulous Press photographers. There was only one slight miscalculation, and that was that the camellia heads which were tossed by the enthusiastic Portuguese into the open bus were hard enough to sting The Queen's cheeks as they came hurtling in. "They hurt!" she said laughingly afterwards.

Another gay and unusual scene for The Queen was when she attended, at her own request, the American football game between the Universities of Maryland ("The Terrapins") and North Carolina ("The Tar-Heels"), at which she thoroughly enjoyed herself, even though the mysteries of the game could not be fully understood in just one session.

The Queen has seen all possible kinds of decorations in her honour, from her royal cipher displayed in diamonds in Amsterdam, to lager bottles in Copenhagen. She was a not very expert bidder at a Dutch flower auction where the price moved from high to low and she "paid" £47 for two pots of orchids valued at £30. In Denmark Queen Ingrid showed The Queen the conical-shaped butter churns which have been introduced "to make the butter flop more", as Queen Ingrid told her, in order to get back to the quality produced by the old-fashioned churn.

Two of the most beautiful occasions which she has attended are visits to exquisite little royal theatres. In Sweden she attended a performance of opera and ballet in the little jewel of a royal theatre at Drottningholm which was unused and untouched for a century and a half, and is in almost the original condition.

The performance of an act of Rameau's *Les Indes Galantes* was the first in the beautiful royal opera house of the Château of Versailles since its reconstruction. This theatre was first used at the marriage of the Dauphin, the future Louis XVI, to Marie Antoinette. With its walls of subtle green, pillars painted like pink marble, turquoise blue silk hangings and dark blue velvet upholstery, in the blaze of beautiful chandeliers, it is an exquisite sight.

The treasures of the countries which The Queen visits are, as far as time and space permit, shown to her. Herself a considerable owner of Rembrandts, she saw some of his greatest works in the Rijks Museum in Amsterdam, and also many magnificent art treasures in the National Gallery of Art in Washington.

She has seen some interesting ships too, the replicas of the ships which brought the first settlers to Jamestown, Virginia, 350 years before ("Such tiny ships," she remarked. "It might be fun to sail in one"). She saw the *Mayflower* replica which had recently sailed the Atlantic during The Queen's sea progress to New York. She visited the Viking ships, similar to those which made considerably earlier crossings of the Atlantic, in Oslo, and there also inspected the *Kon Tiki* raft, and, like all other visitors, drew off her glove to feel the balsa wood of this frail raft for herself.

It is customary, during such visits, for the Heads of two States to exchange presents. The Queen has made this an opportunity to become a patron and donor of some of the best of our British arts and crafts. For instance, to the President of Portugal she took a painting by Graham Sutherland, which was a symbolic interpretation of Britain and her oldest ally, Portugal. To President Coty she took three engraved glass goblets, the work of Laurence Whistler, one of which showed a view of Windsor Castle, another a view of the Palace of Versailles by moonlight, while the third was engraved with an inscription commemorating the visit. (The work of Laurence Whistler is much appreciated by the Royal Family, who possess some specially commissioned pieces.) To President Eisenhower she took an English walnut and black calf hide table, on which was laid out, under glass, a map showing the Battle Order of "D" Day. She also made President and Mrs. Eisenhower a gift of a pair of parula warblers, birds from the south-east of the United States, sculpted in porcelain and perched in a branch of sweet bay-tree or black-stemmed magnolia, the work of a modern artist, Miss Dorothy Doughty from the Worcester Royal Porcelain Co. Ltd.

State Visits are naturally magnificent and memorable. They become something more because of The Queen's sincerity and kindliness.

One occasion which will be remembered was The Queen's visit to the Asscher's Diamant Maatshappij N.V. in Amsterdam, during her first State Visit to the Netherlands. There were diamonds in plenty, but more than that, there was true thoughtfulness. An event of that day, so typical of The Queen, is told best in the words of Mr. Joseph Asscher, Junior, in a letter to me:

When Her Majesty arrived at our factory she was received by my brother, Louis Asscher, Jr., and myself. We at once saw that she was wearing the brooch you mention. This brooch is made up of the Cullinan III and IV respectively, a pear-shaped diamond of 92 carats and a square cushion-shaped diamond of 62 carats respectively. We then accompanied Her Majesty and also the Queen of the Netherlands, the Prince Philip and the two elder Dutch Princesses to our auditorium, where various members of our board and our wives were introduced to the Royal Party.

The oldest member of our board is Mr. Louis Asscher, Senior, who was present when more than 50 years ago the crown jewels you mention were processed by my father and his brothers. When The Queen met him, she took off her brooch and gave it to us with the words: "Will you show these to your uncle, as I brought them along thinking he would like to see them again?" I must say that we indeed were deeply moved by this gesture, as we understood then that The Queen had brought over these stones specially to show them to us in Amsterdam.

(This was actually the first occasion on which The Queen has ever worn this brooch, the most valuable in her possession, and I am told by one well qualified to know, that the thought was entirely her own.)

In our auditorium (where we did not allow any representative of the Press) old Mr. Asscher spoke a few words about the cleaving of the Cullinan and my brother and I then showed the Royal Party the original tools which were used in processing this famous stone.

The Queen at one moment jokingly referred to the Cullinan III and IV as "Granny's chips". [The origin of this expression is that Queen Mary always described the Cullinan brooch as "The Chips"—this can be readily understood when they are compared with the first two stones in the Crown and the Sceptre.]

We then proceeded to show Her Majesty and the other Royal Visitors through our plant, and I may here add that we were deeply impressed by her charming personality . . . if there ever was an example of thoughtfulness on the part of Her Majesty, we feel that it was when she brought this wonderful brooch over to us. I may add that this gesture made a tremendous impression when the press in Holland wrote about it.

It is not the jewels, the beautiful dresses, the devoted entourage and the splendid setting which cause The Queen to shine on the great public occasions. It is The Queen's spirit of devotion, her thoughtfulness, her modesty and her sense of duty which give such splendour a meaning and a heart.

CHAPTER THIRTEEN

The Cost – and the Gain

"Our Monarchy gives us dignity, ceremony and pageantry without vulgarity, ostentation or extravagance. One can also say without disrespect, that it gives us more than value for money."
> Humphry Berkeley in an article "The Finances of the Monarchy"—*The National and English Review*

"The hardest-working professional queen since the first Elizabeth."
> American magazine *Look*, 1957

"The Crown has performed the . . . remarkable feat of converting an Empire into a Commonwealth of independent nations."
> Sir Ivor Jennings, *The Queen's Government*

THE Government grant to The Queen, which is paid entirely by the Government of the United Kingdom, amounts to between twopence and twopence halfpenny per person in the United Kingdom each year. That is the cost of one cigarette.

The incomes from the Crown Lands, handed in to the Exchequer by George III in 1761, and by succeeding sovereigns, in exchange for a fixed annual income known as the Civil List, now amounts to more than double the sum The Queen receives from the country, though it must be remembered that before the surrender of the Crown Lands the Monarchy used to pay for certain services that are now part of the National Budget.

Furthermore, during the Prince of Wales's minority, The Queen gives to the Exchequer eight-ninths of the income of the Duchy of Cornwall until he is eighteen years of age. While the Prince of Wales is between the ages of eighteen and twenty-one, the country receives a very considerable proportion of his income. This free gift from the incomes of the Duchy of Cornwall amounts, in itself, to over £1½ million. Not at all a bad bargain, from the United Kingdom point of view, apart altogether from the priceless and irreplaceable part The Queen plays (although that seems the wrong verb!) in the Commonwealth.

The economic background is little understood by many who, while admiring The Queen and considering the Monarchy "worth every penny", do not realise that it pays for itself. The Chancellor of the Exchequer benefited from this royal property in the year 1950–51 to the tune of £860,000 for the Crown Lands and £352,000 for small branches of hereditary income, a total of £1,212,000. In the year 1956–7 these incomes surrendered by the Sovereign to the Exchequer amounted to a gross income of £2,964,646. Against this there was expenditure amounting to £1,688,566. There were some minor adjustments to be made to these figures, but the profit to the country amounted to well over a million and a quarter pounds.

What were the principal properties surrendered by the Sovereign to the Exchequer and now forming the income of the Crown Lands? This is a question often asked, and generally vaguely answered as, "Aren't they Regent's Park and the Nash terraces?" It is, in fact, a question impossible to answer fully without considerable research, as changes and acquisitions have been made in the property originally handed over. The following is, however, a general picture.

The origins of the Crown Estate go back at least to Edward the Confessor. The present Estate consists in part of ancient demesnes and, in part, of purchases during the last 150 years. It is one of the largest, most varied and most valuable holdings of landed property in Great Britain, with a present gross income, as has just been stated, of close on three million pounds per annum.

In England the most valuable properties are in London. In Central London the Estate includes all properties in, and most of those surrounding, Regent's Park, most of Regent Street and Lower Regent Street, and Carlton House Terrace and Gardens. It also includes properties in Pall Mall, St. James's Street, Piccadilly, Haymarket, Trafalgar Square and Whitehall, in the City of London, Holborn and Kensington. In outer London there are estates at Eltham, Hainault, Hampton, Richmond and Oxshott, and urban property at Dover, Hastings, Ascot, Windsor, Bagshot and Egham.

The agricultural land, amounting to a total of about 180,000 acres, lies in twenty-five English counties.

In Scotland, the holdings are entirely agricultural and moorland, and amount to about 105,000 acres. The oldest possession is King's Park, Stirling, said to have been laid out by King Alexander III in 1257.

In Wales, the agricultural holdings amount to just over 1,000 acres, although the Estate includes very large areas of unenclosed mountain wastes, together with extensive mineral rights.

The Crown Estate includes much of the foreshore (which lies between high and low water mark) round the coasts of Great Britain and Northern Ireland, and also the bed of the sea in territorial waters, which are usually the three-mile limit. This ownership produces revenue from the right to take sand and gravel, from jetties, from oyster beds and (in Scotland) from salmon fishing. (During the war, when working in a Mercantile Marine Office, it used to be my easily-forgotten duty to send accounts for the modest sums charged for use of the foreshore within that area.)

In addition there are considerable investments in Government Stocks.

The Sovereign also surrendered the revenues from such things as wrecks, estrays ("Any beast not wild, found within any Lordship, and not owned by any man"—Cowell) and fisheries; droits of the Admiralty and from Courts of Justice; from fines, recognisances, legal fees and forfeitures; and from prerogatives connected with the Church, such as the temporalities of bishoprics during vacancy.

Certain Post Office revenues; the excise on beer, ale, cider and wine licenses; and when they were in force, the 4 per cent West Indies duties were also surrendered.

Treasure Trove, unwilled money and the income from the foreshores, already mentioned, were included in the surrendered revenues, except where they occur within the boundaries of the Duchy of Lancaster and the Duchy of Cornwall, when they form part of the revenues of the respective Duchies.

So much for the income surrendered by the Sovereign.

As the financial background to the Monarch is more often discussed than understood, it is perhaps also worth setting down in some detail the background of the income the Sovereign receives in exchange from Parliament.

The Queen receives the grant of this annual income, the Civil List, from Parliament. This ceases after the death of a Sovereign, and must be voted afresh in the new reign. Until 1910 it ceased immediately upon the death of the Sovereign, but since then the prevailing Civil List remains in force for six months. On May 19, 1952, Mr. R. A. Butler, then Chancellor of the Exchequer, presented an Address from The Queen to the House of Commons, which was read to the House by the Speaker. It ran as follows:

"The duties of the Crown render it necessary that renewed provision be made for the Civil List. Her Majesty places unreservedly at the disposal of the House of Commons those hereditary revenues which were so placed by her predecessor, and has commanded that the papers necessary for a full consideration of the subject shall be laid before the House.

"Her Majesty desires that provision shall be made for His Royal Highness the Duke of Edinburgh and for Her Majesty's children, other than His Royal Highness the Duke of Cornwall. Her Majesty also desires that provision shall be made for Her Royal Highness the Princess Margaret in the event of her marrying, and for any future wife of His Royal Highness the Duke of Cornwall, in the event of her surviving His Royal Highness.

"It is Her Majesty's intention during the minority of His Royal Highness the Duke of Cornwall to provide for His Royal Highness from the revenues of the Duchy of Cornwall, and to assent to arrangements for applying the balance of these revenues during the minority of His Royal Highness, in relief of the charge of Her Majesty's Civil List. In the event of the revenues of the Duchy of Cornwall vesting in Her Majesty, it is Her Majesty's intention, in so far as these revenues are sufficient, to provide for Her Majesty's Civil List out of these revenues.

"Her Majesty recommends consideration of these several matters to her faithful Commons and relies on their attachment to her person and family to adopt such measures as may be suitable to the occasion."

The Lord Privy Seal, Mr. H. F. C. Crookshank, then read that the Chancellor of the Exchequer, Mr. R. A. Butler, would move a Motion at the beginning of business of the House on the next day, for the appointment of a Select Committee to consider The Queen's Message.

The House of Commons Select Committee was duly appointed and consisted of twenty-two members, of whom twelve were Conservatives, the party in power, nine were Socialists and one Liberal. It included two women, Mrs. E. Hill and Miss Elaine Burton. This Select Committee was given the power to examine all witnesses who would voluntarily appear before them, but had not the power to send for persons, papers and records.

By early July an agreed report was made by the Select Committee to the House of Commons. They recommended that the Civil List should be made up as follows:

H.M.'s Privy Purse	£60,000
Salaries of H.M.'s Household	£185,000
Expenses of H.M.'s Household	£121,800
Royal Bounties, Alms, special services	£13,200
Supplementary Provision	£95,000
	£475,000

The Civil List of King George VI was £410,000, and of that the provision for the Privy Purse was £110,000. King George V had a Civil List of £470,000. Their Civil Lists contained only the first four items listed above, which in the Civil List of Queen Elizabeth II total £380,000.

The Supplementary Provision is there to meet rises in cost and wages which may be expected during The Queen's reign. Savings made during the early years of the reign are handed back to the Royal Trustees, who consist of the Prime Minister and the Chancellor of the Exchequer of the day and the Keeper of the Privy Purse, and are put aside by them in order to be able to meet rising costs in the later years of the reign.

Regarding the income of the Duchy of Cornwall, usually providing during a long minority a very pleasant nest-egg for the Heir Apparent, The Queen has, as already stated, set aside eight-ninths of the income of the Duchy of Cornwall to be put at the disposal of the Exchequer until the Prince of Wales is eighteen. The remaining ninth part of the income is used to provide for the Prince of Wales's expenses, and to give him "a moderate capital sum". Between the ages of eighteen and twenty-one, the Prince of Wales will retain an additional £30,000 per annum. The incomes of the Duchy of Cornwall will entirely revert to him on his twenty-first birthday. This gesture of The Queen's in giving up the incomes of the Duchy of Cornwall on behalf of her Heir Apparent is without precedent. When the Heir to the Throne has a long minority, he generally accumulates a considerable wealth. King Edward VII, for instance, had the estate of Sandringham bought for him by the Prince Consort with the Duchy money. The Queen, when Heiress Presumptive, did not receive the income of the Duchy of Cornwall; this belongs by statute to the eldest son of the Sovereign.

Although The Queen has a very considerable income, she has large expenses, and she suffers from the rise in the cost of living like the rest of us. In the first half of the twentieth century the cost of living trebled, but the rise in the total Civil List, including the money being put aside to meet further rises, has been very slight. A balanced budget has been possible only through careful pruning of expenses and staff. But, of course, Palace expenses, in spite of all care, are like those of other people and continue to rise. For instance, although the Members of the Household are modestly paid in comparison with salaries in industry, while the number of staff employed was reduced by one hundred persons between 1937 and 1951, in the same period salaries rose from £150,000 to nearly £200,000 per annum.

There were eighty-six horses in the Royal Mews in 1937 and only thirty-five in 1951 (there are thirty horses to-day). Yet the cost of fodder rose in that period from £2,000 to £3,200. And so on, and so on.

In fact, the budget was never balanced in the last years of King George VI's reign. Conscientiously, he returned to the Exchequer the money he had saved during the war years through lack of entertaining. At the same time he was meeting from his Privy Purse the annual deficiency on the amount allowed by the Civil List for Household salaries and expenses. The Select Committee report showed that in 1947 this deficiency was £27,053, in 1948 it was £44,079, in 1949 £29,360, in 1950 it was £47,472 and in 1951 it was £42,641.

In addition to the Civil List, some members of the Royal Family are provided for from the Consolidated List, as follows:

Queen Elizabeth the Queen Mother	£70,000
The Duke of Edinburgh	£40,000
The Duke of Gloucester	£35,000
The Princess Margaret	£6,000
The Princess Royal	£6,000

These sums are liable to some Income and Surtax, which The Queen's Civil List is not.

There remain other members of the Royal Family who do considerable public work, but who are not provided for from the Consolidated Fund. It is understood that The Queen will make provision for them from her Civil List, up to a total of £25,000 per annum.

Naturally there are a number of related costs, usual to the heads of great modern states, which are part of the cost of the Head of State, although they are not met from the Civil List. These might possibly, if all added together and lumped on to The Queen's expenses, increase the cost of the Monarchy by perhaps one penny per head per annum, to the trifling amount of just under threepence halfpenny a year, or rather more than the price of a letter.

The cost of transport is partly paid by public money and partly from the Civil List.

The cost of the royal yacht *Britannia* is included in the Navy Estimates. Unlike most of the other naval vessels, whose only rôle is in defence, but which are nevertheless generally recognised to be vital for the safety of this island, the cost of *Britannia* is continually criticised in certain quarters. Ships are apt to be expensive. But it is sometimes forgotten that it is considerably less expensive for a ship to be specially equipped for carrying The Queen and other members of the Royal Family, than to try to adapt a fighting machine like a battleship or cruiser to the totally uncontemplated function of a royal yacht. It is extremely expensive and wasteful to charter a merchantship, designed for high-pressure trading, to fulfil those functions, if other means are possible. As I have already mentioned, the royal yacht is moreover designed for conversion to an efficient hospital carrier in wartime. At present, she gives her complement sea-training, she takes part in naval exercises and is a fitting vessel for the conveyance of the

Sovereign of a great maritime nation. "Showing the Flag" has always been considered a useful function of the Fleet in peacetime. What could be a better way of doing this than by means of the royal yacht *Britannia*?

The Queen's Flight is a charge upon the Air Estimates.

The Royal Train is the property of British Railways, but The Queen pays for its use, and the fares of all those travelling in it.

The Queen buys, maintains and pays the expenses of her cars from her Civil List, and she buys, maintains and pays the expenses of her carriage horses and coaches from the same source.

Buckingham Palace, Windsor Castle, the Palace of Holyroodhouse, St. James's Palace, Hampton Court and Kensington Palace are all Crown property, and are maintained by the Ministry of Works. Sandringham House and Balmoral Castle are the Sovereign's private property, and are maintained by her.

The Crowns and the jewels in them are Crown property, including the Koh-i-noor and the Star of Africa. The Queen has, quite apart from the Crowns, a magnificent collection of personal jewellery, which has been estimated as the most valuable collection of set jewellery—no one knows what unset treasures may be found in the collections of certain Eastern potentates—in the world.

The Queen (it should hardly be necessary to state this, yet it is a question often asked) pays from her Privy Purse for all her dresses and their accessories.

From her Civil List she pays the very considerable total of salaries and wages to her Household. Although the Treasury is empowered to undertake the payment of retired allowances granted by the Sovereign in respect of those Members of the Household paid from the Civil List, the payment of pensions to employees on the Royal private estates is the Sovereign's personal responsibility.

The Queen gives generously both to individuals in need and to good causes. A substantial sum is allocated for Royal Maundy, Christmas and Easter gifts to the aged poor, and to assist in the education of children who have lost their fathers in one of the Armed Services while serving Sovereign and country.

She also subscribes to numerous charities which enjoy her Patronage. She makes Christmas gifts to the comforts fund of numerous hospitals, and at Easter hundreds of daffodils are sent from the Royal Gardens to the wards of London hospitals.

The proceeds from the admission fees to Windsor Castle, Sandringham Gardens, the grounds of Balmoral Castle and the Mews at Buckingham Palace are devoted to helping numerous local charities. At Windsor she makes a Christmas gift of coal to the aged poor of the town.

Many subscription lists for a wide variety of good causes are headed by a generous gift from The Queen.

She also gives numerous prizes and medals to cultural and scientific bodies, to schools and colleges and to Service training academies.

A very considerable expense is that of entertaining, as will be readily understood by those who read the chapter "The Queen, Our Hostess". At Garden Parties at Buckingham Palace and the Palace of Holyroodhouse, The Queen entertains about 25,000 people from all walks of life.

Heads of State on State Visits are always accommodated and entertained at Buckingham Palace, and banquets and receptions are held on special occasions. All this is in addition to the numerous representatives from the Commonwealth, home and overseas, who are daily entertained by The Queen.

There is one other aspect in which the Sovereign's expenses have risen sharply in this reign, and that is with regard to The Queen's travels, both in the Commonwealth and on State Visits to foreign powers. As has already been said in the chapter on "The Commonwealth", when The Queen visits a Commonwealth country, she is the guest of that country, and her accommodation and transport within it are paid by the host. Nevertheless The Queen naturally has many quite considerable incidental expenses in connection with her visits overseas. This increasing and vitally important part of The Queen's duties is bound to be, and to continue to be, costly.

The expenses of our Head of State compared with that of the United States, show that the President of the United States receives *all* his expenses while in office, plus 100,000 dollars a year. The cost of the British Royal Family is about twice that of the Dutch Royal Family, which has far smaller world-wide commitments.

The Queen does not pay Income Tax on the Civil List. The reason is that the Civil List is granted by Parliament to meet the Sovereign's official expenses and that to impose an Income Tax would mean increasing the original grant in order to provide money to pay the tax!

Income from The Queen's private estates and so on is liable for tax.

The estate of the Sovereign, alone, is exempt from death duties.

The Sovereign is not obliged in law to pay Customs duties; but in 1901 His Majesty King Edward VII voluntarily decided to accept an obligation to pay duty on goods imported for the use of their Majesties and the Royal Household, and succeeding Monarchs have continued this practice. The Sovereign does not, however, pay duty on articles which are offered and accepted as official gifts. Exemption is similarly accorded in respect of official gifts imported by other members of the Royal Family.

The baggage of Her Majesty The Queen and other members of the Royal Family, and of members of their suites, is normally delivered to Buckingham Palace or other Royal residence concerned on return from abroad. Customs Officers subsequently attend in order to assess any duty which may be due.

Apart from The Queen's Civil List, the Sovereign inherits the income of the Duchy of Lancaster, which has, since the time of Henry IV been vested in the Sovereign. The Duchy of Lancaster owns considerable property, amounting to about 52,000 acres, principally situated in Lancashire, Cheshire, Staffordshire, Yorkshire and Northamptonshire. Most of the land is agricultural.

Until recently little land lay within Lancashire itself, but for traditional reasons estates were acquired in The Fylde in Lancashire in 1944–5. The Queen has twice visited Duchy of Lancaster property, at Crewe in 1955 and Needwood in Staffordshire in 1957.

She has also her private inheritances, which include the estates of Sandringham and Balmoral, much jewellery and many art treasures. Her inheritance is the outward sign of her long lineage, and is a central treasure-house for the whole nation and Commonwealth. The fact that death duties (which are not paid by The Queen, although they are paid by other members of the Royal

Family) have not dispersed The Queen's treasures, as they have those of many great families, has been immeasurably to the national gain.

As Queen, she has inherited some unusual historic possessions.

As already mentioned, The Queen receives each year two silken flags, one tricolour from the Duke of Wellington as a quit-rent for Stratfield Saye, and one fleur-de-lys from the Duke of Marlborough for Blenheim Palace.

Less regularly presented, but older in origin than either of them, is the one red rose (it was a dark crimson "Madame Louise Laperrière" rose from the garden of the Duke of Argyll) that The Queen received from the Captain of Dunstaffanage on behalf of the Duke of Argyll, who was abroad, when she visited Dunoon in the summer of 1958.

As it is worded in the Historical Manuscripts Commissions report, this is as demanded in a

charter under the great seal by King James III to Colin, Earl of Argyll, Master of the Household, and his heirs, committing to them the keeping of the King's castle at Dunoon, with power to make constables, porters, jailers, watchmen, and other officers necessary for the keeping of the castle, and to remove them at his pleasure and put others in their places; for the keeping of which castle His Majesty grants forever to the Earl the lands of Bordland, extending yearly to 27 merks Scots with other fees belonging to the keeping of the castle; to be held blench of the King and his successors for a red rose yearly at the castle. Dated the 15th of January, 1472.

The last occasion on which the rose was certainly presented to the Sovereign was when Mary, Queen of Scots visited Dunoon in 1563. But the Duke of Argyll tells me that Mary was half-sister of the Countess of Argyll and visited her several times at Inveraray Castle, when she may also have been presented with a rose. Queen Victoria also visited Inveraray Castle several times, when it is possible she may have been presented with a red rose.

The Queen owns all mute swans which are not pinioned or marked, and there is a royal Swan-Keeper. At Swan-Upping each year on the River Thames (a lesser-known ceremony is held also on the Yare and the Wensum near Norwich) the cygnets of swans belonging to the Dyers and the Vintners Companies are marked, to distinguish them from the unmarked royal swans. The sturgeon was created a royal fish by Act of Parliament in the reign of Edward II (1307–27), but the swan's origin as a royal bird is unknown, though this probably took place in or earlier than the twelfth century. The mute swan was, of course, a table bird and in the early days was not really wild. Incidentally, the recent phenomenal increase in the number of mute swans is an ornithologist's puzzle.

The Queen owns other and rarer swans, the only Trumpeter Swans in Europe, which are in the care of the Wildfowl Trust at Slimbridge in Gloucestershire, of which The Queen is Patron. I am indebted to their Honorary Director, Mr. Peter Scott, C.B.E., D.S.C., for the following account of these rare birds:

The Queen's Trumpeter Swans are flourishing. They are in fact the only birds belonging to Her Majesty in our care, and the only Trumpeter Swans in Europe. There are less than 1,500 of them in the world, all living in the Rocky Mountains and Alaska. Five Trumpeters were originally caught at Lonesome Lake in British Columbia and given to Her Majesty as a joint present from the Dominion Government and the Government of British Columbia. They were sent here in 1951, soon after the Royal Tour of Canada. Unfortunately two years later we lost one female through intestinal disease. Two young females were sent to us in 1956, and we now have the three pairs here at Slimbridge. Wild caught swans usually have to be kept in captivity for about ten years before they start to breed, but one male built a nest here last year (1957) and we are hoping that his wife may take the hint this year.

The Queen first came to the Wildfowl Trust on March 4th, 1950. She came again, together with The Duke of Edinburgh, to see the Trumpeter Swans on April 25th, 1952, and honoured us with a third visit, accompanied by the Princess Royal, on April 20th, 1956. The 1952 visit was official, the others unofficial.

Many of The Queen's possessions are, of course, of great value. During the centuries the Sovereign has gathered treasures of every description. These form not only an almost continuous and valuable historical record of the fine products of each age, but also a heritage of ever-increasing and quite irreplaceable value.

Among the most personal of The Queen's inheritance are her jewels, which add lustre and dignity to State and great occasions of many kinds and in many lands. Indeed, they can properly be regarded as part of the job.

The Queen has, as I have said already, the most valuable collection of personal jewellery, set and in use, in the whole world. The jewels have come to The Queen in a variety of ways, but there are five main sections. These are the jewellery which she had before her marriage; her wedding presents; her Accession and Coronation presents; the valuable bequests she received from her grandmother, Queen Mary; and the loyal gifts which have been made to her, notably when she has been making an overseas Commonwealth tour.

Before she was married, Princess Elizabeth was not jewellery-minded. Her most valuable piece of jewellery was undoubtedly the necklace and bracelet pieces of jewellery made from the diamonds presented to her when she celebrated her twenty-first birthday in South Africa. These consisted of finest-quality diamonds, twenty-one stones from the South African Government and one from the Kimberley mines, of which the best is almost ten carats, fifteen set with lesser diamonds in the necklace and seven in the bracelet. Other pieces of jewellery which have been favourites with her are the three strings of pearls she received from her grandfather, King George V, and several brooches. For instance there is the badge of the Grenadier Guards in diamonds, sapphires and enamel, which was presented by the regiment to her as Colonel-in-Chief on her sixteenth birthday. There is the flame lily brooch from the children of Southern Rhodesia. Two favourite brooches are connected with the launching of ships—an antique diamond flower brooch with a little bow at the base of the stem, presented by the famous John Brown's shipbuilding firm when she launched the battleship H.M.S. *Vanguard* in 1944, and a very much used brooch, an oval of sapphires set in diamonds presented when she launched the *British Princess* at Laing's yard at Sunderland, a present from the builders and the owners.

Princess Elizabeth received some lovely presents when she was married. Her engagement ring, a solitaire diamond set with diamond shoulders, is a stone given by Princess Andrew of Greece to Prince Philip. Her wedding ring is a plain, rather broad ring of Welsh gold.

The Queen received from her father a favourite necklace of oblong sapphires set in diamonds and separated by diamond collets (that is, a stone individually set, as in a ring) with matching and beautiful earrings, which are sapphire and diamond drop earrings swinging free in a drop-shape, bordered by diamonds. From her father and mother she received a ruby and diamond necklace, and a superb pair of chandelier earrings in diamonds of every variety of cut except the "rose" cut.

Queen Mary gave her so many pieces of jewellery that it is not possible to recount them all here, but notable was the all-diamond festoon, scroll and collet-spike tiara with twenty-seven collets which The Queen calls "Granny's tiara" and which has the advantage of being very light. Queen Mary also gave The Queen one of three diamond bow brooches, a second of which was given to Lady Mary Cambridge on her marriage.

From the Nizam of Hyderabad she received a triple rose tiara. The large diamond roses are detachable and the larger or the two smaller are sometimes worn as brooches by The Queen. The Shaikh of Bahrain gave her a fine pair of matched Persian Gulf drop-pearl earrings. From Dr. Williamson of Tanganyika she received a fine pink diamond, the size of a sixpence, which has been set as the centre of a five-petal flower with straight stem, mounted with the finest of white diamonds.

It would be impossible to list all Princess Elizabeth's wedding presents; indeed, the catalogue of the wedding presents shown at St. James's Palace amounted to 2,583, and many more presents were afterwards received.

When The Queen came to the Throne in 1952 and on the occasion of her Coronation in 1953 she received further presents, of which there is only room to mention perhaps the gifts of very fine aquamarines received from Brazil. The original gift consisted of a necklace of nine graduated large oblong aquamarines in a scroll setting with one fine aquamarine oblong drop, together with aquamarine earrings similarly set. Later, The Queen had the aquamarines set in a tiara. In the summer of 1958 the gift was completed by a bracelet of seven great aquamarines set in diamonds, which The Queen usually wears on her right wrist. This was the bracelet she wore when the guest of Vice-President Nixon at Winfield House in London. The Queen has also received an aquamarine clip from Brazil.

The Queen received magnificent jewellery as a bequest from

Queen Mary. This included three major tiaras. The Russian style tiara (sometimes called a sun-ray tiara) is so called because Russian royalty and nobility wore jewelled tiaras fashioned in the shape of Russian peasant girls' head-dresses. This truly magnificent present was given to Queen Alexandra by friends and acquaintances at her Silver Wedding in 1888.

A very beautiful tiara of Russian origin consists of fifteen intertwined ovals, in each of which is suspended either drop pearls or emeralds. This was formerly the property of the Grand Duchess Vladimir of Russia. The emeralds belonged to Augusta, Duchess of Cambridge, who presented them to Princess Mary, Duchess of Teck, the mother of Queen Mary. They had originally been won in a lottery in Frankfurt early in the nineteenth century. The other tiara is in diamonds with nineteen hanging drop pearls and a lovers' knot above each drop pearl. It was made for Queen Mary from various ornaments.

The Queen's most valuable brooch, the third and fourth parts of the Cullinan Diamond, named the Star of Africa by King Edward VII, has already been described in the previous chapter.

The Queen also inherited from Queen Mary a very beautiful emerald and diamond necklace, of which the emeralds are from the same source as those in the tiara. Two drops, one a large emerald, the other a marquise pendant diamond, the fifth part of the Cullinan Diamond, hang at uneven lengths.

A most beautiful emerald and diamond brooch with a centre lozenge-shaped emerald, and one large emerald drop is *en suite* with this necklace. The Jubilee Offering Necklace is a very fine pearl and diamond necklace, with a crown at the front, which was a jubilee offering to Queen Victoria with money left over after the building of the Albert Memorial. The Dagmar Necklace, a present to Queen Alexandra, when Princess of Wales, from King Fredrik VII, has already been described in Chapter Twelve.

The last section of The Queen's inheritance of jewels are those loyal gifts which she received during her reign, many of them when visiting regions of Great Britain or the Commonwealth countries overseas. These are far too numerous to be mentioned individually here, but two such brooches which The Queen often wears are the diamond fern brooch, with central spine and twenty leaves, which she received from the women of New Zealand at

Christmas 1953, and the wattle brooch, in the form of a spray of wattle in white and deep yellow diamonds, which was the gift of the Australian Government in 1954.

There are many other fine jewels which The Queen wears.

The well-known diadem is a regal circlet of four diamond cross pattées and four motifs of rose, shamrock and thistle in diamonds. It is mounted on a band of diamond scroll work enclosed in two rows of pearls. It was made for King George IV to wear over a Cap of Maintenance and was remounted for Queen Alexandra in 1902. It fits straight on to The Queen's head.

The Queen wears a magnificent diamond necklace with diamond drop. The necklace was made in 1858 of very large diamonds, which were taken from a Garter Badge and Sword. This necklace was often worn by Queen Victoria. The large diamond drop, weighing 22½ carats, which The Queen wears with this necklace, is one of three very large drop diamonds, which were taken from a fine Indian cut ruby necklace, one of the treasures of Lahore, given to Queen Victoria by the East India Company in 1851. Two other large drop diamonds from this necklace have been mounted as earrings, together with two large collet diamonds from this same Garter Badge and Sword. As I have mentioned earlier, The Queen wore this diamond necklace and earrings at her Coronation.

The large drop from the necklace which was altered in 1937 was used in the Crown of Queen Elizabeth the Queen Mother at her Coronation in 1937. It is detachable.

The triple diamond necklace which The Queen wears on special occasions was made in 1950 for Queen Elizabeth the Queen Mother from 150 diamond collets, taken from a large collection of unmounted diamond collets.

To The Queen a watch is vital. The Queen is never seen without her watch, at which she glances unobtrusively, to keep control of the strictly rationed minutes. For years she wore a fine French watch set on a narrow platinum band, the face being no wider than the band. This had been presented to her parents for her during the State Visit of King George VI to France. This watch was lost at Sandringham, and The Queen missed it greatly. She now wears an almost identical watch, again with a face no wider than the narrow platinum band, which was presented by France to replace the first.

The Queen's pictures form a heritage of ever-increasing value both in the monetary and the artistic sense. It is the only European royal collection to survive as such. The collection is particularly rich in paintings by Holbein, Van Dyck and Canaletto. It contains several fine Rembrandts and half a dozen paintings by Rubens, many sixteenth- and seventeenth-century Venetians, and a good small collection of Italian and Northern Primitives. English portrait painters such as Reynolds, Gainsborough and Lawrence are well represented. There is not space to mention many other artists represented, from Fra Angelico to Zoffany, from Lely to Wilkie, from Stubbs to Landseer.

The collection of drawings is magnificent, and enormous; some of the artists are extraordinarily lavishly represented— Leonardo da Vinci, Michelangelo and Raphael, Holbein and Canaletto, and seventeenth-century Italians.

The first royal collector on a considerable scale was Henry VIII, who employed Hans Holbein as Court Painter.

Both the elder sons of James I were ardent collectors, although Henry, Prince of Wales, died young. Charles I showed both zeal and discrimination in gathering one of the very finest collections of great paintings ever assembled, and was moreover a patron of living artists, including Rubens and Van Dyck. The Commonwealth dispersed many of his art treasures by sale. Many of the paintings which remained in England were found and returned to royal ownership after the Restoration of Charles II, but most of the finest pictures had crossed the Channel for ever. The lost pictures included many Titians, several paintings by Corregio and Raphael and much else.

The later Stuarts continued the collection.

James II made a collection of Van der Velde sea battle-pieces. Little more of importance was added until the time of Frederick, Prince of Wales, son of George II and father of George III. He was a collector of fine plate, and he also purchased a number of important pictures, notably by Rubens and Van Dyck. George III, a man more interested in the arts than he is given credit for, bought considerably and well, notably the Smith collection from Venice, which is the source of the extraordinary richness of the royal collection in Canalettos and other Venetians. The Smith collection also brought two more Rembrandts.

George IV was a collector of pictures as he was of most arts, and he bought discriminatingly and wisely. He was particularly interested in seventeenth-century Dutch and Flemish painting, strengthening the Rubens and Rembrandts and buying many pictures by such artists as Cuyp and Teniers, as well as many of the finest pictures of lesser artists. Many of the paintings he bought were in first-class condition. The next royal collector, the Prince Consort, bought a considerable collection of Primitives. There are fine Primitives of his choice remaining in the royal collection, although some of the best were given to the National Gallery by Queen Victoria after his death.

Since that day, most additions to the royal collection have been portraits or scenes commemorating great royal occasions.

The finest of the royal pictures are on view to the public at Hampton Court and at Windsor. The Queen also generously loans her pictures to special art exhibitions both in Britain and overseas.

There is a collection of drawings at Windsor Castle which contains works by Holbein and Leonardo da Vinci. These drawings have been in royal hands since the seventeenth century and are among the most famous in the world. The collection was greatly enlarged in the eighteenth century by King George III, and there have been subsequent additions. In the main it consists of Italian drawings of the sixteenth and seventeenth centuries, but it also contains good examples of the English, French, Dutch and Flemish Schools.

A selection of the best drawings, which is changed at intervals, is always on view at Windsor Castle. Loans from the collection of drawings are also frequently made to outstanding exhibitions in England.

Although there is a certain amount of English eighteenth-century furniture which has remained in the royal collection ever since the reign of King George III, the most important part of the furnishings of the Royal Palaces consists of French eighteenth-century furniture. The greater part of this was acquired by King George IV in the years immediately before and during the French Revolution, and again after the end of the Napoleonic

Wars. Much of it was originally at Carlton House, George IV's London house, whilst he was Prince of Wales. In forming this part of the collection, which contains a large number of remarkable pieces formerly in the French royal collections, he was advised to a considerable extent by his close friend, the third Marquess of Hertford, who began the celebrated collection of French furniture now housed in the Wallace Collection. During the Revolutionary period he was also able to make use of the services of his French cooks, Benois and Weltje, who acted as his agents on a number of occasions in obtaining furniture from Paris which had come on to the market as a consequence of the French Revolution.

The Queen's collection also includes one of the most notable assemblages of eighteenth-century Sèvres porcelain in the world. This was acquired at the same time and in much the same manner as the French furniture.

The royal collection of armour consists mainly of King Henry VIII's Royal Arsenal. In Mediaeval and Renaissance times the King's armour was distributed amongst a number of Royal Palaces. After the Restoration, when armour was no longer required for military use, the bulk of the remaining armour was assembled and divided between the Tower of London and Windsor Castle, where it remains to this day.

The Queen's racehorses, as has already been mentioned early in the book, belong in part to her, and are in part leased from the National Stud for the period of their racing life. The Queen's own horses are bred at Hampton Court or at Sandringham under the care of her Racing Manager, Captain Charles Moore, C.V.O., and then go on to Captain Cecil Boyd Rochfort at Newmarket for training. The National Stud horses, formerly leased for racing to the late Lord Lonsdale, go for training to Mr. Noel Murless at Warren Place, Newmarket. Usually, the ownership of racehorses is an expensive hobby, but so knowledgeable and astute has been The Queen's ownership that she must have turned what is usually a minus into a plus in the royal books; this without betting, in which, as I have said, The Queen is not interested.

The Queen has also inherited a famous stamp collection, which in itself is a valuable asset, and which has been estimated as worth more than £1,000,000. The Queen as a girl worked on her stamp collection, but she does not have the time nor perhaps the keen interest in philately of her grandfather, King George V, to whom it was a lifelong hobby, and to which he devoted three afternoons a week whenever possible. The collection was continued by King George VI. It is in many respects unique. It contains the rare Mauritius 1847 Penny Orange Red, of which only a few copies are known, and one was sold in London for £4,500 in 1957. The stamps are kept in a special Stamp Room at Buckingham Palace. The Queen generously lends her stamps to exhibitions abroad. Part of the collection was lent, for instance, to the New Zealand stamp centenary in 1955; part went on loan to a philatelic exhibition in Capetown in 1952, and to an exhibition held by the Indian Posts and Telegraph Department in New Delhi in 1954, and also to other exhibitions both in the Commonwealth and on the Continent.

The Queen is undoubtedly a very wealthy woman. She has problems of finance, but they are not the same as those from which most of us suffer, or rather, they are on a vastly different scale.

If The Queen chose to live the life of a wealthy but selfish person, no doubt she would be very well off indeed—if she closed down the great State homes, shut up Buckingham Palace as it was shut in Queen Victoria's reign, and ceased travelling on our business.

But then, you say, she would not be doing her job. And that is unthinkable.

The Queen has a longer lineage than we have, she has greater means than we have, she has more resources and more opportunities. But she has precisely the same number of hours in a day and days in a year as we have. All the alternatives to duty are there —husband, children, lovely places to live in, horses to ride, hills to climb. And what does The Queen do? She spends hours each day reading worrying, dull, difficult papers about the unsolved, and it must often seem insoluble, problems of the world. She spends more hours talking gravely about these same problems to men at least a generation her senior. When she puts on her lovely hat and goes out in her fine Rolls-Royce, it is more often than not to sit on a draughty platform listening with serene courtesy to well-meant but lengthy platitudes. When she travels, she has to pass by the coral beaches for the local hospital, the glorious loneliness of veldt or forest for an overcrowded reception.

Why?

Because The Queen is filled with a sense of duty so deep that it is a feeling of vocation. Because for her the Commonwealth is her life. She knows that if she works incessantly, cheerfully, resolutely and entirely without taking offence, she will do incalculable good.

Paradoxically, The Queen's life will be far more full and satisfying than if she had been able idly to enjoy the fruits of her position, with perhaps a little mild doing-good when it did not seriously inconvenience her. She must derive a deep satisfaction, as do all dedicated persons, from the fulfilment of her works.

But it is a long, hard pull. Some fill their jobs as unstintingly as does The Queen, give as much of their energy, time, patience and thought to *helping* rather than *destroying*. Most of us do not.

Scoffing has always been easy, taking for granted is easier still. We are all given to grumbling. But when we are adding the pros and cons of life to-day, it is well to give thanks that in a position of such leadership and responsibility the people of the Commonwealth have as their Head

QUEEN ELIZABETH
our Queen.

APPENDIX

ABSTRACT OF THE MILEAGE IN VARIOUS KINDS OF VEHICLES DURING THE QUEEN'S VISIT TO NIGERIA IN 1956

From	To	Car	Plane	Other Vehicles	Total
27 January					
Buckingham Palace	London Airport	14			14
London Airport	Idris, Tripoli		1,472		1,486
28 January					
Idris, Tripoli	Ikeja, Lagos		1,911		3,397
Ikeja	Igbobi Roundabout	7			3,404
Igbobi Roundabout	Government House, Lagos	6			3,410
29 January					
Government House	Cathedral	½			3,410½
Cathedral	Government House	½			3,411
Government House	Tarqua			Launch 1½	3,412½
Tarqua	Government House			Launch 1½	3,414
30 January					
Government House	Racecourse	½			3,414½
Drive round Racecourse		1			3,415½
Racecourse	Government House	½			3,416
Government House	Igbobi	7			3,423
Igbobi	W.A.C. Medical Research	1½			3,424½
W.A.C. Medical Research	Government House	6			3,430½
31 January					
Government House	House of Representatives	½			3,431
House of Representatives	Government House	1			3,432
Government House	Law Courts	½			3,432½
Law Courts	Government House	½			3,433
1 February					
Government House	Ikeja	14			3,447
Ikeja	Kaduna Airport		407		3,854
Kaduna Airport	Government House, Kaduna	7			3,861
Government House	Polo Ground	1½			3,862½
Polo Ground via Durbar Camp	Government House	4			3,866½

353

From	To	Car	Plane	Other Vehicles	Total
2 February					
Government House	Racecourse	1½			3,868
Drive round assembly at Racecourse		1½			3,869½
Racecourse	Government House	1½			3,871
3 February					
Government House	Racecourse	1½			3,872½
Drive through children's ranks		1½			3,874
Racecourse	W.A.I.T.R.	1			3,875
W.A.I.T.R.	Officers' Mess	1½			3,876½
Officers' Mess	Government House	1½			3,878
Government House	Lugard Hall	1½			3,879½
Lugard Hall	Government House	1½			3,881
4 February					
Government House	Kaduna Airport	7			3,888
Kaduna Airport	Jos Airport		135		4,023
Jos Airport	Tudun Wada	5			4,028
5 February					
Tudun Wada	St. Pivan's Church	½			4,028½
St. Pivan's Church	Tudun Wada	½			4,029
6 February					
Tudan Wada	Jos Airport	5			4,034
Jos Airport	Makurdi Airport		176		4,210
Drive round Airfield		1			4,211
Majurdi Airport	Enugu Airport		112		4,323
Enugu Airport	Government House	5			4,328
7 February					
Government House	House of Assembly	2½			4,330½
House of Assembly	Government House	2½			4,333
Government House	Welfare Hall	3			4,336
Drive round Housing Estate		1			4,337
Welfare Hall	Government House	3			4,340
Government House	Stadium and Arena	3½			4,343½
Stadium and Arena	Government House	3½			4,347
8 February					
Government House	Enugu Airport	5			4,352
Enugu Airport	Calabar Airport		116		4,468
Calabar Airport	Mission Hill Cemetery	4			4,472
Cemetery	Calabar Residency	2			4,474
Residency	Sports Field	½			4,474½
Drive round ranks of children		1			4,475½
Sports Field	Calabar Airport	2½			4,478
Calabar Airport	Port Harcourt Airport		89		4,567

APPENDIX

From	To	Car	Plane	Other Vehicles	Total
Airport	Residency	6½			4,573½
Residency	Port Area	2			4,575½
Port Area	Sports Field	3			4,578½
Drive round children's ranks		1			4,579½
Sports Field	Airport	5½			4,585
Port Harcourt Airport	Enugu Airport		116		4,701
Enugu Airport	Government House	5			4,706

9 February

From	To	Car	Plane	Other Vehicles	Total
Government House	Oji River Power Station	28			4,734
Oji River Power Station	Oji River Leper Settlement	½			4,734½
Oji River Leper Settlement	Government House	28			4,762½
Government House	Enugu Airport	5			4,767½
Enugu Airport	Benin Airfield		133		4,900½
Drive round Airfield		1			4,901½
Benin Airport	Ikeja Airport		158		5,059½
Ikeja Airport	Lagos Government House	14			5,073½

10 February

From	To	Car	Plane	Other Vehicles	Total
Government House	Apapa Wharf	8			5,081½
Bullnose Steps	Ijori Power Station			Launch 2	5,083½
Ijori Power Station	Government House Steps			Launch 1	5,084½
Government House	Racecourse	½			5,085
Racecourse	Government House	½			5,085½
Government House	Law Courts	½			5,086
Law Courts	Government House	½			5,086½

11 February

From	To	Car	Plane	Other Vehicles	Total
Government House	Lagos Terminus	4			5,090½
Lagos Terminus	Abcokuta			Train 59½	5,150
Abcokuta	Ibadan Station			Train 60	5,210
Ibadan Station	Government House	4			5,214
Government House	Western Hall	1½			5,215½
Western Hall	Government House	1½			5,217

12 February

From	To	Car	Plane	Other Vehicles	Total
Government House	St. James Pro-Cathedral	3			5,220
Pro-Cathedral	Government House	3			5,223

13 February

From	To	Car	Plane	Other Vehicles	Total
Government House	Racecourse	3			5,226
Drive round children's ranks		6			5,232
Racecourse	Moor Plantation	5			5,237
Drive round plantation		2			5,239
Moor Plantation	Government House	7			5,246

APPENDIX

From	To	Car	Plane	Other Vehicles	Total
14 February					
Government House	Teaching Hospital	2			5,248
Teaching Hospital	College of Arts	5½			5,253½
College of Arts	University	5½			5,259
Trenchard Hall	Principal's House	2			5,261
Principal's House	Mellanley Hall	2			5,263
Mellanley Hall	Government House	9			5,272
15 February					
Government House	Parliament Building	1½			5,273½
Parliament Building	Government House	1½			5,275
Government House	Ijebu Ode	47			5,322
Ijebu Ode	Shagamu	24			5,346
Shagamu	Lagos, Government House	36			5,382
16 February					
Government House	Ikeja, Lagos Airport	13			5,395
Lagos Airport	Kano Airport ·		521		5,916
Kano Airport	Residency, Kano	5			5,921
Residency	Emir's Palace	4½			5,925½
Emir's Palace	Residency	4½			5,930
Residency	Kano Airport	5			5,935
Kano	Idris, Tripoli		1,470		7,405
17 February					
Idris, Tripoli	London Airport		1,539		8,944
London Airport	Buckingham Palace	14			8,958
	TOTALS	477½	8,355	125½	8,958

INDEX